TO THE MANNER BORN

The Publication of this book is due in part to a generous gift from the Watson-Brown Foundation.

TO THE MANNER BORN

The Life of
General William H. T. Walker

RUSSELL K. BROWN

MERCER UNIVERSITY PRESS
MACON, GEORGIA

ISBN 0-86554-944-3
MUP/P295

First Edition published by the University of Georgia Press, 1994.
Originally designed by Erin Kirk.

The paper used in this publication meets the minimum
requirements of American National Standard for Information
Sciences—Permanence of Paper for Printed Library Materials,
ANSI Z39.48-1992.

Printed in the United States of America.

Library of Congress Cataloging-in-Publication Data

Brown, Russell K.
To the manner born: the life of General William H. T. Walker /
Russell K. Brown
p. cm.
Includes bibliographical references (p.) and index.
ISBN 0-86554-944-3 (alk. Paper)
1. Walker, William Henry Talbot, 1816-1864.
2. Generals—Confederate States of America—Biography.
3. Generals—United States—Biography. 4. Confederate States of
America. Army—Biography. I. Title.
E467.1.W19B76 2005
973.7'42'092—dc20
[B]   93-9954 [CIP]

Title page portrait of William H. T. Walker courtesy of U. S.
Military Academy Archives.

For Jin

CONTENTS

ILLUSTRATIONS

MAPS

PREFACE

SOME FEW MEN are noted for their thoughts, most only for their deeds. The ordinary man, toiling through life, is usually recollected, by those who care, for what he did and was. Those more exposed to the public eye may make some philosophical impression. Far too often, they, too, are remembered only for their actions. William Henry Talbot Walker was no exception. One hundred thirty years after his death, historians usually remember him for three things: his death at the battle of Atlanta in 1864, his intemperate resignation from Confederate service in 1861, and his bad-tempered behavior throughout his life. In the town where he was born and lies buried his statue adorns the Confederate monument. Those of a historical bent know that his grave and his father's home are on the grounds of the local college. Many fewer are aware that the residence of his adult life still stands in the county of his birth.

W. H. T. Walker was a man of action, but he was also a man of passionate convictions passionately expressed; of strong likes and dislikes; of hot temper but of tender compassion. He could boast of his accomplishments, but he could be humbled by sorrow. He could appear reduced in integrity by his ambition, but he could be redeemed by service to his country or to his family. He held a philosophy of life that his contemporaries found admirable, however it might be judged by modern society. To dismiss him as merely a militant proslavery general is to do him less than justice. The evidence shows that he was that, but also much more.

For more than fifty years, the special collections of the William R. Perkins Library, Duke University, have been the repository for a set of manuscript documents known as the W. H. T. Walker Papers. The original acquisition of some two hundred items, from a source that is no longer recorded, occurred in 1940. Another two hundred pieces were added to the papers in 1964, acquired from a dealer in Florida. For years, historians interested in researching events, principally Civil War battles, in which Walker was involved, have skimmed the papers, looking for information to satisfy their own particular interests. No one has ever attempted to organize the whole; no one has ever made an effort to use them to reconstruct the life of the man who wrote many of the letters. The principal focus has always been on gleaning material for an examination of Walker's Civil War career. Perhaps part of the problem lies in the opinion of the anonymous archivist who, after cataloging the letters, termed them "of little historic value, principally dealing with personal and family matters." Few researchers, looking for details to explain battlefield conduct or to explore their own theses on personality, would waste time on a collection of personal and family papers.

The W. H. T. Walker Papers at Duke contain 406 items, more or less, depending on how some fragments are counted. Approximately 200 of these are letters written by Walker to his wife and daughter. Another 150 pieces were written by different family members to each other, about half during the general's lifetime. The balance of the collection is made up of memos, receipts, snatches of poetry, newspaper clippings, and other miscellany.

Besides the Walker Papers at Duke, another major collection of source material is in the Military Records Branch at the National Archives. This collection consists of hundreds of pieces of official correspondence, principally located in the Records of the Adjutant General's Office and in the War Department Collection of Confederate Records. Other important collections are in the U.S. Military Academy Archives at West Point and at the Georgia Department of Archives and History in Atlanta.

There is a wealth of information available. How much rich color can be added, how well can the life story of an individual be rounded out, how exhaustively can his public actions be explained from a careful reading of his personal letters? William H. T. Walker has come down to us across history as the gallant young officer who sometime in middle age turned temperamental and dyspeptic and allowed his oversensitivity to insult to deny him the realization of his talents. At what might have been the height of his career, he was denied full participation in events by his own overweening pride, and for the last years of his life he served on the fringes of history. Was that all there was to the man? Were there not other facets of his personality? Why was this one-dimensional figure selected to represent Augusta when that city built its Confederate monument in the last century? Why is there a monument at the place he fell in Atlanta in 1864? Why does a local commemorative society bear his name? Who *was* W. H. T. Walker?

Magazine articles have been written about him as recently as 1993. An entry on Walker is included in the *Dictionary of American Biography*. Several museums hold some of his artifacts. Numerous books by good historians and volumes of reminiscences by old veterans mention his name, but most only add to the legend of the "Georgia firebrand." How would one go about reconstructing the life of this man in terms other than those already in print?

The general's personal letters span the years 1846 to 1864. The first letter was written to his bride of two months while he was on recruiting duty during the Mexican War; the last was written four days before his death, to his wife of eighteen years. In between, it is possible to measure the times they were apart and the times they were together by the grouping of the letters: many in 1846 and 1847, none from 1848 to 1851; a burst in the fall of 1852 during a two-month separation; a few in the fall of 1853 during a trip to New York; and so on up through the Civil War years and the absences while Walker was campaigning. In the letters Walker pours out his heart: his plans, his frustrations, his desires, his insecurities, in the way any husband might write to his wife. They cover personal and family matters, but they also illuminate the character of their author. The letters reveal W. H. T. Walker not as a soldier stick figure but a real human being. He smokes cigars; likes fried chicken; drinks Catawba wine; loves to waltz and polka; is angry with his superiors or his brother-in-law; admires the eyes of Mexican women; hopes for advancement; worries about his wife alone in society while he is away; voices his disdain for Yankees, foreigners, and slaves, in that order; complains of his health; and cares for his children. There is hardly a letter in the entire collection in which he does not speak of his children, his concern for their health, his pride in their accomplishments, his care for their education, and his sorrow at their deaths. He fathered eight children and buried four of them before he was laid in the ground himself.

Can this be the harsh, arrogant martinet who would rather resign than be "overslaughed," the warrior whose face was "lit by the gleam of battle"? Of course it can. These are the other faces missed by the researchers rushing to explain the actions of the Reserve Corps at Chickamauga or looking for further evidence of the "ranting" commander of the defenses of Savannah. These facets of personality help to explain the whole man. What husband and father is not a bundle of personalities spread among his domestic, professional, and social lives? The portrait limned in the W. H. T. Walker Papers is of a man with fears and ambitions, triumphs and tribulations, burdens and enrichments. It is the *real* W. H. T. Walker.

A playwright asked to dramatize the life of Walker would probably produce a tragedy in two acts. Act I, a long prologue, would consist of brief scenes, each portraying an antebellum episode: youth, young soldier, war hero, paterfamilias, tyro businessman, commandant of cadets, and gentleman farmer. In each scene the hero would stand large at center stage, dominating the action. Act II, the climax, would be short but intense, full of frenzied activity. The hero now fades into the enlarged cast, still a speaking part but overshadowed by and at the command of other, more important characters. Although he leaves the stage completely in only one scene, he is forced to share the limelight with, even yield it to, others who have the power and authority to make him do their bidding, several of whom he regards as antagonists. At the end he takes center stage once more to act out his death scene.

The reader will easily perceive this pattern in Walker's biography. Walker is the focus of attention in the chapters leading up to the Civil War. From secession onward the scope of the action becomes so large that he is only an important secondary figure. To place his service in proper context it is necessary to describe events in which he took no part but which provide a framework for his activities. His actions and opinions are tracked for the last few years of his life, but they are submerged in the drama unfolding around him. It is not the purpose of this book to rewrite the history of the American Civil War; however, in those chapters dealing with Walker's participation in wartime events it has been necessary to recreate those events to clarify his role. In some instances this has led to a full recounting of battles or even whole campaigns. In a few cases this retelling has led the author to uncover perceived discrepancies or point out corrections.

On this point a word of criticism on sources may be appropriate. Primary source material such as reports, diaries, and letters should give us the best firsthand version of events. Usually this is the case. Vanity, opinion, apology, or braggadocio, however, can cause a writer to present facts best calculated to improve his own reputation or to tarnish someone else's. This is especially true in postwar reminiscences, no more glaring example of which exists than the memoirs of Joseph E. Johnston and John Bell Hood.

My original intent was to organize, transcribe, and annotate the Walker Papers at Duke. To these I hoped to add what other pieces of the general's correspondence I could collect, and I found more than four hundred such items. It soon became evident that the mass of personal correspondence, with notes, would run to hundreds of pages of text. It was also evident that the whole would be of little interest to the general public. The letters, newspaper clippings, official documents, recollections, and other items, however, were studded with nuggets of information worth recording or useful for better understanding of Walker. From this refinement of intent came the plan to write a biography. This effort was remarkably assisted by the award of a grant to write a biography of Walker. So this book came about. The goal of publishing Walker's papers has not been abandoned, merely postponed. The general's annotated papers may yet appear in print, but for now that remains a remote objective.

The spate of recent publications containing material important to a study of W. H. T. Walker's life and times has been both rewarding and frustrating. Albert Castel's writing on the Atlanta campaign, Peter Cozzens's book on Chickamauga, T. Michael Parrish's life of Richard Taylor, and Christopher Losson's life of Benjamin F. Cheatham are all full of useful data and insight, but trying to keep up with the flood while producing and editing my own manuscript has been a pleasant strain. In some instances my own work was so far along that I elected not to try to incorporate any more material. In others, it was impossible to neglect another author's ideas or opinions, and revision of my own draft was necessary.

My opinions and drawn conclusions about my subject and his actions are based on my reading of the evidence; some of them are at variance with conventional wisdom. In a few instances I have turned up what I think is new or previously unused material; some of it contradicts what other writers have had to say about Walker and his life. Although I have received copious advice and assistance from various sources, any errors of fact or conclusion are my sole responsibility. I hope only that I have done justice to General Walker.

PREFACE TO THE PAPERBACK EDITION

MERCER UNIVERSITY PRESS'S generous offer to produce a new edition of the biography of General William H. T. Walker is a welcome opportunity for me to make a few comments about the book, my research, and the general. First published in 1994, the book received critical acclaim in the main, but suffered from only modest sales, in part due to the high selling price. A more reasonably priced soft-cover edition promises to make the volume available to a wider range of readers.

Aside from pricing and availability, this is also an opportunity to correct several factual errors that appeared in the original text. Most of them were my own; several of them were pointed out by alert reviewers and readers. These errors have been corrected here, as has been at least one glaring typo. There may be others that I have overlooked but they will have to await another reprint. As for differences of opinion about aspects of the general's life or my presentation of events concerning him, I have changed nothing. For those authors and others who have taken me to task about my conclusion on the circumstances of Walker's death at the Battle of Atlanta, I admit that more first-hand accounts have come to my attention than I was aware of a dozen years ago. However, my reading of the situation is as it was before. In the absence of a definitive statement by Walker's faithful chief of staff, I concur in the opinion of Wilbur Kurz, that master of Atlanta Civil War history, that Walker was killed by a sniper before the battle was fairly begun. This is an opinion shared by members of the Walker family, past and present. Several more of the general's wartime letters have come to light in recent years. They have not changed my view; rather, they serve to reinforce my previously offered opinion of him as a man of action and a consummate leader and motivator. William H. T. Walker was a classic representative of his time and of his region; as a soldier and a general, he was "to the manner born."

The earlier edition of this book was dedicated to my mother, since deceased. In no way detracting from that memorial, I dedicate this new edition to my faithfully supportive wife, Jin, who has seen me uncomplainingly through four publications up to now. She has asked me to do no more because each is so stressful for me, but she knows there probably will be others. Thanks, Jin.

—Russell K. Brown

ACKNOWLEDGMENTS

TO ACKNOWLEDGE the help of all who have been so generous to me over the last two years would be impossible. I must begin with the grants of the Porter Fleming Foundation given to me in 1989 and 1991. Without them, I would have been totally helpless in my search for Walker materials. Next, I must mention Karen Mitchell Allmond, Walker's great-great-granddaughter, whose unfailing enthusiasm for this project has recharged my flagging energies many times. Other family members who gave me support through time and information were Hugh Walker, Jr., the general's great-grandson, and Adele Shearer and Laurie Wolfe, collateral descendants.

It would have been impossible to proceed with my research into certain aspects of Walker's life without the help of two gentlemen with whom I have spoken and corresponded but whom I have never met. I hereby acknowledge my debt to Steve Davis of Atlanta and Paul McCain of Decatur, Georgia. Others who have helped me sort out some of my ideas about Walker and his activities or character are Brian Cisco, the biographer of Walker's principal subordinate of Civil War days, States Rights Gist, Albert Castel, Richard McMurry, Nathaniel C. Hughes, Jr., and Eugene Jones of Goose Creek, South Carolina, the leading expert on Ellison Capers and the 24th South Carolina. My thanks go also to William Garrett Piston, biographer of James Longstreet, who read my typescript in draft. I received great encouragement from his positive response and constructive comments.

I am deeply in the debt of Jeff Mosser of Aiken, South Carolina, and Steve Davis (another one), director of the Augusta College Media Center, Augusta, Georgia, for assistance with photographic work. I am also grateful to William R. Scaife of Atlanta for permission to use three maps that he originally prepared for his *The Campaign for Atlanta.* Because of the different time spans of his book and mine, there are some differences between data displayed on the maps and details described in my text.

For research assistance I remain indebted, as always, to Fred Danes of Woodworth Library at Fort Gordon, Georgia, who retrieved for me through interlibrary loan every arcane and out-of-the-way request imaginable. Even when his library was flooded in late 1992 Fred continued to support me as much as he could. Other research support was provided by Linda Orne of the Conrad Technical Library at Fort Gordon after Fred Danes was overwhelmed by the elements.

My research has taken me to many institutions throughout the South and East. I owe a great deal to William Lind and Stuart Butler at the Military Records Branch, National Archives, for steering me in the right directions among their byzantine maze of holdings. I should also mention Suzanne Christoff at the U.S. Military Academy Archives, who provided dozens of useful items of information through correspondence and during my visit to her facility. Charlotte Ray of the Georgia Department of Archives and History has been helpful in making available documents I could not have found otherwise. Dennis Kelly and other staff members at the Kennesaw Mountain National Battlefield Park helped me through correspondence and during my visit to their well-preserved historic area. A special note of thanks is due the entire staff in the Special Collections Library at Duke University. I have not space to name others who have aided me either in person, by telephone, or through the mails, but if they remember me or my requests, I now thank them.

When I first submitted my manuscript for publication, it was only a mass of loosely related information. It took the concentrated effort of the editorial team at the University of Georgia Press to turn my mass into a coherent whole. Besides acknowledging the support of Malcolm Call, director of the press, I must also mention Matt Brook, my production editor, who deftly guided me through the publication process. A special word of thanks is due Trudie Calvert, nonpareil among copy editors. Not only did Trudie sort out my jumbled grammar and syntax, but she made many valuable suggestions to improve my laborious prose.

In addition to the foregoing, I acknowledge permission of the following institutions and individuals to quote from their material: Special Collections Library, Duke University, Durham, North Carolina, the W. H. T.

Walker Papers and the Samuel Wragg Ferguson Papers; Southern Historical Collection, University of North Carolina at Chapel Hill, the W. W.
Mackall Papers; Western Reserve Historical Society, Cleveland, Ohio,
the Braxton Bragg Papers and the William P. Palmer Civil War Collec-
tion; the Georgia Historical Society, Savannah, Mercer Family Papers;
Huntington Library, San Marino, California, W. H. T. Walker correspon-
dence in the Civil War Collection; Richmond County Historical Society,
Augusta, Georgia, Cumming Family Papers and *A Northern Daughter and a
Southern Wife;* Transylvania University Library, Lexington, Kentucky, the
Jefferson Davis Papers; South Caroliniana Library, University of South
Carolina, the Williams-Chesnut-Manning Family Papers; Colonel Law-
son W. Magruder, Jr., Waco, Texas, Magruder Family Papers; McKinney
Library, Albany Institute of History and Art, Albany, New York, Frederick
Townsend Papers; Hargrett Rare Book and Manuscript Library, Univer-
sity of Georgia, Athens, Hamilton Branch Letters and John M. Davis Let-
ters; Nathaniel C. Hughes, Jr., Chattanooga, Tennessee, and Morningside
Press, Dayton, Ohio, *Liddell's Record;* Pat Bevis, Atlanta, Georgia, on be-
half of Edisto Press, *Madame LeVert;* the editors of the Georgia Historical
Quarterly, Athens, "The Memoirs of Charles Olmstead" and "Some Letters from Henry C. Wayne to Hamilton Fish"; Louisiana State University
Library, Baton Rouge, "War Memoirs" of Philip D. Stephenson.

Two other special people contributed immeasurably to this work. My
wife, Jin, has exhibited a degree of patience which only another writer's
spouse could comprehend. She has forsworn interesting vacations for research field trips, spent innumerable weekends and evenings "alone" in
the house, reheated meals gone cold, listened to pages of text read aloud,
and otherwise served as a sounding board for ideas and opinions about
a man dead 125 years. Not a murmur of complaint has passed her lips.
Second, I need to mention the leader of my lifelong cheering section, my
mother, Marie Brown. Her support for all of my undertakings, literary or
otherwise, has been to the full measure in every case, sometimes with a
quizzically raised eyebrow, but never lacking in enthusiasm and encouragement. In a previous book I failed to give her the recognition she deserves;
I hope to make up for it now.

I

PREPARATION OF A SOLDIER

1816–1837

LONG BEFORE most of his Civil War contemporaries, W. H. T. Walker was a national military hero. His exploits on the battlefield in two wars made his name a household word in Georgia, throughout the South, and across the nation. As a young army captain, he was on familiar terms with governors, senators, cabinet members, Supreme Court justices, and others among the rich and powerful. Ties of blood and marriage enabled him to move freely in the high society of both North and South. Yet when his star of fame was near its zenith, by a peculiar quirk of self-induced circumstances he allowed it to wane almost to extinction. Although he continued to render faithful service in the few years remaining to him, and although he retained the warm regard of his family, friends, and the citizens of his native state, his career never regained the full luster it had in his youth.

William Henry Talbot Walker was born November 26, 1816, in Augusta, Georgia. He was the third of the five children of Freeman and Mary Garlington Cresswell Walker who survived to adulthood. His two older siblings were George Augustus Beverly, born in 1805, and Ann(a) Eliza Amanda, born in 1809. After William's birth came Sarah Wyatt Minge in 1823 and John David in 1825. One source says there was another brother, Freeman, who was born in 1819 and died in 1846, but this child was not mentioned in William's father's will in 1827.[1]

William came from several distinguished family lines, all of them Virginian in their antecedents. Freeman Walker, born in 1780 in Charles City County, Virginia, was the son of Freeman and Sarah Minge Walker of that county. The younger Freeman had come to Augusta near the turn of the nineteenth century with his three older brothers, George, Valentine, and

Robert. All trained in the law, George and Freeman setting themselves up in legal partnership as Walker and Walker. They were all active in local politics, Valentine becoming a justice of the peace and eventually a state legislator and Robert a judge of the superior court and mayor of Augusta. Freeman and Valentine also entered the local militia. To the days of their deaths they were known respectively as Major and General Walker. All four also acquired large landholdings in Augusta and surrounding Richmond County.[2]

George Walker married Eliza Talbot, sired at least six children, and died in 1825 at the age of sixty-three. His most famous descendant was his granddaughter Octavia Walton LeVert, the epitome of the Southern belle, who toured Europe, was presented to Queen Victoria in 1853, and was on close terms with the rich and powerful of two continents. Valentine Walker married twice, first to Mary Arrington in 1807 and, after her death, to Zemula Cresswell Whitehead, a widow, in 1819. Valentine had no children. He died in 1852 at age seventy-two. Robert Walker married Ann Cooper and fathered three daughters and possibly one son. He died in 1825, having had a locally prominent career.[3]

On April 29, 1803, Freeman was married to Mary Garlington Cresswell at Bellevue, the home of his brother George, by George Walton, chief justice of the Georgia Supreme Court. Mary was the child of David, a surveyor, and Phoebe Talbot Cresswell. The Cresswells (sometimes spelled Creswell) had come to Georgia by way of South Carolina. Phoebe was the daughter of John Talbot, a wealthy Virginia planter, who moved to Wilkes County, Georgia, with his entire retinue of family, slaves, livestock, and household goods in 1783. John Talbot, a former member of the House of Burgesses in the Old Dominion, had helped to write the Virginia Bill of Rights and Constitution. He quickly established himself as one of the leading lights on the Georgia frontier. Following Talbot's death in 1798, his son Thomas carried on the family plantation in Wilkes County. Another son, Matthew, was briefly governor of the state and later became the Georgia state treasurer. Apparently, there was a third son, William Henry. In later years W. H. T. Walker wrote that he had been named for his grandmother's brother. John Talbot's daughter Eliza was the wife of George Walker, Freeman's brother. Mary G. Cresswell's sister Zemula was Valentine Walker's second wife. Frequent family intermarriage was common in the early days of the republic.[4]

Freeman Walker prospered both in the law and in politics. The income from his practice enabled him to support his family in style. He maintained a winter home on Greene Street in Augusta, a summer residence, Belle-vue, in the sand hills above the city on the tract of land he acquired from his brother George, and a farm, Spring Hill, on Spirit Creek in Richmond County. The Walkers appear to have lived well, spending money as quickly as they made it. Freeman was a state legislator from 1807 to 1808 and served two terms as mayor of Augusta, 1818–19 and 1822–23. In 1819 he was elected to fill an unexpired term in the U.S. Senate and held that post until 1821.[5]

Young William enjoyed the happy life of a high-born youth in the semi-rural nineteenth-century South. Where he attended school depended on the family's location. When in town, he attended classes at the Academy of Richmond County, just a city block from his father's house at the corner of Greene and McIntosh. When the family was at Spring Hill, William had to travel farther to the school at Richmond Bath, a small community of summer residences in the southern part of the county. In neither place did he obtain a strong formal education, a deficiency from which he was to suffer when he went on to higher learning.[6]

The bubble of William's happiness burst in September 1827. The Spring Hill house burned to the ground. Worse yet, Freeman Walker took a chill in the damp evening air while trying to save his possessions and died a few days later on September 23. This calamity rendered Mary and her five children nearly destitute. The sand hills property, Bellevue, had been sold to the U.S. government in 1826 as a new site for the Augusta Arsenal. Spring Hill was gone as a dwelling place. Freeman had sunk heavily into debt to support his opulent life-style. Mary was left with the house on Greene Street and Freeman's personal possessions, plus his debts. To his sons, Freeman left only his personal library. George, or Beverly, as he was known in the family, was appointed guardian for Ann Eliza and William. Sarah and John David were left to their mother's care.

Despite their straitened circumstances, the Walkers continued to live to the limit of their resources. Some of their expenses were met by selling what assets remained. For other assistance Mary turned to her sister and brother-in-law, Zemula and Valentine. In the fall of 1843 Valentine deeded to Mary a piece of land and built her a house near his own place, Belleville, at Windsor Spring in Richmond County. This house, called Seclusaval, eventually became William Walker's residence whenever he and his family were in Georgia.[7]

As William, known to his family throughout his life as Willie, ap-proached his midteens, the question of a career for him became a matter of concern to the family. Beverly had recently married and was interested in moving to Alabama to take up planting near some of his cousins. Before he left he wanted to see that his ward was properly educated and placed in a profession. William had always looked up to the uncle whose name he bore and who he termed "my heroic namesake." A history of military ardor and love of military titles was evident in the family line. A military career seemed to be ideal for the young man.[8]

At that time, all appointments to the U.S. Military Academy at West Point were made by the president through the secretary of war. It was the policy of the War Department to give preference for appointments to sons of military families and to young men of meager means whose families could not otherwise afford to educate them. In the latter category, the secretary usually accepted recommendations for appointment from members of Congress. So it was that in January 1831 six of the seven members of the Georgia delegation to the U.S. Congress wrote to Andrew Jackson's secretary of war, Lewis Cass, recommending the son of their former colleague Senator Freeman Walker as a suitable candidate for appointment on the basis of need. In April 1832, Cass offered Walker an appointment in the class of 1836. In a letter dated April 23, 1832, the earliest known example of his handwriting, Walker accepted the appointment and agreed to report for examination for admission the following June. His letter was accompanied by one from Beverly, agreeing to allow his ward to attend the Military Academy. Thus was the fifteen-year-old boy entered on the path of Mars.[9]

The West Point of 1832 was not the stable, highly renowned institution it was to become in another generation. Still, it was far superior both as a center for scientific education and as a school for military professionals than it had been fifteen years earlier. The great Sylvanus Thayer was nearing the end of his superintendency; the equally illustrious Dennis Hart Mahan was just beginning his career as the foremost American military theorist of the nineteenth century. Thayer had rescued the academy from anarchy in 1817, turned the Corps of Cadets into a real military organization, and molded the curriculum to fit the needs of practical military and civil engineering as well as classical education. West Point was the only four-year engineering school in the United States at that time. Mahan, an academy graduate, had studied and traveled in France and was teaching military art and theory, using the notes taken during his travels.

Under the regimen then in practice, candidates for admission reported to the academy in June, were examined for their aptitude, and then were admitted as new cadets. The first year's training began with a two-month summer camp in July and August, followed by the two-semester academic year that opened in September. Although the entrance examination could be ridiculously easy, in some cases consisting of a single oral question, normally more candidates were turned away than admitted. Some traveled hundreds or thousands of miles to be examined, only to be told that they were not accepted.

Walker, despite his sketchy formal education, was one of about ninety-five candidates who successfully negotiated the entrance exam for his class. Among others who passed were his fellow Georgian John Jones, who never graduated, and Marcus C. M. Hammond of the South Carolina Hammonds, whose home was in Beech Island, just across the Savannah River from Augusta. Graduates of the class of 1836 were not greatly distinguished in later years. The best-known member was probably Montgomery C. Meigs, quartermaster general of the Union army during the Civil War years and early construction engineer of the U.S. Capitol.

Summer camp was a living hell for the new cadets. The camp was situated near the present Koskiuszko Monument overlooking the Hudson River shoreline. The upper-class cadets welcomed the break in the academic grind and were glad to be living out of barracks in the open, but part of their initiation into military service was a system of extreme, at times brutal, hazing. Most of the training of the new cadets was in the hands of upperclassmen. Despite the best attempts of the army officers present, they were frequently unable to prevent harassment of the new men.

The training included drill, guard duty, artillery practice, camp police, and other military necessities. The older cadets used every opportunity to confound the fifteen- to twenty-year-old youths under their tutelage. On one occasion, a young cadet was placed on guard duty at a location remote from the encampment. A group of upperclassmen crept up to his guard post, covered themselves with sheets, and ran toward him out of the dark. The young man was terrorized. In another incident, a cadet fired off the lock of his (unloaded) musket directly in the face of a new cadet, nearly blinding the youth and frightening him out of his wits. Tactical training was equally arduous. An older cadet told of watching the newer ones learning artillery drill. Some of them were so young and so small that they were not tall enough to see down the barrels of the smoothbore cannon they were serving.

Despite these drawbacks, by the end of the summer the new cadets had become well-trained recruits and were accepted into the corps for academic classes. Yet another useful aspect of this basic training was the socialization of these boys from every walk of life in America. Summer camp was the height of the social season at West Point. Balls and parties were frequent, dancing instruction was provided for the young men, and girls were invited from nearby towns and from as far away as New York City to join in the entertainment. We have no record of the young Walker at this period other than the academic, but, judging from his later life, he must have been in his element during his social opportunities. If later performance can be judged, he must also have taken well to military discipline and training. It was in the academic field that he was to prove weakest.[10]

Walker's problem was not uncommon. Statistics show that cadets from southern and western states, where formal early education was hard to come by, consistently did less well in the classroom than their northeastern comrades. The curriculum was not especially difficult. In their first year the cadets had to master only two academic subjects, French and mathematics. They were examined twice yearly, in January and June. Those found deficient could be dismissed from the academy; a few were allowed to continue with a lower class ("turned back" was the phrase used).[11]

By the end of the examinations in January 1833, Walker's deficiencies were becoming obvious. He placed sixty-second in his class in math and fifty-sixth in French. By June 1833, out of fifty-nine cadets remaining of those who had entered a year before, his overall standing was fifty-eighth. Whether the problem was lack of application, inaptitude, or poor health is impossible to say, but Walker was very near ejection from the academy. It has been suggested that poor health was the principal cause of his tribulations, but we can only guess at the psychological impact of his near failure.[12]

Summer camp in 1833 was a welcome respite. Now it was Walker's turn to bedevil the new cadets under the guise of discipline and instruction. The academy had a new superintendent, René E. DeRussy, whose tenure would extend for the remainder of Walker's stay, and a new commandant of cadets, Captain John Fowle, who replaced Captain Ethan Allen Hitchcock. Walker probably enjoyed camp much more than he had the previous summer. September brought the return of the corps to barracks and to the classroom.

The course of study for the second-year cadets, who were known as third classmen, included more French, more math, and drawing. The drawing instructor was the noted American artist Robert Weir. Despite this inspired example, January 1834 found Walker deficient in drawing, forty-third in French, and fifty-fifth in math. By June 1834, he stood fifty-seventh out of fifty-seven who were deemed proficient. The four cadets below him were dismissed for deficiency in their studies. The apparent discrepancy in numbers from the end of the first year is accounted for by the cadets who had been turned back from the class of 1835.[13]

Second class summer was the occasion for a month's home leave, the first opportunity Walker had had to visit Georgia in two years. His visit proved to be not a happy one because he returned to the academy too sick to participate in the routine. The returns for the academy show him present but sick in September 1834. From October 1834 to March 1835 he was absent sick. Where he spent this period is not known. Presumably, as he did in later years, he came south for the more congenial climate.

Walker has been described as small in stature and of a frail constitution. As an adult he suffered terribly from asthma, a malady he may have developed in childhood, and this may have been the reason for his absence from West Point in the winter of 1835. The record shows that he was not examined academically in January 1835 because of his absence. In June 1835, despite his return, he was not examined "in consequence of his previous absence," and he was turned back to the class of 1837.[14]

Among his new classmates were several whose names would be at least as prominent as his own twenty-five years hence. From the South were Braxton Bragg and William W. Mackall. John Pemberton, a Pennsylvanian who would later side with the South, was also a class member. Future Union generals included Joseph Hooker and John Sedgwick. Other members of the class were future Union adjutant general Edward D. Townsend, future Union chief of ordnance Alexander Dyer, Jubal A. Early of Army of Northern Virginia fame, and Randolph Ridgely, a future Mexican War hero.[15]

Walker's academic performance was not improved by his prolonged absence. The curriculum for second class cadets was chemistry, natural philosophy (natural sciences), and drawing. Again, he fared poorly. In January 1836 he stood deficient in drawing and near the bottom of his class in the other two subjects. By June he had managed to eke out proficient grades, but he was still near the bottom of his class.[16]

Although Walker had not shone as a scholar, his behavior while a cadet and his military bearing had been exemplary. In August 1836, during his first class summer camp, he was rewarded with an appointment as cadet lieutenant. Alas, he held this position for only two months. On a night near the end of October he was discovered absent from his room during a bed check and was broken back to the ranks. Apparently he had succumbed to the greater privileges afforded first classmen and had gone over the wall, perhaps to the establishment of Benny Havens, a congenial dispenser of strong drink, perhaps to a romantic rendezvous with a female visitor.

Not having learned from this episode, Walker was found absent from his room once again in November. This time he was placed in arrest and confined to his room pending court-martial. Arrested cadets were allowed out of their rooms only for classes, drill, and necessary personal functions. They were not even permitted to eat in the mess hall with other cadets. Walker remained in this limbo until February 1837, when a general court-martial found him guilty of the charge. He was given the relatively mild sentence of having to walk three extra tours of guard duty and was released from arrest.[17]

June 1837 brought release in the form of graduation and commissioning in the army. At the final tally Walker stood forty-sixth in a class of fifty. After five years of study and discipline and one severe bout of illness, William H. T. Walker was finally launched on his professional military career.

What were Walker's prospects in his new career? In 1836, the year before he graduated, the adjutant general prepared a memorandum on army promotion for the secretary of war. In it he predicted that a newly graduated cadet could expect to wait eight years to become a first lieutenant. It would be eighteen years before he attained his captaincy and thirty-eight years before promotion to major. After fifty-eight years, if he lived that long, he might make colonel. Of course, this pattern made no allowances for the attrition of war or expansion of the army.[18]

Although the Military Academy had originally been intended as a school for engineers and engineering dominated the curriculum, few new graduates found positions in that branch of the army. The graduates with highest standing in each class went to the more technical branches, engineers and artillery, while the lower men, the "goats," were destined for the infantry. Walker, among the lowest of goats, could expect nothing else.

If, as frequently happened, insufficient vacancies existed in the Regular Army for new officers when they graduated, they would be appointed brevet (acting) second lieutenants until a vacancy occurred. All graduates were commissioned from July 1 in their year of graduation. Walker became a brevet second lieutenant of infantry, unassigned, on July 1, 1837. He took advantage of this opportunity to take a leave to visit his mother in Georgia and his brother Beverly at his estate, Tranquila, in Lowndes County, Alabama, near present-day Selma. It was here that Walker learned belatedly of his appointment as a second lieutenant in the 6th Infantry to date from July 31, 1837, with orders to report immediately to his regiment in Florida. He was already late when the message reached him, it having been sent to his home in Augusta. On August 13, 1837, from Pleasant Hill, Alabama, Walker acknowledged receipt of the secretary of war's message and reported his imminent departure for the seat of war against the Seminole Indians.[19]

2

GLORY AND AGONY

1837–1844

BY THE TIME Walker arrived in Florida in October, the Second Seminole War had been dragging on for almost two years. Five different generals had been in command up to this point, all with indifferent success. Many more were to follow before the termination of this longest and most frustrating of all of the Indian wars of the United States.

The war had its origins in two recurring themes of antebellum America: Indian removal and the return of fugitive slaves. The administration of President Andrew Jackson had vigorously pursued the policy of removing the Indians of the southeastern states to the West to make way for the advancing tide of white population. The saga of the Cherokee "Trail of Tears" is well-known. Other tribes, Creek, Choctaw, and Chickasaw, had also agreed to emigrate to Arkansas and Oklahoma. Only the Seminole of Florida Territory were intransigent.[1]

The Seminole, numbering only about five thousand souls, were not a real tribe at all. Many of them were Creeks who had gone to Florida and joined with small local tribes. A significant number were Negroes, free blacks, runaway slaves, or even slaves of the Indians, who lived in a condition of bondage much more lax than under their white owners in Alabama or Georgia. As long as the Seminoles remained in Florida, they could provide a haven for the runaways. Parties of whites crossing into Florida to hunt for their slaves were resisted by the Indians, who frequently conducted counterraids into neighboring states.

By 1835 it was obvious that the Indians would have to go west, and the new superintendent of Florida Indians, General Wiley Thompson of Georgia, worked assiduously toward that goal. Some chiefs finally agreed to removal on condition that they be allowed to examine the land they would be given. By fair means or foul, they were coerced or cajoled into accepting a tract in the Indian Territory, and plans went forward for collecting the emigrants near Tampa Bay and transporting them to the West.

At this juncture several younger chiefs, Osceola among them, denounced the agreement for removal, claiming that the delegation that had accepted the Indian Territory land spoke only for themselves, not for the whole tribe. Despite this disclaimer, Thompson and the army commander, General Duncan L. Clinch, insisted on compliance, by force if necessary.

On December 28, 1835, while Thompson and his aide were walking outside the defenses of Fort King, they were set upon and murdered by Osceola and his band.[2] On the same day, two companies of U.S. troops under Major Francis L. Dade were ambushed and massacred. Only 3 men survived of the 120 who were present. The Dade Massacre and the murder of Thompson electrified the nation, galvanized the Jackson administration, and launched the Second Seminole War. For the next two years a succession of commanders led their troops, both regulars and volunteers, on fruitless sweeps through the swamps of Florida. Few Indians were ever seen, fewer still killed or captured. Some small numbers, destitute and starving, did turn themselves in for removal, but the bulk of the Indians and their black allies remained at large. By the fall of 1837, the theater of war had been divided into two sectors, that northeast of Tampa Bay under the overall commander, General Thomas Jesup, and that to the southeast under Colonel Zachary Taylor of the 1st U.S. Infantry.

In December 1837 Taylor marched out of Tampa Bay to the east with a force of over a thousand men. He had three regiments of regulars, the 1st (his own), 4th, and 6th; a regiment of Missouri volunteers; and a band of Delaware and Shawnee Indians acting as scouts. Among the ranks of the 6th Infantry was Second Lieutenant William H. T. Walker, who, because he was the only officer present with it, commanded Company G. Going on his first active campaign, and only a few weeks after his twenty-first birthday, the new lieutenant was to be responsible for the actions of a company of infantry.[3]

After establishing a base on the Kissimmee River, Taylor pressed forward with eight hundred men. They passed several abandoned hostile campsites but on the morning of Christmas Day caught up with the Indians in a fortified position in a swamp on the shore of Lake Okeechobee. Taylor deployed his men in three lines, the volunteers in front, the 4th and 6th Infantry in the second line, and the 1st Infantry in reserve. Then he ordered a frontal assault, the only feasible tactic in the swamp, which Taylor described as "totally impassable for horse, and nearly so for foot, covered with a thick growth of sawgrass, five feet high, and about knee deep in mud and water."[4]

Through this morass the troops advanced into a withering musket fire from the entrenched Indians. The volunteers fled en masse when their commander was wounded, and the regulars moved to the fore. For three hours the battle continued until the Seminoles were finally driven from their position—but at great cost. Taylor had sustained losses of 26 killed and 112 wounded, more than 17 percent of the total engaged. Only 14 Indian bodies were found on the field.

Lieutenant Walker was one of the 112 wounded. At the head of his company he had sustained at least three wounds while traversing the swamp. Although shot in the leg, the neck, the shoulder, and with a broken arm, he continued the advance. When the commander of the 6th, Lieutenant Colonel Alexander Thompson, fell mortally wounded, Walker stopped to aid him and was struck in the chest by another ball that incapacitated him. A story was told years later that while he lay near death on the field, an Indian scavenging among the dead stole his wallet and other valuables. Some months later the same Indian was captured, and Walker's belongings were returned to him.

After the battle, when Taylor was able to turn his attention to the dead and wounded, the unconscious Walker was removed to camp for burial. As the story was later told, the bearers stopped to rest and laid their burden down in the swamp water. Walker was sufficiently revived by the sudden cold to speak out, much to the surprise of witnesses. But except for efforts to make him comfortable, the surgeons thought him a hopeless case and transported him to Fort Brooke at Tampa Bay for probable interment.[5]

In his official report, Taylor cited Walker for gallantry while describing the exploits of the 6th Infantry:

> I am not sufficiently master of words to express my admiration of the gallantry and steadiness of the officers and soldiers of the Sixth Regiment of Infantry. It was their fortune to bear the brunt of the battle. The report of the killed and wounded, which accompanies this, is more conclusive evidence of their merits than anything I can say. After five companies of this regiment, against which the enemy directed the most deadly fire, were nearly cut up—there being only four men left uninjured in one of them, and every officer and orderly sergeant of those companies with one exception were either killed or wounded—Captain Noel, with the remaining two companies, his own Co. K

and Crossman's B, commanded by 2nd Lt. Woods, which was the left of the regiment, formed on the right of the 4th Infantry, entered the hammock with that regiment and continued the fight and the pursuit until its termination. It is due to Capt. Andrews and Lt. Walker to say they commanded two of the five companies mentioned above and they continued to direct them until they were both severely wounded and carried from the field, the latter receiving three separate balls.[6]

The 6th went into action with 175 men and lost 75 in killed and wounded, more than 40 percent casualties. The regimental commander and regimental adjutant were killed; the sergeant major was wounded. In Company G, Walker and his first sergeant were wounded; two privates were killed and eleven wounded. Taylor was breveted a brigadier general for his victory at Lake Okeechobee. In January 1838 Walker was advanced to the rank of first lieutenant by brevet, and in February he was promoted to that grade permanently.[7]

As Walker liked to say in later life, he got well "to spite the doctors." He convalesced slowly at Tampa, but his always fragile health and the enervating climate prevented a full recovery. Walker asked for and received a leave of absence to go home and recuperate. Because of the absence of water transportation from Tampa Bay and his perennial impatience, he decided to ride seventy-five miles across to the east coast of Florida and catch a steamer from the St. Johns River to Savannah. He was able neither to mount nor dismount a horse unaided.

In company with another invalid officer in equal distress, Walker set out from Fort Brooke. Each morning they were strapped into their saddles and rode in agony all day to the next way station, where they were unstrapped for the overnight stay. By slow stages, they made their way to Black Creek, a tributary of the St. Johns. From there, a sort of inertia of momentum kept Walker going until he reached Augusta. Drained of strength, he gave out and had to be carried from the boat dock to his mother's home in Augusta.[8]

Walker remained at home recovering through that spring and summer. On May 31, 1838, he forwarded to the adjutant general a surgeon's certificate concerning his health. Dr. Alexander Cunningham of Augusta wrote that "the injury sustained from gunshot wound received in his left arm and side . . . was sufficient to deprive him . . . of the use of the left arm." Also, "His whole arm is still useless and will require nearly or quite another twelve months before he will be able to discharge his duties as an officer."[9]

In October 1838 Walker's leave of absence expired and he thought he would have to return to his regiment. Still a novice in the ways of the army, he apparently did not know that he could ask for an extension of his leave so he resigned rather than report in a sickly condition.[10] Apparently believing that his military career was behind him, Walker cast about for another profession. Probably influenced by his uncle Valentine, and with memories of his father's calling, he decided to go into law. What funding he used is not clear, but in the fall of 1839 he went to New Haven, Connecticut, and enrolled in Yale Law School. Tuition was $100 per term.

Law school was less formal in the nineteenth century than it is now. Students read law in the offices of established attorneys, attended a few lectures by prominent judges or lawyers, practiced their skills in moot courts, and then went into business for themselves. The course of instruction was two years long, but Yale did not begin to grant law degrees until 1843. None of this was of much concern to Walker because he remained in New Haven less than a year. While there he lived in a boardinghouse and apparently made a few friends, but he did not find the action and adventure that army life had provided.[11]

In the fall of 1839 he applied for reinstatement in the army. Several of the junior officers of the 6th Infantry petitioned for his reinstatement to the regiment in his former rank, making a place for him in his old lineal seniority. Other officers protested that such action would set an unfortunate precedent, but with the endorsement of General Zachary Taylor, Secretary of State John Forsyth, and others, Walker's commission was restored in November 1840 and sent to the Senate for confirmation in December.[12] When he rejoined his regiment in Florida in December, he reentered the world of patrols, sweeps, and raids in search of the ever-elusive Seminole. But within a few months of returning to duty he showed the first flash of mercurial spirit that would mark the rest of his career.

A small portion of the 6th Infantry had been mounted and served as a separate scouting detachment. In February 1841, command of this detachment was given to First Lieutenant Charles S. Lovell. Lovell had been commissioned about three months after Walker had, was his junior as a first lieutenant, and was a former enlisted man. Serving in a subordinate position as a company lieutenant while a junior had a semiautonomous command did not sit well with Walker. In amazing disregard of military protocol, he dashed off a hotheaded letter, dated March 18, to the regimental commander, Lieutenant Colonel Gustavus Loomis, a fifty-three-year-old veteran of the War of 1812. Walker did not mince his words.

The recent detail that has been made of my junior to a separate command whilst I am present and acting in a subordinate capacity has been to me a matter of no little astonishment. I did not resent it immediately, hoping that I might have some good reason assigned for it. As I have had none, I have to be guided by my own reason and I am necessarily drawn to one of two conclusions, that my junior was better capable of performing the duty than I was (which grant that he is, you certainly don't know it), or that you made the detail without reflection. I do not write this communication for the purpose or with the hope of changing the detail. My motive is higher than any such selfish consideration. I would demand it if I desired it. I do not, nor would not take it if it was offered to me. I write merely and simply to let you fully understand that I am not so ignorant of the rights that the officer can claim as not to know that mine has been infringed upon, nor so weak and submissive as not to let my commanding officer know that I as an officer feel the slight and have the spirit to resent it.[13]

Loomis took this affront to his authority about as well as might be expected. He had Walker relieved from his company and placed in arrest, and he preferred charges against him to be resolved by court-martial.

After considerable correspondence between Loomis and department headquarters at Tampa Bay, a court was convened at the latter place on April 25 with Lieutenant Colonel Newman S. Clarke, 8th Infantry, as president. Walker was charged with three offenses: disrespect to his commanding officer expressed in the letter of March 18; failure to follow army regulations in addressing the letter directly to the regimental commander instead of through his adjutant; and failure to follow army regulations in addressing an appeal directly to the adjutant general of the army instead of through channels. Loomis added the last charge on April 15 when he learned that Walker had appealed to the adjutant general to have the commanding general of the army, Alexander Macomb, review the correspondence and throw out the case before it came to trial. To Loomis, this must have been just one more example of Walker's inability to play by the established rules. Although the adjutant general eventually returned Walker's letter to the department commander, General Walker K. Armistead, without action, this was not known at the time of the trial.[14]

Walker admitted having done everything he was accused of but entered pleas of not guilty on the basis that none of his transgressions were criminal acts. Relying, no doubt, on the meager legal skills he had acquired at Yale, he presented a rather sophomoric argument against each charge. To the first, disrespect, he replied that even if Colonel Loomis thought his letter was disrespectful, he (Walker) did not. In response to the second charge, disobedience of orders in wrongly addressing his letter, Walker wrote that the charge had no foundation in itself and if he were found not guilty of the first charge, he could not be found guilty of the second. As for the additional charge, direct communication with the adjutant general, Walker fell back on the lame excuses that, first, it was none of Colonel Loomis's business and, second, no one could prove he wrote the letter to Washington because there was no witness who could identify his signature.

A parade of witnesses was called testifying to the effect that Walker had, indeed, intended no disrespect to the colonel, and that, indeed, there was no one who could confirm that the signature on the letter to the adjutant general was his. After two days of this sham, the court returned a verdict of not guilty on the first and third charges. On the second charge he was found guilty, but the offense was reduced from disobedience of orders to neglect of duty. He was sentenced to be privately admonished by General Armistead. Walker was then returned to duty.[15]

This incident was early evidence of a character trait that would often result in self-destructive behavior over the coming years. Walker was extremely sensitive to what he perceived as personal insult or any activity that reflected on his well-developed pride and sense of honor or his social or professional standing. In this case, the appointment of a junior to a semiautonomous position while Walker remained in a subordinate capacity was perceived as a slap at his professional ability. His reaction was not as simple as an explosive temper or youthful hotheadedness. Rather, it was a declaration of manhood and a claim to justice and integrity. As he was to write some years later, "Take from me anything but my self-respect and my pride and I will feel rich. To part with them would be to part with life, and what is dearer to me than life, honor."[16]

Perhaps it was the insecurity of his fatherless childhood, perhaps the effect of physical frailty, perhaps the need to prove his manhood, perhaps resentment at ever-present financial embarrassment; whatever the cause, Walker never accepted any slight, no matter how trivial. In this he was not alone among Southern gentlemen or his military contemporaries. Bertram Wyatt-Brown uses the case of Edmund Ruffin as an example of the Southern concept of honor.

Ruffin was a sickly child and suffered the loss of his mother and father at an early age. His stepmother had numerous children of her own and left the boy to fend for himself emotionally. Ruffin grew up with a permanent sense of repressed inferiority, expressed through sensitivity about personal and sectional honor. He overcame these inner inadequacies by engaging in disputes and quarrels with anyone unfortunate enough to disagree with him.[17]

Walker lost his father at an early age. His mother, burdened with two minor children and the responsibility of his father's indebtedness, had little time for her ten-year-old son. His two older siblings had already attained their majority and were little disposed to look after a ten-year-old. Beverly Walker was appointed guardian for his younger brother and sister and apparently carried out his duties conscientiously, but it was not the same as having a male parent. Walker wrote to his wife once of his lonely days as a youth wandering the hills of Richmond County and musing over his fate. Wyatt-Brown notes that the touchiness of such well-known men as Alexander Hamilton and Andrew Jackson might be traced to youthful solitariness springing from loss of parents at an early age or low community respect for the family. The efforts of the Georgia legislative delegation to have Walker appointed to West Point could be construed as community pity for the wretched offspring of Freeman Walker. Not that military service itself was dishonorable. Far from it, for in the South, next to planters, lawyers, and doctors, no profession was more esteemed than the military despite its dim prospects for advancement.[18]

One other problem Walker might have felt he had to overcome was lack of physical stature. The importance of this attribute is evident in every description of Walker available, all of which remark on his achievements despite his small stature. Slight build could be a curse, but also incentive to excel. Alexander Stephens, Walker's fellow Georgian, overcame both small stature and physical frailty to become politically prominent. Walker wanted to do the same.[19]

The parallels between Walker and Ruffin are clear. In Walker's response to life's humiliations there was the intimation that he would carry his demand for redress to any length rather than submit. The sequence just described would be repeated time and again: resentment, complaint, demand for redress. If the sought-after relief was not forthcoming, Walker might find surcease in the ultimate option, resignation. Damn the consequences, his own need for self-approbation would be satisfied. His honor had been sullied; he would state his displeasure and then, if necessary, withdraw from the situation to prevent further unbearable distress. "I could not stand it and would not for worlds" was the way he described one such

situation to his wife, and he meant every word. Thus did so simple an incident as the command of the mounted detachment foreshadow a pattern of
behavior that would be his pride and curse through the years, sustaining
his own sense of honor but frequently proving injurious to his hopes for
advancement.[20]

If Walker's behavior was injurious, it was not unique in the pre–Civil
War U.S. Army. Officers occasionally resorted to resignation as a means
to right real or supposed wrongs. Perhaps the classic example was that of
William Jenkins Worth on the eve of the Mexican War. Worth, a native
New Yorker, had been colonel of the 8th Infantry since 1838 and brevet
brigadier general from 1842 for his Florida war service. David E. Twiggs,
like William Walker, born in Richmond County, Georgia, was colonel of
the 2d Dragoons from 1836 and outranked Worth as a colonel. Zachary
Taylor, a brevet brigadier general since Okeechobee in 1837, was commander of the Army of Observation in Texas. Taylor named Twiggs his
second in command as senior colonel. Worth protested on the basis of his
brevet rank and appealed to the War Department. Taylor ignored Worth,
who left the army to go to Washington intending to submit his resignation if his claim was not sustained. Unfortunately for Worth, this was on
the eve of the battles of Palo Alto and Resaca de la Palma, May 8 and 9,
1846, both of which he missed. Upon hearing the news of the battles, he
returned immediately to the war zone and eventually won a good name
and further brevet promotion for himself at Monterrey and on the road to
Mexico City. But Congress rewarded Taylor and Twiggs with permanent
promotions to major general and brigadier general, respectively, for their
actions on May 8 and 9. Worth remained colonel of the 8th Infantry until
his death in 1849, forever subordinate to his adversary, Twiggs. He had
satisfied his honor but sacrificed his career.[21]

Over the next year the Florida war continued to wind down as more and
more of the Indians surrendered and were transported to the West. Walker
served at different times as company commander and post commander.
In November 1841 he commanded the regiment's mounted detachment
for about three months. By the time the 6th Infantry left Florida in the
spring of 1842 his service had been sufficiently noteworthy that he was
recommended for a brevet promotion to captain by General Worth, the
new department commander, for "high chivalry and excellent qualities."
This recommendation, for obvious reasons, was not approved by the War
Department.[22]

With the conclusion of the Florida war, the 6th Infantry was moved to the Indian Territory, and Walker spent two dreary years in frontier garrison at Forts Towson and Gibson. For about half the time he was assigned in the West, Walker was absent from his post, either sick or on leave. He went to Fort Towson in May 1842 and in June obtained a two-month sick leave of absence from his department commander, Brevet Brigadier General Zachary Taylor. Using various excuses, Walker managed to stretch the leave to January 1843. His monthly reports and requests for extension of his leave were sent at different times from Pleasant Hill, Alabama, Augusta, Georgia, and Charleston, South Carolina. He finally returned to the frontier in January 1843 but not before he had been reported absent without leave for several weeks. He was assigned to Fort Gibson, where his company had been transferred in November 1842. Gibson was noted as being the most unhealthy post in the army, and Walker spent a miserable fifteen months there. For at least two months, although he remained at his post, he was carried on the returns as too sick to perform duty. Finally, in May 1844, relief came in the form of assignment as a recruiting officer in the East.[23]

While Walker was fighting Indians in Florida, struggling to get himself reinstated in the army, and dealing with the boredom of frontier life, changes had been taking place at home in Augusta. His two sisters had married during his absence. First, Ann Eliza married Adam Johnston, a wholesale grocer who had moved to Augusta from Charleston, South Carolina. In Augusta in 1840, Sarah, affectionately called "Sister," married Johnston's younger brother, Walter Ewing Johnston, a physician. Adam and Ann Eliza were childless, but Sarah had one son, Walter Ewing, Jr., born in 1841. Adam soon left the grocery business and by the early 1850s was the successful president and manager of Richmond Factory, a textile mill on Spirit Creek near the site of Freeman Walker's old Spring Hill place. Walter and Sister took up residence at their own estate, Alta Vista, in south Richmond County. After Mary Garlington Walker occupied the Seclusaval property provided for her by Valentine and Zemula Walker in 1843, Adam and Ann Eliza moved in with her. Seclusaval became the home in Augusta to which William Walker would return time and again until his death and from which much of his correspondence, both personal and official, would emanate.[24]

3

HIGH SOCIETY

1844–1846

THE UNITED STATES ARMY in the years before the Mexican War had a strength of less than ten thousand men, of whom fewer than a thousand were officers. Despite these small numbers, recruiting up to strength was a constant problem. Miserable pay, deplorable conditions, and unlimited opportunity in civilian life made soldiering an undesirable and unrewarding profession for the enlisted ranks. Most recruits were either immigrants or misfits. As a consequence, the army kept up a large recruiting service made up of officers detached from their regiments and assigned to the various cities and large towns throughout the nation. The superintendent of recruiting, as the officer in charge of that service was called, had his headquarters in New York City, and it was there that Walker reported for duty about June 7, 1844.[1]

His hopes for a plush assignment in New York or Boston were soon dashed. Because he had to travel all the way from Indian Territory, Walker was one of the last of those assigned that spring to arrive in New York. As a result, all the good posts had been taken and Walker was assigned to the relative wilderness of Utica, New York. His protests that he had had to travel so far and that posts should be awarded on the basis of seniority were of no avail. Both the commanding general and the adjutant general of the army turned deaf ears to his pleas. The decision on Walker's station was left to the superintendent of recruiting, Lieutenant Colonel Newman S. Clarke, who had been the president of Walker's court-martial three years earlier.

Clarke reasoned that the order for recruiting duty had specified a reporting date of May 1. He gave no weight to Walker's argument that the order had been delivered to him at Fort Gibson on May 13. Clarke followed a strict rule of first come, first choice. As far as he was concerned, seniority had nothing to do with recruiting; one officer could drum up recruits as well as another, regardless of location. Utica needed a recruiter, Walker was available, and he would go to Utica.[2]

Life in Utica was not all bad. The duty was easy. Noncommissioned officers performed the actual tasks of finding recruits. Officers were required only to examine the new men and swear them into service. When possible, an army surgeon would conduct a physical examination of the prospective soldier. Any controversy that occurred in his recruiting duty was of Walker's own making. After each recruit was sworn in, he was forwarded to a permanent army installation where he would be given a formal examination. In some cases boards of officers, known as survey boards, would be convened to review the findings and either accept or reject the recruit. On such matters Lieutenant Walker often differed with official opinion.

Apparently, in his zeal to find recruits, Walker took almost any man who offered himself for service. He appealed to Colonel Clarke on numerous occasions for advice on whether a man was acceptable. When a survey board rejected one of Walker's recruits, however, he took it as a personal affront to his judgment and reputation and fired off a letter of protest. In at least three instances he wrote directly to the adjutant general explaining in exhaustive detail why he, a simple lieutenant with little medical training, could not be expected to discern defects that only a professional physician could diagnose. If Walker was unhappy in Utica, he certainly gave Colonel Clarke no cause for comfort in New York.[3]

After ten months of laboring in the wilderness, Walker won a transfer to the more congenial recruiting station in Albany, New York. Hudson River Valley society was undergoing a groundswell of change at that time. By acts of the New York State legislature, the great estates that had existed since the Dutch land grants of the seventeenth century were being broken up and the land given to the tenants, or "anti-renters," as they were known. One of the great landowners, General Stephen Van Rensselaer, the "Last Patroon," resisted to the end, hence his nickname, and the state militia had to be called out to quell the resultant riots. Walker, a member of the aristocratic class in his native Georgia, naturally sided with the patroons, who took to him as readily as he to them.[4]

One of Walker's first acquaintances in Albany seems to have been Justine ("Tiny" or "Teeny") Van Rensselaer, daughter of the Last Patroon. Through "Tiny," Walker broke into Albany high society. He entered into a round of parties, picnics, canal boat excursions, even mock tournaments the likes of which he had probably never seen in Georgia. By late 1845 or early 1846 he had met and become smitten with seventeen-year-old Mary Townsend. "Tiny" was enjoying the special attentions of Dr. Howard Townsend, Mary's brother, who had recently completed his medical studies, and it was doubtless through them that Walker and Mary became acquainted.[5]

The Townsend name was important in Albany. The family forebears, three brothers, had come to Massachusetts, then to Long Island, about the time of the English Civil War. They and their descendants prospered mightily as merchants and seamen. Some of them had moved into the area just north of New York City before the American Revolution. In 1799 the brothers Isaiah and John Townsend moved to Albany from Orange County, New York, and went into business as iron founders, brick and barrel stave makers, and anything else they could lay their hands to. They also dabbled in local politics, serving as aldermen, occasionally as mayor, members of school boards, and other civic pursuits. The brothers maintained sumptuous mansions at 144 and 146 State Street in the heart of Albany, directly across the street from the present state capitol.

In 1808 Isaiah Townsend took as his second wife his distant cousin Hannah Townsend of Oyster Bay, Long Island. She bore him seven children who lived to maturity: Isaiah, Anna, Robert, Franklin, Howard, Frederick, and Mary. All of them except Isaiah became or married men of prominence. Robert became a captain in the U.S. Navy, Franklin was mayor of Albany and adjutant general of New York during the Civil War, Howard was a noted physician, Frederick was a brevet brigadier general in the Civil War and afterward New York adjutant general, Anna married one of the wealthiest bankers in America, and Mary married W. H. T. Walker. The younger Isaiah spent many of his early years carousing in Europe and later settled in Cornwall, New York. The elder Isaiah died in 1838, and the reins of the family interests were passed to Franklin, who continued the partnership with his uncle John and, later, John's son Theodore.[6]

In November 1845 Walker was promoted to captain and assigned as commander of Company F, 6th Infantry. His company was on duty at Fort Smith, Arkansas, but Walker was allowed to remain on recruiting duty in Albany (and to continue to pay court to "Molly" Townsend). His recruiting tour was due to end in May 1846, and that January he received orders to report to his company at the end of May.

Walker protested. On the basis of his late arrival in New York in 1844, he asked that his tour of duty as a recruiter be extended to September 1846. In his letter to Colonel Clarke he wrote, "I have very *particular* reasons (which are private)" for asking for the extension. Clarke forwarded the letter to the adjutant general, who refused the extension. Walker then traveled to Washington to appeal to Adjutant General Roger Jones and Major General Winfield Scott, the commanding general, in person. Returning to Albany, he wrote to Jones on April 16 asking that he be granted an eight-month leave of absence. Always willing to stretch a point in his own favor, he asked that the leave begin not in May but in July, two years from the time he had commenced duty in Utica. Then, strangely, on April 21, Walker wrote to Jones again, asking that his application for leave be withdrawn and that he be ordered to report to his regiment forthwith. His only stipulation was that he be allowed reasonable travel time to visit his family in Georgia en route to Arkansas.[7]

There are two possible explanations for this change of mind. One is that he asked Molly Townsend to marry him and was rejected by her brothers, most probably Franklin, the acting head of the family. Whatever they thought of this young hero as a social acquaintance, they could not have regarded him too highly as a suitor for the hand of their underaged sister. Proud but poor, with only his military pay to live on, and from the alien South, he did not come from the type of family into which the Townsends were used to marrying. Certainly there was a falling-out between the young men, as attested to by Walker's letters to Molly later that summer when the subject of his staying at her mother's house on his return to Albany arose. In one impassioned passage he wrote: "Your brother has taken his stand and *I have taken mine*. Your mother's house is no place for us to meet nor is it a place that my dignity will let me go to *avoid him*. *He is your brother* and I hope we will never meet."[8]

The other possible reason for Walker's sudden reversal was the prospect of war with Mexico. Tensions on the U.S.-Mexican border were high. Texas had been annexed by the United States and had become a state in the Union in 1845. Troops under Zachary Taylor had advanced into Texas to protect U.S. interests in June 1845. In March 1846, Taylor's little Army of Observation had advanced to the Rio Grande to sustain the U.S. claim for that river to be the southern boundary of the new state. Clashes between U.S. and Mexican troops on the north side of the river seemed unavoidable and war appeared imminent. On April 10, the chief quartermaster of Taylor's army disappeared, probably the victim of bandits, but a patrol sent out to find him was ambushed and its officer, Lieutenant Theodoric

Mary Townsend
"Molly" Walker,
W. H. T. Walker's wife
(courtesy of Hugh M.
Walker, Jr.)

Porter, son of Commodore David D. Porter, was killed. News of these events was published nationwide by April 21. That this was the catalyst for Walker's interest in returning to duty was suggested in a memorial printed in August 1864, a few weeks after his death.[9]

Whatever the circumstances, and possibly as a result of both factors, Walker was ready to return to active duty. The adjutant general granted the request for a delayed transit to Arkansas by way of Georgia. Against the wishes of her family, Walker and Mollie impetuously decided to get married so that she could accompany him. On May 9, 1846, they were married by Reverend John N. Campbell in the First Presbyterian Church in Albany. There were no members of the groom's family present. The witnesses were Mollie's brother-in-law Henry H. Martin and a lawyer, Julius Rhoads.[10]

Meanwhile, in Texas, another event had occurred which put a completely different complexion on Walker's future. On May 8 and 9 Taylor's army was victorious in the two small but hard-fought battles of Palo Alto and Resaca de la Palma. These two battles had been preceded by an attack on a party of Americans on the Texas side of the Rio Grande on April 25 and by a Mexican siege of the American fort opposite Matamoros on May 3. It took some time for the news to reach Washington, but on the same day as the Walker wedding President James K. Polk asked Congress to declare war against Mexico. The bill was passed rapidly, and on May 13 the president declared that a state of war existed. Walker had already left Albany on his way to Arkansas and was in Washington when the declaration of war was made. The next day the adjutant general ordered him to Frederick, Maryland, "much against his will," to resume recruiting to bring the army up to strength for war duty. The commander at Fort Smith, Gustavus Loomis, was directed to break up Walker's company and use its men to fill up the other understrength companies of the 6th Infantry.[11]

Recruiting in Maryland proved to be anything but easy. Competition from volunteer organizations being raised for the war caused a poor response for regular recruits. Walker was hampered by a lack of materials and by noncommissioned officers he considered incompetent. The lack of cooperation, as Walker saw it, following his now well-established pattern of self-vindication, of the commanding officer at Fort McHenry, to which place Walker's recruits were to be directed, only compounded his problems. To make matters worse, his asthma began to flare up, as it frequently did when he was under tension, and his old arm wound needed attention. The one bright aspect of the change of scene was that Molly was with him. She joined him in Frederick, Maryland, where they lived cozily in a boardinghouse. When he went out of town to visit his substations, he kept in touch with her by mail. The earliest item in the W. H. T. Walker Papers at Duke University is a letter he wrote her from Cumberland, Maryland, on July 13, 1846.[12]

From Frederick, Walker was moved in August to Easton, Pennsylvania, to recruit for the 6th Infantry. Molly grew tired of the hotel life and decided to visit her mother in Albany. Walker took her home and returned to Easton alone. Finally, on September 10 he was ordered to set up a recruiting rendezvous (collecting point for recruits) in Brooklyn, New York. While there he had frequent opportunity to visit in Albany. Although he made plans for Molly to live with him in Brooklyn, it is not clear whether she ever did so.[13]

Walker had been agitating the War Department to allow him to go to Mexico since July. On October 14, from Brooklyn, he proposed that he organize a company from the recruits on Governor's Island in New York Harbor and take them to Mexico. His suggestion was endorsed by the superintendent of recruiting and the adjutant general and approved by Commanding General Scott. On October 31, he was ordered to form the recruits on Governor's Island into a new Company F, 6th Infantry, to replace the one that had been broken up the previous September, and to take ship for Point Isabel, Texas, to join Taylor's army.

The company was officially mustered into service on November 17. The first muster roll and return, prepared at Tampico, Mexico, the following December 31, showed one officer and ninety men present for duty. Walker spent the six weeks after October 14 organizing his company, arranging shipping, and generally preparing for war service. He selected four sergeants and four corporals from among his recruits. The first, or orderly sergeant, was a veteran, Hiram P. Downs, whose wife would eventually accompany him to Mexico City.

Walker ordered weapons and camp equipment from the chief of ordnance and the quartermaster general, respectively. One of his principal problems was obtaining adequate transportation. Army quartermasters were scrambling to charter, lease, or buy any available vessel at every port in the United States to supply and reinforce Taylor's army. Many vessels were unsuitable, shipping rates naturally soared, and troops and material were backed up waiting their turn to sail.

Walker's flurry of activity was punctuated by his outbursts of impatience at the delay. When not so occupied, he was visiting Molly in Albany with consequences to be realized the following summer.[14]

4

A NEW ADVENTURE

1846–1847

WALKER BADE FAREWELL to Molly in Albany about November 26 (his birthday). On December 1 he and his company of ninety recruits with three camp women departed New York Harbor in the chartered brig *J. Peterson* of Rhode Island registry. At the last minute, to his great delight, Walker's destination was changed from Point Isabel to Tampico, Mexico, a port that had been captured by the U.S. Navy only on November 14. For Walker the change meant that he would be joining the army being formed for the invasion of Mexico rather than that occupying the northern areas along the Rio Grande.[1]

Under the terms of charter then in effect, a ship's captain could be paid either a flat fee for a voyage or a daily rate over a period of time. He was required to provide subsistence for himself and crew. Normally, a copy of the charter document would be given to the troop commander. The captain of the vessel would not receive payment until the charter was handed over to the quartermaster officer at the destination port. The troops brought government-provided rations with them. Water, cooking facilities, and accommodations were to be provided on board. Conditions on most transports proved to be chaotic on the long trip to Mexico. Accommodations were woeful, provisions inadequate or unpalatable, and sickness rife. Bad weather only added to the misery of the passengers.[2]

The voyage of the *Peterson* was destined to be a long one and, initially, very rough. On the first night out, a sudden storm forced the captain to put back to New York after having barely passed the southern tip of Staten Island. The brig remained in quarantine for several days before putting to sea again. Walker had promised Molly that he would keep a journal during his voyage. On December 2 he noted, "Company F, 6th Inf[antry], could be flogged very easily by the Mexicans at the present moment. You never saw such a ghastly looking set." By December 6 the *Peterson* had advanced as far south as Georgia but was forced hundreds of miles east of her proposed course by prevailing winds. That day he wrote that all of his men were awfully sick and "the three camp women, poor things, are nearly dead."[3]

The young army captain also suffered horribly from seasickness. He was the only officer on board and had a cabin to himself but had to serve as doctor, chaplain, and commissary to his men as well as commander. The crew of the brig consisted of the captain of the vessel, a mate, a steward, and a cabin boy, none of whom Walker ever named in his journal. The diet was a monotonous fare of codfish and chowder served up in liberal doses by the steward, who was drunk most of the time. There was little to relieve the tedium at sea. Walker had brought along a Spanish grammar, a book on philosophy, and a book on the lives of Napoleon's marshals. He found the marshals boring and the grammar worthless (no doubt it was to a man who had almost failed French). For the most part he read philosophy and wrote letters to Molly, quoting and misquoting the romantic poets, giving her advice on proper behavior in society for young married ladies, speculating on his prospects in Mexico, and promising undying love.[4]

He also reported humorous or enlightening incidents and observations. On December 6 he related the case of a man who came to him with a complaint of lockjaw. Walker decided that the best way to unlock the jaw was to offer the patient a drink of brandy. The cure worked so well that the "doctor" was afraid he would be besieged with cases of lockjaw for the rest of the voyage.

In the more personal comments, Walker revealed some of his underlying insecurity. He advised Molly on December 9 not to allow any of her male cousins to kiss her and to make them call her "Mrs. Walker" now that she was married. The same day he advised her against sitting on window seats with her male relatives in a manner so that their bodies might touch. In other letters he gave long discourses on the low regard men have for women who act flirtatiously in society. Molly, barely turned eighteen years old, must have been annoyed and surprised by her new husband's apparent mistrust.[5]

The wind finally shifted on December 12. The *Peterson* had been blown almost as far east as Bermuda. Now she began to run back toward the Bahamas, headed for the landfall known to seamen as "the Hole in the

Rock," a point on Great Abaco Island on the Northeast Providence Channel. Walker hoped for a chance to go ashore and stretch his legs and also to mail his journal back to Albany. The skipper of the brig estimated that they would be in Tampico in seven days. Estimate and hope were both dashed. By the fourteenth the wind had dropped to little more than three knots. The weather was delightful, but forward progress was practically nil. It was not until December 16 that they reached the Bahamas.[6]

His hope of mailing letters faded when plans to land on Stirrup Key on December 18 were disappointed by a sudden gale-force wind that blew the vessel away from its anchorage. Walker had been close enough to see and smell the oranges, lemons, and coconuts, but the storm blew them fifty miles away. He contented himself with plans to stop and mail his letters from Key West. Meanwhile, he kept up the journal. On the sixteenth he wrote that he looked forward to a naval engagement before arriving at Tampico. Because the Mexican navy was practically nonexistent, it is not clear who he expected to fight. He reported to Molly on the eighteenth on a pistol her brother Frank had presented him as a gift before he left Albany. Walker had taken it apart to find out why it would not fire. The result of his effort: "I . . . am not mechanic enough to put it together again." [7]

The *Peterson* passed Key West December 21. Because so much time had been lost in the voyage, the captain did not stop. Walker's hopes of mailing letters were once again disappointed. He was also denied the pleasure of meeting an army friend, Lieutenant Massilon Harrison, an engineer at the Key West garrison. Nevertheless, the brig plowed on with its cargo of ninety-plus souls. By this time Walker had taught the cook to prepare chicken soup and buckwheat cakes. Where the ingredients came from he did not say although they might have been part of his private larder. The *Peterson* came upon a school of porpoises while crossing the Gulf of Mexico on December 23. The men were delighted and threw sticks of firewood at the marine creatures. Walker was disdainful of his men's actions but ended that passage in his journal by mentioning that "I amused myself firing a pistol at [the porpoises]." By now he was especially anxious to get to Mexico. A case of measles had occurred in his company. He attempted to quarantine the victim, but in such cramped quarters it was impossible. He feared that the disease would spread through the entire company if he could not soon separate the sick from the well. On a more positive note, he boasted that he had not suffered from asthma a single day since leaving New York.[8]

Christmas Day passed quietly. The captain of the brig and the captain

of Company F shared a dinner of chicken soup and a glass of port wine.
The Mexican coast finally came in sight on December 27. After so many
tribulations the captain had made a perfect landfall at the mouth of the
Panuco River. The joy of the soldiers was soon turned to disappointment.
They had arrived at Tampico, but it took three days to stand into the river
because of the strong offshore breezes. But on December 30 Walker was
finally ashore in Mexico.[9]

Walker next endured two more months of boredom in a tent outside
Tampico, drilling his company, withstanding the "northers" of the winter
season on the Gulf Coast, and awaiting the assembly of General Winfield
Scott's army that would later seize the Mexican port of Vera Cruz. To ease
the boredom, he had reunions with old army friends, tours of the city,
horse riding and hunting, and letter writing. Company F was joined at this
time by Second Lieutenant Rudolph Ernst, a native of Germany and an
1846 graduate of West Point, assigned as Walker's second in command.[10]

The painfully slow buildup of the American army was the result of
several factors. After Zachary Taylor's capture of Monterrey in northern
Mexico in September 1846, it became obvious to the Polk administration
that only a thrust at the heart of Mexico would cause General Antonio
López de Santa Anna's government to sue for peace. An advance by Taylor's army on Mexico City was not feasible. The alternative was seizure
of a Mexican port followed by an overland advance to the capital city. At
first it was thought that Tampico might serve as a base of operations, but
it soon became apparent that the route from there to Mexico City was too
difficult. The next choice was Vera Cruz, whose vulnerability had been
proven by its capture by the French during the "Pastry War" of 1838.

Another decision to be made was the choice of a commander of the army
of invasion. President James K. Polk was a Democrat. His two leading
generals, Winfield Scott, commanding general of the army, and Zachary
Taylor, commanding the Army of Occupation in northern Mexico, were
both Whigs. It was unthinkable for Polk to allow a Whig to gain the glory
of the conquest of Mexico, but there was no other choice. Scott, the pre-
eminent American commander of the antebellum period and one of the
finest military strategists in our nation's history, was given the task.

By the time President Polk made his decision, it was already mid-
November 1846. Scott needed to organize his army, transport it to Mexico,
land on the hostile coast, capture Vera Cruz, and advance away from the
coastal plain before the onset of the yellow fever, or black *vomito*, season, which normally began in April. His transportation problems would

be complicated by the winter storms. By prodigious effort, equipment was purchased or fabricated, shipping arranged, and units identified and sent to Mexico. So it was that Walker's destination had been changed from Point Isabel and Taylor's army to Tampico, one of Scott's assembly points. Despite Scott's best efforts, the available shipping was inadequate to the task at hand and the months of January and February slipped by while the troops already at Tampico sat in the mud and the rain and awaited the arrival of the "mighty man of war."[11]

Like professional soldiers throughout history, Walker was disdainful of the volunteers who had flocked to the colors and many of whom were now camped around him. He mentioned to his wife several times his desire not to have to serve under volunteer officers who outranked him. When a division of Zachary Taylor's army arrived at Tampico, Walker vented his spleen on the two Irish-born volunteer generals in Scott's army, Robert Patterson and James Shields. Walker complained of Shields, "We native Americans . . . find ourselves commanded by a wild Irishman. 'Tis disgusting in the extreme and such contemptible appointments make me feel like quitting my country in disgust." It was a theme he would return to over the years.[12]

Some of Walker's most graphic descriptions of his life in camp are in his letters from Tampico. He spoke with astonishment of the abundance in the Tampico market, he reassured Molly that Mexican women were ugly, and he described himself and his living conditions in great detail. In a letter of January 22, 1847, he described his life in camp: "My orderly sergeant's wife [Mrs. Downs] cooks for us [Walker and Lieutenant Ernst] and we have a servant who waits on us, sets the table, attends to our tents, etc. For breakfast generally we have *buckwheat* cakes, and eggs, for dinner either venison, goose or duck, and vegetables."[13]

Later he complained that he was so well fed that "my coats I can't button so much stouter am I growing." After telling of the varieties and prices of food in the Tampico market, he proceeded with a description of his tent and its furnishings.

As for my tent, I will describe it to you just as it is. The table that I am now writing on is made of two rough pine planks supported by two other rough pine planks sunk in the ground. On it is three cracked tumblers, a sugar dish with the top lost and the handle broken, a pitcher with the mouth broken, a bottle with a candle in it, and two or three bad pens, scribbled paper, and a portable inkstand. Under it, and resting on mother earth, is a pile of pamphlets, books and papers on which is a hairbrush, a razor (dull), and a cracked looking glass, and to the left, under this same table reposes very quietly and unpretendingly, a tin wash basin. All these things you see to the left as you enter the tent. Next on the left comes an empty demijohn, my valise on which is a clothes brush, a hairbrush and two books, and in front of which are three pamphlets on the ground. To the left of this valise and on the same line is my trunk on which are oranges, pistols and overcoats, and in the corner between the trunk and the corner of the tent a pile of haversacks, canteens etc. Between the corner and the center of the back of the tent there is nothing but a pole passing up the center of the back of the tent serving to support the back of the tent. Then comes a barrel and between which and the right wall of the tent as you enter is my bed which extends all the length of this wall. I cannot describe to you my bed so as to convey an idea of its construction. Four uprights with forks to them were sunk in the ground, two at the head and two at the foot. Poles were put connecting these uprights and the staves from a barrel laid across them. On these staves my bed is laid. Sheets and pillow cases, of course, I cut. I have no chairs. My visitors sit on trunks, boxes and my bed. I have a dirt floor. A carpet would be a curiosity. So much for my tent.[14]

Walker was pleased early in February to meet for the first time Mary's brother Robert Townsend, an officer in the USS *Princeton* with the U.S. Navy's Home Squadron. He was also mightily cheered by the arrival of Scott with a staff "as long as a comet's tail" on February 18, not that he was impressed by the size of the staff but that so many of them were his friends and acquaintances. Action soon followed Scott's arrival. With the troops already assembled at Tampico, more arriving from the East Coast of the United States, and a large portion of Taylor's army transferred to his command, Scott was prepared to advance to Vera Cruz. On March 2 Walker and his company boarded the steamer *Alabama* for the run down the Mexican coast to the rendezvous with the Home Squadron at Anton Lizardo, fourteen miles below Vera Cruz. Also aboard were General Patterson and his staff and three hundred men of Colonel William Campbell's 1st Tennessee regiment. Among the officers present, besides Walker and Lieutenant Ernst, were Lieutenants Pierre G. T. Beauregard and George B. McClellan of the engineers and Captain Abram C. Myers of the Quartermaster Department, future quartermaster general of the Confederate army. At Anton Lizardo Walker was overjoyed to be united on March 4 with four more companies of his regiment and to meet on March 6 or 7 his brother John David, a sergeant in the South Carolina Palmetto Regiment.[15]

Scott and the navy's Commodore David Conner decided on a landing as early as possible to avoid damage to the shipping from another norther. First, Scott, Conner, and some of their principal staff officers performed a reconnaissance of Vera Cruz harbor and its protecting fortress of San Juan de Ulúa. They determined that the best landing place would be on the south side of the city. From there they could gradually extend their siege line around to the west and north. After some changes in plans, March 9 was picked as the date for the invasion.[16]

5

TO THE HALLS OF MONTEZUMA

1847–1848

FOR THE LANDING at Vera Cruz Scott organized his army into three divisions, two of regulars commanded by Generals William J. Worth and David E. Twiggs, and one of volunteers under General Patterson. Worth's division was given the honor of leading the amphibious assault. Specially built surfboats were to be used to convey the troops from their transports to the beach. After the initial force had landed and cleared the beach of defenders, the rest of the army could come ashore, encircle the city, and begin the siege.

Walker's company, assigned to Worth's division with the rest of the 6th Infantry, was among the first to land. Although preparations for the landing began early in the morning of March 9, it was not until past five in the afternoon that the first troops waded ashore. General Worth and his staff led the way, followed by the twenty-six hundred men of his division. Without meeting an opposing shot, they rushed across the beach and planted the Stars and Stripes in the dunes to the accompaniment of "The Star Spangled Banner" played by the bands in the fleet offshore. By 11:00 that same night Scott's entire army of eighty-six hundred men, except for the siege batteries, had been landed without the loss of a single life.[1]

Beginning on the morning of March 10 the American troops started their encircling movement. While Worth's division remained south of Vera Cruz, Patterson moved past them to the western side, and Twiggs followed him around to take up position on the north. With Conner's squadron in the bay on the eastern side, Vera Cruz was completely invested. While this investment was taking place, Walker met again with his younger brother, John David, and with Mary's brother Robert.

Investment was one thing; reduction of the fortress and surrender of the city quite another. As Walker noted numerous times in his letters, the Mexicans refused to come out and fight on the plain so the city would have to be taken by artillery barrage. The encirclement was completed by March 13, but lack of suitable transportation and continued bad weather greatly hampered the landing of the siege artillery. Not until March 22 were Scott's batteries ready to begin their bombardment.[2]

Scott's army faced a bastion which many military experts believed nearly impregnable despite the easy victory of the French in 1838. The city held a population of about fifteen thousand and a garrison, under Brigadier General Juan Morales, of some thirty-three hundred. Almost 250 guns were emplaced, nearly evenly divided between the city and its protecting fort of San Juan de Ulúa, but many of the guns were unserviceable or improperly mounted and the gunners were hampered by a serious shortage of powder. Beyond the garrison itself, there were several thousand Mexican troops outside the American lines who throughout the siege launched continued but ineffectual attacks against the besiegers. Contrary to expert opinion, General Morales, who had an intimate knowledge of his position, considered Vera Cruz indefensible.[3]

It was during the period of construction of the American emplacements and movement of the heavy guns that Walker put in his most arduous service of the siege. His company was detached from the 6th Infantry and sent on outpost duty in advance of the American lines. His mission was to provide protection for the engineers against forays from Vera Cruz. Although no such raids took place, Walker's company and others similarly selected were subjected to fierce, continuous cannonading. Once a company was posted, it could not be withdrawn or relieved except under cover of darkness. As Walker described one such incident to his wife, "When day broke my position was discovered and from ten o'clock in the morning until eight at night an incessant firing was kept up by the enemy from their batteries. . . . I made my men lie flat on their faces from eleven o'clock until dark." Ever nonchalant, Walker added, "I got tired of lying on my face and quietly turned my face to heaven, put an overcoat under my head, and resorted to my comforter, a segar."[4]

Captain Ephraim Kirby Smith, whose younger brother, Edmund Kirby Smith, would achieve fame in the Civil War, had duty similar to Walker's. In a letter to his wife on conditions in the front lines, he reported:

On the morning of the fifteenth [of March] . . . General Worth came to our position and ordered us to advance. Captain Walker was thrown forward with his company to a large cemetery near the wall of the city, and I was ordered to remain about two hundred yards in his rear to support him in case he was attacked. Towards night Walker thought himself threatened by cavalry from the city, and I advanced to his assistance. It was, however, only a small reconnoitering party which soon retired. It rained nearly all night and by morning we were all pretty well worn out by two nights' picket duty. We . . . returned to camp dirty, wet, cold, and hungry.

Walker's version of this incident, less graphic than Smith's, included the detail that he had captured three members of the reconnoitering party.[5]

The Americans were frustrated by what they considered the cowardliness of the Mexicans in not coming out for an open fight. There was little glory to be won in skirmishes and picket duty. But the bombardment had the desired effect, and on March 29 the Mexican commander surrendered. The defenders marched out of the city and laid down their arms; the Americans marched in and raised the Stars and Stripes. Mexican losses were estimated at about two hundred killed and wounded. The U.S. forces lost thirteen killed and fifty-five wounded. Walker had nothing but contempt for the Mexicans and said so forcefully in his report to Mary on the surrender: "These Mexicans are not men. They seem to have all the bad blood of Spain and Africa and the Indians in their veins. I have no sympathy for them. They have made themselves the laughingstocks of their women and children. I dislike to look at such a band of cowards."[6]

Throughout his stay in Mexico, Walker gave full vent to his white, Anglo-Saxon chauvinism. He inveighed against Irish-born generals put over native-born American officers and freely expressed his disdain for his Mexican opponents, but he saved his strongest vitriol for volunteer officers given positions of responsibility over regulars or regular officers who had left the service and returned as volunteers in a higher grade.

Writing to Mary from Tampico, Walker voiced the lament of professional soldiers in every army.

The army is completely swallowed by the volunteers. Col[onel]s and majors and gen[era]ls are as thick as bees and a capt[ain] in the U.S. Army is a very small man in the midst of so many gentlemen of rank. What I object to is that they should throw the regular and volunteer forces together. . . . All these citizen political soldiers imagine because they are great Jackson men that they must have his soldierly qualities but, alas, how little they are aware what complete fools some of them are in the military. They annoy us by their ridiculous blunders and ignorance and we have only rank enough to criticize.[7]

In another letter, he referred to volunteer General Gideon Pillow of Tennessee as a "mushroom general." For having appointed such officers, Walker called President Polk, Pillow's former law partner, "a fifth rate Tennessee lawyer."[8]

With Vera Cruz taken, Scott had to resolve the logistical problems of his advance into the Mexican interior. Concurrent with his desire to see that his army was properly outfitted was his need to move away from the coast before the onset of the fever season, the dreaded *vomito*. The need to move overcame the need to organize, and on April 2 Scott began his advance to Jalapa, seventy-four miles inland and forty-seven hundred feet above sea level and the fever zone. At the same time, measures were set in motion to arrange for supplies and transportation. Twiggs's division moved off first, followed by Patterson's. For lack of transportation, Worth's division, with Walker's company now reunited with its regiment, remained at Vera Cruz. Scott remained in Vera Cruz to work on his supply problems.[9]

At this juncture six of the 6th Infantry's ten companies were present in Mexico. The regimental commander was Colonel Newman S. Clarke. The second in command was Major Benjamin L.E. Bonneville, the noted western explorer whose name is now best remembered from the racing flats near Salt Lake City and from a model of automobile. Bonneville had made a name for himself in the West, but of his service in Mexico Justin Smith said that he "proved himself incompetent or worse." Besides Walker's company, which had sailed from New York, four had sailed from New Orleans or Brazos Santiagos under Colonel Clarke, and three had marched overland from Texas to Zachary Taylor's army under Bonneville. Only one of Bonneville's companies had joined Scott's army, but the other two were on the way. Walker's company lieutenant was Rudolph F. Ernst, with whom he had shared meals at Tampico. Officers besides Walker whose names would later become prominent were Lieutenants Lewis A. Armistead, Edward "Alleghany" Johnson, Simon Bolivar Buckner, and Winfield Scott Hancock. Lieutenant Colonel Loomis was left behind with the two companies that remained in Indian Territory. Of his service with Walker in Mexico, Buckner would later be quoted as saying, "It was my good fortune to serve through the Mexican War under General Walker of Georgia . . . and, sir, it is to him I am indebted for whatever military enthusiasm I now possess."[10]

A Mexican army of twelve thousand troops under the personal command of General Santa Anna had chosen a strongly laid-out defensive position on the Jalapa road at Cerro Gordo. Twiggs arrived there on April 11 and attempted to push his way through on the twelfth. When his advance troops met enemy fire, the entire division withdrew. Twiggs ordered a frontal assault for the morning of April 13, but General Patterson, who had come up and was the senior officer present, canceled the attack until Scott could come forward.

Scott had received word of Twiggs's encounter with Mexican forces late on the eleventh. He immediately set out for Cerro Gordo, ordering Worth's division to follow him. Because of the lack of transportation, the men had to carry everything they needed on their backs. Walker, as an infantry company officer, marched on foot with his men. The heat was intolerable, and men fell out of ranks by the hundreds. Thirty men in Walker's company fell behind on the three-day march, but they all caught up by the time the division arrived near Twiggs's position. Despite their fatigue, officers and men alike were enthusiastic over an opportunity to meet the Mexicans in battle.[11]

After three months in Mexico, and at the far end of an inadequate supply line, the American troops were beginning to look like a band of brigands. Walker described himself to his wife: "I have no shirt but a flannel one. I have on a sailor's shirt over that made [from] a frock coat. No stock or cravat, a pair of pantaloons that were once white but, alas, are so no longer, a pair of thick soldier's shoes, a head of hair that scissors have been a stranger to since my arrival in Mexico, and a beard that has cut the acquaintance of razors. This is my marching trim."[12]

As events turned out, Worth's division had little to do at Cerro Gordo. Twiggs's regulars and Patterson's volunteers carried out the assaults on April 17 and 18, with the regulars doing the bulk of the fighting. Worth's role was to follow behind Twiggs to join the battle if necessary. When Worth's men arrived on the field, they were in time only to assist in rounding up prisoners. Said Walker, "You may well imagine how disgusted I was when, after running up several heights to participate in the action, to find when we came in view the enemy had surrendered." So rapidly had Santa Anna decamped that he left behind his personal carriage and his wooden leg. The road was now open to Jalapa.[13]

While the main body of Scott's army stopped at that garden spot of the Mexican highlands to recuperate, Worth's division pushed ahead to Perote. Walker had no time to stop, but he noted: "The Xalapa [sic] girls are very pretty. I only had a peep at them as I marched through the streets, but as their bright, black eyes beamed from behind their lattices, one really thought that night had come and he was gazing on a firmament of stars." Apparently, the more time passed and the farther he got from Albany, the better the Mexican girls appeared. Walker had written from the camp near Vera Cruz that his bachelor friends were much taken with the "pretty figures, pretty feet and hands, and sweet voices of the Mexican girls," but "they do not claim from me even a passing glance."[14]

Once arrived in Perote, he received a dinner invitation from a Spanish gentleman but was embarrassed to have no shirt to wear. He told Mary: "A soldier I had at Vera Cruz deserted and ran off with all my shirts and cravats, my sword and revolver. I have cut shirts since this catastrophe (except flannel) . . . . Wearing shirts is altogether a mere idle fashion. . . . I have discarded razors and . . . I don't think it was intended that hair should ever be cut."[15]

The vicissitudes of campaigning and the social possibilities of Mexico, however, did not distract Walker from his habitual occupation, defending his honor and dignity. While at Perote he prepared his bimonthly muster roll for Company F for the period March 1 to April 30. In it he noted that Corporal Joseph Kerwin, the man he credited with saving his life in Florida in 1837, had transferred into the company as a sergeant. Major Bonneville, the acting regimental commander, made some comments on the roll which Walker regarded as highly derogatory. There was a space on the form to rate the company for quality of discipline and instruction, military appearance, and condition of arms, equipment, and clothing. Bonneville rated Company F as "improving" in discipline and instruction, "indifferent" in appearance, "good" in condition of arms and equipment, but "wasted" in condition of clothing. If Walker's description of himself was any indication, Bonneville's ratings on appearance and clothing may have been accurate.[16]

At any rate, Walker begged to differ and was not put off by Bonneville's lofty reputation. He addressed a letter to the adjutant general on the topic on May 14. The opening sentence told the story: "I cannot permit the remarks of Major Bonneville . . . to be read . . . without some explanatory remarks for they incidentally reflect upon me as the Captain of the company." Then he went on to explain, convincingly to the objective reader, the various defects perceived by Major Bonneville. He did not neglect to take a swipe at Bonneville. "The discipline of the company when it was in Tampico [i.e., an independent command] . . . was more to my taste than it has been under the direction of Major Bonneville." He closed with one more reminder of the real purpose of the letter: "I make these remarks because I deem them due to myself." The complaint had the desired effect. On future muster rolls the company was rated good in all categories except clothing, which was marked "much worn and none on hand [for replacement]."[17]

At Perote, on May 2, the 6th Infantry was joined by several officers, the regimental band, and 180 recruits from Fort Gibson who had come to Vera Cruz from New Orleans and then marched up to join the army. Among the new officers were Lieutenants Anderson D. Nelson, who had charge of the party of recruits, and Ralph W. Kirkham, regimental adjutant. Colonel Clarke retained Kirkham in his position in the regiment and also appointed him assistant adjutant general for the brigade. Kirkham's wife was the niece by marriage of Lieutenant Colonel Loomis.[18]

On May 10 Worth advanced from Perote, reaching Puebla on the fifteenth. En route, there was a slight brush on the fourteenth with Mexican cavalry at Amozoca. The brigade of which Walker's regiment was a part advanced out of the little town to meet the enemy, but the Mexicans fled when the American artillery opened up on them.

Puebla was the point of no return for Scott's army. When he left there to continue his advance to Mexico City he would sever his line of communications with his base at Vera Cruz. Also, his army would be greatly reduced in size. The terms of service of the volunteer regiments that had enlisted for twelve months in May and June 1846 were about to expire. Only about 10 percent of them agreed to remain with Scott. Rather than attempt to hold them involuntarily, Scott allowed them to march off to Vera Cruz early in June. He was now tied to Puebla until newly raised regiments of regulars and volunteers could arrive from the United States.[19]

Walker was completely smitten by the women of Puebla. On May 26, he wrote: "The ladies of Puebla are remarkable for their small feet and hands, fine figures, pretty black hair and eyes. They dance waltzes and walk more gracefully as a body than any females I have seen. They are remarkable for their suavity of manner and kindness of heart. Their beauty is talked of much by those who admire their style." This was a far cry from the "mulattoes" of Vera Cruz, but he added, lamely, "Give me the eye that has heaven's blue in it and the heart that has heaven's virtue and goodness." One wonders how closely he had assessed the Puebla women's ability to waltz and kindness of heart. If Walker did succumb to Mexican beauty, he was only one of many.[20]

After two months of rest, recuperation, and reinforcement at Puebla, Scott's army, now organized in three regular divisions commanded by Generals Worth, Twiggs, and Gideon Pillow, and one of volunteers, led by John A. Quitman, was ready for its final advance. Scott had fourteen thousand men, of whom eleven thousand were fit for the march to Mexico. On August 7 they moved out from Puebla. Walker was still assigned to Worth's division. Colonel Newman S. Clarke was now the brigade commander, and the temporary commander of the 6th Infantry was Major Bonneville.

The first stage of the march was to Ayotla, placing Scott about twenty miles from Mexico City and giving him a choice of four routes in his final approach to the capital. He chose to move around the south side of Lakes Chalco and Xochimilco to the villages of San Agustín and San Antonio, directly south of Mexico City, and then advance to Tacubaya, about three miles from the southern gate of the city. This route would take him up against the strong Mexican defenses at Churubusco, where the access way narrowed between the lakes on the east and a vast lava bed known as the *pedregal* on the west. This movement was conducted between August 15 and 18 with Worth's division and the cavalry in the lead.[21]

In an attempt to get around the *pedregal* to the west to bypass the Mexican defenses, American reconnaissance found a route past the village of Contreras. Scott concluded to go that way and ordered that a road be cut across the *pedregal*. Work began on the road on the morning of August 19 by the divisions of Generals Pillow and Twiggs, supervised by engineer Captain Robert E. Lee. Worth's division remained at San Antonio in front of the defenses at Churubusco. The work on the road progressed until the Americans came under fire from a Mexican division that had posted itself at Contreras and nearby Padierna. The Americans continued their advance on the evening of the nineteenth, setting the stage for the twin battles of Contreras and Churubusco.[22]

At daylight on August 20 three American brigades launched their attack at Contreras. Within seventeen minutes the Mexican force had been converted from an army to a mob fleeing in retreat. Scott, however, dared not advance too far on his left (Contreras) for fear of leaving Worth's flank on his right unprotected at San Antonio. Therefore, he ordered Worth to try to outflank the Mexicans at San Antonio and keep pace with the American movement from Contreras.

Worth's first move was to send the brigade of Colonel Clarke, including the 6th Infantry, across the *pedregal* and around the Mexican position. Upon seeing this movement, the Mexicans fell back on Churubusco. Their position there consisted chiefly of a fortified convent and a strong point built up at the south end of the bridge across the Churubusco River. To take advantage of the disorganization of the retreating Mexican column,

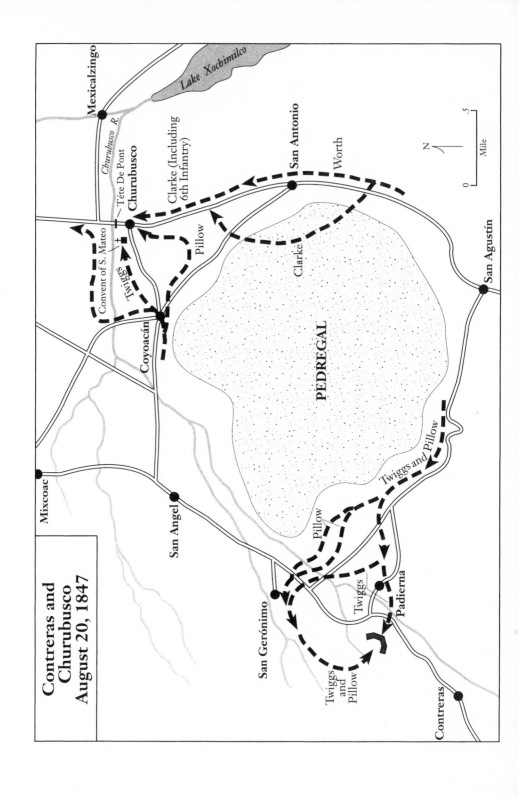

Contreras and Churubusco August 20, 1847

Lake Xochimilco

Mexicalzingo

Churubusco R.

Téte De Pont
Churubusco

Convent of S. Mateo

Clarke (Including 6th Infantry)

Pillow

Twiggs

Twiggs

Coyoacán

San Antonio

Worth

Clarke

PEDREGAL

San Agustín

Twiggs and Pillow

Mixcoac

San Angel

Pillow

Twiggs

San Gerónimo

Padierna

Twiggs and Pillow

Contreras

N

0   .5

Mile

Scott ordered an attack on the convent to clear the way for capturing the bridge and the road. Both convent and bridgehead were strongly defended and masked by thick fields of corn.[23]

The men of Clarke's brigade had crossed the *pedregal* in single file because of the broken nature of the terrain. When the first four companies of the 6th Infantry, which was in advance, had crossed, and before they were completely formed in line, someone, probably Major Bonneville, gave the order to attack. The four companies crossed the road and entered a cornfield, leaving the other four companies behind. The thick corn made it difficult to maintain formation, and when they emerged into an open meadow on the other side of the corn only the color company, Walker's, maintained its dress. Some men from other companies also dressed on the colors and followed Walker to a second road. Here they were halted by Captain William Hoffman, who tried to form some semblance of order.[24]

Major Bonneville then had the battalion formed on the road in a column of platoons with the colors in the lead, and the men advanced rapidly toward the enemy. In the words of one participant, they ran "butt-end" into heavy Mexican fire. In response, the Americans broke for cover to the right and left of the road. On the left side they sheltered among some adobe buildings and on the right behind some trees on the side of the road. Here they began an ineffectual musket fire against the Mexicans until their officers were able to get them to stop and withdraw.

Captain Hoffman tried once more to organize an advance, but the men would not move under the galling Mexican fire. He appealed to the other officers to help him, and Walker promptly responded that he would follow. In a few moments the whole command was on the road again, but as they approached the enemy lines, they found the road blocked by ammunition wagons abandoned by the Mexicans fleeing before them. Captain Hoffman, who had only parts of two companies, including Walker's Company F, remaining with him, went into a cornfield on the right so thick and so high the men could not see each other. They quickly became separated and lost all semblance of a military formation. Hoffman was left with Lieutenant Simon Bolivar Buckner and a few men. He sent Buckner back to Bonneville for instructions, and Bonneville told them to withdraw.[25]

Meanwhile, Walker, with the regimental colors and a few men of his own, had pushed to the leading edge of the field where he could see the Mexican position. Here, Lieutenant Lewis A. Armistead, who was acting as his company lieutenant while Lieutenant Ernst served as regimental adjutant, joined him with a few more men. Their collective strength was

The 6th U.S. Infantry's Mexican War Regimental Colors
(West Point Museum Collections)

only a dozen, and they concluded they could take no action. The colors made their position perfectly obvious to the Mexicans, and, in the words of Armistead, "they cut everything to pieces around us." Walker did not get Hoffman's order to withdraw because Hoffman could not find them. Indeed, for a time it was thought at regimental headquarters that the colors had been lost. On his own, Walker finally decided to drop back to the rest of the regiment.[26]

While the 6th Infantry was thrown into confusion, Twiggs's division advancing from Contreras made the assault on the convent. Worth finally sent Clarke's brigade directly up the road at a dead run to the bridge. The 6th Infantry, "perhaps the best regiment in the army" in Bauer's estimation, and of which Smith said, "probably the army contained no better corps," had finally collected itself and was on the road with the 5th and 8th

regiments in the fields of corn to the right. Worth ordered the 6th to capture the battery at the bridgehead. Hoffman led forward the reconstituted
battalion which Walker had somehow rejoined. They captured the battery
and then swung around the Mexican left flank, joined by some companies
of the 2d Artillery serving as infantry. This final rush took them to and
across the river on the left of the Mexican position in advance of any other
of the attacking forces. Thus threatened, the defenders of the bridgehead
began to withdraw.[27]

In the meantime, a number of bloody assaults had forced the defenders
of the convent and the road to surrender. During the latter fight, John
David Walker, in the South Carolina Regiment in Quitman's division, was
shot through both legs, but neither bone was broken and his wounds were
not considered serious. The American infantry pursued the Mexicans for
two miles north of the river before Scott called a halt. Some of the American dragoons went as far as the walls of Mexico City before turning back.
Future Union general John Sedgwick, Walker's West Point classmate, was
in one of the companies of the 2d Artillery. After the battle he wrote his
sister, "Our regiment with the 6th Infantry were the first in pursuit and
followed them nearly to the gates of the city." [28]

Walker had distinguished himself greatly in this battle. In his report
of the action, General Worth, noting that "the 6th Regiment of Infantry
moved with a steadiness worthy of its established reputation," mentioned
Walker by name, among others, as having been "conspicuously presented
by [his] commander." Colonel Clarke also gave Walker honorable mention. Captain Hoffman wrote, "Among the officers who distinguished
themselves, I may be permitted to mention Capt. Walker particularly, who
was conspicuous by his gallantry in the whole affair." Major Bonneville,
in the regimental report, added to the chorus of praise: "I cannot but
feel proud of the manner in which the regiment advanced until literally
cut to pieces. Observing Captains Hoffman, Alexander, Walker, and also
Lieutenants Hendrickson, Armistead and Nelson with Lieutenants Ernst
and Buckner, together with Sergeant Major Thompson, Battalion Sergeant
Major Owens, and Sergeant Steinecker in front leading the charge along
with the color guard, I cannot speak of them too highly to the general
commanding on this important and brilliant occasion." [29]

For his gallantry at Churubusco, Walker later received a brevet promotion to major. In his laconic fashion, he reported to Mary in a letter from
Tacubaya a few days after the battle: "You came very near being made a
widow for your humble servant came very near being numbered in the

ranks of death having received three shots through his clothes and having been knocked down once with a cannon ball but he is happy in saying that he has not been hurt though, of course, very badly scared. Our regiment was ordered into the thickest of the fight and led into it. We had ninety odd killed and wounded out of about four hundred and fifty."[30]

Scott's losses overall numbered almost exactly a thousand killed and wounded of eighty-five hundred engaged while the Mexican losses were estimated at just under seven thousand of some twelve thousand engaged. In the 6th Infantry, Major Bonneville, Captain Hoffman, and Lieutenants John D. Bacon and Thomas Hendrickson were wounded, the latter severely. Bacon later died of his wounds.[31]

Bonneville's wound was not serious. While standing in the road before the battery was captured, he was struck in the left breast by a musket ball with sufficient force to knock him into a ditch. He later surmised that a leather-covered flask in his inside pocket saved him from more serious injury. As it was, the blow severely bruised the left side of his chest and upper left arm. In addition, Bonneville was unable to clamber out of the waist-deep water in the ditch and had to wait for one or two enlisted men to extricate him. These details would later come to light when he was court-martialed for his lack of activity during the battle.[32]

Rather than launch an attack on the walls of Mexico City, Scott agreed to a truce to allow the American peace commissioner to try to come to terms with the Mexican government. For two weeks the American army fretted over this delay when the prize they had marched so far and fought so hard to capture lay within their sight. Walker joined in the carping over being denied the fruits of victory, but he felt that the war was already over and the Mexicans had been whipped. Yet some of the martial spirit had gone out of him too. Previously he had expressed dissatisfaction with the Polk administration's management of the war and staffing of the army. Now, for the first time, he expressed an interest in leaving the army. In a letter from Tacubaya he asked Mary if the members of her family could influence Secretary of War William Marcy, a New Yorker, to grant Walker a leave so that he could come home. Events would intervene before he could get an answer.[33]

When the truce expired without results, Scott prepared to take Mexico City. In planning with his principal staff officers on September 6, he decided to advance on the city from the south, but on the seventh he heard a rumor that the Mexicans were melting down church bells to mold into cannon just southwest of the city gate at a row of stone buildings called Molino del Rey. Although this rumor later proved unfounded, Scott thought he should take the Molino.[34]

The attack was launched by Worth's entire division of 3,250 men at dawn on September 8. It was a traditional frontal assault. Each of the two brigades of the division was assigned one end of the building to attack. In advance, a picked command of the best 500 men in the division, organized into five companies of 100 men each, was to attack the front of the building. Walker was given the command of the men selected from the 1st Infantry. Under the false impression that the buildings had been abandoned, the Americans advanced freely in the open. When they came within range, the hidden Mexican gunners opened fire. Of the fourteen officers in the picked battalion, eleven were gunned down in the first shock, Walker among them. The battalion reeled back in disarray. The exultant Mexican infantry ran from the buildings among the wounded, bayoneting every man who moved. In Walker's company only he and one private escaped the butchery, probably because they appeared to be already dead. Bauer says the Americans believed the Mexicans slit the throats of the wounded. Smith reported that the wounded were butchered and robbed. Robert Kirkham gives a graphic description of a wounded officer who was stabbed to death before being robbed and stripped of his clothing. Raphael Semmes, a naval officer with Scott's army, wrote that the Mexicans were *"bayoneting the wounded* with savage delight." [35]

Walker had taken a musket or carbine ball in the back. Unable to move under the hail of Mexican fire, he lay immobile on the field. Each time he attempted to lift his head or shift his position he drew more musketry. Not until the defenders were driven from the buildings after about two hours of fighting could he be carried to safety. A more detailed description of Walker's wound is not available. Kirkham said he was shot through the body, possibly near the hip, because the bullet struck a miniature of Mary that Walker had in his pocket. Eleven months later he wrote that his hip was improved and he could again walk without a cane. This information indicates that he was shot in the lower back near the hip or pelvis.[36]

This costly victory had been a hollow one for Scott. At a price of about eight hundred casualties he had killed or wounded some two thousand Mexicans, captured seven hundred more, and occupied some empty stone buildings. Clarke's brigade lost half of its officers and a third of its men, among them Captain Kirby Smith, Walker's companion in outpost duty at Vera Cruz. In the 6th Infantry, besides Walker, Lieutenant Ernst was mortally wounded and Captain Albemarle Cady was wounded. To make matters worse, after the battle Scott withdrew his men to their original positions. The attack on Molino del Rey is judged by historians to have been Scott's most serious tactical error in the Mexico City campaign.[37]

The battle at Molino del Rey ended Walker's fighting in Mexico. His conduct earned him another brevet promotion, this time to lieutenant colonel, but it would be months before he could stand upright again. From his hospital bed in Mexico City, where he had been carried on a stretcher after the city was finally taken, he wrote to Mary that the wound itself was not so debilitating as the fevers and side effects that accompanied it. The fever was so bad that his condition became critical and his life was feared for. Three months after the battle he was still flat on his back and hoping to return to Albany in a month at best.[38]

William Montgomery Gardner, another Augustan with Scott's army, had been critically wounded at Churubusco. He was already in the hospital when Walker was brought in. Gardner recalled several incidents that reflected Walker's irrepressible nature. On being told by the surgeons, as he had been ten years before in Florida, that they could offer him no hope of recovery, Walker is reputed to have replied, "If I could only be certain that I had no chance to get well, I'd send to the market for a turtle, the biggest to be found, dine on turtle soup, and die like a gentleman." A more likely tale recounted by Gardner concerned another officer who had received a minor injury when struck by a fragment of stone broken off by a cannonball. This young man lay in the bed next to Walker, emitting terrible moans and groans. Walker, who had been suffering in silence, finally said, "Lieutenant, are you suffering very much?' "Not so very much," was the reply. "Then, confound it, shut up," said Walker, "I am!"[39]

While Walker lay near death in Mexico City, the actions of his battalion commander at Churubusco and elsewhere came under scrutiny. On October 5, a court-martial convened in Mexico City to consider the grave charge of misbehavior before the enemy against Major Benjamin L. E. Bonneville. For three weeks the court considered a list of ten specifications of shortcomings on Bonneville's part at the battles of Churubusco and Molino del Rey. Almost thirty witnesses, most of whom were critical of Bonneville, presented far more detailed accounts of the two battles than appeared in the official reports. Bonneville took nothing away from the 6th Infantry's luster in his own defense statement when he said, "I commanded a regiment second to none in point of reputation." In the end, he was found guilty of only three of the specifications. The final verdict was that he was guilty of "want of due exertion and activity." He was sentenced to be admonished in general orders by the general in chief. Walker was listed as a witness but was too ill to appear at the trial. He must have been aware of its progress.[40]

Although Walker's misery was to continue for some time, there was one bright new star on his horizon, and help, although slow, was on its way.

6

HERO AND FAMILY MAN

1848–1854

WHILE CAPTAIN WALKER had been tramping and fighting across Mexico, events of great interest to him had been transpiring in Albany. By April, at the latest, Walker was aware that he was soon to be a father. Several of his letters that spring contained veiled notes of pride and longing at the thought of the impending birth. By July 27 he wrote that he was "dying" to see his child, and in August, "Kiss him, her, or it [for me]." On July 7, 1847, Mary Townsend Walker gave birth to a healthy baby girl. The name Molly proposed to her husband was Mary Cresswell Walker, after his mother. He gladly acceded to her suggestion, although he said he would have been equally happy with calling the child Mary Townsend. The baby quickly became known as "little Molly" after her mother, and her uncles sometimes called her "Molina" from the place where her father had been wounded.

In a letter to her brother Fred in January 1848, Mary described the baby, now six months old: "She has two teeth, she is so bald, plays bo peep, plays with and kisses her father's daguerrotype; not a pretty child but a bright one." In the same letter, commenting on a letter dated November 1847, which she had received from Walker, Mary complained, "The letter before that was, 'Oh, I am dying to see you, my Molly,' and now he don't speak so of me at all. Still, I would feel hurt if he did not express just such a desire [to see the baby]." [1]

While Walker strengthened himself with thoughts of his child, the Townsend family was setting in motion plans to rescue him from Mexico and the army doctors. There is no record of when the family first heard of Walker's wound, but by December 1847 they were aware of his condition in the Mexico City hospital. Walker had written to Mary that his mother wanted him to return to Georgia. Instead, Franklin, by now over his displeasure at his sister's marriage, and Robert Townsend determined to go to Mexico and bring him back. On January 6, 1848, Franklin sailed for Vera Cruz. En route he was to meet Robert, and the two would work out a plan for Walker's return.[2]

Evidently they were not too successful, for the army took matters into its own hands. By a special order issued on February 29, 1848, Walker was to "repair" to Albany, New York. On March 3 an army doctor was ordered to accompany him as far as New Orleans, and on March 4, an enlisted soldier of his own company was assigned to Walker as personal attendant all the way to Albany. Presumably, shortly thereafter Walker came down from Mexico City by army convoy to Vera Cruz, where he may have been met by the Townsend brothers and carried to New Orleans. Possibly, John David Walker accompanied them.[3]

Walker's older brother, Beverly, journeyed to New Orleans to meet the returning party. He attempted to induce William to return to Augusta with him, but the invalid was adamant; he would go to Albany to see his wife and daughter even if it killed him. Unknown to Walker, Mary had come to Augusta en route to New Orleans. Only after her arrival in Georgia did she learn, perhaps from the disappointed Beverly, that her husband had already proceeded up the Mississippi, using the inland water route to get to Albany. His journey was slow because he had to be carried on a litter the entire way. It was not until May 2 that the little caravan reached Albany.[4]

The day after his arrival there, Mary returned to Albany from Augusta, bringing Mary Cresswell Walker to see her ailing son. The elder Mrs. Walker's letters back to Augusta were gloomy and not encouraging. By the time she returned to Georgia near the end of June, however, Walker's brother-in-law Dr. Walter Ewing Johnston was able to write, "[We are glad to hear] our dear friend, the Lieutenant Colonel, has again assumed the vertical." Walker continued to improve. By August, although he still complained of problems with his hip, he was well enough to travel to West Point and spoke of thriving on a diet of "roast beef and exercise," and he had dispensed with the services of his hospital attendant.[5]

The winter climate in the North had never agreed with Walker and, as was to become his custom in later years, he took his family south in November 1848. The citizens of Augusta were ready to welcome their hero home. The *Augusta Constitutionalist* for Saturday, November 18, and the

Augusta Chronicle and Sentinel for Monday, November 20, 1848, reported, under the heading "Complimentary Ball for Colonel Walker":

> One of the most brilliant and showy affairs that Augusta has produced for many seasons was the complimentary ball of Thursday evening. Col. Wm. Henry Walker, the honored guest of the evening, was present, the cynosure of all eyes, and received the greetings of a large assemblage of his friends and fellow citizens of both sexes. The young, the fair, and the gay, gave grace and hilarity to the scene, while many of our staid matrons and sober citizens made their appearance, for the first time in many years, to give evidence of their high appreciation of the gallant conduct and soldierly qualities of the honored guest. Augusta is proud of her gallant son who has been preserved, almost by a miracle, from a soldier's grave, and receives him again with a beating heart and open arms to the home of his childhood where he has ever been known and esteemed for every estimable quality. After his dreadful wound at Molino del Rey, from which he lingered many weary months in pain and agony, upon the verge of the grave, he comes among us in high health and spirits with his fair and accomplished lady and infant daughter, to find among his early friends and companions a brief and grateful repose from the toils of the camp and the field. Green be the laurels that grace his manly brow, and long may he live to wear them.
>
> We should not omit to mention that among the guests of the evening was . . . Mr. John David Walker, now of Charleston, brother of Col. Walker, a member of the Palmetto regiment, who was severely wounded in the battle of Churubusco.

Despite improvements in his condition, Walker continued to feel the effects of his wound, reporting to the adjutant general in December, "My wound has given me much trouble and yesterday the cause was explained by a piece of bone coming out of it."[6]

The Walkers remained in Augusta until February 1849, when William brought his family to Washington, D.C., to receive his new orders. It was now nearly eighteen months since he had been wounded and he was ready to return to active duty, though in a limited capacity. The 6th Infantry had returned to the western frontier with headquarters at St. Louis. Company F was at Fort Crawford, Wisconsin. Walker was still nominally commander of Company F, but he was manifestly unfit for life at a frontier post, especially so far north. Walker and the Townsends pulled all the political strings they could to get him an assignment in Washington.

The aged inspector general of the army, Colonel George Croghan, who had held his post since 1825, died in January 1849. Walker was one of those who hoped to replace him. Furthering this goal was the purpose of the family trip to Washington in February. Walker prevailed on several prominent citizens to write to President-elect Zachary Taylor in his behalf, but the post went to Colonel James Duncan, another young Mexican War hero. Duncan had been one of the agents through whom outgoing President Polk engineered General Scott's removal from command in Mexico in 1848, and the inspector generalcy was his reward.[7]

Walker returned to Albany and continued to furnish the adjutant general with monthly reports on the delicacy of his health. Then in July 1849, Colonel Duncan died suddenly at Mobile, Alabama, following the wedding of Braxton Bragg, at which he had been best man. Walker's hopes were renewed, and he appealed directly to Secretary of War George W. Crawford, a Georgian, for the appointment. This time he enlisted the aid of prominent Whig politicians such as William Seward of New York and Arthur Hoskins of Alabama to intercede with President Taylor. Again, the appointment went to another. This minor episode in his career demonstrated how political Walker could be when seeking a promotion. He considered himself a man of integrity, and he was, but he was never above the most blatant exploitation when personal advancement was at stake.[8]

In August, the adjutant general offered Walker command of the recruiting rendezvous in New York City, and he accepted. He was ordered to take up his new responsibilities on August 31, which he did. Alas, the winter weather was too cruel for him, and on December 31 he asked for relief so that he could travel to the South for his health. Walker remained in Georgia by himself that winter. Mary stayed with her mother in Albany. On September 11, 1849, she had given birth to a boy, Freeman Walker, named after his paternal grandfather and usually called "Freemy." Wrote Walker to his wife, "He is a boy that is worth rearing."[9]

In April 1850, Walker reported himself well enough to resume duty in New York but asked for relief from having to report to his company, now at Fort Kearny, Nebraska. The adjutant general had other plans for him. Walker had been back from Mexico for two years and had seen only four months of active service in that period, all in New York City. Colonel Jones wrote a tactful letter explaining that other officers had been on the frontier without relief for years and deserved a turn in the civilized cities of the East. Walker would have to go to duty in the West. After his arrival in Albany in June, Walker wrote again, this time to the Headquarters of the Army in New York, asking for a temporary extension on recruiting duty, and it was granted to him.[10]

This geographical separation of army authority bears a note of explanation. Although the War Department and the various staff department heads were always located in Washington, the commanding general or general in chief of the army was free to locate his headquarters wherever he desired. After his return from the Mexican War, Winfield Scott, feeling he had been badly used by the War Department and jealous of Zachary Taylor's election to the presidency, moved his headquarters to New York City. Later still, he moved to West Point, which was his headquarters at the outbreak of the Civil War. Scott was not the only commanding general to do this. During his tenure, William T. Sherman moved the Headquarters of the Army to St. Louis, also to get away from official Washington.[11]

Before leaving Augusta to go to Albany and pick up his family, Walker had a piece of deferred personal business to attend to. In November 1847, when the news of his heroic deeds had been reported back to Georgia, the state legislature had adopted a resolution authorizing that he be presented a sword:

> Whereas Captain William H. T. Walker of the 6th Regiment, U.S. Infantry, achieved for himself under the command of General Zachary Taylor during the Florida War a reputation creditable to himself and his native state, and more recently under General Worth at the battles around Mexico City sustained with signal gallantry his former high position, be it therefore unanimously resolved that his Excellency the Governor is hereby requested to have purchased and presented an elegant sword suited to an officer of his rank as a testimony by the General Assembly that the said Captain William H. T. Walker has deserved well of his country.[12]

Delays in manufacture and lack of opportunities had prevented a presentation of the sword, but now the citizens of Augusta were anxious to carry out their pleasant duty in the name of the governor. A polite correspondence between the governor's representative, James Gardner, publisher of the *Augusta Constitutionalist*, and the colonel, and a series of meetings to arrange a suitable presentation, were reported in the press. A date and time were finally agreed upon. The mayor and city council of Augusta and a committee of distinguished citizens hastened to arrange the festivities. On the appointed night, May 23, 1850, the event came off magnificently.

> A temporary stage had been erected at the platform on the eastern side of City Hall, the back of which was framed by two Star Spangled Banners and the corners in front ornamented with two military standards, one a portrait of the gallant General [Duncan L.] Clinch and the other, the Rattle Snake flag of

Georgia. A few minutes before six o'clock a single gun announced the arrival of the Committee of Arrangements who attended Colonel Walker to the stage and took their seats upon it with him. The band played "Hail, Columbia," and His Honor, the mayor [Thomas W. Miller], presented Colonel Walker to James Gardner, Jr., Esquire, the representative of His Excellency, the Governor. Mr. Gardner addressed Colonel Walker in a few remarks on his gallant service and the local scene in sight of the house where he drew his first breath, the Academy where he learned his lessons and the hall which had echoed his father, then he presented the sword. Colonel Walker responded by saying he was not eloquent, but his remarks were greeted by repeated bursts of applause. A national salute ended the ceremony and after a short interval the platform was occupied for the rest of the evening by dancers. The City Hall was brilliantly illuminated and the trees were hung with lamps. Behind the orchestra a large transparency showed the name of Colonel Walker and the battles in which he distinguished himself in Florida and Mexico. The appearance of this gallant officer with his fine, frank military bearing after having been twice *riddled* with enemy's bullets — with all the associations which surrounded him — moistened the cheek of many a mother on the platform and caused many a father's eye to glisten.

Fredrika Bremer, the Swedish traveler and chronicler, who had been staying in Augusta, elaborated:

I was pleased that the young hero of the day, in his speech, mentioned with affection and praise many of his comrades in the war, who had, he said, deserved this distinction better than he; and he related their achievements. He seemed to have a heartfelt delight in speaking of the deeds of his comrades-in-arms. [After the ceremony] the hero of the day descended from the platform amid a host of friends and acquaintances; his sword of honor, with its handsome silver hilt, its inscription and belt, was passed from hand to hand among the spectators. After this, music struck up, and the company proceeded in a promenade dance under the trees . . . the young hero at a given sign taking the lead. . . . A heavy shower of rain, which came on quite unexpectedly, put a sudden end to the fete, and sent everybody helter-skelter home.

The sword was engraved with the names of Walker's battles, "Okeechobee, Vera Cruz, Churubusco, Molino del Rey." [13]

Walker took up recruiting duty in Albany after reporting as ordered in New York. After only three months, as had now become the norm, he asked for relief from the northern climate. This was quickly followed by a request to withdraw his application for relief and then by another to be allowed to travel in Europe for his health. Sometime after October 26,

1850, Walker set sail for Europe. Whether Mary and the children accompanied him is not known, but they probably did not. Mary gave birth to another child the month after Walker returned from Europe so her condition may have prevented her from going with him.

The tour took Walker to England, France, and northern Italy, where he visited the scenes of Napoleon's campaigns. In Rome, he apparently teamed up with Captain George W. Cullum and another gentleman and the trio traveled on through Egypt, Palestine, and Turkey. It was reported that Walker kept a journal on this trip, but it has not been found. All that remains is his annotated guidebook to Rome with the flyleaf inscribed with the date December 18, 1850.[14]

Walker returned to the United States in June 1851 and requested a return to recruiting duty in Albany. His request was denied by the adjutant general, but apparently he once again appealed to the Headquarters of the Army, for on July 11, with the approval of Winfield Scott's assistant adjutant general in New York, Walker was ordered to duty as a recruiter. The family rented a house at 93 Eagle Street. He stayed at this post for a year, even weathering the Albany winter, before asking for a month's leave to go to Georgia, probably because of the death of his uncle Valentine Walker. By June 1, he was back in Albany, but in July he asked for and was granted a twelve-month leave of absence to take care of personal business affairs, "which if neglected will involve me in serious pecuniary embarrassment." Walker left for Georgia hurriedly in September 1852, accompanied by his sister Sarah, who had been visiting in Albany.[15]

The reason for his request for leave and his haste in getting to Georgia was that Walker had been bitten by the entrepreneurial bug. By some happenstance he had fallen in with George W. Beardslee of Albany, New York, later the inventor of the magnetic telegraph. Beardslee had perfected and patented a process for making paper from wood shavings and had set up a planing and papermaking mill in Little Falls, New York. Either through his own inspiration or by someone else's suggestion, Walker quickly saw the value of such a process in the piney woods of Georgia. He struck a deal with Beardslee for exclusive rights to the use of the patent in Georgia, borrowed some capital from Mary's uncle, and went off to Augusta to buy a planing machine and find a place to set it up.[16]

Now Walker's network of military acquaintances came into play. His West Point classmate Marcus C. M. Hammond had left the army and was living across the Savannah River from Augusta in Hamburg, South Carolina. Hammond's wife's stepfather, Major Wyatt W. Starke, also lived in

Hamburg. Major Starke's natural daughter was married to an army officer, Colonel George Talcott, former commander of the Augusta Arsenal. Through these connections, Walker learned that Starke, a man of vast and intricate business dealings, who had recently fallen on hard times, had for sale a planing machine on an island in the Savannah River near the city of Savannah. Starke had been using the machine in an ordinary lumber mill operation.

After some difficulties, Walker bought the machine from Starke, but he used up most of his capital in so doing and did not have an engine to power the machine. He knew he could not borrow more from the Townsend family. He was on the point of abandoning the project, giving up his leave, and reporting to his regiment when he made another fortuitous meeting. This time his benefactor was Robert A. Allen, a wealthy Savannah merchant who was a native of and maintained a farm in south Richmond County, in the area now known as Allen's Station. Somehow Walker convinced Allen of the viability of the project, and Allen agreed to take charge. As Walker wrote to Mary, "I play in the performance that very interesting character, the 'gentleman.'" Despite his role as nearly silent partner in the project, it is apparent that Walker was one of the early leaders in introducing wood pulping, now one of the state's economic mainstays, to Georgia.[17]

Archibald Johnston, the brother of Walker's brothers-in-law, Adam and Walter, found an engine at an excellent price in Charleston. Allen engaged a good mechanic, William Kine, by offering him a share of the venture. On October 18, 1852, Walker and Allen signed a contract to build a lumber and planing mill in Savannah, to be operated by Allen and sundry of his other business partners. Walker's share was based on his holding the right to use the Beardslee patent in Georgia. The contract granted Allen's company the right to exclusive use of the patent in Savannah and an area within ten miles of that city. Allen promised to begin construction on the mill by December 1852.[18]

In January 1854 the Georgia General Assembly granted a charter to the partners to operate their mill under the name of Savannah Lumber Manufacturing and Planing Machine Company. William L. [sic] Walker was named as a director of the company. In May 1854 Kine apparently lost interest and backed out of the project. The remaining partners reincorporated as the Savannah Planing Machine Company. The company continued to operate and generate profits for Walker until 1861, when the impending crisis apparently shut it down and the assets were put up for sale. As late as 1863 Walker was still receiving money from Allen, but whether it was from investments or from sale of the company assets is not known.[19]

Another piece of business Walker had to attend to was helping his aunt Zemula settle the affairs of her late husband. On his death the previous April Valentine Walker had left a substantial estate to be administered by his executor, George Schley. Large numbers of Walker's Negroes had been hired out to the Central of Georgia Railroad for construction of the line from Waynesboro to Augusta. They worked in appalling conditions, and William Walker intervened on their behalf. Writing to his wife on the severity of their labor, he noted that they had been "playing patty from morning to night." This comment reveals the relative standing on his social scale of Negro slaves and Irish immigrant laborers.[20]

Walker had one last piece of business on his mind before leaving Augusta. Just before his departure from Albany in September, he had written to the commissioner of pensions in Washington to claim his bounty land warrant. Under the act of September 28, 1850, a veteran of the Mexican War was entitled to 160 acres of government land to be selected by the recipient from any public lands. It was no doubt with an eye to the future that Walker submitted his application. He had asked that the warrant be forwarded to him at Savannah, and he probably planned to choose land in northern Georgia. Although Walker spoke several times of looking for land, he never actually staked his claim.[21]

Having concluded his business deal so successfully, Walker dashed off to Albany about November 1 to pick up his family and bring them to Georgia for the winter. His business success notwithstanding, he faced other problems.

Shortly after Walker had returned from Europe, Mary had borne another son, William Henry Talbot Walker, in July 1851. The baby, usually called Talbot or "Tally," had been sickly at birth but then seemed to recover. By the time Walker left for Augusta in the fall of 1852, Tally was ailing again, this time with the croup, causing his father some anxiety. When Walker returned to Albany in November, Tally was well again and able to travel to Georgia. Yet the family had barely settled in Augusta when the baby died on November 30, 1852. He was the first of Walker's children to be buried in the family cemetery at the arsenal.[22]

Walker's grief over this first loss of a child provides an opportunity to examine some of his values as a Southern gentleman. For his gallantry in the Seminole and Mexican wars Walker had achieved a degree of glory that was much esteemed by his countrymen, as witnessed by the welcome home and the sword presentation ceremony. By marrying well and producing offspring he had gained further prestige. As a father he displayed the casual devotion to his children common in the South. Distracted though he was by affairs of career and business, nevertheless he always had time for a thought or a word about Molly or Freemy or Tally. The loss of one of them, and more than one as time passed, would always be marked by an outpouring of grief not expected in a man of otherwise severe mien and behavior.[23]

Another concern of Walker's that fall of 1852 was his wife's financial status, which was directly connected with his honor and his good name. Mary's father, Isaiah Townsend, had died intestate in 1838. There was no problem at that time. Isaiah's brother John continued to run the family businesses, and Hannah and her children received their fair share of the income, which was considerable. As Mary's brother Franklin grew older, he moved into the business, as did John's son Theodore. Eventually, Franklin and Theodore were running the business, although John remained the nominal head. In about 1852 Robert Townsend left the navy and came home to Albany to enter private business. This may have been the catalyst for the division of the estate, or perhaps it was John's advanced age, for he was now sixty-nine and in failing health. In any event, the Townsends petitioned the county court to divide the property of Isaiah Townsend among his heirs, and it was done.

The result left Walker furious. By the terms of the division, and at the behest of her brothers, Mary Walker's share was left to her in full and could be passed on to her children, but it could not be touched by her husband. Also, although the specific terms are unknown, apparently she could draw the income but was not allowed to dispose of the capital. The protection of a woman's inheritance against a profligate husband was relatively rare at that time. In the social conditions of nineteenth-century America, when women had almost no rights and whatever a woman owned was almost always automatically the property of her husband, Walker took this as an outrageous insult to his personal honor. He was astounded that anyone could impugn his character by suspecting that he might make off with his wife's property, and he said so forcefully in writing to Mary. His always delicate relations with his brothers-in-law were not improved by this episode.[24]

Beyond the seeming insult, the caution of the Townsend brothers had deprived Walker of one of the essentials for his honor. He had personal prestige from his own exploits, he had the respect of the community due a man with a devoted and growing family, but he lacked the wealth that would have given him even higher status. His father's profligacy had robbed him of an inheritance. There is no reason to believe Walker married Mary Townsend merely for her money, but the glimpses he had of the Townsends' palatial life-style must have suggested to him that when his wife came into her inheritance he could restore himself to his rightful status in society.[25]

His lack of an inheritance led Walker to concern for his financial self-sufficiency, another prerequisite of personal honor. He had tired of army life. He had never liked the boredom of peacetime service, and he realized that he could not go on as a recruiting officer forever. Life at a frontier post held no temptations for him, and he knew it did not for Mary. She was Albany born and bred and seldom cared to stray far from her native city. Walker was seriously interested in taking up a new career, but he knew that without capital or credit he would have a hard time getting started. His hopes for capital from the Townsend inheritance had come to nothing. So Walker turned to the world of industry for wealth and esteem. He was fortunate in finding a partner who had both capital and expertise to get the project started. Even so, the planing machine company would not be a source of substantial income for years. Walker could see no future for himself except the bleak one of continued military service with his salary supplemented by his wife's private income. This was a problem for which he could find no immediate solution and one that would plague him for the next five years.[26]

Within a few weeks, Walker's mind was relieved of this last burden. Rather than reporting to his regiment, he was selected in November 1852 to assume duty as the deputy governor of the Military Asylum at East Pascagoula, Mississippi. In 1851 Congress had authorized a set of three such asylums for the care of retired or invalid soldiers. The one in Mississippi was sited at the location where General David E. Twiggs had set up a hospital for sick soldiers returning from Mexico. Not many soldiers took advantage of this benefit, and the number in residence in Pascagoula averaged fewer than ten during the four years it was in operation. Because of this low response, the two branches were closed in 1855 and the inmates were transferred to the main asylum in Washington, D.C., the forerunner of the Old Soldiers Home.[27]

There is some doubt whether Walker ever actually took up his duties in Mississippi. Official records do not indicate that the post of deputy governor at Pascagoula was ever filled. In December 1852, when Walker received his orders, he was informed by the Western Department in New Orleans that his leave of absence need not be interrupted. When his leave expired the following August, the department commander, General Twiggs, wrote Walker that he was not needed because there were only five inmates, the buildings were in a run-down condition, and no new construction had been started. It was suggested that he could await further orders at the discretion of the Headquarters of the Army. General Scott generously allowed Walker to choose his own site, and he chose Albany and Augusta. For every month from December 1852 to June 1854, Walker's letters of report to the adjutant general, to the Headquarters of the Army, and to the Western Division at New Orleans, the parent organization of the western branch of the asylum, were written from either Augusta or Albany. For all the time Walker was nominally assigned there, the correspondence of the asylum was signed by First Lieutenant and Brevet Major Earl Van Dorn, its secretary. Walker's mother-in-law, Hannah Townsend, however, made a reference in a letter in May 1854 to the inconvenience of having to travel to Pascagoula, indicating that he may have at least visited the asylum.[28]

Whatever the details of the Pascagoula assignment and whatever burdens lay on Walker's mind, his military career was about to take another dramatic turn.

7

COMMANDANT OF CADETS

1854–1856

THE NATIONAL ELECTION of November 1852 had brought the Democratic candidate, Franklin Pierce, to the presidency. The Whig candidate, General Winfield Scott, was easily defeated and the lackluster caretaker administration of Millard Fillmore was swept out of office. President Pierce was a Mexican War veteran. He had been a general commanding a brigade in Scott's march to Mexico City. Although a Northern man, he looked favorably on states' rights, manifest destiny, and the extension of slavery to the new territories if acceptable to the inhabitants, the so-called popular sovereignty doctrine endorsed by the Compromise of 1850. For his secretary of war, Pierce selected another Mexican War veteran, Senator Jefferson Davis of Mississippi, who had supported Pierce wholeheartedly during the election campaign.

Davis was one of the true political giants of his time. Educated at West Point, he had been a soldier, a hero of the battle of Buena Vista in 1847, a state legislator, a successful planter, a U.S. congressman, and a senator. Now he was called on to be an administrator. Davis was one of the most able men ever to head the War Department. He had his shortcomings, especially vindictiveness, but he brought to office a zeal for progress and improvement, an attention to detail, and a level of energy that are the characteristics of the good administrator. Although he had the welfare of the nation as a whole at heart, Davis was not immune to the pleadings of his section, the South, nor was he likely to turn a deaf ear to the demands of other veterans, especially wounded war heroes. When the national interest could be combined with his personal predilections, he was happy to respond.[1]

In December 1853, nine months after taking office, Davis found just such an opportunity. The position of commandant of cadets at the U.S. Military Academy was due to become vacant in the summer of 1854. The incumbent, Captain Robert S. Garnett, had held the position for two years and was ready for reassignment. Davis knew there was an officer in Augusta, Georgia, who was filling an unnecessary position at the military asylum in Mississippi and was unfit for normal field duty. He deftly resolved both issues by offering Walker the vacancy at West Point. If Davis knew or cared, and it may have made no difference, Walker was a sound Democrat, having supported Pierce in the election of 1852, but politics was not the most vital issue in filling one of the most important professional positions in the army.

Walker was pleased and flattered by the offer. It is possible that he had been politicking for the appointment for he had been to see General Scott in New York the previous October. Nonetheless, not only did the position fit his health and family needs, but it was a great compliment. Whereas the superintendent at West Point was responsible for the all-around education of the cadets, the commandant provided for their military instruction and oversaw their discipline. He had a great influence on their molding as officers and men. Walker hastened to accept the offer, telling Davis with unusual humility: "I do not flatter myself that I have attained the standard established by the Army for him who assumes the responsibility of Commandant of the Corps of Cadets and in accepting the appointment I do so with a full sense of my unworthiness. The delicacy which has prompted you to desire not to expose me to a duty which my services might have rendered me physically incapable of discharging is fully appreciated by me. My health is not robust but is always better when I am actively employed and I feel willing to expose it to the trial." [2]

Walker remained in the South until spring, conserving his frail health and attending to the organization of his planing machine company. His pleasure at his new position was severely tested in March by the sudden loss to the croup of his firstborn son, Freeman, that "boy worth rearing." Freemy was buried in the family plot in Augusta next to Tally. In June 1854, Walker received his orders to report to West Point and assumed command of the Corps of Cadets by his own special order on July 31, 1854. [3]

The academy to which Walker reported was undergoing its greatest ferment of change in twenty years. Jefferson Davis and the superintendent believed that four years was an insufficient period of time to teach the cadets all they needed to know to be leaders of soldiers and good engineers.

Davis had convinced Congress, and the curriculum had been changed to five years beginning with the class that was admitted in June 1854. That class was divided between those young men of eighteen years or older who would graduate in 1858, a four-year course, and those under eighteen who would be required to stay for five years. Each subsequent class would be of five years' duration. Walker arrived just a month after this division of assignments had been made.[4]

At the head of the staff and faculty in 1854 was that American military genius Captain and Brevet Colonel Robert E. Lee. Other prominent faculty members were Dennis Hart Mahan, in charge of military engineering as he had been when Walker was a cadet; Robert W. Weir, still professor of drawing; George Washington Cullum, Walker's former traveling companion, instructor in practical military engineering; and Patrice de Janon, instructor in sword exercises or "Master of the Sword."

In addition to his duties as commandant, Walker was an instructor in tactics, that is, the practical military training of the cadets other than their engineering courses. To assist him he found a staff of eight other officers and a detachment of enlisted men. Such future well-known names as Fitz John Porter, John Gibbon, and Cadmus M. Wilcox were on Walker's staff when he arrived. Other officers at the academy who were to achieve national prominence in another decade included John M. Schofield, Quincy Gillmore, John G. Foster, and Adam J. Slemmer. In his principal assistant, First Lieutenant Anderson D. Nelson, who had served in Mexico with the 6th Infantry, Walker found a disciplinary soul mate. Nelson, remembered as "Sides" by Samuel Wragg Ferguson, was hated for his strict application of regulations, his caginess in ferreting out cadet misbehavior, and his unbending imposition of the most severe penalties for infractions. Cadmus Wilcox, another tactical officer, was remembered for wearing rubber-soled shoes so that he could approach unheard and catch cadets committing infractions in their rooms. Walker liked Nelson and Wilcox and approved of everything they did. In fact, strict application of discipline was a necessity.[5]

The behavior of the upper-class cadets toward the new men had not improved since Walker's time seventeen years before. Serious incidents of hazing such as firing an unloaded musket in a new cadet's face still occurred. Hazing became so bad in the summer of 1855 that Walker authorized the new cadets to use their bayonets to defend themselves. The hot-tempered young men sometimes physically threatened the academy staff such as raising a saber to an instructor or striking a waiter in the mess hall. Walker issued or had issued in his name a steady stream of orders and directives dealing with infractions of regulations: improper uniform, being off-limits from the summer camp area or academy grounds without a pass, leaving quarters after hours, being absent from guard mount or from post while on guard duty, sleeping on post, or being under the influence of liquor. The last charge was once made against Cadet Leroy Napier of Georgia, who later served as company and battalion commander under Walker in the war. S. W. Ferguson had reason to complain of Nelson's strictness: he was the cadet accused of striking the mess hall waiter; another time he was caught out of his room without permission.[6]

Some of the incidents were laughable in retrospect, such as one cadet getting another to act as substitute on guard so that the first man could slip off post, marching in a boisterous manner, being caught in the West Point hotel without a pass, or forging an officer's signature on a letter to the *New York Times*. Others showed immaturity, such as cadets committing "nuisances" in the camp rather than going to the latrine or "sinks." Some were very serious, as was the incident of the unknown cadet who sexually assaulted a female resident at the academy in the dark and the sectional conflict foreshadowed in fights between cadets. No infraction was too great or too small to escape the eagle eyes of Walker, "Sides" Nelson, or the other members of the tactical staff.[7]

Besides enforcing strict discipline, the officers of the tactical training staff tried to find recreations that would hold the cadets' interest. Dances were always popular because of the opportunity for female companionship. During summer camp in 1855, Walker permitted the cadets to play chess. Although all games were forbidden by academy regulation, he introduced this innovation as a means to "diminish inducements to unlawful indulgences." Lee's successor as superintendent, Major John G. Barnard, later petitioned the chief of engineers to allow a change in the regulation to permit cadets to play chess on a regular basis.[8]

The ready availability of whiskey both on and off the post added greatly to the unruliness of the cadets and the disciplinary problems encountered by the officers. The famous establishment of Benny Havens and Cozzen's Hotel were only two of many places where the cadets could get liquor for immediate consumption or to carry back to the barracks. It was an era of hard drinking; many of the officers of the army were drinkers, if not drunkards, and the cadets were only living up to the standard of the times.

One of the more infamous incidents of Walker's tenure as commandant occurred at Christmas 1854 and New Year 1855. On both holidays the cadets drank heavily all day. On Christmas Day, when the dinner meal was served in the mess hall, rather than eat, the cadets danced, sang, and kicked the food off the table. A week later the situation was even worse. The mood in the mess hall turned ugly, a riot started, and several cadets were stabbed with carving knives snatched from the festive spread. To make matters worse, the first captain, the senior cadet, was induced to leave the mess hall rather than intervene.

Walker acted promptly. On January 2 he placed in arrest for insubordinate conduct the three principal perpetrators of the riot and two cadet captains and, for leaving his post, the first captain. On January 3 he broke the first captain to the ranks, saying, "The scenes which occurred in the Mess Hall on the 1st of January are a disgrace to any institution. . . . Whilst the Comm[an]d[an]t, under all the circumstances, does not for a moment suppose that there was any want of nerve on the part of the First Captain, he made a military blunder in being persuaded from the proper discharge of his duties and therefore he has recommended that he be reduced to the ranks." [9]

A particular thorn in the commandant's side was Cadet Samuel Selden Hetzel, class of 1857. His father, Abner Hetzel, had graduated from West Point in 1827 but had died during the Mexican War. His mother was the daughter of Samuel Selden, an influential judge in Rochester, New York. Hetzel did not take well to discipline. He was unruly at drill, inattentive in class, and intractable before his superiors. Hetzel had been recommended to be turned back to the next lower class in January 1855 for not responding promptly to an order and for "muttering" in ranks. He had also been placed in arrest for violating orders by being off-limits. He appealed to Secretary of War Davis, through the chief of engineers. Davis sustained his appeal. Hetzel, however, continued his incorrigible conduct. In August 1855 he was arrested for breach of confinement and in February 1856 for insubordinate conduct in the mess hall and while marching to barracks. In March 1856 Davis ordered him suspended without pay, confined to camp, and turned back to the class of 1858 as of July 1, 1856.

Hetzel's mother kept up a steady correspondence in her son's defense. Superintendent Lee had to tell her that he thought some of the details were better forgotten than remembered. Walker once complained to his wife about receiving a "scorcher" from Mrs. Hetzel on his treatment of her son. Some months after Walker's departure from the academy, Hetzel was discharged.[10]

Most cadets never gave cause for concern. Six classes (1855–60) came

under Walker's military and disciplinary tutelage while he was commandant, and 128 of their members graduated. Some 30 later became general officers for the North or South in the Civil War. A few served long
enough to lead divisions and corps in the Spanish-American War of 1898.
Prominent on the Southern side six to ten years hence would be Joseph
Wheeler (class of 1859), Fitzhugh Lee (1856), E. Porter Alexander (1857),
and Stephen Dodson Ramseur (1860). Francis Shoup (1855) was chief of
artillery in the Army of Tennessee in 1864; Robert Houston Anderson
(1857) was Walker's first aide when the latter was a Confederate brigadier
and later became a Confederate cavalry general under Wheeler. Other rec-
ognizable Confederate names were Lunsford Lomax, James P. Major, and
William H. Jackson, who later commanded a cavalry division in Mississippi and Georgia (1856), and Samuel Wragg Ferguson and Joseph Marma-
duke (1857).

Among future Union leaders were Godfrey Weitzel, David M. Gregg,
Alexander Webb, Alfred T. A. Torbert, W. W. Averell, and William B.
Hazen (1855); George Bayard, John W. Forsyth, John K. Mizner, William
P. Sanders, and Samuel S. Carroll (1856); George C. Strong (1857); Charles
G. Harker (1858); Martin D. Hardin (1859); and James H. Wilson (1860).
Wesley Merritt (1860) commanded a cavalry division under General Philip
Sheridan in 1864–65 and led an army corps to capture Manila in the Phil-
ippines in 1898. Marcus Reno of Custer Massacre fame was a member of
the class of 1857. Ulysses S. Grant's aides-de-camp Cyrus B. Comstock
(1855) and Horace Porter (1860) and Sherman's chief engineer, Orlando
Poe (1856), also served under Walker's stern eye. Ramseur, Bayard, Strong,
Sanders, and Harker gave their lives for their respective causes.[11]

Just a month before Jefferson Davis offered the appointment at West
Point to Walker, he gave a special assignment to another young officer
from Georgia. As part of his plan to update the U.S. Army, Davis was interested in preparing a new tactics manual to reflect changes in technology
and maneuver as practiced in Europe. The introduction of the quick-firing
rifle and the killing power of the new ammunition made the slow, pon-
derous evolutions of an earlier generation of tactics obsolete. To adapt the
new French tactics manual for American use, Davis selected Captain and
Brevet Lieutenant Colonel William J. Hardee, an 1838 academy graduate
and a dragoon officer who had studied in France before the Mexican War.[12]

Hardee spent most of the spring and early summer of 1854 in Washington working on the manual. By the end of July his manuscript was
complete. Davis quickly gave his approval to the work and directed that a

testing board be assembled at West Point to put the new tactics into practice. The board, with Hardee as adviser, convened at the Military Academy
on August 15. Prominent among its members was the new commandant of
cadets. This was the first professional association of Walker and Hardee,
and it would culminate some ten years hence.[13]

West Point was first and foremost a military installation. The Military
Academy was the showplace of the army, and each commandant jealously
guarded the reputation of the Corps of Cadets as the finest marching unit
in the nation. Whenever new drills or tactics were introduced, they were
first studied by the academy staff and practiced by the corps and then
shown off to others. So it was with Hardee's new tactics manual. The
cadets practiced the accelerated pace and quick evolutions of the French
light infantry from August to October. Cadets complained of being drilled
until they were too tired to study, but Walker kept them at it. In October, Secretary Davis came to West Point and observed the drill. He was
obviously pleased with the result. In his official report to the adjutant general on the new drill, Walker pronounced it a vast improvement over the
old "heavy infantry" drill. Although Hardee, who succeeded Walker as
commandant, justly deserves credit for his publication of *Rifle and Light
Infantry Tactics*, it was Walker and the Corps of Cadets who tested the tactics for the U.S. Army. In 1855, similarly, Walker and the corps practiced
the new light artillery drill that was under consideration.[14]

The commandant was, because of his office, much sought after to render
opinions and to be the final arbiter on questions of military etiquette or
protocol. Walker enjoyed his role and corresponded at length with military notables across the nation. Mary Walker settled into the life of the
academy from the comfort of the commandant's quarters, a spacious two-
story brick house with a kitchen in the cellar, which had been built in
1819. The Walkers were next-door neighbors to the Lees and must have
shared formal and informal social events although no record now exists.
Besides housekeeping, Mary also kept up a garden to supplement their
ration allowance. Whenever she was away from West Point, she was always
anxious to return, something that could not be said of many of the places
her husband's career took her.[15]

While Walker was concerned about the press of official business and
Mary was adjusting to her new home, two personal tragedies occurred in
their lives. Robert Townsend Walker, a third son, born in Albany in September 1853, died of the croup, the same ailment that had carried off his
two brothers, at West Point on October 1, 1854. Seven-year-old Molly was

now the only child left to Walker and his wife. To heap an even greater burden on the distraught Mary Walker, her mother, Hannah Townsend, who had come to West Point to console her daughter, died suddenly at the academy on October 31, 1854.[16]

These family crises coupled with his military responsibilities caused Walker to defer his annual leave of absence in 1854 longer than usual. It was not until late January 1855 that he was able to get away from West Point on a seventy-day leave. He felt that it was imperative for him to go, for he needed to tend to business at the mill in Savannah and wanted to stake out a claim to land in north Georgia. He had received his Mexican War bounty land warrant in December 1852, and now he wanted to inspect possible locations. Walker arrived in Augusta on February 8, rested for several days, and went to Savannah the next week. He was encouraged enough by what he found to think that the time might be right for him to leave the army, especially if he was denied the promotion he aspired to. Although he spoke of going to north Georgia to claim his bounty land, apparently he never did.[17]

In 1854 a bill had been introduced in Congress to provide for two additional regiments each of infantry and cavalry. The expansion of U.S. territory following the war with Mexico had given the army a much greater area to protect and control. Vast new lands, longer lines of communications, and many more hostile tribes of Indians called for a larger army. This military increase was one of the improvements Jefferson Davis was working for. There would be some increase in War Department staff officers and one new general officer position. Walker had heard that General James Shields of Mexican War fame might receive the appointment, and he reverted to an old theme. Writing to Molly on March 7, he said, "[Shields] is not to the manor [sic] born and there is no earthly reason why he should be appointed . . . over native Americans." Time had not relieved Walker of his xenophobia.[18]

The higher-level vacancies in the new regiments would be filled by promotions of serving officers; competition would be keen. There were many officers who thought their seniority or gallant service in Mexico made them eligible for promotion. Walker thought he qualified on both counts; he had been a captain for more than nine years and he had twice been breveted for service in Mexico. If the army did not reward his faithful service, it would be time for him to seek another profession. Finally, on March 4, 1855, the bill passed Congress, and the names of the selectees were quickly forthcoming. Walker was promoted to major in the new 10th

Infantry, but he would continue at West Point until his tour there was complete. The superintendent of the academy, R. E. Lee, was appointed lieutenant colonel of the new 2d Cavalry Regiment and ordered to Texas immediately.[19]

Walker returned to West Point about the first of April, just as Lee was leaving. In substantive rank he was now the senior officer on the post, and in his opinion this made him de facto superintendent and post commander. The Corps of Engineers, however, disagreed. West Point had been founded as an engineer school. By academy regulation, the superintendent was always an engineer officer and was also post commander. The academy was part of the Corps of Engineers, and the superintendent took his orders from the chief of engineers, Brevet Brigadier General Joseph G. Totten. In Totten's opinion, the acting superintendent at West Point was the senior engineer officer there, Captain and Brevet Major John G. Barnard.

In a letter to the adjutant general, Walker immediately challenged Barnard's appointment. He based his case on the Articles of War, which explicitly stated that the senior officer present should take command unless orders to the contrary were issued by the president. The adjutant general replied that Barnard was taking charge in his brevet rank of major, which dated from the Mexican War, whereas Walker's majority, though substantive, was less than a month old. Walker's rejoinder could have been that in his brevet grade (lieutenant colonel) he still outranked Barnard, but he accepted the dictum. A War Department special order on April 11 settled the matter in Barnard's favor.[20]

That order should have ended the dispute, but it did not. Walker continued to agitate for a change in the regulation giving preference to engineer officers. In November 1855, while on a trip to Georgia, he stopped in Washington to ask for relief from having to serve under an officer he considered his junior in rank. As he put it, "I could not, consistently with my sense of military propriety, do duty under [Major Barnard]." He explained further that he bore Barnard no personal animosity, that he thought the arrangement of April 1855 was only temporary, and therefore he had not protested further at that time. Now, however, as it was evident that no permanent solution would soon be forthcoming, Walker felt bound to ask for relief. Necessarily, he had to direct his request through the chief of engineers to the secretary of war, and General Totten recommended retention of the system of having the senior engineer officer in charge. Davis sustained Totten, saying cryptically, "No decision is required, the change of circumstances having removed the difficulty presented," as if he did not really understand the problem. Davis may have been sympathetic to Walker's plight. In his annual report as secretary in December 1855, he recommended that the system be changed so that officers of any branch of the service could command at West Point. In its annual report in June 1856, however, the Military Academy's Board of Visitors recommended that the traditional restriction be kept in effect. The board relied on the recommendation of Major Barnard, not exactly a disinterested witness, as the basis of its report. In his written endorsement of the board's report, Davis still favored a change.[21]

Walker was not mollified by Davis's recommendations. He wrote to his wife: "Though legitimate authority I bend to, at West Point though they rather piled it on too high. I could not stand it and would not for worlds." In May 1856 Walker journeyed to Washington once more, this time to resign from the vaunted position as commandant of cadets. His dislike and distrust of Jefferson Davis seems to have dated from this time.

Walker's action seemed to shock the army into a realization that the situation at West Point needed to be regulated. Although engineer officers retained their hold on the superintendency for another ten years, beginning in 1858 the superintendent was given the local rank of colonel and the commandant would henceforth be a lieutenant colonel while serving at the academy, effectively removing any question of rank or precedence.[22]

8

FAREWELL TO ARMY BLUE

1856–1861

MARY WAS AGHAST at Walker's action, horrified for what the change would mean for him in service and bereft at the idea of leaving their cozy quarters at the academy for an unknown future. She had given birth again in the midst of the seniority ordeal and was hardly ready to handle another crisis. On February 3, 1856, William Henry Talbot Walker, Jr., the second son to bear that name, was born at West Point. The new baby was lovingly described by his eight-year-old sister Molly in a letter to her grandmother in Georgia: "The baby is growing very large and is a very bright little fellow. . . . He is a plump little fellow and has a good deal of hair. I love him more and more every day because he grows brighter every day. . . . He cries very little and loves to be undressed. I hold him sometimes but Mama is always afraid I shall let him fall." To her cousin Anna in Augusta, Molly wrote a few days later: "At first Mama thought his eyes were brown but now we think they are blue. . . . He was weighed when he was born and weighed seven pounds and a half. He has a good deal of hair. I am very glad to have such a dear little brother. . . . Mama calls him Willie." [1]

The birth of another son filled the Walker household with pride and joy, but it did nothing to assuage the feelings of anxiety over the future. From Georgia Walker attempted to comfort Mary's concern over his resignation, explaining his pride and his ambitions. "You speak of *many* thinking me foolish in throwing up my place at West Point. Nothing could induce me to lower my military self-respect and dignity by serving under a junior. On your account I regret the necessity that compelled me to leave but I would do the same thing tomorrow for my own military reputation demands it." [2]

William Henry Talbot
Walker, Jr., age nine
(courtesy of Karen
Allmond)

In response to a rumor Mary had heard that William J. Worth had
served as commandant at West Point while Sylvanus Thayer was superintendent, even though Worth outranked Thayer, Walker wrote, "If [Worth]
did condescend to serve that long under a junior it is only an evidence that
he preferred place to principle which I am very sure . . . your husband
will never do." Once again, Walker had gone through his regular cycle of
injury, complaint, and appeal. He felt he had been wronged by Barnard's
appointment over him; he had complained to the adjutant general in April
1855 and been rebuffed. When he appealed to the chief of engineers and
secretary of war in December 1855, his case was rejected again. In Florida
in April 1841, Walker had been mollified after his court-martial by a mere
counseling by the department commander. After his confrontation with

Major Bonneville in Mexico in 1847 concerning the company muster roll, Bonneville had softened his criticism and Walker had been satisfied. This time there was no way out of the intolerable situation except resignation. "I would rather, if I remained in the army, live on the top of the Rocky Mountains and maintain my self-respect than to live at the most eligible place in the world and lead a life offensive to my dignity." This was no posturing; Walker was attempting to explain to his wife of ten years why he would never sacrifice principle to place.[3]

After turning in his resignation in Washington on May 20, 1856, Walker was directed to New York to report to the Headquarters of the Army for orders. Arriving there, he was granted four months' leave of absence and then went to Augusta to take care of family matters. Among other things, he had the body of baby Robert exhumed from the cemetery at West Point and reburied in the family plot at the Augusta Arsenal. Now the three boys lay together under simple markers inscribed, respectively, "WHTW," "FW," and "RTW." Walker always intended to put up more imposing monuments but never did.[4]

As often seemed to happen when he was undergoing emotional crises, Walker was struck with an attack of asthma that was so serious he was not sure he would recover. His illness so enervated him that he was unable to return to the North for almost a month. Writing to Mary from Augusta, he said, "Judging from the violent streaks of sickness I have had, and from my delicate constitution . . . it is reasonable to conclude that I will not live to an old age." The manner of dealing with the disease was rather quaint. Walker's family doctor prescribed "three drinks of brandy or whiskey per day and three . . . pieces of red pepper." In a revealing moment of self-knowledge Walker commented, "One would have supposed that I was fiery enough without the addition of so much steam."[5]

While Walker was traveling to Georgia and convalescing from his illness, the headquarters of the 10th Infantry Regiment was preparing for his return to troop duty. Walker had been appointed senior major of the regiment in March 1854 but had not yet spent any time with the unit. The 10th Infantry was stationed at three posts in the Minnesota Territory. The regimental headquarters under Colonel Edmund B. Alexander had been at the largest post, Fort Snelling, near St. Paul, but in June 1856 it was moved to Fort Ridgely. Several companies were at Snelling under a senior captain, and two companies were at Fort Ripley under Lieutenant Colonel Charles F. Smith, who had been commandant of cadets at West Point in the 1840s. Later a Union major general, Smith has been credited with being U. S. Grant's mentor in the early days of the latter's military career. Smith suffered an unusual fate during the Shiloh campaign of 1862 when he injured his leg while boarding a boat, developed an infection, and died of the complications of his injury. The 10th Infantry's junior major, Edward R. S. Canby, another future Union commander, was also absent from the regiment in the summer of 1856.[6]

On June 12, 10th Infantry headquarters issued regimental order 45 directing Walker to proceed to Fort Ripley and take command there, relieving Smith so that he could move to Fort Snelling. Walker was resigned to going to the frontier. Although he was tired of army life and would have resigned if he felt more secure financially, he felt bound by his oath to serve wherever assigned. Following his departure from West Point, he recognized that he could ask no special favors. He had held one of the most prized positions the army could offer and had surrendered it voluntarily. Now he would have to take his chances in routine garrison duty. He wrote to his wife, "I am at present (much to my regret) an officer of the U. States Army and liable to go wherever the government chooses to order me and as long as I wear a sword . . . I will always obey orders no matter to what point of the compass they carry me."[7]

High on the list of decisions he had to make that summer was what to do with his family while he was in Minnesota. He wanted them settled before he left. Mary and the children were still living at West Point. They would have to vacate the commandant's quarters soon, but he did not want to settle them with her sister Anna Martin in Albany. The best course seemed for them to take up temporary residence in her native city while he scouted out the situation in Minnesota. Mary, however, wanted to go to Minnesota with him so they could face the wilds together. Eventually Walker conceded that they would go together to "spy the land" so that Mary could see for herself it was no place for a family. Walker returned north from Georgia at the end of July and spent the next two months moving from West Point and working out the details of their move to the West.[8]

For better or worse, Mary persuaded Walker to bring the whole family, and the four of them arrived at Fort Snelling on September 24, 1856. From there, they pushed on up to their new home at Fort Ripley, more than one hundred miles north of St. Paul on the Mississippi River, with the northern winter almost upon them. When they arrived at Ripley, Walker, as expected, was the senior officer present and therefore the post commander. The two companies present were A and C, commanded by Captains Anderson D. "Sides" Nelson and Joseph L. Tidball, respectively.

Nelson was Walker's old friend from Mexico and West Point. Tidball was an 1849 West Point graduate who was too young to have seen service in the Mexican War.[9]

This was Walker's first duty with troops, not counting the Corps of Cadets, in nine years. He threw himself into his duties with his usual vigor and professionalism, bad health and cold weather notwithstanding. The combination proved too much for him. Over the next two months he suffered three bouts of asthma. Mary described the effects of one in a letter to her niece in Albany on November 9.

> The Col[onel] was so ill and is still confined to his bed, too feeble to sit up. He had had an attack of asthma and gotten nearly over it, and on muster day, the last of October, he thought it necessary to be present and out he went altho' I urged and entreated him not to expose himself so much. He came in in an hour so weak that he could not say one word. I sent for the Dr. and immediately applied blisters and calomel and he has been as near death's door as ever a mortal was with engorgement of the lungs. His cough is leaving him now. . . . We are having intense cold weather, the thermometer 6 degrees below zero.[10]

This severe attack made it clear that Walker was unfit for further field service, at least in such a northerly clime. On November 25, he asked for an extended leave of absence, and four days later, without waiting for an answer, he was on his way southward. Although he did not know it at the time, he would never again wear the uniform of a United States officer on active duty. The combined effects of the asthma attacks of June and October 1856 had finally broken down his constitution. So bad was the congestion in his lungs that for nights on end he could not lie down to sleep. Although from time to time he expressed hope of returning to duty, he never did.[11]

When Walker had been in Georgia on leave in June and July 1856, he had been casting about for a career alternative to the army. He had received two substantial offers but had turned them both down. Robert Allen had asked him to come to Savannah and take over direct management of the mill. Walker refused on the grounds that he could not commit himself to a life of commerce. Thomas Barrett, a prominent Augusta banker, had offered to back Walker financially in any venture he wanted to try. Again Walker had demurred. But in reporting these offers to Mary, he had hinted that the civilian occupation of most interest to him was that of gentleman farmer.[12]

Now he realized that ambition. Whether he sought or obtained the help of Thomas Barrett or Robert Allen or whether he gained access to some of his wife's money is unknown. But Walker bought a plantation. On March 7, 1857, while he was still convalescing, Walker, his mother, and her two sisters, Zemula Walker and Betsy Cresswell, traveled to Savannah to sign promissory notes to the Marine Bank for some $35,000, to be secured by mortgaging twenty-five slaves belonging to the three women. No cash changed hands. Instead, the notes were for the amount still outstanding on a repossessed farm, Mobley Pond plantation.

Walker did not own the property outright. He had a one-quarter interest in a four-thousand-acre plantation in Screven County, Georgia, about fifty miles south of Augusta. His three partners, each with a quarter interest, provided the capital and the hands, and Walker was the operating manager, assisted by his brother John David and an overseer. The farm lay in the extreme northeast corner of Screven County, in the angle formed by the Burke County line and the Savannah River. Mobley Pond is not a pond at all, but a long, oval-shaped depression in the ground, one of what are called Carolina bays. Some geologists theorize that they were formed and so shaped by gigantic splinters from the crash of a heavenly body many millennia ago. Mobley Pond is about a mile long and about seven miles around.[13]

Mobley Pond had been discovered and named at least seventy-five years before Walker acquired the property. British colonel Archibald Campbell's men had marched past it on their way from Savannah to the conquest of Augusta in 1779, noting that "Mobile's [sic] Pond [was] a good extensive plantation, clear and open . . . for a considerable extent." The plantation there was owned by a man named Telfair. In 1842 his widow, Margaret Telfair, of Chatham County, Georgia, sold the land to Wyatt W. Starke, who was in the process of buying up most of that part of Screven County known as Fork of Briar Creek. This was the only part of Screven County in those days where cotton prospered. The fertile soil and the transportation facilities on the adjacent Savannah made agriculture a profitable venture.

When Starke bought Mobley Pond, the bay was under eight feet of water. Starke had paid $50,000 for the property and was determined to make every inch of it useful. He soon set about draining the pond. A series of drainage ditches was dug from the pond to the river by hand by imported Irish laborers. The main ditch was four miles long and, in some places, twenty feet deep. Starke did not say how long the work took, but he did say it cost him $10,000. When the job was completed, he estimated that his property had doubled in value from his original investment. The cypress that covered the lower part of the pond was harvested for wood for building and fencing. The exposed upper part yielded lush grass for fodder at the rate of two tons per acre. Starke was justly proud of his effort.[14]

Starke's empire began to crumble in the 1850s. Much of his land and many of his other assets were seized by his creditors to satisfy his debts. In April 1854 Starke mortgaged Mobley Pond and much of the rest of his Screven County land to the Marine and Fire Insurance Bank of Savannah to pay off some of those debts. After Starke died in 1855, the bank repossessed the property and was only too glad to find a buyer in 1857.[15]

The farm became Walker's refuge and his obsession for the rest of his life. He divided his time between Seclusaval and Mobley. In all the monthly status reports he sent to the adjutant general between January 1857 and December 1860, only one, in November 1858, was dated from Albany. All the rest bore datelines of Augusta or Mobley Pond. Mary continued to make pilgrimages to her family home, but it was much less home for her now that her mother was gone. She went back to Albany for the birth of another daughter, Hannah Townsend, in August 1858, but Freeman Valentine was born in July 1860 in Augusta. Albany, West Point, and Minnesota were far-away memories. The Walkers settled down to the life of the planter class in the rural South, slightly decadent, slightly backward, but generally relaxed and comfortable. Sectional conflict loomed over the horizon, but more pressing were issues like finding ready cash, educating the children, and getting in the crops.[16]

At Mobley Walker planted cotton and corn. He grew watermelon and peaches, but mostly for personal consumption. Pigs were raised on the farm, too. Cotton was a lucrative enough business that Walker needed a broker and a banker. His broker was Dr. James B. Walker of Augusta, no kin, a physician who had turned to commerce. His bankers were Gazaway Bugg Lamar of Savannah and his son Charles Augustus Lafayette Lamar, notorious for his exploits in the African slave trade. G. B. Lamar's first wife had been a Cresswell, cousin to Walker's mother. The Walker family income was supplemented by his military pay, the proceeds from the mill, and the income from Mary's property in New York. Though the Panic of 1857 crippled the American economy during this period, it was felt less in the agrarian South than in the industrial North, and cotton remained a staple of the U.S. export industry.[17]

The census of 1860 gives a picture of the Walker family in the last days of the prewar period. On October 18, 1860, the day of the enumeration in

Richmond County, Mary G. Walker, age seventy-two, was living alone, presumably at Seclusaval. Walker, his wife, and three children lived with their aunts Zemula, sixty-two, and Elizabeth Cresswell, fifty-six, apparently in Valentine Walker's old residence, Belleville, which was contiguous to Seclusaval. His sister Sarah Johnston lived with her son Ewing in a separate residence nearby.

The census counted one hundred slaves on the Walker property at Mobley. That year Walker told the census marshal, or enumerator, that his net worth was $28,000 in real estate and $8,400 in personal property. For overseer at Mobley he hired a man he did not name but took on the reference that he was a member of the local Methodist church. Walker's closest neighbors in Screven County were Seaborn Jones, Reverend Peyton Wade, and Dr. Robert W. Lovett. All three had much more extensive landholdings, but they welcomed the national hero to their world.[18]

Walker would probably have been content to continue this existence for the rest of his life. His military career intruded only when the commander of the 10th Infantry tried to coerce his senior major back to active duty. Twice during the Utah expedition of 1858–60 Walker received orders to rejoin his regiment; twice he pleaded bad health and was let off. His monthly reports were rendered faithfully to Washington and New York. For several months in a row he would report improving health and then a relapse. Lack of sleep was a constant problem. In December 1858 he wrote the adjutant general, "An attack of asthma . . . has kept me out of my bed for seven nights." Again, in May 1859 he reported, "Nearly five nights out of seven I am not able to lay down at night." Several times he was required to submit surgeons' certificates, but he had no trouble either in obtaining them or having them accepted at headquarters. In one, the surgeon described Walker's condition as "an organic lesion of the left lung consequent upon gunshot wounds received in the Florida and Mexican Wars." His content with the bucolic life was less than an impetus to return to uniform and the mission of subduing far-off Mormons. In one of his letters in 1860, Walker revealed an event that would prove a hindrance to future biographers, "A few months ago my house was burned and my books and papers consumed."[19]

Although Walker's leave of absence from 1856 to 1860 was longer than average, he was not unique in being away from active duty for an extended period of time. The army at that time was very liberal in granting officers long leaves for a variety of reasons. Robert E. Lee took a leave of twenty-seven months to look after his wife's affairs; Major Samuel P. Heintzelman spent eighteen months away from the army tending to personal business interests much as Walker had done in 1852. Numerous officers took leave for health reasons. George Washington Cullum traveled in Europe for a year in 1850–51, part of that time accompanied by William Walker. General David E. Twiggs went on leave from the Department of Texas in December 1859, ostensibly to travel in Europe for his health; he returned in November 1860 in time to surrender his command to the state authorities.[20]

Walker's illness and disabilities were real enough, and he was honorable enough not to lie about his health, but his physical condition gave him a plausible excuse not to return to a life he loathed. Although he continued to enjoy the pay of an army officer and the prestige of being a military hero he had no desire to spend his life in dreary frontier posts. After more than twenty years of military service, Walker knew that the only time he was satisfied to be in uniform was when action was in the offing. He had yet to be associated with Richard Taylor or William L. Cabell, but their characterizations of him in years to come were apt. After meeting Walker in 1861, Taylor said, "No enterprise was too rash to awaken his ardor if it necessitated dashing courage and self[less] devotion." Cabell, who also met Walker in Virginia in 1861, wrote, "The breath of battle always brought an unusual glitter to his eye." Walker thrived on military action or even the preparation for it. It was not just the glory that he loved; it was an opportunity to display his manhood, to prove to himself as much as to the world that whatever his defects, and he recognized there were some, no one could best him in his own arena. For Walker life itself was honor or nothing; as a corollary, military service was active campaigning or nothing.[21]

Meanwhile, events in Kansas, in Washington, in Illinois, and in a dozen cities in the North were conspiring to bring to an end the uneasy sectional peace of the decade following the Compromise of 1850. The Kansas-Nebraska Act, the Dred Scott decision, the nullification of the Missouri Compromise, the Lincoln-Douglas debates, the enforcement of the Fugitive Slave Act in the cities of the North against the wishes of their inhabitants, and the subsequent passage of local laws in those cities to prevent enforcement of the act, all had kept a constant focus on and a pressure to do something about the slavery issue. The abolitionists were in full cry as never before. Harriet Beecher Stowe romanticized the plight of the slaves; John Brown gave his life for them. The abolitionists and other antislavery men now had their own political party. The Republicans had done well in their first election in 1854 but had not been able to elect a president in 1856. The election of 1860 promised to be another story.

When the Democrats met in their national convention at Charleston, South Carolina, in April 1860, the Southern delegates would not accept any candidate unless he promised to allow slavery in the territories where it already existed. The Northerners would not accept such a condition. The convention adjourned without selecting a presidential candidate. The delegates met again in June in Baltimore but with the same result. Finally, the two wings of the party met separately and the Northerners nominated Senator Stephen A. Douglas of Illinois while the Southerners chose John C. Breckinridge of Kentucky, who was vice-president in the Buchanan administration. Douglas's running mate was an unusual choice, conservative Herschel V. Johnson of Georgia. The Republican convention in Chicago, after several inconclusive ballots, nominated Abraham Lincoln, an attractive dark-horse candidate. The Republican party platform came out clearly for prohibition of slavery from all federal territories.

Lincoln's election was a foregone conclusion. With the Democrats so deeply split, neither of their candidates could gain a majority of electoral votes. The election was further splintered by the creation of the compromise Constitutional Union party that nominated John Bell of Tennessee for president. In November, Lincoln carried almost every Northern state as well as California and Oregon. Although he had less than a majority of the popular vote, he had a clear majority in the electoral college. Breckinridge carried the South, and Bell took the border states of Virginia, Tennessee, and Kentucky. Douglas won only in Missouri and garnered a few electoral votes in New Jersey.

In Georgia there was no support for Lincoln, of course. Governor Joseph E. Brown backed Breckinridge, former congressman Alexander Stephens supported Douglas and Johnson, and a small group led by Benjamin H. Hill favored Bell. The vote in Georgia was fragmented. Breckinridge took fifty-one thousand popular votes, Bell, forty-two thousand, and Douglas, eleven thousand. The election was thrown into the state legislature, which awarded all ten electoral votes to Breckinridge on the basis of his plurality even though the two more conservative candidates polled a majority between them.[22]

The political situation in Augusta and Richmond County was equally confusing. The *Augusta Chronicle and Sentinel* and its subscribers supported Bell's Constitutional Union ticket. The *Augusta Constitutionalist* came out for Douglas and Johnson, while a third paper, the *Evening Dispatch*, threw its editorial weight behind Breckinridge. The election results that November were somewhat different than those from across the state. Of some twenty-three hundred votes cast, Douglas received 46 percent and Bell 37 percent. Breckinridge trailed with only 17 percent. Obviously, conservatism was strong in Richmond County.[23]

On the day of Lincoln's election, November 7, but before the results were known, activist Governor Brown, predicting a Republican victory, sent the Georgia legislature a message calling for a special convention to determine what course of action the state should take to protect its rights. He had received an invitation from South Carolina to attend a regional convention in the event of Lincoln's election, but he recommended against any joint action until Georgia could determine its own course. On November 18 the legislature, after hearing addresses on the issue from leading spokesmen, including Thomas R. R. Cobb in favor of secession and Alexander Stephens against, passed a bill in response to the governor's message calling for elections in each county. These elections were to be held on the first Wednesday in January 1861 (January 2) and the convention would meet in Milledgeville, the state capital, on January 16. Brown issued a proclamation calling for the elections on November 21. He also asked for and received an appropriation of $1 million for state defense.[24]

The news of Lincoln's victory brought consternation in other states across the South. Within days of the election the South Carolina legislature voted to assemble a special convention to determine the state's future status. The doctrine of states' rights proclaimed by John C. Calhoun and his cohorts in 1832 once again prevailed in the Palmetto State. On December 20, 1860, South Carolina voted to secede from the Union and "resume her position among the nations of the world."[25]

While the South Carolina convention was deliberating, Governor Brown published an open letter on December 7 advocating immediate secession. At about the same time, in response to his requests, the legislature passed measures incorporating the volunteer companies already in existence throughout the state, appointing a state adjutant and inspector general, authorizing the governor to call for ten thousand volunteers to be organized into brigades and divisions for the defense of the state, and furnishing arms to volunteer companies even if they had no uniforms. With these measures in hand, Brown looked forward confidently to the January convention.[26]

During this time William Walker faced a personal decision. He had been a lifelong Democrat. He owed his appointment to West Point to a Democratic president. Although he admired Winfield Scott personally, Walker was on record as having supported Pierce in 1852. As a Georgian and a slave owner he had probably backed the Breckinridge ticket in 1860.

Like others of his class, he was determined not to submit to the regime of a "black" Republican. Despite more than twenty-five years of service to the United States, Walker now showed his loyalty to the South by a dramatic move. On December 15, 1860, even before South Carolina had seceded, he submitted his resignation from the U.S. Army. It was received and accepted by the adjutant general to be effective on December 20. As he was proud to boast in the remaining years of his life, Walker was the first officer of the Old Army to give up his commission.

Although the move was in keeping with his social and political mores, there was some hint of self-interest in Walker's decision. The governor had received authority to appoint an adjutant and inspector general only three days before, December 12. Brown had nominated Captain Henry C. Wayne, a U.S. Army quartermaster officer and a member of a prominent Savannah family, for the new vacancy, but other nominations could be made from the floor of the legislature. As Walker admitted to Wayne in a letter a few weeks later, his name had been mentioned by his friends as an alternate candidate. Perhaps he saw himself as better qualified to take the leading role in the state's military affairs and felt that by shedding his Old Army commission he could demonstrate his complete loyalty to Georgia. As it turned out, Wayne won the appointment and resigned from the U.S. Army on December 31, 1860.[27]

Henry Wayne was a graduate of West Point in 1838 and the son of an associate justice of the U.S. Supreme Court. He had been a quartermaster officer for almost twenty years and was selected by Secretary of War Jefferson Davis to conduct the army's camel experiments in the 1850s. He and his Northern-born wife and their children maintained a residence in Washington, where they were neighbors of and socially intimate with the Davis family, even though Wayne was only a captain and brevet major for his Mexican War service. Wayne gave up a lot to accept Brown's appointment. He had left his family in Washington and did not see them for the duration of the war. His father remained with the North, although he did not disapprove of his son's choice.[28]

Wayne was lauded by Governor Brown as "the first man who responded to the call of his State," but he was still an active serving officer in the U.S. Army when he accepted the state appointment and did not resign his federal commission until nearly three weeks later. Although Walker could claim to be the first to give up his Old Army commission, Wayne could claim to be the first to take service with Georgia.[29]

Throughout Georgia following the enactment of the convention bill and the governor's proclamation, slates of delegates began making known their intentions to stand for election on January 2. Following the inclinations indicated by the November general election, the announced candidates from Richmond County were three conservative cooperationists, that is, men who were opposed to precipitate secession, preferring to confer with other states before taking such drastic action. The three were Georgia Supreme Court justice Charles J. Jenkins, president of the Georgia Railroad John Pendleton King, and president of the Augusta Gas Company Henry Harford Cumming. This ticket was warmly supported by the *Chronicle and Sentinel* and by the city's mayor, Foster Blodgett, Jr. Despite these public demonstrations of conservatism, there was a strong movement for secession in the county, abetted by the editorials of the opposition *Constitutionalist.*

On December 21, hoping to clarify sentiment in the county and supported by a petition signed by several hundred citizens, the mayor called for a meeting to be held at city hall at noon on December 24. At the appointed time and place the adherents of the announced candidates gathered to ratify their selection as representatives in Milledgeville. Unfortunately for the conservatives, taking the newspaper announcements of the meetings as an open invitation, a large number of secessionists and "minute men," companies of irregular volunteers, gathered with them.

The situation was described by the *Augusta Constitutionalist.* "The excitement was great and the meeting opened with every symptom for a free fight. As the Hon. Charles J. Jenkins was proceeding to speak and the prospect of ill-advised interference became imminent, Col. William Henry Walker, late of the U.S. Army, called upon the secessionists to follow him from the meeting. This was promptly done and much the larger crowd gathered in front of the steps. Col. Walker was elected chairman by acclamation and proceeded in a few eloquent words to address the crowd."[30]

The group assembled with Walker then adopted a resolution for immediate secession which was later forwarded to Milledgeville and read before the legislature. Then they selected their own slate of radical candidates. "Upon appeals of Messrs. [Ambrose R.] Wright and Walker, the crowd resolved not to disturb in any way the little meeting of the conservatives and with renewed cheers for all sorts of things adjourned." The radical candidates were John Phinizy, Sr., Dr. Ignatius P. Garvin, and George W. Crawford, former governor of Georgia and secretary of war in the Taylor administration. The minority party inside the hall meanwhile voted in favor of the restraint candidates, only replacing Cumming with businessman Alexander C. Walker.[31]

In a letter in the *Chronicle and Sentinel* on January 8, 1861, entitled "Resistance and Submission," "Georgian" criticized Walker for using inflammatory language at the meeting on December 24 in having threatened to take up arms against Georgia before he would allow her to submit tamely to the new administration. Never one to accept criticism, however accurate, Walker responded on January 9 in a letter that was printed on January 11. First he mentioned that he had not even planned on being at the meeting but, being in town and hearing of the gathering, he decided to stop by. He went on:

> I will rise "with uplifted arm" against the rule of a renegade southern abolitionist (Lincoln), let Georgia go as she may in her convention. With my consent, Lincoln's flag shall never wave over the remains of my ancestors and I flatter myself there is too much of the old revolutionary treason in the land such as those rebels, George Washington and Patrick Henry, had to submit to Black Republican rule. "If this be treason, make the most of it." I war against fanaticism and not against Georgia. I war for freedom, against tyranny; I war for the South to govern the South, and when I die, to leave my children free men and not the slaves of an arrogant and presumptuous North.

"Georgian" replied on January 13, saying he had not intended to single Walker out for criticism, and, in fact, "his conduct was highly commendable." The matter rested there.[32]

The possibility of a whiff of gunpowder provoked Walker into action more intense than attending meetings or writing letters. The night before the Augusta election he went to Charleston to aid in the defense of that city against an attack by U.S. forces, probably in response to the news that Major Robert Anderson had removed his garrison from Fort Moultrie to Fort Sumter on December 26. The rumored attack did not materialize, and Walker returned home sometime early in the new year. But the time was approaching for this son of Georgia to leave his fields and join in the defense of his native state.[33]

9

ANTICIPATION AND FRUSTRATION

1861

JANUARY 2, 1861, was a stormy day in Georgia. Many would-be voters were likely deterred from going to the polls by the wintry conditions. When the day's ballots had been counted, the radical secessionists won, fifty-thousand to thirty-seven thousand. If the vote had been a referendum, the people of Georgia would have supported immediate secession by a margin of only four to three. In Richmond County the secessionist slate received a large majority in the city of Augusta but only a small one in the rural areas. These results were mirrored across the state. Cities and towns were more heavily secessionist than the countryside. Beyond the bare results, there was a suggestion by a letter writer that at some of the polling places in Richmond County there had been some unruliness, even extending to interfering with cooperationists who wanted to vote. In his letter "Georgian" wondered out loud if Colonel Walker would have been as successful in preventing disturbance, if he had been there, as he had been at the open meeting on December 24. The latter comment lends credence to the conclusion that Walker had been in Charleston on election day.[1]

The three-hundred-odd county delegates to the state convention met at Milledgeville on January 16. Three prominent politicians, Governor Brown, Justice Charles J. Jenkins, and Howell Cobb, though not elected, were admitted to the convention's deliberations. Cobb was newly returned to Georgia, having resigned his post as secretary of the treasury in the Buchanan administration. George W. Crawford of Richmond County was elected president of the convention, and the debate began. Impassioned speeches were made by representatives of both sides, those who favored immediate secession such as Howell and Thomas R. R. Cobb, Judge

Eugenius Nisbet, and Robert Toombs, and those who were in favor of waiting for and cooperating with the other Southern states. Among the latter were Alexander and Linton Stephens, Herschel V. Johnson, and Benjamin H. Hill.

On the third day, January 18, Judge Nisbet introduced a resolution asking that Georgia seek immediate secession and that a committee be named to write a secession ordinance. Herschel Johnson proposed a resolution calling for a convention of all the Southern states. Instead of addressing Johnson's motion, the convention approved Nisbet's by a vote of 166 to 130. The next day, January 19, the ordinance committee reported back its draft for a vote. Benjamin Hill first reintroduced Johnson's measure for a Southern convention, which was voted down 164 to 133. Then the ordinance was introduced and approved 208 to 89. Following this lopsided victory all of the delegates signed the ordinance in a gesture of unity. The convention remained in session ten more days and before adjourning on January 29 authorized the governor to raise two regiments for possible future use, selected delegates to go to a Southern convention at Montgomery, Alabama, on February 4, and agreed to meet again in Savannah to make necessary changes to the state constitution. In at least two of these measures the convention had probably usurped the power of the state legislature, but never mind, Georgia was out of the Union.[2]

Secession was generally but not universally greeted with elation. Even those who had reservations felt bound to support their state's new independence. As was to be expected, the jubilation was greatest in the cities. Among the former cooperationists there was a feeling more of sadness than of anger as they contemplated a future outside the Union.[3]

When Georgia severed its ties with the Union, the state began to take over Federal functions and property. Even before the convention had met and while voting for delegates was still in progress, Governor Brown acted. There were two United States military posts in Georgia, Fort Pulaski at the mouth of the Savannah River and the arsenal at Augusta. Fort Pulaski had no garrison. Following the movement of the Charleston garrison from Fort Moultrie to Fort Sumter on December 26 Brown feared an attempt might be made to place Federal troops in Pulaski. On January 1, 1861, he went to Savannah to organize a takeover of the fort by state troops. On January 3, after some discussion, he directed Colonel Alexander R. Lawton of the 1st Regiment of Volunteers to occupy and fortify Pulaski. Lawton was a local railroad executive and 1839 graduate of West Point.[4]

The arsenal at Augusta, in the Sand Hills or Summerville community, stood on the land Freeman Walker had sold to the U.S. government in 1826. In 1861 it was garrisoned by a company of the 2d Artillery of some eighty men, commanded by Captain Arnold Elzey, a Marylander, who had been Walker's 1837 classmate at West Point. Immediately following the passage of the secession ordinance, Governor Brown came to Augusta to demand the surrender of the arsenal. To back up his words he had a force of a thousand men in eleven companies of volunteers, minute men, and militia from the surrounding counties. Their commander was another Augustan, Lieutenant Colonel Alfred Cumming, son of Henry Harford Cumming and late captain of the 10th U.S. Infantry, Walker's old regiment. Cumming had resigned his Old Army commission on the day Georgia seceded and Brown had hastily appointed him commander of what was styled the Augusta Independent Volunteer Battalion. At Brown's side, among other members of his staff, was his volunteer civilian aide, William H. T. Walker.

Governor Brown sent in his demand for the surrender of the arsenal on January 23. He called for the volunteers to be available to take the arsenal by force, if necessary, at 1:00 P.M. on January 24. When Cumming assembled his troops at the appointed time, they found that Elzey, on instructions from the War Department in Washington, seeing discretion as the better part of valor and being himself in sympathy with the secessionists, had surrendered at noon that day. As the *Augusta Constitutionalist* reported on January 25:

> After the arrangements were completed, Col. Wm. Henry Walker, late of the U.S.A., crossed the room and taking the hand of Captain Elzey stated that as his old brother in arms and lately an officer in the same army, he felt it his duty to state that the honor of the officer he held by the hand was in no way compromised but he had done [all] which any government could require or a true man perform. A silent embrace was all the reply Captain Elzey could make and the embrace of two such men filled with tears the eyes of all who saw it. Col. Walker was at West Point with Capt. Elzey and the endorsement given by one who has been three times shot down under the Stars and Stripes is not unworthy of him who received it.

By the surrender of the arsenal, Georgia obtained twenty-two thousand muskets, four pieces of artillery, and sundry other munitions of war. The company of Federal artillery departed on the twenty-ninth to go north. Elzey would eventually become a Confederate major general.[5]

Having disposed of the enemy in his midst and accumulated considerable materials of war in the process, energetic Governor Brown was now ready to set up his army. The secession convention had authorized him two regiments for the future use of a Southern confederacy. On February 1, Brown, through Adjutant and Inspector General Wayne, organized the two infantry regiments of the Georgia Army. The colonel of the 1st Regiment, at Savannah, was William J. Hardee. The colonel of the 2d, at Augusta, was Walker. The rosters of the officers of the two regiments read like a Who's Who of Georgia distinction for the next four years. The two majors of Hardee's regiment were Lafayette McLaws and William Montgomery Gardner; two of his captains were Alfred Iverson and John David Walker, William's younger brother; and one of the lieutenants was Joseph Wheeler. In Walker's regiment one of his majors was Alfred Cumming and one of his lieutenants was H. D. D. Twiggs, nephew of the general of the same family name. Others equally gallant, though less well-known, such as Peyton L. Wade, Jr., were also present.[6]

The next six weeks were a blur of activity as the officers prepared their forces for the expected conflict. Officers of the new regiments fanned out across the state to begin recruiting. Walker was involved in a flurry of correspondence, recommending appointments, requisitioning equipment, procuring training manuals, and overseeing the activities of his regiment. From February 1 to 4 he was in Milledgeville making administrative arrangements with Adjutant General Wayne. On February 22 Walker was able to report his regiment organized for field duty, but in the same letter he also reported that he had been invited to Montgomery, Alabama, to appear before the Military Affairs Committee of the Provisional Confederate Congress.[7]

The Georgia Army, like other state armies, was to be short-lived. The delegates to the Southern convention met at Montgomery on February 4 with Howell Cobb of Georgia as president. In short order the convention produced a Confederate Constitution, largely the work of Thomas R. R. Cobb, organized a Provisional Congress, and elected Jefferson Davis of Mississippi as provisional president and Alexander H. Stephens as provisional vice-president. Robert Toombs of Georgia became secretary of state and Leroy P. Walker of Alabama was named secretary of war.[8]

The new Confederate government moved fairly quickly to take over its responsibilities. On February 28 an act was passed authorizing the president to take over all external matters for the constituent states; to accept control from the states of the forts, arsenals, arms, and munitions formerly the property of the United States; and to form a provisional army. The provisional army would be composed of such troops as the states might tender for twelve months' service, to be received in regiments, battalions, and companies with their officers. The Confederate government would appoint general officers. Georgia's first quota could be filled by the two regiments authorized in January. Governor Brown was informed of these actions and stipulations on March 1 and the Georgia convention, during its second session, transferred the said property to the Confederate government on March 20 and 23. The reception of the two regiments was a different situation.[9]

The reason Walker was summoned to appear before the congressional committee in Montgomery was to offer him (along with Hardee) a colonelcy in the Confederate States Army, the regular army of the new government, which was to consist of ten regiments. Walker did not reach Montgomery until early in March. On March 9 the central government had issued its first call to Georgia for 1,000 men each for Pensacola and Fort Pulaski. In a controversy that extended into the next month, Brown and Secretary Walker wrangled over how to satisfy the quota. Governor Brown offered the two regiments that had been formed for that purpose although they were not yet filled up, one of them having only 200 men and the other 250. Walker would not take them because they did not conform to the requirements of the act of February 28 and the companies were not yet fully formed. Brown offered to fill up what companies he could and send the rest with their officers later; Walker objected. Walker asked for 750 volunteers and 250 of the recruits for each location; Brown demurred, preferring to send the regiments designated for the purpose. Eventually Brown yielded and sent all volunteers to both locations.[10]

The Confederate government issued its first call for state troops on March 9 in conformance with the act of February 28. When the troops entered Confederate service, the national government would not recognize state commissions of the officers unless the units were fully formed. If single companies went, the central government would organize them into regiments and appoint the officers, thus taking away much of the governor's patronage power. The officers in the two regiments would have to be recommissioned by the Confederate government. Those who were not acceptable would be denied commissions. This was contrary to the intent of the ordinance of the Georgia convention in January, which had specified that the term of service of the regiments would be three years and that they would serve in the regular Confederate army. The regiments, complete with officers appointed by the governor, were to be embodied into the Confederate service as whole units.

Walker was incensed at the demands of the Montgomery government.

He was insulted at the low rank offered him. In a letter to Governor Brown he pointed out that Braxton Bragg and P. G. T. Beauregard, both of Louisiana, had been made Confederate brigadiers, while he and Hardee had been offered only colonelcies. Beauregard had been Walker's junior in rank in the Old Army, and Bragg, who was his contemporary, had left the army in 1856 to settle in Louisiana as a planter. Walker, who saw no parallel between Bragg's resignation and his own extended sick leave, spurned the Confederate offer. He also ignored the fact that Bragg was already a state major general commanding the troops Louisiana was preparing for Confederate service. Hardee accepted and was posted to Fort Morgan, Alabama.

Walker thought the policy would be ruinous to the morale of Georgia officers. Their regiments would not be part of the regular army under the call of March 9 but would be disbanded after their terms of enlistment had expired. The president would appoint all of the officers of the ten projected regular regiments without reference to the governors' wishes. Walker advised Brown to stop enlistments, saying he did not want command of the regiment under such conditions and would rather join the volunteers. In a show of support for Brown, he wrote, "We are both in the same boat and I will float or sink with you." [11]

By March 21 the two Georgia regiments had between six and seven hundred men. Robert Toombs asked Secretary Walker to take the regiments into the provisional army, but Walker insisted that they must meet the requirements of the law. In the event, the two regiments were combined into one and went to Virginia in June 1861 as part of Georgia's quota to reinforce that front. From then to the end of the war they were known as the 1st Georgia Regulars. This was of no moment to William Walker. On March 14 he had resigned his commission as colonel of the 2d Regiment. Once again, when he saw that he could not get his way, he withdrew from the situation. This time, however, he had prospects for something better. [12]

With the likely loss of the Georgia Army, Governor Brown began to organize the state volunteers to be prepared for entry into the Confederate States Army when called. Under the act of the state legislature of December 1860, Brown planned to set up two divisions of two brigades each from the 250 or more volunteer companies in the state. Command of the 1st Division was offered to Henry R. Jackson of Savannah, who had briefly commanded all the state's forces between the Georgia convention and the takeover by the provisional Confederate government, and the 2d was offered to Walker. [13]

Unlike Walker and Henry C. Wayne, Henry Rootes Jackson was not a professional soldier. Related to the Cobb family and son of a college professor, Jackson was a lawyer and a Democratic politician. His credentials included graduation from Yale College, federal district attorney for Savannah, volunteer service in the Mexican War, and minister to Austria in the Pierce administration. He had been a delegate to the two Democratic party conventions in 1860, a Breckinridge presidential elector, and a delegate to the Georgia secession convention. Jackson was a political ally of Governor Brown, whom he had served as aide-de-camp at the seizure of the Augusta Arsenal in January.[14]

When it was determined that only one division would be activated, Jackson withdrew in Walker's favor. The latter accepted his commission as major general in the Georgia volunteers on March 22 to rank from March 13. The new division consisted of the 2d and 4th Brigades, which were based on the old state militia organization. The two brigadiers were Paul J. Semmes, brother of Raphael Semmes, and William Phillips.[15]

Walker's new task was to raise, organize, outfit, and train complete regiments for muster into Confederate service. Some eight thousand men were organized, a far larger force than Walker had ever hoped to command, but his role was principally an administrative one and he chafed under his inability to go on active field service. When peace negotiations broke down, the Confederate government increased its demands on the states for troops. Georgia was asked for three thousand more men on April 8 and, after the firing on Fort Sumter, five thousand more on April 16. The secession of Virginia on April 17 prompted a call for regiments and companies to go to that state. There was a call for another regiment for Pensacola. During April Walker and Governor Brown urged the Confederate secretary of war, Leroy P. Walker, to accept the Georgia troops in brigades and divisions rather than as regiments. When General Walker queried the governor directly, Brown replied that it was a matter he had no control over, and Secretary Walker answered a direct query by saying that by law he could accept no organization larger than a regiment and then only through the governor. William Walker even appealed to Robert E. Lee, new commander of the Virginia forces, volunteering to come at the head of five thousand troops or as an aide. Fearing Lee might have forgotten him, Walker signed himself, "Y[ou]r friend . . . former Com[mandant] of Corps of Cadets." Lee replied politely that help from Georgia was not needed at that time.[16]

By late April Walker had had enough. This time his unrest was not bad temper at not getting his own way but fear that he might miss the war.

Thousands of men were going off from Georgia to the fronts while he was immobilized in a desk job. The prospect of action and glory could stir him like nothing else. In exasperation he resigned his state commission, which the governor accepted on May 4, and began to pull whatever political strings he could to get a general's commission in Confederate service. Prominent citizens of Augusta wrote to Secretary Walker on his behalf, as did his well-placed cousin Madame Octavia LeVert of Mobile. Thomas R. R. Cobb in Montgomery told his wife on April 30 that he had received a letter from Walker that day and that he would intercede with President Davis on the general's behalf. Either the barrage of mail or the dire needs of the service for trained officers had the desired effect. On May 25, 1861, Walker was appointed brigadier general in the Provisional Army of the Confederate States. He was still junior to Bragg and Beauregard, and it was only a temporary commission, but he was off to war. As the *Augusta Chronicle and Sentinel* reported on May 28:

We are glad to see that the president has appointed Colonel William H. T. Walker a brigadier general. It has been a source of much mortification to his many admirers that he has not sooner been placed in position where he could be effective. It has seemed very strange, indeed, that one of our most brilliant and daring military men has been allowed to rest upon his well-earned Florida and Mexican laurels rather than be placed where he could achieve new honors for himself and render distinguished services to his native land. General Walker was, we believe, the first officer of the U.S. Army to throw up his commission upon the election of Lincoln. He deserves well of his country for his past deeds and we are glad that now he is to be again in active service. He will make his mark wherever he goes.[17]

Walker wanted to go to the front in Virginia, but that would have to wait for the future. The *Chronicle* reported the next day: "Brigadier General Walker is ordered to report forthwith to Pensacola and therefore does not go to Virginia yet. After the surrender of [Fort] Pickens he will possibly go to the Old Dominion, that is, provided the war does not end too soon. He ought to have been sent to Virginia at first." On May 30 Walker notified the War Department that he had selected Lieutenant Robert H. Anderson to be his aide. That day or the next, with his body servant and a horse, he departed by rail for a thirty-six-hour trip to Pensacola. At the age of forty-four William Walker was off to war again.[18]

Following the secession of the Southern states, most Federal military posts within their boundaries had either been captured by state forces or had been abandoned by their garrisons. The most notorious of these incidents had been the surrender of the entire Department of Texas to state forces by Brevet Major General David E. Twiggs in February 1861, even before Texas formally seceded. Only three U.S. coast defense forts held out against state attempts at takeover. The most famous of these was Fort Sumter in Charleston Harbor. Sumter had been reduced by bombardment on April 12, the act that precipitated the war. The other two holdouts were Fort Monroe, Virginia, and Fort Pickens, blocking the entrance to the harbor at Pensacola, Florida. Pensacola was the site of the only U.S. navy yard on the Gulf Coast, and before the Confederate government could make use of the navy yard it would have to take Pickens.[19]

Even before Florida seceded in January 1861, state leaders had given attention to gaining control of Pensacola Bay and the important navy yard there. The only obstacle was the garrison, a single company of artillery at Fort Barrancas near the yard. The commander of the post, the bookish Lieutenant Adam J. Slemmer, had attempted to coordinate protective measures with the commandant of the navy yard, but that aged worthy, although he put some of his men and vessels at Slemmer's disposal, tamely surrendered the yard to state forces when they demanded it. Slemmer thwarted the designs of the Florida authorities by moving his small garrison at Fort Barrancas on the mainland to Pickens on Santa Rosa Island. His total force was only eighty-odd, including thirty sailors who had volunteered to go with him. In addition, a number of U.S. war vessels lay off the island to support him. Slemmer's action effectively blocked the use of the bay by Confederate authorities and ensured the Federal forces a vital base of operations in the Gulf of Mexico.

By early February 1861 another company had arrived at Pickens from Fort Monroe, although the men remained in their vessel until April. On March 17 Captain Israel Vogdes reported to the adjutant general that he had four hundred men available to defend Pickens, including marines and sailors from the ships. Early in April more forces were dispatched from New York under Colonel Harvey Brown, who was named commander of the Department of Florida. Meanwhile, following the firing on Sumter, additional troops were landed on Santa Rosa Island to protect Pickens. When Harvey Brown arrived there on April 17, he could dispose of some twenty-six hundred men ashore and afloat, and by May 2 he had four hundred in the fort.[20]

After taking over the navy yard on January 12, the Florida state authorities had made their first demand for the surrender of Pickens. Slemmer refused, knowing he was safe for the moment isolated on Santa Rosa Island. There was no doubt that an assault would be made eventually on the fort, but the U.S. authorities hoped to have reinforcements in place before it came. A standoff was reached, however, through an agreement on January 28 between former senator Stephen Mallory of Florida and the Buchanan administration. The U.S. secretaries of navy and war agreed not to place additional troops in Pickens or take offensive actions with their vessels, and Mallory undertook to speak for the state forces when he agreed that there would be no attack on Fort Pickens. This was why Captain Vogdes and his company remained on shipboard for two uncomfortable months after their arrival.[21]

There matters rested while both sides continued to build their forces. Florida was too weak to capture the Union fort by itself. Most of the troops gathering on the Southern side came from Alabama. When the first demand was made on Slemmer, the Florida representative gave his strength as eight or nine hundred. By January 28 Mallory was able to say that it had increased to seventeen hundred. Despite the truce, each side feared an eventual attack from the other. Those at Pickens thought a landing would be made on Santa Rosa Island, followed by an attack on the fort; the Southerners worried about an attempt to retake the navy yard.[22]

The Confederate Congress's act of February 28, 1861, taking responsibility for external affairs of all the seceded states, also extended to the situation in Pensacola Bay. On March 7, Braxton Bragg of Louisiana, former captain of U.S. artillery and West Point classmate of W. H. T. Walker, was commissioned brigadier general in the Confederate army and ordered to Pensacola. He arrived there on March 10 and assumed command the next day. The force at Bragg's disposal was less than a thousand men consisting of a regiment and a company from Alabama and two Florida companies, which soon decamped. By the end of the month one company from Georgia and the first company of a battalion of Louisiana Zouaves had arrived, but this untrained mass was not sufficient to overcome a fortified place. More troops were en route, however. On March 9, the secretary of war had issued a call for five thousand men, one thousand each from Georgia, Alabama, and Louisiana, fifteen hundred from Mississippi, and five hundred from Florida. Bragg was a good organizer and trainer, and he hoped to put together a force capable of taking Pickens and opening up Pensacola Bay for the Confederacy.[23]

The breakdown of peace negotiations at the beginning of April caused the Confederate authorities correctly to think that the Union forces might end the truce and land more troops. On April 7, Bragg informed the Confederate War Department that he would fire on reinforcements unless ordered not to. Vogdes had been agitating all along to make a landing in compliance with the orders he had received from the commanding general of the army on March 12, but Captain H. A. Adams, the senior naval officer present, acting under the agreement of January 28, refused to sanction such action. Finally, on April 6, the new Republican navy secretary, Gideon Welles, issued a confidential order for Adams to land Vogdes and his company. The problem was how to get the order to Adams in the most expeditious manner.[24]

Navy lieutenant John L. Worden, later to command the *Monitor* against the *Merrimac*, was dispatched overland to make contact with Adams at Pensacola. Traveling by boat and train, he went to Richmond, on to Atlanta, and eventually to Pensacola. He left Washington on the morning of April 7 and arrived at Pensacola late on the tenth. En route, fearing detection, he memorized his message and destroyed the compromising document. When Worden asked Bragg for permission to go out to the U.S. squadron, Bragg naturally asked the nature of his business. Worden replied that he had only a verbal message of a pacific nature. Bragg let him go, and he made his way to Adams's vessel on April 12. That very night Adams landed Vogdes's company and a company of marines at Pickens. Worden was arrested at Montgomery on his way back to Washington but was eventually released.[25]

Bragg protested to Adams when he learned of the reinforcement, but Adams replied that he was acting in accord with his instructions. When Harvey Brown's contingent arrived on April 16, it was landed immediately without incident. By this time Bragg had close to five thousand men available and two thousand more on the way. The heterogeneous organization included an Alabama regiment, two Mississippi regiments, a Georgia regiment, one Georgia company, part of a battalion of Louisiana Zouaves, and two Florida companies. Secretary Walker advised Bragg against rashness in landing on Santa Rosa Island; in keeping with his constant worry of a Union descent on the navy yard, Bragg replied that his first priority was a secure defense, followed by a lodgment on the island.[26]

Bragg's organizational efforts were seriously handicapped by a lack of trained officers. Colonel Adley Gladden, who had served as a regimental officer in the Mexican War, arrived at the head of the 1st Louisiana Regiment early in May, but besides Bragg himself there were scant few to whom he could entrust higher command. To remedy that, on May 11 he asked Cooper for two or three officers to command his brigades. This request may have been the catalyst that won William Walker his Confederate general's commission. Bragg was asking for brigade commanders; Walker, who had recently headed a division of Georgia volunteers, was looking for a job. Bragg asked for some brigade commanders on May 11; Walker was commissioned on May 25 and ordered to Pensacola on May 28.[27]

Walker arrived at Pensacola late on the night of June 1. The next morning he traveled nine miles by steam tug to meet Bragg at the navy yard. If Walker had been one to reflect about coincidences, he might have had an eerie feeling. Bragg had been his classmate at West Point; so had Captain Israel Vogdes, one of Harvey Brown's company commanders. Slemmer had been on the staff at West Point during Walker's last year as commandant. Another officer at Pickens, Lieutenant Samuel F. Chalfin, had been one of Walker's tactical officers at the academy and retained enough regard for his old commander to agree to smuggle a letter from Walker to Mary's family in Albany later in the siege. Such was the stuff of the War Between the States.[28]

Bragg's army at Pensacola consisted of four brigades of mixed arms, principally infantry and artillery. Their major occupation, besides drilling, was manning the batteries that Bragg had erected for defense of the navy yard and for bombardment of Pickens if the long-awaited attack ever materialized. Despite having sent twenty-five hundred men to Virginia in May, Bragg still maintained a strength of more than seven thousand aggregate although a large number were sick and unfit at any one time.

Walker took command of the 2d Brigade, which contained the 1st and 7th Alabama regiments under Colonels Henry D. Clayton and S. A. M. Wood, the 1st Georgia Battalion of five companies commanded by Major John B. Villepigue, and two independent companies, for a total strength of about twenty-three hundred men. Walker's opinion of volunteers had not improved since the Mexican War. He wrote to his wife: "A perfectly raw, undisciplined, undrilled brigade. . . . The company officers and the field officers elected by the privates. The privates, many of them, congressmen, lawyers, doctors etc. The consequence is I have to play Col., captain, corporal, officer of the day, and dry nurse generally to the whole concern." His headquarters was at Fort Barrancas, and he had most of the siege artillery under his control. The other brigade commanders were Colonels Adley Gladden, James Chalmers of Mississippi, and John K. Jackson, an Augusta lawyer and militia officer who had come to Pensacola at the head of the 5th Georgia Regiment. Walker referred to these three as a

The Clinch Rifles, Company A, 5th Georgia, one of the volunteer units at
Pensacola, Florida, in May 1861. The 5th Georgia served under Walker's
command in the Atlanta campaign in 1864.

New Orleans merchant, a young lawyer from Mississippi, and a young lawyer from Georgia. As the only general present besides Bragg, Walker was
second in command.[29]

One of his separate companies was a familiar unit, the Washington
Artillery battery of Augusta, under Captain I. P. Girardy, which Governor
Brown had called the best-drilled volunteer artillery company in Geor-
gia. Unfortunately, Girardy's men had come to Florida without their field
guns. Upon arrival they found two guns belonging to the Alabama troops.
When they test-fired these, one was found to be defective, leaving them
with one gun. In early August, a few days after Walker's departure from
Pensacola, Bragg converted the company to infantry and added it to the 1st
Georgia Battalion. Two other Augusta companies, the Clinch Rifles and
the Irish Volunteers, were also at Pensacola as part of the 5th Georgia.[30]

Walker was pleased to be on active duty, but his enthusiasm soon waned.
He was unhappy with the condition of the fortifications: "I am here behind

a set of miserable sandbags that are rotting"; with the state of discipline of the troops: "I fight raw troops I never drilled"; with the qualifications of the volunteer officers; with the strength of the army: "We are certain to be used up unless we get reinforcements"; with the progress of the campaign: "This sitting down and waiting to be whipped . . . is to me the most disgusting"; but most of all with having to play "second fiddle" to Bragg. On June 13, he wrote his wife; "I am very much disgusted at being stuck in the sand here where if we really have a fight the Commanding Gen[era]l gets the credit of if successful. If not, I bear my share of the responsibility." Again, on July 3, he wrote, "I am here playing second fiddle to Bragg without the slightest showing." To his daughter Molly about July 10 Walker wrote, "As I am not in command I cannot act and I have merely to sit with my fingers in my mouth and await orders." His disgust with his position led him to write in the same letter, "This order to Pensacola has given me many a grey hair." [31]

Walker had no doubt about where the responsibility for the problems at Pensacola lay. As he put it on July 12, "There is a great responsibility somewhere and Jeff Davis as the head of the nation must be responsible. Posterity will hold him responsible." He also hinted at his advice to the congressional Military Affairs Committee in Montgomery the previous March: "Had my counsels prevailed four months ago . . . Fort Pickens would have been ours." Walker, like Joseph Brown, was probably an advocate of an assault on Pickens before it could be reinforced. [32]

Besides his discontent with the situation at Pensacola, Walker harbored resentments against the administration in Richmond. In the letter of July 3, Walker had said, "This government has shelved me. I shall have cause to remember the new government; I owe it one." He informed his daughter on July 10, "My friend, J[ohn] J[ames] W[alker] of Mobile [thinks] it was an outrage the way I was treated." To his wife on July 12, Walker complained, "I frequently had a bigger command twenty five years ago. It is a crying shame. It is a d——d insult to me." Walker longed to be in Virginia, where he foresaw much more opportunity for action and advancement, especially after hearing the electrifying news of the victory at Manassas. On July 13, he wrote to Adjutant and Inspector General Samuel Cooper in Richmond, applying for a transfer on the basis of seniority in the Old Army. Comparing himself to the other brigade commanders, he wrote, "My position is neither more nor less than theirs, though I am an old officer of the army of twenty five years standing and a general and they have been in service a few months and are colonels." He added, "I do most respectfully request that I be removed from behind these 'sandbags' and transferred to an open field." Later he wrote to Mary, "I will come on the telegraph wires if I am ordered to Virginia, the cars will be too slow."[33]

Walker's state of mind soon affected his health. By early July he was suffering from a severe bout of asthma. He could barely drag himself from his tent to perform his duties. The damp climate and humid summer weather did nothing to improve his condition. Smoking saltpeter to clear his lungs was probably more detrimental than helpful to his overall health. He was only one of hundreds debilitated by the climate and disease, but the state of his health became so much a matter of concern to Bragg that he claimed he feared for Walker's life. When Walker wrote to Richmond for a transfer on July 13, Bragg endorsed the request, "Respectfully forwarded but with regret and reluctance." By August 2 Bragg himself wrote to Cooper, informing the adjutant general that he was allowing Walker to leave immediately for health reasons so severe that "he is very feeble and failing daily." Bragg asked that Walker be replaced and suggested that Colonel Richard Taylor of the Louisiana volunteers, son of former president Zachary Taylor, would be suitable. Walker departed Pensacola with his aide on his way to Richmond and a new, more healthful and hopefully more active assignment.[34]

En route to Virginia, Walker stopped in Augusta for a quick visit. The citizens of his native city were delighted both to see him and to hear that he was going to Virginia. The *Chronicle and Sentinel* noted his arrival from Pensacola on August 6 and his departure for Richmond on the tenth. To the first notice was appended the warning, "Now look out, ye insolent invaders."[35]

Traveling by train, Walker arrived in Richmond in one day. He and his aide, Lieutenant Robert H. Anderson, made different impressions. Anderson attracted attention as the best-looking man in Richmond. Walker's notoriety was of a more questionable variety. His poor health, his frustration from two months at Pensacola, his displeasure in the delay over his appointment as general in the Confederate army, and his disappointment over having missed the battle at Manassas the previous month were not disposed to put him in the best frame of mind. A day or two after his arrival, he got into an argument with an official in the adjutant general's office over whether he had an appointment for an interview. Soon thereafter, he engaged in a shouting match at a dinner party with Senator Robert Barnwell of South Carolina concerning the treatment of Yankee deserters. Although Walker was admired for his courage and military accomplishments, these incidents did not sit well with the Confederate administration or with Richmond society. Nevertheless, within a few weeks, Walker received what he had come for, command of a brigade of infantry. General Joseph E. Johnston, commander of the Confederate Army of the Potomac at Centreville, Virginia, hearing that Walker was in Richmond, asked for him specifically to take over one of his new brigades.[36]

Walker arrived at Centreville on August 31. He found, to his delight, that he would be commanding one of the best brigades in the Army of the Potomac. Following the victory at Manassas in July, army organization had been improved. Johnston endeavored, whenever possible, to place regular officers at the head of the volunteer troops. Walker's brigade, the 8th, consisting of the 6th, 7th, 8th, and 9th Louisiana regiments and the 1st Louisiana Special Battalion, Roberdeau C. Wheat's fabled Louisiana Tigers, had been under the command of its senior colonel before his arrival. They were good men but wild and undisciplined. The Tigers had made a name at Manassas for courage and one in camp for intractability. The other regiments, of equally good quality but equally wild, were recruited from the streets of New Orleans as well as the Louisiana countryside. Crime in camp was commonplace. At one time during his tenure as commander Walker reported he had three murderers in confinement. The officers had "that New Orleans dare-deviltry which is encouraging to a commander" but does nothing for discipline. Walker commented good-naturedly on the number of Irish in the ranks, especially in the New Orleans regiments. Despite his past diatribes against Irish officers, it was clear that Irishmen in their rightful places in the ranks were not a threat to his native Americanism. Besides Rob Wheat, Walker had as commanders Colonel Richard Taylor, at the head of the 9th Regiment, and Colonel Harry T. Hays, brother of Jack Hays of the Texas Rangers, in the 7th. Colonels Isaac Seymour and Henry Kelly led the 6th and 8th regiments, respectively. The strength of the brigade was about forty-five hundred men.[37]

If the troops made a good impression on Walker, he made an equally good impression on them. Taylor wrote in his memoirs: "[Walker's] ability as an instructor and his lofty martial bearing deeply impressed his new brigade and prepared it for stern work." Taylor also noted Walker's health problems: "Always a martyr to asthma, he rarely enjoyed sleep but in a sitting position; yet he was cheerful and full of restless activity."[38]

The reporter for the *New Orleans Picayune* was also taken by what he saw at Manassas.

Gen. Walker is . . . one of the most gallant and best tried officers of the old
army. As a field officer, indeed, he has not probably a superior in the world. . . .
He is just the man to lead our brave and gallant Louisianians on to glory and
to victory. . . . In person, Gen. Walker is very slight; but few persons I ever
met have a more dashing and soldier-like appearance. . . . He stands straight
as an arrow, rides with a grace seldom attained by the most expert horseman,
and altogether, on the field, has the appearance of the brilliant and dashing
soldier his comrades on the plains of Mexico have always represented him
to be.[39]

Perhaps a more realistic appraisal of Walker's physical appearance was
provided by another soldier: "The permanent evidences of his sufferings
remained in a painfully spare frame and a pale cadaverous complexion,
which always suggested a ghost on horse back." Possibly this witness had
seen Walker during one of his bouts of sickness.[40]

One of the most colorful characters in Walker's colorful brigade was
Lieutenant Colonel Roberdeau C. Wheat of the 1st Special Battalion. Rob
Wheat was Virginia-born and trained to the law, but his adventurous
personality had made him a soldier of fortune. He had fought in Nicara-
gua with William Walker, the filibusterer, in Mexico as a revolutionary,
and in Italy with Garibaldi. At the outbreak of the Civil War, Wheat returned to New Orleans, recruited his battalion from the toughs of the
city wharves and slums, and led them to Virginia. One company called
itself the "Tigers," a name that soon attached itself to the whole battalion
and later to all the Louisiana troops in Virginia. At Manassas Wheat had
been critically wounded, shot through both lungs. The army doctors, as
was their wont in serious cases, gave him up for lost. "I don't feel like
dying yet," said Wheat. The doctor reiterated that there had never been
a recorded case of anyone recovering from such a wound. "Well, then,"
responded the determined victim, "I will put my case on record." This
was a sentiment with which Walker could agree and a man with whom he
would be proud to fight. Wheat was still convalescing when Walker arrived
in Virginia, and the Tigers were temporarily commanded by Lieutenant
Colonel Charles DeChoiseul.[41]

While Walker and his new brigade were adjusting to each other, he
found time to make contact with the Georgians in Johnston's army.
Toombs's brigade of the 1st Regulars, 2d, 8th, and 9th Georgia was only
a few miles from Walker's camp. On September 7, John David Walker, a
company commander in the 1st Regulars, paid his brother a call. On subsequent days Walker visited with his old comrades, Cadmus Wilcox of the

rubber-soled shoes at West Point, Arnold Elzey, his West Point classmate, whom he had last seen at the Augusta Arsenal in January, and William Montgomery Gardner, new colonel of the 8th Georgia, who had been grievously wounded at Manassas. Gardner had succeeded to the command of his regiment on the death at Manassas of its colonel, Francis Bartow, whom Walker had once referred to as "a pet of Davis." There was also a constant flow of civilians at Walker's headquarters, coming from home to visit their family members and friends in the army. These included James Gardner, publisher of the *Augusta Constitutionalist*, who had come to visit his younger brother, the wounded colonel, and a Mrs. Wilson, probably the wife of Reverend Joseph Wilson, minister of the First Presbyterian Church in Augusta where Walker's wife and mother attended services. Reverend Wilson was visiting the Georgia troops that September as a representative of the Augusta committee of the Georgia Relief and Hospital Association. At home in Augusta the Wilsons had a four-year-old son, Thomas Woodrow Wilson.[42]

Walker's personal staff at this time was small. Lieutenant Anderson, soon promoted to captain and then major, was the brigade adjutant. This left a vacancy for a regular aide. Walker tried twice to have Lieutenant Joseph Wheeler, a fellow Augustan, brought from Pensacola, but Wheeler was destined for bigger and more important things. As volunteer aide, Walker had Commander Henry J. Hartstene, CSN, a friend from before Mexican War days and a former member of the Wilkes Antarctic expedition of 1841. Also present was Lieutenant Eustace Surget, a Louisianian who had been adjutant before Walker arrived and now became Anderson's assistant. During September Walker appointed Captain Thomas R. Heard of the 6th Louisiana to be major and brigade quartermaster and Lieutenant Aaron Davis, 7th Louisiana, to be captain and brigade commissary. In early October Surgeon Stokes A. Smith of the 7th Louisiana became brigade surgeon.[43]

Activities in the 8th Brigade were those normally found in a military organization preparing for active operations while in the face of the enemy. Regiments were provided for outpost duty, skilled workmen were detailed for bridge building, work parties were formed, a special detail was sent to guard the Confederate signal station on Bull Run Mountain, action was taken to suppress that bane of every army, the whiskey vendors, the sick had to be cared for, baggage disposed of, disciplinary actions carried out. In October, the brigade was augmented by its own artillery, Captain Thomas Bowyer's Virginia Light Battery, and a cavalry detail.[44]

Besides meeting old friends and attending to official business, Walker had another pleasant duty to perform that September. Whatever else could be said about him, Walker always strived to improve the morale and training as well as the discipline of his units. As proof of the high regard in which he was held by the men under his command at Pensacola, the Washington Light Artillery Company commissioned a presentation sword to be given him. The sword was not ready until after he had left for Virginia, but it was forwarded to him under cover of a gracious note:

> Desirous of evincing our respect and esteem for you and our regrets at the severance of the relationship existing between yourself, as general commanding the 2d Brigade, and our company, we beg your acceptance of the accompanying sword. Under ordinary circumstances, and in ordinary times, we would be loath to present a sword so devoid of ornament or beauty, but in this crisis of our government, and tendered to one who has to the country and to history shown to what good use the sword can be wielded in defense of honor and of liberty, and manufactured within the limits of our own state, we feel that it will be accepted and acceptable. In the hope that the bright flash of the blade will prove as the eye of a basilisk to our enemies, and confident that honor and success will follow in its track when in your grasp, we remain respectfully and with esteem, [the officers of the Washington Light Artillery].

Walker was not to be outdone in flourish of phrasing or graciousness of thought. He replied to the company commander on September 17: "I received the very handsome Georgia made sword which the Washington Light Artillery of Augusta, Ga. did me the honor to present me. Please accept for yourself and express to the company my thanks for the distinguished compliment paid me. Rest assured, sir, that I will remember on the battlefield that I am a native Georgian, proud of my native state, and that I wear a Georgia made sword presented to me by a company from my native city." The sword had previously been described in a newspaper article: "The sword, though not as elaborately wrought or ornamented as some made at the north, is nevertheless neat, well finished, and exceedingly serviceable. On the blade is engraved the following inscription: 'Gen. W. H. T. Walker, C.S.A., from the Washington Artillery, Augusta, Georgia, 1861,' with ornamental flourishes; on the reverse, the letters 'C.S.,' with flags and ornamental flourishes. The scabbard is of black leather with brass mountings." [45]

The military situation in northern Virginia was at a virtual standstill in the fall of 1861. There were reconnaissances and affairs of outposts but little more. Since July 21 and the smashing Confederate victory at Bull Run or Manassas each side had been eyeing the other warily and building strength. The principal Union force had recently been renamed; it was now also called the Army of the Potomac. It had a new commander, George B. McClellan, brought from western Virginia. The Confederate Army of the Potomac remained under Joseph E. Johnston with General Pierre G. T. Beauregard as his chief assistant.

McClellan took as his first priority the rebuilding of his shattered army. In August 1861 he claimed an effective strength of 50,000 men for the defense of Washington and operations in Virginia. By the end of September he had over 140,000 troops under arms. McClellan, a cautious man by nature, saw defense of Washington and its environs as his main military mission. He devoted some 50,000 of his men to that task. After accounting for lines of communications, absentees, and so on, he felt that he had only some 80,000 for offensive operations and most of those were not yet ready for field service.[46]

On the Confederate side, Johnston was husbanding his strength around Manassas and Centreville, but he was also closing his force up to the Potomac with a view to controlling the crossings of that river in its upper and lower reaches. Under Johnston, Beauregard led the semi-independent, self-styled 1st Corps. Walker's brigade was in Beauregard's corps. Johnston's strength overall was about forty-five thousand organized in thirteen brigades, eight of them under Beauregard. As the victor of Manassas, Johnston had less to do in improving army organization and morale than McClellan, but his men also spent much time in the school of the soldier. Johnston and Beauregard themselves spent much of their time in controversy with the president and the War Department.[47]

William Walker was happy in the Army of the Potomac, probably happier than at any other time in the three years he served in Confederate gray. He had a fine brigade, he was a member of a victorious army, his good reputation had preceded him, and he was serving under a man he liked and respected, Joseph E. Johnston. The two had been acquainted for many years. When Walker was a cadet at West Point his classmate and possibly roommate was Robert Milligan McLane of Delaware, son of a diplomat, cabinet member, and railroad magnate. McLane resigned from the army in 1843 to pursue a successful career in politics. During his years of military duty McLane had served twice with Joseph E. Johnston, whom he introduced to his sister Lydia. In 1845 Lydia and Johnston were married. Evidence suggests that if the Walkers and Johnstons were not intimate, they were at least on friendly terms over the years. Writing to his wife in 1864, Walker reminded her that he and Johnston had been friends for twenty-five years. After Walker's death, Mrs. Johnston, in a note of condolence to Mary Walker, commented on that friendship.[48]

Besides the social connection, Walker was much like Johnston physically and in personality. Both men were short in stature and slender in build but stiff and erect in carriage and in the saddle. The Georgian had an air of elegance about him, especially in uniform, similar to Johnston's. A full-length photograph that has survived in the family collection (see p. 289) shows Walker in the uniform of a Confederate general officer, complete to the full-dress black chapeau, rarely worn by officers and probably infrequently manufactured. Another photograph shows penetrating eyes under a frowning brow. From various accounts, though, he could as quickly smile as frown.

Walker was popular with men and women alike as attested by the many references in his letters to renewing old acquaintances or meeting friends in out-of-the-way places. Also like Johnston, Walker had married into a better class of society than he had known as a youth. His marriage provided an entrée into the highest social circles of the nation. If Johnston's subordinates and close friends were intensely loyal to him and he to them, so were Walker's. Joseph B. Cumming, who served on the staffs of Generals Walker, Johnston, Hood, Hardee, and J. K. Jackson, said of Walker that "membership of [his] staff was in itself a certificate that such member was performing his full soldierly duty." E. T. Sykes, one of Walker's critics, said that he treated his staff "with the utmost consideration and deferential courtesy," as if they were "superior to the ordinary subaltern."[49]

The most significant similarities of character were in their quick resentment at real or supposed slights and their cantankerous dealings with superiors and equals. This propensity on Walker's part has already been amply demonstrated. Johnston's problems with the Confederate administration were just developing.

Johnston's main issue at that time was a question of promotion and date of rank. In the Old Army, before his resignation, he had been a brigadier general and the quartermaster general. After Brevet Major General David E. Twiggs, Johnston was the senior officer of the U.S. Army to join the Confederacy. When he entered Confederate service, he accepted the rank, like most others, of brigadier, the highest then available. In August 1861 the grade of general was created and five officers were nominated and confirmed to that rank. They were, in order of date of confirmed rank,

Samuel Cooper, the adjutant and inspector general, Robert E. Lee, Albert Sidney Johnston, Joseph E. Johnston, and Beauregard. J. E. Johnston had outranked all of the other four in the U.S. Army and he protested that fact in a rash letter to President Davis. His request to be placed at the head of the promotion list was denied by Davis, and there the matter rested for some time. The new secretary of war, Judah P. Benjamin, later contended that seniority in the Old Army or in the new was not a factor in the selection of general officers; the president was empowered by law to appoint whomever he chose. This episode is instructive in understanding William Walker's own promotion controversy, which developed in due time.[50]

Beauregard's problems with the Richmond administration were of his own making. They had little direct bearing on Walker's forthcoming problems, except for the timing involved, but they are illustrative of the condition of the higher command in the Confederate Army of the Potomac at that time.

When Beauregard made his report in October of the battle at Manassas the previous July, by design or by poor construction, probably the former, he magnified his own strategic planning and role while belittling that of President Davis. Further, implications were made, not by Beauregard himself, that the president had obstructed the pursuit of the enemy as they fled toward Washington. When challenged by Davis, Beauregard naturally retracted his rash comments, but his troubles were not over. Beauregard considered himself as semi-independent of Johnston's command and had styled his own organization the 1st Corps. Walker's brigade was part of Beauregard's corps. On this matter Beauregard ran afoul of Secretary of War Benjamin. Confederate law did not allow for the army corps level of organization at that time. As Benjamin succinctly put it, Beauregard was "second in command of the whole [army] and not first in command of half the army." This latter issue was not definitively resolved until Beauregard left the Army of the Potomac early in 1862.[51]

While Walker was drilling his men and visiting with his friends that September 1861, a new officer arrived in Johnston's army. Gustavus W. Smith was a Kentuckian by birth and a West Pointer, but he had resigned his commission in 1854 to go into civil engineering. Most recently he had been a New York Democratic politician and street commissioner of New York City. The city administration, from the mayor on down, was sympathetic to states' rights, secession, and the Southern cause. By political belief and by birth Smith leaned toward the South and so, in September 1861, he resigned his commissioner's position and threw in his lot with

the Confederate States. The South could always use another profession-
ally trained officer, and Smith was welcomed. In fact, Johnston had asked
for him as early as August while Smith was still waiting to see which way
Kentucky would go. President Davis rewarded Smith with a major generalcy to date from September 19, and he was assigned command of all the
troops not under Beauregard. Smith was accepted immediately into the
high councils of the army.[52]

Among the important topics under review by the generals that fall was
the organization of the army. Beauregard's differences with the Davis administration over his place in the command scheme had already arisen.
Also under discussion was the proper arrangement of the brigades into
divisions and the selection of officers to command the divisions. Since before the battle at Manassas in July, the Army of the Potomac had been
an organization of brigades reporting directly to the army commander.
Johnston, Beauregard, and Smith all felt that the traditional arrangement
of brigades organized into divisions and divisions reporting to corps or
army commanders should be implemented. This was especially important
because the army had grown to sixteen brigades, nine under Beauregard
and seven under Smith. Late in September, Secretary of War Benjamin
sent a note to Beauregard asking for recommendations for promotion to
major general. On September 28, the three senior generals addressed a
polite letter to Benjamin outlining their proposal to organize seven divisions of two brigades each and naming the seven officers they thought
should become major generals to command the divisions. Beauregard followed this up with a separate note of his own to the secretary, urging
the importance of a decision and stressing the qualifications of the officers
named. He went so far as to say, "They have few equals, and none superior,
in any service." The seven recommended officers were then listed in the
following order:

1.	Brig. Gen. W. H. T. Walker	P.A.C.S.
2.	Lt. Col. W. W. McKall [sic]	C.S.A.
3.	Brig. Gen. Earl Van Dorn	P.A.C.S. (already appointed)
4.	Brig. Gen. James Longstreet	P.A.C.S.
5.	Mr. Mansfield Lovell	formerly U.S.A.
6.	Brig. Gen. J. T. Jackson [sic]	P.A.C.S.
7.	Brig. Gen. W. H. C. Whiting	P.A.C.S.

These were the choices of the three senior generals of the Army of the
Potomac to command the divisions under them. The serial ranking was

almost strictly by West Point graduation date without regard to rank or achievement since.[53]

At about the same time as the personality conflicts were developing and reorganization was being considered, Beauregard decided he was ready to show off the skills of the Louisiana brigade. On September 28, Walker was ordered to take his three best regiments and a battery or two of artillery and make a reconnaissance in force to feel out Yankee positions on the Maryland side of the upper Potomac River and to make a military demonstration along the river as rapidly and at as many locations as possible. The purpose of the operation was not to engage the enemy but to make an "ostentatious demonstration." [54]

On September 25, Walker's brigade had been ordered from Centreville to Camp Beauregard, near Germantown and a few miles west of Fairfax Courthouse. At daylight on September 29, the brigade broke camp and the 6th, 7th, and 8th Louisiana regiments, with H. G. Latham's Virginia battery, a section of rifled guns of J. B. Walton's New Orleans Washington Artillery Battalion, and Whitehead's company of the 2d Virginia Cavalry marched out in a northerly direction. The 9th Louisiana was left behind because of its sickly condition. The brigade marched twelve miles and halted about 1:00 P.M. They rested until 2:00 A.M. on the thirtieth and then moved a few more miles to stop just short of the Potomac near the Great Falls. Here Walker gave the order that at daylight they would show themselves to the Federal garrison on the Maryland side and shell a large depot building that was being used as a Yankee billet and storehouse.

As daylight began to break, the gunners stood to their pieces with matches lighted, but a dense morning fog rendered the target invisible. The fog did not clear until after eight, but when it did it revealed hundreds of tents and perhaps two thousand Yankee soldiers bathing, relaxing, and drilling on a Sunday morning. The batteries opened up, causing the Union troops to scatter, much to the glee of the Rebels. Some 150 rounds were fired, including hot shot at the warehouse, but it was not set afire. A reporter with Walker's column claimed to have seen at least two dead carried off the scene. The Louisianians suffered no casualties.

Having completed the first phase of the mission, Walker and his brigade then moved successively to Kohn's (or Coon's) Landing and Seneca Falls, repeating the demonstration at each location. On October 1, the brigade returned to camp after a march of fifty-eight miles, footsore but happy. Walker was proud of his men, and they were proud of themselves. The soldiers found their excursion pleasant, the more so because the only casualties were a few blistered feet. Walker informed Mary by letter of his foray, and accounts were carried in several newspapers, especially in Augusta and New Orleans. The stories varied in minor details but generally substantiated each other. In his letter to his wife Walker mentioned that his total force was two thousand and that he had been in the midst of some thirty to forty thousand U.S. troops on both sides of the river, who, if they had caught him, easily could have destroyed his brigade.[55]

A New Orleans newspaper correspondent told his readers that in a review of the Louisiana brigade by President Davis and General Beauregard on October 3, Davis told Walker that his was the "boldest and most daring expedition of the war" and "creditable" to the general and all who took part. The report may have been prompted by local boosterism, but there is no reason to doubt that Davis would have congratulated Walker on the fine showing by his brigade. Unfortunately for Walker, this was to be the only active service the Tigers would perform under his command.[56]

George McClellan, in a private letter, commented on the foray: "We almost expected a little row up the river yesterday, but it amounted to nothing. The enemy fired 112 shots with artillery at our people at Great Falls, slightly grazing one man's arm and wounding a horse slightly. Fine shooting that! They must learn to do better if they hope to accomplish anything." He would learn before a year had passed what kind of shooting the Southern soldiers were capable of.[57]

The impromptu reconnaissance must be examined in light of other events that were occurring at the same time. On the same day that Beauregard issued his order to Walker to move to the Potomac, he, Johnston, and Smith had written their letter to President Davis urging the appointment of more major generals. The president had been invited to visit the camp to discuss strategy issues only a few days before. The commanders intended to recommend to the chief executive that their army, reinforced of course, should take the offensive by crossing the Potomac at the nearest ford, placing itself behind Washington, and then forcing McClellan to battle on their terms. They expected this action to bring Maryland into the Confederacy and shift the war zone to the northern border of that state.[58]

It takes no great stretch of imagination to understand that the purpose of Walker's foray was to feel out defenses at the several fords nearest the army. Walker's appointment to command this exercise was also deliberate. His success in this enterprise would aid in demonstrating his suitability for promotion to major general. Of course, the words of compliment to Walker during the review on October 3 may have come from Davis's mouth, but they were certainly urged on him by General Beauregard in furtherance of the generals' plan for promotion of their nominees.

The response of President Davis and Secretary Benjamin to the proposal for more generals was cool. Benjamin wrote to Johnston on October 7 that the president thought the number of generals was inflated and that two more major generals, in addition to G. W. Smith and Van Dorn, plus a few more brigadier generals, would be sufficient. On October 10, Davis wrote directly to Smith expounding on his reasoning. Davis said he felt that an army of thirty-seven thousand infantry should be divided into no more than four divisions and that to do otherwise would decrease the value of the commissions of the generals holding them. He admonished Smith in his best didactic style not to allow commissions to assume "militia value." Then he reviewed the organization of the army and the numbers of troops and of generals from each state, noting, significantly, that Louisiana had enough regiments for two brigades but no brigadiers, whereas Georgia had two brigades and two brigadiers, but one of them (Walker) was serving with troops from another state.[59]

Even before Davis wrote to Smith the die had been cast. On October 7, James Longstreet and T. J. Jackson from Johnston's army, Hardee in the west, Theophilus Holmes, Benjamin Huger, and John B. Magruder, all of whom commanded separate departments in Virginia, and Mansfield Lovell, who had held no previous Confederate commission, were appointed major generals. On October 11, Edmund Kirby Smith, another of Johnston's brigadiers, was added to the list. Of the seven officers on the list submitted to the secretary of war less than two weeks before, only three were selected, Longstreet, Jackson, and Lovell.[60]

These promotions were followed on October 22 by a general order from the adjutant and inspector general's office announcing a realignment of Johnston's army into divisions and brigades with state homogeneity whenever possible. This was a follow-up to the president's letter of October 10. In this general reshuffling of the army, Walker was removed from the head of the Louisiana brigade and it was given to its junior colonel, Richard Taylor, who was promoted to fill the vacancy. Taylor was the brother of Jefferson Davis's first wife. Walker felt that his old antagonist of West Point days was again playing favorites at his expense. Walker was not mollified by being offered a Georgia brigade. Nor did it matter that Taylor had a reputation nearly as stern as Walker's in maintaining discipline among his New Orleans "wharf rats." And it helped not at all that his new division commander, Edmund Kirby Smith, was eight years Walker's junior in the U.S. Army. Kirby Smith was a hero of Manassas, but it was more than Walker's pride could bear.[61]

Walker exploded in writing. On October 27, he addressed his letter of resignation to the secretary of war, Judah P. Benjamin. In it he expressed his outrage at Davis's handling of promotions and his unwillingness to serve further under such a leader.

> I have the honor to resign my appointment as a brigadier general in the Provisional Army, which my self respect as a gentleman and pride as a soldier will not allow me any longer to hold. I was the first officer of the old army to resign and offer my services to the south. I was in the old service oftener wounded than any [other] officer in it, and as often breveted for gallantry on the field of battle, and left it without a stain on my character as a gentleman and a soldier. I was honored by my native State (Georgia) with the commission of Major General of the Provisional Army. In order to be in active service I have been on the Potomac several months in command of a brigade and nearly every mail recently has brought me intelligence of my being over-slaughed by some young officer I ranked in the old service, and this in the face of an enemy. Young men have been put over me here who had not graduated at the West Point Academy until after I had been wounded several times in the service, and recommended by no less a soldier than Gen. [Zachary] Taylor for high military promotion. Not content with putting my own countrymen over me, an officeholder (Gen. Lovell from New York City, who was there under pay of New York when our countrymen were gallantly fighting at Manassas and elsewhere) has been brought to the south and made major general over men "to the manor born" [sic] and to cap the climax, the Brigade which I now command, and which I have been months drilling and putting in a proper state of discipline, is to be taken from me and one of my junior colonels put in command of it. I leave my name with the brigade. I know I have its confidence. One would have supposed that an Executive who had himself been a soldier would have scorned to have wounded the sensibilities of an old and tried soldier. The sacred cause for which I drew my sword I will fight for in my native state but I will not condescend to submit any longer to the insults and indignities of the Executive.

General Beauregard, Walker's immediate commander, discreetly endorsed this missive "Respectfully forwarded" and sent it to the War Department.[62]

Although Walker hit out at Richard Taylor and Kirby Smith, he took most deliberate aim at Mansfield Lovell, who had been G. W. Smith's assistant in New York and had come to Richmond seeking an appointment. Lovell had resigned from the U.S. Army in 1854 to engage in filibustering activities in Cuba and had held no military appointment since. Now he was being sent to command the crucial defenses at New Orleans. Walker's complaint was reminiscent of the remarks he had made about Bragg the previous March.[63]

If Walker believed in conspiracy theories, there was evidence at hand to support such belief. When the Louisiana Brigade went on its foray to the Potomac at the end of September, the 9th Louisiana had been left behind because of the high sick rate in the regiment. One of those absent sick was the regiment's colonel, Richard Taylor. During his absence, Taylor went to Richmond to stay at the house of fellow Louisianian Secretary of War Judah P. Benjamin. On October 2, Benjamin addressed Walker a note telling him that Taylor was sick at his house and he had extended Taylor's leave of absence by fifteen days. Besides preempting Walker's authority as brigade commander, this memo could have sustained his belief that Davis, Benjamin, and Taylor had hatched a plot to supplant him, and he could certainly guess when and where it happened. Taylor later wrote that when he learned of his promotion he begged President Davis to rescind the order. Instead, Davis wrote to the other officers of the brigade explaining the promotion in soothing terms and allowed it to stand. Surely, Walker was not a recipient of such a letter.[64]

Benjamin could not let the insults in Walker's letter of resignation go unanswered. On October 29 he replied:

> Your letter of the 27th instant has been received. In it, you tender your resignation as brigadier general in the Provisional Army. It is due to self respect that I should remark on the impropriety of your using this department as the channel for conveying disrespectful and insulting comments on the action of the Commander-in-Chief of the army and the Chief Magistrate of the Confederacy. His sole offense, according to the statements of your letter, consists in not selecting you to be a major general, for there is no question of promotion involved in the appointment of general officers. The law expressly vests in him the power to choose officers to command brigades and divisions and it is no disparagement to any officer, whatever may have been his services, that the President prefers another as a division commander. Your statement, therefore, that you have been overslaughed and that you have thus been subjected to the insults and indignities of the Executive is based on a total misapprehension of his duties and your rights according to the laws which govern the army. Your communication has been submitted to the President and by his direction your resignation is accepted.[65]

Reason and the law were on Benjamin's side, but Walker would have none of it. In a parting shot, as he prepared to leave Virginia, he got in the last word.

Your communication informing me of the acceptance of my resignation has been received. You state that "it is due to self respect that I should remark on the impropriety of your using this department as the channel for conveying disrespectful and insulting comments on the action of the Commander-in-Chief of the army and the Chief Magistrate of the Confederacy." My resignation had to be sent through your department. It is the proper military channel which your short sojourn in the department made you ignorant of. How your self respect could have been wounded by the plain, unvarnished statement of an old soldier I am at a loss to divine. Suffice it to say that my communication was intended for the Executive and though you have attempted to hoist your self-respect before the country in defense of an Executive who chooses to do this and to do that in the face of the public opinion of the army and the country, I doubt very much whether in trying to preserve your own self-respect (which has not been assailed) you will not lose the respect of the country.[66]

By October 31 this correspondence had been leaked to the press, possibly by Walker himself. The publication of Walker's and Benjamin's letters caused a sensation across the South. Except in Georgia, public opinion seemed to side with Davis. Mary Boykin Chesnut wrote in her diary, "Forgetting their country—quarreling for their own glory. For shame!" The *Richmond Examiner*, one of Davis's severest critics, took his side. On Walker's behalf, the correspondent of the *Augusta Constitutionalist* reported from Centreville on October 29 that Generals Johnston and Beauregard had recommended the Georgian for promotion. He went on to say that many of the officers of the Louisiana brigade were dissatisfied with the change and had threatened to resign, which was true. They were no happier than Walker at the change in command. Only Walker's counseling caused them to rethink their actions. In the end, only Robert Anderson resigned with his general, returning to Georgia to take a position in the Georgia State Troops. By war's end, Anderson was a brigadier general of Confederate cavalry under former Lieutenant Joe Wheeler.[67]

Walker issued a farewell order to the troops thanking them for their support and commending them for their spirit. In return he received several resolutions from the officers of the regiments expressing their regret at his departure. According to the reporter for the *Picayune*, Walker and Taylor parted on good terms, the former giving the latter his camp equipage.[68]

The letter of September 28, 1861, from the generals of the Army of the Potomac to the secretary of war is of some significance in explaining Walker's abrupt resignation. Although alluded to in the *Official Records*, a footnote states that the letter was "not found" during the compilation of those records. Previous researchers have either overlooked it or not bothered to cite it in discussing Walker's decision to leave the army. It seems fairly clear that Walker was aware that he was on a short list of nominees for promotion. He may even have known his name was at the head of the list. His reaction when, worse than being selected behind men lower on the list, he was not selected at all is understandable. This, coupled with being reorganized out of his brigade, constituted a double blow from President Davis.[69]

Although Walker resigned in no small part because of personal pride and this action fits the pattern of his career when faced with unpleasant circumstances, it should also be examined in the light of relations between the Confederate administration in Richmond and the Joe Brown clique in Georgia. Throughout the four-year life of the Confederacy, Brown and his adherents felt that they had traded one violator of states' rights for another. The fear of the black Republicans which had caused Georgia to secede in 1861 was replaced with an abhorrence of the central regime headed by Jefferson Davis. As the war progressed and the pressures on the Richmond government became greater, the Confederate government, personified by Davis, usurped (in the minds of the state leaders) more and more state powers. First it was the naming of officers for volunteer units, then the control of arms and munitions, later direct enlistment of units into Confederate service, and then conscription. All of these actions reduced the powers and patronage of the governors while strengthening the hand of the president.[70]

If Governor Brown had his political allies, such as Vice-President Alexander Stephens, he also had supporters among the Georgia generals. Walker, who a few years later would note that "[Governor Brown], you know, has always been a great friend to me," was one of them. Two others were Henry R. Jackson and Henry C. Wayne. Jackson had been a leader of state troops early in 1861 and had received a Confederate commission as brigadier after Walker. Wayne had left the U.S. service almost simultaneously with Walker to accept Brown's appointment as state adjutant general. Wayne did not receive even an offer of commission in the Confederate army until January 1862. When such offer of appointment did come, Wayne spurned it, telling Secretary of War Benjamin, "If I am fit to be a general now, I was equally fit for the place months ago when I could have been properly ranked with my associates in the old Army and the neophyte generals from civil life."[71]

It is clear that some Georgia generals were thoroughly disillusioned with the military policies of the Richmond administration and preferred state service to Confederate. Walker was one of them. Governor Brown, in a letter to Walker in November 1861, intimated that he had not known the latter was going to resign, but it is not unfair to assume that Walker was aware of events in Georgia and the prospect of appointment there. His resignation from Confederate service was probably made up of equal parts of personal dudgeon, disgust with the Davis administration, abetted by admiration for Governor Brown, and hope for duty in Georgia. Perhaps he even aspired to the command of the division Brown shortly after offered to Jackson. While Walker was willing to burn his boats in Virginia, he may already have had plans for a new launching in Georgia.[72]

There appears to be nothing to the story that Walker resigned because of ill health. He had complained of asthmatic attacks while at Centreville, but in his letters to his wife he never mentioned that as a reason for discontent. As late as October 24 he was making plans to bring his family to Virginia for the winter and looking forward to a general engagement with McClellan's army. It was the announced reorganization of the army that led him to resign.[73]

Walker returned to Georgia on November 2, his dignity satisfied and his head held high, but the anticipation of the previous spring had been soured by the frustrations of Pensacola and Centreville. The vacancy caused by his resignation was first offered to Henry R. Jackson, and after that officer's resignation it was filled by the promotion of the convalescent colonel William Montgomery Gardner.[74]

IO

GEORGIA CINCINNATUS

1861–1862

WHILE THE OPPOSING ARMIES, North and South, maneuvered for position in Virginia and Tennessee in late 1861, the South's most vulnerable area, its coastline, lay virtually unprotected. Effectively, there was no Confederate navy. The only defensive positions were the former Federal forts lying at the entrances to the major harbors and rivers. The U.S. Navy's Atlantic Squadron, feeble as it was, was free to land an invading force on any stretch of the long arc between Hampton Roads, Virginia, and Brownsville, Texas.

Expeditions toward such a goal were being fitted out in the North as autumn wore on. In August 1861, a combined naval and military force under Flag Officer Silas H. Stringham and General Benjamin F. Butler had sailed from Annapolis, Maryland, and captured the forts at the entrance to Hatteras Inlet, making a lodgment on the North Carolina coast. Even as William Walker was resigning from the army and returning to Georgia, another Union fleet and army were preparing to leave Hampton Roads, Virginia, bound for an unknown destination on the Southern coast.[1]

This second expedition consisted of more than twelve thousand troops under Brigadier General Thomas W. Sherman in over thirty transports escorted by a fleet of seventeen warships under Flag Officer Samuel F. DuPont. Their mission was to seize two unspecified locations on the Southern coast and set up bases for protection of the blockading squadrons. They departed Hampton Roads on October 29 and arrived off Port Royal Sound, South Carolina, on November 4. On November 7, the fleet bombarded and captured the two forts at the entrance to the sound and landed troops at Hilton Head. As well as being a base for fleet operations, this point would serve as a staging area for future operations against the Carolina and Georgia coasts.[2]

The Confederate army had a weak coast defense organization in place, but it was fragmented into several independent departments. To meet this new and potentially disastrous threat, President Davis, on November 5, created the Department of South Carolina, Georgia, and Florida and appointed General Robert E. Lee as its commander. Lee's subordinates were, in the District of Georgia, with headquarters at Savannah, Brigadier General Alexander R. Lawton, who had captured Fort Pulaski the previous January; in the District of South Carolina, with headquarters at Charleston, Brigadier General Roswell S. Ripley; and in the District of East and Middle Florida, Brigadier General James H. Trapier. Lee arrived in South Carolina on November 7 and proceeded directly to Coosawhatchie Station on the Charleston and Savannah Railroad, while the bombardment of the forts at Port Royal Sound was in progress. On November 8, he established his headquarters at Coosawhatchie, midway between the two cities which he expected would be the most likely targets of Union attacks, Charleston and Savannah.[3]

Lee found the strength of his command less than reassuring. In South Carolina, Ripley had some sixty-eight hundred men posted from the Savannah River north to Charleston, naturally concentrated around the latter place. Lawton in Georgia had about thirty-five hundred men around Savannah and another two thousand from the Altamaha River to the Florida line, principally at Brunswick. Trapier's strength was approximately four thousand for the entire state of Florida except the western panhandle, which was still under Braxton Bragg's command at Pensacola. A few gunboats of the Confederate navy under Commodore Josiah Tattnall were available for river and harbor defense, but the Confederacy had nothing that could seriously challenge the Federal cruisers.[4]

Upon arrival in his new department Lee realized that defense of the entire coastline was impossible with the means he had at hand. He determined upon a three-part plan of action. He would defend Charleston, Savannah, Fort Pulaski, and other strong points; block the waterways leading to the interior; and give up weak positions, concentrating his forces for rapid response. He also understood the necessity of protecting the Charleston and Savannah Railroad, the vital communications link that ran lateral to his front. Finally, knowing he could not hold at all points along the coast, he planned an interior line of works to protect Savannah and the railroad. He realized his resources were insufficient for these purposes, and he asked for permission from Richmond to bring transient troops under his command, which request was granted.[5]

The condition of coast defenses in Georgia was reported to Lee by his ordnance officer, Lieutenant Colonel W. H. Gill. There was a battery on Jekyll Island and another on St. Simon's Island, both protecting access to Brunswick. For protection of Savannah, Fort Pulaski, a brick and masonry structure on whose construction Lee had worked as a young lieutenant, stood on Cockspur Island near the mouth of the Savannah River. Closer in to the city were Fort Jackson, Thunderbolt battery, and the Green Island battery. Brigadier General Hugh W. Mercer commanded the troops and batteries in the Brunswick area while General Lawton had the bulk of his troops in Savannah and at nearby forts and camps.[6]

The governors of the coastal Southern states were not unmindful of the pending threats, but they had been dispatching their best troops to make up the regiments of volunteers that entered Confederate service for field duty. In addition, there was a great shortage of arms even if men could be found for new units. Governor Brown of Georgia moved energetically to remedy both problems. As early as July 1861, he had begun to collect old guns from the citizenry for state use and to encourage the people to form volunteer companies in their counties. After an inspection of the coast of Georgia in September, he determined that the Confederate defenses were inadequate, and he called up the volunteer companies to form a new organization, the Georgia State Troops, enlisted for six months. The response was so great that in October he had to curtail the volunteering.[7]

This first call resulted in the formation of two brigades. Brigadier Generals Frank Capers, former commandant of the Georgia Military Institute at Marietta, and George P. Harrison, Sr., a Savannah aristocrat, were appointed to command them. The combined strength was about fifty-five hundred. The response to Brown's call for men was large enough that he hoped he could raise a third brigade, if needed. The attack at Port Royal in November caused him to issue a proclamation asking for thirty more companies, which were formed into three regiments totaling twenty-five hundred more men. W. H. T. Walker arrived home from Virginia just at this time. Events there had not tarnished his reputation in Georgia; rather the opposite. Governor Brown approved of any man who would stand up for his rights and honor against the overbearing central government. Soon after his return to Georgia, Walker offered his services to the governor to command the Georgia State Troops. In polite letters on November 11 and 16, Brown informed Walker that the major generalcy had already been offered to Henry Jackson, who was being invited to resign his Confederate commission to take command of the state troops. Brown went so far as to tell Walker that had he known the latter would be available, he would have given him command of the division. Brown then offered Walker command of the newly raised third brigade, which Walker gladly accepted, saying he would be most pleased to serve under Henry Jackson. On November 26, Brown nominated Walker to the Georgia Senate, and the appointment was confirmed.[8]

Walker's arrival was viewed with some concern by the Confederate authorities because of the circumstances of his resignation. On November 1, while Walker was still en route from Virginia, Lawton wrote to Secretary Benjamin about the imminent arrival of state troops. After reporting the organization of the first brigade, he went on:

> It is now well understood that Governor Brown will at once appoint General W. H. T. Walker a major general [sic], and his commission will no doubt bear date before the time that this note will reach you. General Walker is an old friend of mine, and under other circumstances I could have no objections whatever to serving under him, as he is several years my senior, but I fear that the feelings with which he has now left the Confederate service, fomented by the temper which Governor Brown has (in the past at least) exhibited toward the War Department, might cause great embarrassment here, if he is permitted to assume command under State authority.[9]

Lawton's fears and Brown's temperament notwithstanding, relations between national and state forces were reasonably good. As Douglas Southall Freeman said of Lee's relations with another officer in his department, "With the self control that always marked his acts, Lee ignored [his] peculiarities and made the most of his abilities." Governor Brown welcomed the appointment of General Lee as department commander. Lee and Jackson got along well from the start, as did Wayne and Lawton once the rules for use of the Georgia troops had been established. As early as October 1, Wayne had suggested to Governor Brown that "it is absolutely necessary . . . for the state to cooperate with the Confederacy heartily in all matters." Wayne informed Lawton that the state troops would be subject to Confederate orders and would always cooperate during emergencies but recognized the governor as their ultimate authority for administrative purposes. Lee and Lawton accepted this. Lee planned to use the state troops as a reserve for his own forces. Lawton was sufficiently impressed with the spirit of cooperation shown by Brown and Wayne to remark on it.[10]

Even before assuming command of his brigade, Walker had made a visit to Savannah in an unofficial capacity, presumably to check the state of the defenses but no doubt also to look after his business interests. Earlier in the year, the planing machine company had folded and was now selling off its assets. Walker continued to receive disbursements from Robert Allen, either from return of capital or long-term dividends, but he would certainly have wanted to take a firsthand look at his property after having been away for more than five months.

On December 6, he received an order from the adjutant general to report, as quickly as he could get ready, to Camp Harrison at Station Number 7 on the Savannah, Albany, and Gulf Railroad Line, which was located about seventy miles south of Savannah near Screven in Wayne County. The camp was the assembly point for the thirty or so companies that were to make up the three regiments of Walker's 3d Brigade, Georgia State Troops. The camp was located on the railroad because of the delineation of responsibility between state and Confederate troops. Lawton's units were to man the coast defenses while Jackson's division, acting as a reserve, would form a second line some miles inland and along the railroad for convenience in moving to any threatened point.[11]

Under the system the state had adopted, anyone who raised a company of fifty to eighty men was commissioned captain. If another man could convince the governor that he could get ten captains with their companies to rally to him, he would become a colonel. Colonels were plentiful; captains wiling to swear allegiance to them were scarcer. As Walker telegraphed to Adjutant General Wayne soon after his arrival, "[Colonel] Harris has eight companies, Nunally six, Wright two, Johnson two. Do you intend Nunally to have six. Do you wish me to wait on Wright till he gets eight more companies. Until these questions are answered I can't [get] organized. Answer." [12]

The companies were available; the problem was inducing them to join a particular regiment. For example, the Jack Browns, a company from Marion County, had only forty-three privates, less than the requisite number. The captain had a dispensation from the governor to take more time to fill up his ranks. The captain wanted his men mustered in and made a part of the 10th Regiment. The men refused, preferring to be part of a different battalion in a different brigade. Walker wanted them in his brigade. He wrote to Henry Jackson asking for instructions: "Let me know [if] I have the right to make them obey me at the point of a bayonet." Jackson's answer is not recorded, but the Jack Browns wound up in the 10th Regiment.[13]

A colonel who could not form a regiment would lose his commission.

The various colonels kept asking for more time to fill up their regiments. Walker was anxious to get on with his organization because the situation was changing rapidly. His task was not helped by Governor Brown's meddling to help his friends. When William F. Wright and another officer could not muster sufficient companies to form regiments, Brown telegraphed and then wrote Walker to delay his organization until enough men could arrive. He ordered Walker to take whatever arms he needed from the Savannah arsenal for the next two or three companies arriving so that they could be attached to the deficient regiments. When Henry Jackson protested these orders, Brown told him flatly, "My order has not been countermanded and must be obeyed." Walker finally got the governor to agree to allow him to muster in his brigade on January 31, 1862. The regiments least ready by that time would be disbanded and their companies used to fill up the others.[14]

Men in companies with such names as the Jack Browns, the Freemen of Floyd, the Sunny South Guards, the Gilmer Tigers, and the Brown Lookouts volunteered in the thousands from all over the state. Armaments were a perennial problem. The militia companies and gunshops of Augusta were denuded of weapons to arm Colonel Robert Y. Harris's regiment. Governor Brown even conceived a plan for a battalion of men armed with pikes. It was the job of Jackson, Walker, and the other generals and colonels to mold this unruly mass into a fighting force. Finding weapons for the formed companies was another problem. Brown's original call had asked for men "armed with a good country rifle or double barreled shot gun, or a good military gun, fit for immediate use." These were the weapons they had brought to camp with them. They were gradually replaced with standardized arms, but it took time, and the men expected to be reimbursed for the personal guns they turned in.[15]

Squabbling among the officers did not help. Not only were they competing for the men to join their regiments, they also engaged in personal affrays. When Walker's adjutant, Major Octavius Cohen Myers, gave an order to Colonel Elijah W. Chastain of the 8th Regiment, Chastain responded, "Go to hell, God damn you; don't talk to me, I hate you." When this was reported to Walker, he had no choice but to order Chastain's court-martial. In the midst of his other problems Walker had to find officers to sit on the court, send other officers as witnesses, testify himself, and then approve the sentence. Chastain was found guilty of one of the three charges brought against him. He was sentenced to forty-eight hours' suspension from command, but Governor Brown, an old friend of Chastain's, allowed no punishment beyond arrest.[16]

While the national and state forces were aligning themselves in Georgia and the other states in Lee's department, Thomas W. Sherman's division at Hilton Head had been cooperatively quiescent. On November 24, however, a Union landing was made on Tybee Island at the mouth of the Savannah, threatening to blockade the river. It was also perceived as a possible first step toward attacks on Fort Pulaski or the city of Savannah. Additional forays were made along the South Carolina and Georgia coast in December. These moves brought renewed appeals from Governor Brown for Confederate help and for strengthening of Georgia's defenses. Brown asked that Georgia units sent to Virginia be brought back and that additional arms be made available for the state troops.[17]

When Brown asked the legislature for more money to support his state troops, those officials countered with a bill to turn the troops over to the Confederate government. The governor was strongly opposed and said so, but the house passed the measure. In conference with the senate, the bill was toned down to read that the troops would be offered to the Confederacy only if they consented. Brown thereupon contacted the secretary of war and offered his full division. Benjamin reiterated the dreary old refrain of "regiments, battalions and companies." Brown was delighted. Next he ordered a referendum among the troops. Almost unanimously they refused a transfer. For the time being, Jackson's division remained under state control.[18]

Jackson brought Walker's 3d Brigade to Savannah early in January and made him commandant of the city. From his headquarters at Camp Walker he not only commanded twenty-five hundred troops but also issued orders to the civilian population. The brigade, after final muster, was composed of the 8th, 9th, and 10th regiments and the 3rd Battalion, Georgia State Troops. The regimental and battalion commanders were, respectively, Colonels Elijah W. Chastain, Robert Y. Harris, William F. Wright, and Lieutenant Colonel Aaron D. Nunnally. There was usually a battery of artillery attached, either Captain Frederick H. Burghardt's Macon German Artillery or Captain Leroy Napier's Macon Light Artillery. Napier had been a cadet at West Point when Walker was commandant. Once arrived in Savannah, Walker found that a company of cavalry was necessary for policing his lines. At his request, a company was attached. At different times, he had either the Bibb Cavalry, Captain Abner M. Lockett, later Captain Thaddeus G. Holt, the Thomas County Dragoons, Captain Samuel B. Spencer, or Captain Arch C. Davenport's Independent Company of Volunteer Georgia Cavalry, the Tattnall Guards, a sixty-day company.[19]

Keeping the troops in camp and out of the fleshpots of the city was as much a problem as had been keeping the cadets on the reservation at West Point. The dram shop keepers were all too eager to sell their product to the soldiers. Jackson and Walker were forced to publish restrictive orders. Jackson issued his General Order No. 16 controlling the disorderly conduct of soldiers entering the city. Walker published his own edict on February 10: "Notice. It is hereby ordered that any individual who shall sell, or furnish in any manner whatever, liquors of any kind to any soldier within the limits of this city and suburbs, will have his shop or store or barroom immediately closed, and his liquors emptied into the street." Whatever the means, the resulting order was much appreciated by the population, some of whom felt their city had never been more peaceful or quiet. Lieutenant George Anderson Mercer, son and aide to Brigadier General Mercer, wrote in his diary of his native city: "All is as quiet as in profound peace." The correspondent of the *Charleston Tri-Weekly Mercury* told his readers that "the citizens [of Savannah] assured me they had never in peace known their city kept in such perfect order and quiet," and he added, "Such is the spirit of one man." So thorough was Walker's control of Savannah that General Lawton gave him jurisdiction over Confederate troops stationed in the city.[20]

While Walker was preparing his brigade and maintaining order in Savannah, the crisis at Fort Pulaski was looming. General Thomas W. Sherman, the Union commander, had been uncertain about what his objective should be in Georgia, but under urging from McClellan in Washington, he finally decided to capture Fort Pulaski. By January 1862, the fort was garrisoned by four hundred men in five companies of the 1st Georgia Volunteers, a Confederate regiment under Colonel Charles H. Olmstead. It came under the jurisdiction of the Confederate District of Georgia. In February 1862, Sherman strengthened the force on Tybee Island and construction of batteries was begun. At the same time, another Union force, making use of the many streams and bywaters in the area, bypassed Pulaski, removed the obstructions Lee had had placed in the channels, landed four miles upstream, and began building two more batteries. The Confederate fort was thought to be nearly impregnable by its defenders, but the Union commanders brought to their batteries ten-inch mortars and rifled cannon which were calculated to make short work of the masonry walls.[21]

Federal gunboats, making use of the cleared channels, approached within four miles below the city. This threat was serious enough to bring the governor and his adjutant general to Savannah to confer with Generals Lee,

Lawton, Jackson, and Walker. Lee moved his headquarters to Savannah from South Carolina. The defenders at Pulaski were supplied with food and ammunition to withstand a siege. Work on the defensive line before Savannah intensified with most of the work being done by details from the Georgia State Troops. There was no thought yet of Pulaski being captured, but the authorities feared an invading force landing above the fort. Lee also abandoned Brunswick about this time, with Governor Brown's concurrence, to strengthen his defenses in the Savannah area.[22]

Although additional troops had been sent from Virginia earlier, in response to Lee's and Brown's requests, the threat to the interior of the Confederacy from U. S. Grant's army advancing along the Tennessee River had caused the Confederate government to draw some regiments from Lee to strengthen Albert Sidney Johnston's army in Mississippi. In response to Lee's warning that Savannah, as well as Brunswick, might have to be abandoned, Brown wrote that Lee was the best judge of what to do, but "I would leave [Savannah] in smoking ruins when driven from it." Walker certainly concurred with the governor's sentiment when he told the correspondent of the *Charleston Tri-Weekly Mercury* that he would "hang any man who makes such a proposition [for surrender] as soon as the rope can be adjusted around his neck," and "he openly announces his decision to burn the city rather than it shall fall into the enemy's hands."[23]

About this time Walker contracted pneumonia. His always frail health, the wet weather, and the constant strain of work had further weakened his body's defense against disease. Nevertheless, he wanted to take his brigade out, first to attack the Federal batteries and later to capture the gunboats in the narrow passes of the river below Savannah. These plans were taken under advisement by his superiors but never acted upon. Walker's plan to capture or destroy gunboats with land forces was not as harebrained as some might think. Ellison Capers, E. Milby Burton, and accounts in the *Official Records of the Union and Confederate Navies* describe in detail an incident in which concealed land batteries destroyed or captured Union gunboats in South Carolina in early 1863. At any rate, the defensive line was finished by the labor of the Georgia State Troops. Several times Walker's brigade was drafted for labor details of five hundred men. The location of the line remains uncertain. Freeman, in *Lee's Lieutenants*, says no source describes exactly the interior line Lee had proposed for protection of the rail line and Savannah. In March 1863, General Benjamin Huger prepared a report of the defenses of Savannah complete with sketches showing every fort and battery erected along the river approaches to the city. It is not known precisely how many of those works were put up under Lee's direction, but Governor Brown wrote to General Hugh Mercer on April 24, 1863, that "the state troops last year built the line of fortifications . . . with the exception probably of the masonry." Before Lee could complete his projected work, he was summoned to Richmond, not to return. His place was taken by recently promoted Major General John Pemberton, Walker's West Point classmate, a Pennsylvanian who had sided with the South, and former commander of a district in South Carolina.[24]

On April 10, 1862, the Federal batteries on both sides of Fort Pulaski began their bombardment. Early in the morning Colonel Olmstead was sent a summons to surrender, which he refused. At about 7 : 30 A.M. the batteries opened up, first seeking the range. The distance from Tybee Island to Pulaski was about fourteen hundred yards at the nearest battery and twenty-four hundred at the furthest. At first, the gunners had to adjust their range and later began the actual battering work. By the end of the first day a breach in the angle of the southeast corner of the fort was apparent. Guns were fired at intervals all night long, more as harassment of the defenders than for damaging effect.

At dawn the morning of the eleventh the fire was recommenced. Throughout the morning large sections of wall were gradually dislodged and fell into the moat, forming a bridge into the breach. By early afternoon shells were passing through the openings and battering down the rear walls (blindments) of the casemates. When a shell passed completely through the fort and exploded in the passage to the magazine on the northwest side, but fortunately without detonating the powder stored therein, Olmstead realized his position was hopeless. The white flag was run up and the fort surrendered. Some 385 men were captured, including officers, of whom 18 were sick and wounded.

The success of the rifled guns astonished even those who were employing them. The walls of Pulaski were seven feet thick. The maximum range for smoothbore artillery for battering operations was about nine hundred yards, and a wall of that thickness was expected to hold out for weeks. At Pulaski round shot and shell were fired from ranges of up to seventeen hundred yards and reduced the fort in two days. It was found that an eighty-four-pound projectile fired from a forty-two-pounder rifled cannon could make an indentation twenty-six inches deep in the masonry structure. Three or four such hits in close proximity could effect a breach. This was the first use of rifled siege artillery except in experimentation. Quincy Gillmore said the effect was as radical for land warfare as the introduction of the ironclad was at sea. The mortars were a disappointment. They were not well served and those shells that did strike the fort did little damage. General Lee had had the foresight to have Olmstead plow up the parade ground. The mortar shells merely buried themselves in the soft earth. The two batteries that had been established upstream of the fort participated in the bombardment but with little effect because the weight of their metal was too light.[25]

A soldier who had been at the fort left just before the surrender and carried the word to Savannah. The citizens of the city were thrown into a panic. Many began to pack their belongings and made arrangements to move into the interior of the state. Walker had predicted such a reaction about the time the first Union gunboats appeared in the river. On the night of the bombardment of Pulaski he stormed into a Savannah hotel filled with worried and angry citizens. Addressing the gathering in scathing tones, he told them he had no concern for their personal safety or material belongings. True to the philosophy he had revealed earlier, he let the crowd know there would not be a Savannah to surrender if the Yankee gunboats ever arrived. "I'll never surrender anything more than the ashes of Savannah," he told them. "I'll stay here and I'll keep you here till every shingle burns and every brick gets knocked into bits the size of my thumb nail and then I'll send the Yankees word that there isn't any Savannah to surrender. I've had a convenient limb trimmed up on the tree in front of my headquarters and I'll string up every man that dares say surrender." The young Confederate soldier who was an eyewitness and wrote these words many years later may have freely paraphrased them, but there is no doubt the sentiments and the promised actions were pure Walker.[26]

The Union forces did not advance upon Savannah, but if they had, Walker would not have been in a position to carry out his threat. Two months previously, the Confederate government had decreed that its manpower needs would henceforth take priority over any state's. At that time Governor Brown had ordered his officers to stop all recruiting efforts. On April 12, the day after the surrender of Pulaski, the Confederate Congress passed the Conscription Act. In the wording of the law all men between the ages of eighteen and thirty-five were automatically members of the national army. All men in the Georgia State Troops in that category were liable for Confederate service.

Some three thousand of Jackson's men had gone home at the expiration of their six months' service despite the crisis at Savannah. Rather than quibble about the matter, Brown offered all those remaining to the Con-

federate government in complete units. He thought he could easily bring
back the rest to make a full division under Jackson and his three brigadiers.
As usual, the secretary of war, by now George W. Randolph, stood on the
legal position that he could accept nothing larger than a regiment.

Governor Brown urged Randolph to take the entire Georgia State
Troops division with its four general officers but was refused. The state
troops evaporated as an organization. Some of the regiments and battalions
became units of Georgia volunteers in the Confederate States Army, but
many of the men enlisted as individuals. Henry Jackson disappeared temporarily into oblivion. No biographical sketch records what he did from
the spring of 1862 to the fall of 1863 when he was recommissioned as a
Confederate brigadier. Frank Capers went back to his academy at Marietta, and George Harrison went back to his plantation to take no more
part in the war except as a prisoner of William T. Sherman's army when
it approached Savannah in 1864. On April 15, the *Augusta Chronicle and
Sentinel* reported, "General W. H. T. Walker arrived here Sunday morning
from Savannah. He is still in a very feeble condition but is convalescing."
The *Constitutionalist* reported tersely, "Gen. W. H. T. Walker arrived here
yesterday. His health is improving."[27]

The value of the Georgia State Troops in 1861–62 deserves a brief assessment. Joseph E. Brown's concerns about the defense of the Georgia
coast were real, but his response was as much political as military. Facing
a campaign for reelection in November 1861 and under heavy attack in
the press for his actions in regard to availability of arms and men for coast
defense, Brown probably felt that he had to do something. Whether it was
necessary to raise his own army to solve these problems is the issue. He denied the Confederate government critically needed men and munitions by
using them for state service, yet he satisfied the complaints of his constitu-
ents and raised, trained, and equipped a full division of infantry at no cost
to the central government. He materially aided in the defense of Savannah
when the local Confederate commander had not the means to protect the
long coastline with the slender resources at hand. Most of Brown's men
were later enrolled in Confederate forces; all of them benefited from their
experience as state troops. Later in the war Brown's military posturing was
counterproductive to Confederate goals. In 1862, the Confederate States
ultimately profited from the existence of the Georgia State Troops.[28]

The Augusta that William Walker returned to in April 1862 was a different city than the one he had left eleven months earlier. The effects of the
Union sea blockade were beginning to be felt. The South, never an indus-

trial area, was cut off from its sources of supply in Europe and the North. Augusta became a center for war production. Colonel George Washington Rains built the Confederate Powder Works there in 1862. Other factories turned out shoes and boots, uniforms, muskets and revolvers, cannon, ammunition, wagons, and even belt buckles. By April 1862, the city and county had furnished twenty-four companies of men to Confederate service. As a result, a large portion of the work force in the new factories was female.

Women provided other services. Sewing circles knitted mittens, scarves, and socks for soldiers. Augusta's location on the railroad made it a through point for troop trains. The women of the city provided a canteen service for the young men on their way to war. In April 1862, the first sick and wounded from Savannah and Fort Pulaski arrived in Augusta, presaging its prominence as a hospital center. The local women added nursing and bandage making to their other wartime duties. Briefly, the city experienced boom times, but food and housing shortages, inflation, and an influx of refugees from areas overrun by the Yankees brought a quick end to prosperity.[29]

Elsewhere in the South, 1862 was a year of mixed fortunes. In the Valley of Virginia that spring, Thomas J. "Stonewall" Jackson conducted his classic campaign with troops which included Walker's former Louisiana brigade under General Dick Taylor. Robert E. Lee's transfer from Savannah to Richmond was followed by almost uninterrupted victory in that theater. McClellan's Peninsula Campaign ended in failure in July; another Union army under John Pope was dealt a humiliating defeat on the old Manassas battlefield in August. That battle cost John David Walker his life. In September, Lee's invasion of Maryland brought him defeat, but this was followed by a triumph over Ambrose Burnside at Fredericksburg in December. There another prominent Georgian, Thomas R. R. Cobb, gave up his life.

If the Confederacy, despite mourning its losses, could find hope in victory in the East, events on the other fronts told a different story. While Walker was still at Savannah, Burnside's North Carolina expedition had found success in February 1862. Braxton Bragg had abandoned his operations at Pensacola and with Walker's former comrades, John K. Jackson and S. A. M. Wood, and the Washington Artillery, had joined Albert Sidney Johnston's army in Mississippi. Johnston was in Mississippi because he had been driven out of most of Kentucky and Tennessee by U. S. Grant's advance up the Tennessee and Cumberland rivers. It was this crisis that had cost Lee's coastal department so many men sent to reinforce Johnston. Just before Walker's return home to Augusta in April, the South was saddened by the news of the death of Johnston and thousands of others at Shiloh. Shortly after Walker's return, the shattering news of the loss of New Orleans and the closing of the Mississippi outlet for Confederate commerce befell the South. Still to come were Bragg and Kirby Smith's abortive invasion of Kentucky and the bloody but indecisive battle at Stones River at year's end. Grant's and W. T. Sherman's campaign to capture Vicksburg would also begin before 1862 closed.

As the days and months passed, Walker worked his farm and looked after family matters. Even in the midst of his duties on the Georgia coast, Mobley Pond had been on his mind. Writing to his daughter from Camp Walker in January, he had said, "I sigh for private life." When Governor Brown asked the legislature for an act to encourage volunteering that did not exempt overseers, Walker wrote to Henry Wayne, asking for an exemption for his overseer on the grounds that "the country will be ruined if our plantations are deprived of their overseers." Back on his farm, he sold his crops and banked what money he did not need for immediate living expenses. The bucolic serenity was disturbed by two personal losses and one gain. In June Walker's mother died at the age of seventy-five and was buried in the old arsenal cemetery. In August, John David, a major with the 1st Georgia Regulars in the Army of Northern Virginia, was critically wounded in the leg at Second Manassas. He was carried to a hospital at Winchester, Virginia, where the surgeons wanted to amputate the leg. Remembering his experience in Mexico, John refused. Gangrene set in, and he died on October 3, 1862. He was buried at Winchester, and the body was not returned to Augusta until 1871. In August 1862, Mary bore her last child, a son, who was named Adam Johnston Walker.[30]

On his farm, as Walker assessed the achievements and failures of his first year in Confederate service, he might have mulled over these facts. As a junior officer, he had excelled in leadership by example. He possessed to a high degree the skills required to lead small units of men in battle: personal bravery, a disregard of danger, and coolness under fire. With the tactics of frontal assault then in vogue among American commanders, those characteristics were necessary to stimulate men to advance with confidence into the face of lethal enemy fire. At Okeechobee, Churubusco, and Molino del Rey, Walker provided the leadership expected of him by his seniors, his subordinates, and his peers. Twice, at Okeechobee and Molino del Rey, his personal recklessness nearly cost him his life, but on two of the three occasions, Okeechobee and Churubusco, the wild forward rush in which he delighted was sufficient to win the day. At Vera Cruz, Walker showed another facet of his character, coolness under fire. While pinned down by enemy artillery, the young captain lay on his back smoking a cigar with his overcoat under his head as a pillow. Who could fail to be inspired by such coolness and confidence? His actions won for him glory, promotion, and national fame, the very things he had gone to Mexico to seek.

As a professional academy-trained officer, Walker had the regular army knack for maintaining discipline and simultaneously looking after the welfare of his men. He could empathize with and bear up under the same hardships as his troops. As an infantry officer he marched on foot with his company. He made the long trek from Vera Cruz to Mexico City on his own two feet the same as the lowliest private. He slept in the open with the men, ate much the same fare while on campaign, and was reduced to wearing the same nondescript garb so common to veteran soldiers in every war. He had the complete respect of his brother officers. His iron-willed ride from Tampa Bay to Black Creek in 1838 ensured for him a place in the 6th Infantry whenever he wanted it. When he returned to active duty in 1840, his peers willingly made a place for him with his old rank and seniority, giving up one promotion place themselves. Walker's bearing inspired not only his men but also the junior officers who served with him. Simon Bolivar Buckner recorded his high opinion of Walker during their service together in Mexico.

His two attributes, professionalism and élan, made Walker a great success as a leader of small units, but in the dozen years between the wars, he lost touch with the troops and with his profession. Between 1848 and 1861 he spent only two months on troop duty, with the 10th Infantry at Fort Ripley, and twenty-one months as commandant of cadets. For four years, 1857–60, he was completely out of military service. In fairness, it must be noted that this interval was not as damaging as it might have been. Although technology was changing warfare, even officers who remained on active duty through this period were only dimly aware of the impact of those changes. American tactical thinking was still wedded to the frontal assault. The army to which Walker returned in 1861 was virtually unchanged in its thinking from the one he had left in 1856.

What was different was the level of command at which Walker was functioning. In 1861 he was no longer the company commander leading bold charges against enemy strongholds. Instead, he was an organizer, a trainer, and an administrator of large units. His professional background still stood him in good stead and was the basis for his selection as a senior commander. He carried out his tasks ably, as both colonel and general of Georgia volunteers, but he chafed at the inaction. Not for the first time he resigned from an uncomfortable position.

War at Pensacola turned out to be far from what Walker desired. The tedium of the siege ground down his nerves and his health. There was no scope for display of gallantry or even of sound generalship. Again he was limited to the role of administrator and trainer. As he said, he "played second fiddle to Bragg," commanding "raw troops I never drilled behind sandbags I never built." Walker's effect on the sideshow at Pensacola was negligible. An objective observer would have to conclude that his two-month presence there contributed nothing to the operation.

By the time Walker arrived in northern Virginia, the war there had settled down into a "sitzkrieg." The opposing armies eyed each other warily while building their strength for future operations. The Georgia general was fortunate in receiving command of one of the finest brigades in the army. Here his professional background was put to good use. There can be no doubt that this veteran regular was deliberately selected to lead the Louisianians. Even their own officers admitted them to be "turbulent in camp and requiring a strong hand," but all observers agreed that Walker turned them into one of the best-drilled brigades in Virginia.

In the one opportunity Walker had for independent action, his reconnaissance to the Potomac, he fulfilled his mission to the letter, performing competently in the presence of large enemy forces. He might have gone on to a gallant and distinguished career with the Army of Northern Virginia, health permitting, if his pride had allowed him to accept the overslaughing by junior officers and the transfer to command of a Georgia brigade under Kirby Smith.

Back on the Georgia coast, Walker again faced the problems of organizing and training green troops. Once again the task was administrative rather than tactical: finding weapons, supervising organization, making appointments and promotions, administering discipline. For several months he assumed the burden of military governance over a populated area. On the administrative side, his work was very useful. It laid the basis for organization of several units that later entered Confederate service. As a civil administrator in Savannah, a city in which he was personally popular, Walker had the reputation of being firm but fair. He was admirably prescient in predicting the civilian response to a Yankee attack. His efforts to become involved in field operations in defense of Fort Pulaski were thwarted by his superiors, his health, and the Conscription Act.

At the end of the first year of the war, Walker's contribution had been almost entirely in organizing, training, and disciplining green troops. He had conducted no field operations save one, had had no opportunity to lead men in battle, had seriously impaired his health, and had managed to insult the president and the secretary of war of the Confederacy. Little wonder, then, that Jefferson Davis showed no eagerness to reappoint this volatile general to command during 1862.

As the year drew to its close, the Georgia Cincinnatus waited on his farm brooding over his and his country's future.

II

RETURN TO THE FRAY

February–August 1863

THE MILITARY SITUATION along the coast of Georgia and South Carolina did not change significantly during the rest of 1862. General Pemberton continued work on the defensive system designed by General Lee. The main areas of concern were still Charleston, Savannah, and the rail line between the two. Pemberton also continued Lee's program of giving up indefensible areas to concentrate his forces where they were more needed. Lee had won the reluctant consent of Governor Joseph E. Brown to evacuate Brunswick and the Georgia coastal islands. When Pemberton withdrew troops and heavy guns from positions protecting Georgetown harbor and access to the Stono River south of Charleston, he was less successful in winning the consent of South Carolina governor Francis W. Pickens.

Pickens, sensitive to the fears of the residents of the evacuated areas and concerned with laying open landward approaches to Charleston, insisted on holding the line everywhere. He appealed to Richmond to overrule Pemberton. President Davis and General Lee both supported the department commander. As a result, much heavy ordnance was removed from Cole's and James islands protecting the Stono and displaced to positions closer to Charleston. Pemberton set up a new line on James Island, closer to Charleston but more easily defended.[1]

On the Union side, Major General David Hunter had replaced General Thomas W. Sherman as commander of the Department of the South on March 31, 1862. Activity in his department following the capture of Fort Pulaski was marked by few offensive actions. In Georgia, the army confined itself to small combined operations along the coast, mostly raids to obtain materials or to deny them to the Southern forces and population. Brigadier General Alfred H. Terry commanded at Pulaski, but his garrison amounted to little more than a single regiment. In South Carolina, such operations as were undertaken were aimed at the prime targets, Charleston or the railroad. Late in May, an attempt was made to cut the railroad at Old Pocotaligo; it was driven back with some effort on the part of the defenders but without damage to the rail line. Toward the end of October, another, more serious expedition, involving over four thousand Federal troops, was transported by boat to try again at Pocotaligo. This one was a two-pronged attempt with separate forces going to Pocotaligo and Coosawhatchie. Both units were driven back with only minor damage to the railroad. The plan Lee had devised the year before seemed to be working.[2]

The major Union military offensive that year was initiated by a strange set of circumstances and ended in a serious defeat for the Northern forces.

The black crew of a small steamer being used to carry ordnance from the coastal estuaries to Charleston Harbor took control of their vessel one night in May 1862 and steamed out to join the Yankee fleet. Flag Officer DuPont tested their information on the abandonment of the defenses and found it to be true. General Hunter devised a plan for a land attack on Charleston from the south, landing on James Island, advancing against the Confederate works at Secessionville, and then moving on to Charleston.

A division of nine thousand men under Brigadier General Henry W. Benham, Walker's West Point classmate, was landed on the south end of James Island beginning June 2. By mid-June Benham was ready to assault the Rebel works at Secessionville, which were commanded by Brigadier General Nathan G. "Shank" Evans. Hunter had ordered Benham to take no offensive action without his approval. Nevertheless, and with only the reluctant agreement of his three brigade commanders, Benham launched his attack on June 16. By this time, Pemberton, by judicious shifting of forces, had given Evans a strength equal to Benham's.

In a battle that lasted two and a half hours and involved three assaults on the Confederate defenses, Benham lost over six hundred men out of some six thousand engaged. Confederate losses were about two hundred. For disobeying orders (and for losing the battle), Benham was relieved of command, placed under arrest, and briefly reduced to his permanent grade of major of engineers. The fight at Secessionville was the end of major land operations in the Department of the South for 1862.[3]

The sea blockade of Southern ports continued. More Northern ships were available, and new armored vessels were brought into use on both sides. The South made several attempts to produce ironclad steamers. In Charleston the *Chicora* and *Palmetto State* were built in 1862 and challenged the blockade briefly and with limited success in January 1863. At Savannah the former blockade runner *Fingal*, renamed *Atlanta*, was given an iron cladding and steamed to Fort Pulaski but proved to be too slow and unwieldy for useful operations. Some few fast steamers continued to run the blockade. One of these, the *Nashville*, managed to get into Savannah in 1861 but could not get out again. She took refuge in the Ogeechee River behind the guns of Fort McAllister until the spring of 1863.[4]

Victory at Secessionville had not improved General Pemberton's relations with the civil authorities in South Carolina. Governor Pickens, prominent citizens, and even some of Pemberton's subordinates, notably the prickly Roswell S. Ripley, called for his replacement. Finally, the War Department bowed to the inevitable and Pemberton was summoned to Richmond to be dispatched to Vicksburg, Mississippi. Command of the Department of South Carolina and Georgia passed in September 1862 to General Pierre G. T. Beauregard, the "hero of Sumter." The District of Georgia was now under Brigadier General Hugh W. Mercer. South Carolina was divided into four districts headed by Generals James H. Trapier at Georgetown, S. R. Gist at Charleston, and Johnson Hagood and William S. "Live Oak" Walker in the area between Charleston and Savannah. Florida was a separate command when Beauregard arrived, but it came under his orders in October. About a month after his arrival, Beauregard asked that the locally popular Roswell Ripley, who had been sent to Virginia, be placed in command of the Charleston defenses again. When Ripley was brought back, Gist served under him as commander on James Island. Early in 1863 Trapier's district was brought under Ripley's command also.[5]

Before Pemberton left the command, he gave Beauregard a written estimate of the defense needs of the department. In it he detailed the requirement for 50,000 men to hold the two states of South Carolina and Georgia. In addition to his written evaluation, Pemberton accompanied Beauregard on an inspection of the South Carolina coast September 16–18. Beauregard found extensive works in progress or completed, but he concluded that until all the work was finished and properly garrisoned Charleston could not be adequately defended. He reported that on September 24 he had only 12,500 effective men in South Carolina and 7,200 in Georgia.[6]

In mid-October 1862 Beauregard was warned by the War Department that DuPont's South Atlantic Blockading Squadron had sailed from its base at Port Royal. An attack on Charleston was expected, but what occurred was the attempt on the Pocotaligo bridge. On October 17, DuPont had been called to Washington to confer with Secretary of the Navy Welles about plans for an attack on Charleston, but one did not materialize in 1862. The consensus was that the Union fleet should wait for the arrival of the monitors that were being built. At the end of November, the squadron moved to North Carolina to support Major General John G. Foster's expedition from New Bern to Goldsboro. When Confederate troops were moved from Wilmington to Goldsboro, Beauregard was ordered to supply their replacements. A division of two brigades, one from South Carolina and one from Georgia, under S. R. Gist was sent to Wilmington and stayed until midwinter 1863.[7]

While Beauregard and DuPont were preparing their opposing measures for the inevitable attack on Charleston, the Union admiral had another matter on his mind, this one in Georgia. Beginning on July 29, 1862, and continuing until March 1863, six separate attacks were made on Fort McAllister. These attacks served several purposes: testing the fort's defenses, testing the capabilities of the new ironclads, and looking for the *Nashville*. On the fifth try, on February 28, 1863, the steamer was discovered aground in the Ogeechee. Commander John L. Worden, who had carried the message to the Union squadron at Pensacola in 1861 and had commanded the *Monitor* in its fight with the *Merrimac* in 1862, in his ironclad steamer *Montauk* with three supporting vessels braved the fire of the fort and approached within twelve hundred yards of the *Nashville*. The *Montauk* opened fire at 7:30 A.M. and set the *Nashville* afire within thirty minutes. After burning for an hour and a half, the Rebel steamer blew up at 9:30. The commander of Southern forces at Fort McAllister and along the Ogeechee was Robert H. Anderson, formerly Walker's aide, now restored to Confederate service as a colonel of cavalry.[8]

With his already feeble strength further reduced by detachments to North Carolina and the condition of his defenses less ready than he would have liked, Beauregard faced 1863 and the sure prospect of DuPont's attack on Charleston, the seat of secession. Beginning in February with the feeling out of Fort McAllister, Beauregard expected a major attack. At first, he was sure the blow would fall on Savannah, but he soon decided that either of the two major port cities might be the target.[9]

On February 4, 1863, Beauregard telegraphed to the secretary of war, James A. Seddon, that Union gunboats had sailed from Beaufort, South Carolina, on January 31 and he could not tell if their destination was

Charleston or Savannah. In addition to his other problems, he felt that there was an insufficient number of general officers to command the troops at the critical points. This was especially true in Georgia, where Hugh Mercer was the only general on duty. To bolster the command at the latter place Beauregard asked for the assignment of Henry Wayne "or other competent brigadier general." Seddon endorsed the report to the president, who responded, somewhat surprisingly, "Who is General Wayne? Where is ex-Brig. Gen. W. H. T. Walker? Is he a candidate for appointment?" Through the intermediation of Congressman Augustus H. Kenan of Georgia, Walker gave his affirmative response.[10]

Walker's return to active duty had been anticipated, despite his own reluctance. If William Walker had been content to lead the pastoral life at Seclusaval and Mobley, others had been less satisfied that he should. A writer signing himself "Justice" had complained to the editor of a newspaper of the unfairness of Walker being kept out of service. As early as June 1862, Beauregard, recently relieved from command of the army in Mississippi, had written to Octavia LeVert that he hoped to have Walker under his command, wherever he might be assigned when his health improved. In October 1862, after taking command at Charleston, Beauregard wrote again to Madame LeVert, "Gen. Walker is not here with me yet, for he is still a little unwell. But he is to come at the first gun." In December 1862, Beauregard corresponded directly with Walker on the topic of an appointment for Major Robert H. Anderson. Beauregard closed his letter, "Hoping you will be well enough to join us whenever (?) the abol[itionists] get here, I remain your friend, G. T. Beauregard."[11]

Walker was not sure he wanted to return to the army. In a letter from Mobley to his wife in Augusta, he wrote, "I am now so mixed up with business that requires my personal supervision that I am perfectly indifferent and doubt whether I would, under any circumstances, go back. I feel a perfect disgust and shall never feel in the army as I once did. Besides, my health is too bad." In the same letter he wrote that he wished "Mr. K[enan?]" had not pushed the issue of his reinstatement. At least one of his military acquaintances remarked on the sacrifice Walker made in returning to the army. William R. Boggs wrote, "With ample means he might have lived comfortably in his forced retirement, but every inch a soldier, he once more entered the Confederate service."[12]

It is not generally known that Walker had taken a drastic step in September 1862 to reinstate himself into the good graces of the Richmond administration. Perhaps he was influenced by John David's critical wound, perhaps by the persistent lobbying of Augustus Kenan. At any rate, that September Walker ingested a huge dose of humble pie. The outgoing correspondence of the Confederate War Department contains the following extraordinary communication from Secretary George Randolph to Kenan: "I have the honor to acknowledge the receipt of your letter of this date stating that you are authorized by General W. H. T. Walker to withdraw the insubordinate and disrespectful language used by him in his correspondence with the Honorable Judah P. Benjamin when Secretary of War." Walker must have struggled mightily with his pride to issue that authorization, even at second hand. Either his desire to return to the field was overwhelming or he was a patriot of a higher order than he has been given credit for.[13]

William Boggs's supportive attitude was representative of feeling toward Walker in Georgia. When a group of citizens presented him with a horse, their accompanying letter made reference to his previous separation from the service as a "misunderstanding with the cabinet" and noted, "[your] generous patriotism [in returning] commends [our] respect and esteem." In reply to these sentiments, Walker wrote, "My return to the army, in a position lower than the one I had resigned, was caused by the same self-respect that induced me to leave it; and I have reentered the list of champions of Southern rights and Southern honor with no higher motive than to use my utmost efforts to assist in an humble way in achieving Southern independence." Perhaps he really meant it.[14]

There is no doubt that he returned to service with a pang of regret. Echoing his comment of January 1862 about "sighing for quiet life," in his first letter from Savannah in March 1863 he wrote: "I am as calm and cool as if I was at Mobley Pond where I would infinitely prefer to be. Nothing but a high sense of duty causes me to be where I am. The pride of rank and command which of yore I was so full of I have entirely lost and like a well broken cart horse I pull in the traces with an even, steady pace." Indicating that he viewed his active service as only temporary, he added, "Having accepted, it is my duty to serve, *at least during the emergency*."[15]

This last sentence is critical to interpreting Walker's motive for returning to service in 1863. There is no reason to believe that Walker would dissemble before his fifteen-year-old daughter. The crisis was genuine; the situation on the Georgia coast desperately cried out for a professional military hand. Hugh Mercer, a West Point graduate of 1828, had been out of the army since 1835 and had been a bank cashier for twenty of those twenty-five years. He owed his Confederate commission to his lengthy militia and volunteer service. He manifestly needed help at Savannah. Whatever Walker's personal ambitions and truculence of character, he could be moved by appeals of patriotism to "his mother, Georgia," if not to the Confederacy or the Davis administration. Hence his "self-respect" would not allow him to sit at home while the defense of Georgia rested in the hands of amateurs. Very likely, he intended to stay only until the coastal crisis was resolved. Possibly, he expected to supplant Mercer in command at Savannah. As he noted with some chagrin in his letter to little Molly, "As I was ordered to report to Mercer, it fixes my state at the foot of the list of brigadiers."[16]

Beauregard, after making his request to Seddon, was eager to have some general join his command. On February 16, he wired Seddon, "General Walker has not yet reported." His impatience was understandable because on February 17 the *Augusta Constitutionalist* had reported Walker's appointment in the Confederate army. The reason for the delay cannot be determined, but on March 2, 1863, Walker was confirmed brigadier general in the Provisional Army of the Confederate States to rank from February 9 and ordered on March 3 to report to Beauregard at Charleston.[17]

Walker had already gone to Savannah on March 2 with members of his new staff. When news of his reinstatement was publicized, two junior officers from the Augusta area volunteered to accompany him to his new command. The first of these was Captain Joseph B. Cumming, who had recently been left without assignment. Cumming was the younger brother of General Alfred Cumming and the son of Henry Harford Cumming, who had been a candidate for election to the Georgia secession convention in 1860. Joseph Cumming had been adjutant of General John K. Jackson's brigade and in a foolish controversy with Jackson over an endorsement had resigned his commission. He was subject to conscription and happy for the opportunity to attach himself to Walker's staff. The other officer was Lieutenant G. DeRosset Lamar, son and half-brother of Walker's bankers, Gazaway and Charles A. L. Lamar. Walker made Cumming his volunteer adjutant and "Derry" Lamar his volunteer aide pending official Confederate appointments. Cumming remained Walker's alter ego for the rest of the latter's life. Lamar served with the general until unfortunate family squabbles broke up their relationship a year later. The three traveled by engine especially arranged for the purpose from Augusta to Savannah.[18]

At Savannah, Walker found that he was to command a brigade of three Georgia regiments, the 25th, 29th, and 30th. His brigade would be deployed at Greenwich in the area below the city where the Wilmington

River intersects with St. Augustine Creek. The former brigade commander, who had led the men to Charleston and Wilmington and back, was Colonel Claudius C. Wilson, of the 25th Georgia, a thirty-one-year-old lawyer. The colonels of the 29th and 30th regiments were William J. Young and Thomas W. Mangham, respectively.[19]

One of the first duties Walker undertook was as a member of a board formed to assess the strengths and weaknesses of the state's defenses. Beauregard had directed the review, and Generals Mercer, Walker, and William B. Taliaferro, another new brigade commander, were the board members. The panel met seven times from March 17 to March 30 and issued a voluminous report, which is printed in the *Official Records*. Walker must have found this task onerous; he had returned to active duty to defend his country, not to count cannon.[20]

Walker took advantage of this period to formalize some of his staff appointments. As a matter of protocol, he offered the position of aide to Henry R. Jackson, who was still without commission. Jackson, recognizing the gesture for what it was, gracefully declined. Walker asked for official appointments for Cumming and Lamar, which were duly received. Lieutenant Thomas H. Kenan, nephew of A. H. Kenan, became an additional aide; Captain Nathaniel O. Tilton was borrowed from the 25th Georgia to be acting brigade quartermaster. Captain Samuel H. Crump, formerly clerk of Augusta City Council and a company commander in the 12th Georgia Artillery Battalion, became acting brigade inspector, and Cadet Henry R. Jackson, son of the general, was made brigade ordnance officer. This last appointment was allowed to stand despite the policy of the Ordnance Department that generals were not allowed to select their own ordnance officers. Walker's request for Surgeon Charles C. Schley to be brigade surgeon was denied on the grounds that brigades were not authorized surgeons. In April 1863, Tilton's and Crump's positions were regularized. Another who joined the staff about this time or soon after arrival in Mississippi was Major Alfred C. Dearing, brigade commissary.[21]

Meanwhile, the large Union fleet was hovering off the coast and Beauregard was attempting to divine its intentions. On February 28, Federal ironclads attacked and destroyed the *Nashville* in the Ogeechee River estuary under the guns of Fort McAllister. On March 3, the day after Walker's arrival in Savannah, Union gunboats shelled Fort McAllister itself. It appeared that Savannah might be the target. In a letter to his wife Walker mentioned that he had boats out along the coast watching for the "cannibals" to make another descent.[22]

In early April the Union ironclads, accompanied by a fleet of transports, at last appeared off Charleston. Landings began on Folly Island,
presumably in preparation for an assault on Morris Island and a land bombardment of Sumter from that location. Beauregard had only thirty-two
thousand men available to protect three states, twenty thousand in South
Carolina, ten thousand in Georgia, and two thousand in Florida. The defense of Charleston was provided by some eleven thousand effectives in
Ripley's First District. Beauregard summoned whatever reserves he could
for the defense of the city. Volunteers were called for from South Carolina and Georgia. Among those responding was the Augusta Volunteers
under Captain George T. Jackson. Coming first to Savannah, they traveled to Charleston and were made a part of a South Carolina volunteer
battalion under Major John P. Thomas. One of the Augusta volunteers
was Walker's fifty-seven-year-old brother, Beverly. Walker's brigade, reinforced by the two regiments of the Georgia State Line, Governor Joe
Brown's latest "army," and several light batteries, was brought on short
notice from Savannah, arriving on April 6. Walker was made commander
of that part of St. Andrew's Parish subdistrict on the Cooper River west of
Wappoo Creek. S. R. Gist commanded the subdistrict proper from James
Island. Walker's position was important because he would protect the vital
rail line, the Savannah Turnpike, and three bridges across the Ashley River
into Charleston in the event of a land attack. His headquarters was within
sight of Charleston's church steeples and the Confederate bastion at Fort
Sumter. Thomas's battalion was assigned to Walker's subdistrict guarding
the Wappoo Bridge. On April 7, 1863, from his vantage point, Walker was
able to observe the unsuccessful attempt of the fleet to subdue Fort Sumter
and lay Charleston open to the Union army, which had been collected on
Folly Island for its invasion.[23]

Since the historic struggle between the *Monitor* and the *Merrimac* (*Virginia*) in March 1862, the U.S. Navy Department had bent every effort
toward building more ironclad steamers. By February 1863 nine were ready
and were assigned to DuPont's squadron for the attack on Charleston.
The largest, the *New Ironsides*, was a thirty-five-hundred-ton behemoth
mounting fourteen broadside guns, that is, guns along both sides of the
ship. Seven others were the more familiar "cheesebox on a raft" turreted
steamers of about eight hundred tons, mounting two guns each. These
were *Passaic, Weehawken, Montauk, Patapsco, Catskill, Nantucket,* and *Nahant*.
The ninth vessel, the *Keokuk*, was of unusual design, a double turret, but
she had only one gun mounted. The nine ships carried seven 15-inch guns,

twenty-two 11-inch guns, and three 8-inch rifled cannon. It has been estimated that it was the most powerful fleet ever to sail or steam up to that date. DuPont had had reservations about the capabilities of the ironclads and for that reason had tested some of them against Fort McAllister earlier in the year. Although the conclusion at McAllister was that the steamers were more vulnerable than expected, the sense of the department was to go ahead at Charleston.[24]

The battle of April 7, 1863, between the ironclads and the Confederate forts lasted only two and a half hours, 3:00 P.M. to 5:30 P.M. The fleet crossed Charleston bar on the sixth but was prevented by fog from entering the harbor. Adverse tides delayed the advance until noon on the seventh. At that time, in line ahead, the nine ironclads steamed majestically up the channel with Fort Sumter and Batteries Wagner and Gregg on their left and the Morris Island positions, Fort Moultrie and Batteries Beauregard and Bee, on their right. The battle was opened with a shot from the Morris Island side. All the Confederate batteries joined in when the ships reached marker buoys in the channel. The Union fleet concentrated its fire on Sumter, advancing to fire and then reversing to reload. DuPont allowed the ships to maneuver independently, presenting a somewhat haphazard appearance to observers.

DuPont's worst fears about using ironclads against fortifications were borne out. His squadron was easily bested by the heavy and concentrated fire brought to bear from the Confederate batteries. The monitors got off only 139 rounds in two and a half hours. The forts fired 2,200 rounds of which over 500 found their targets. One ironclad, the *Keokuk*, was sunk and three others had to return to base at Port Royal for repair.[25]

DuPont withdrew at the end of the day to spare further damage to his vessels. In his report to the Navy Department, he admitted that "Charleston can not be taken by a purely naval attack." Writing to General Hunter, the army commander, the day after the battle, DuPont bluntly explained what had happened: "I attempted to take the bull by the horns but he was too much for us. These monitors are miserable failures where forts are concerned." His decision not to renew the battle on April 8 ultimately cost him his command. It was only the imperative urgings of President Lincoln that persuaded DuPont to remain off Charleston bar after his defeat.[26]

When the Union fleet did not leave immediately, Beauregard expected it to land a force on the islands north or south of Charleston and take up siege operations. Every point seemed threatened. On April 9, Walker was alerted to hold his brigade with three days' rations in readiness for instant movement to Mount Pleasant, north of Charleston. This order was super-seded on April 17 by another to return to Georgia without delay, leaving one regiment on Morris Island. Even then, the 29th and 30th Georgia were brought back to South Carolina to protect the Pocotaligo bridge. It was not until May 3 that Walker's brigade was reunited in Georgia. The volunteers under Major Thomas were released by Beauregard on April 15.[27]

The period was not one of uninterrupted anxiety. Walker took the op-portunity during his sojourn in South Carolina to make the acquaintance of Colonel Isaac Bull, descendant of early royal governors of the colony. He managed to find time also for a social engagement with Belle Schley, by birth a McAlpin of Savannah, with whom he apparently carried on a long-standing flirtation over the years. Belle was the daughter of Henry McAlpin, an immigrant Scot who founded the Hermitage plantation near Savannah. Her husband, William Schley, was a lawyer in Augusta. Belle's sister married William's brother; her brother married his sister. Belle is mentioned several times in Walker's letters to his wife between 1852 and 1863, frequently in provocative references. If there was a liaison between her and Walker, it was not a very discreet one.[28]

If Mary Walker found one fault in her husband it was his open and obvious attention to other women. As a young captain in Mexico he had written more frankly than he needed to of his admiration for Mexican women. On the eve of his departure for Pensacola he had been accused of being seen in the street with a certain Madame C. He denied this last accusation vigorously, but as his own sister was the eyewitness, there is no doubt he was there. Although Walker pledged his love to his wife, and no doubt meant it, it seems he was not above peccadilloes, or at least flirta-tions. As he explained to Mary in one letter: "The only thing that ever gets you excited is my attention to someone else. You are not generous on this subject for I was nearly 29 [sic] when married and had some ways which I have found it difficult to break myself of all at once." The inference was that he expected Mary to accept him the way he was.[29]

Once returned to Georgia, the brigade took up post at Isle of Hope, a balmy location on the coast. Various social pleasantries were held, Captain Cumming brought his wife and son down from Augusta, and Walker made plans for Mary and the children to join him. Also during this time, Walker was presented a gift of a handsome horse, which with furniture was valued at $2,000, paid for by donations by prominent citizens of Georgia and South Carolina. This idyllic interlude was rudely shattered early in May.[30]

While Beauregard was contending with assaults on the Atlantic coast, another serious threat to the existence of the Confederacy had been developing in Mississippi. Federal forces had captured New Orleans in April 1862, closing the mouth of the Mississippi River to Rebel commerce. Memphis had been taken by the U.S. Navy. The Confederacy's lifeline to its western states was now maintained only by the two posts at Port Hudson, Louisiana, and Vicksburg, Mississippi, and the length of river between them. Since November 1862, Federal troops under U. S. Grant had been looking for ways to approach and capture the latter city. First Grant had tried to move overland along the Mississippi Central Railroad. Earl Van Dorn's and Nathan Bedford Forrest's raids on Grant's line of communications had caused the Federal army to retreat precipitously to Tennessee. The next effort was to have Sherman's corps float down the Yazoo River, land at Chickasaw Bayou, and advance on Vicksburg from the north. This expedition ended with Sherman's botched attack at Chickasaw Bluff on December 29, 1862.[31]

Now Grant turned his attention to the Mississippi. Between January and March 1863 four efforts were made at using circuitous waterways to get at Vicksburg from its landward side. First, work was resumed on a canal across a neck of land where the river made a hairpin turn in front of the city. The project had been started and abandoned in the summer of 1862. This effort failed because the original project was poorly planned. Another, more roundabout route to bypass Vicksburg on its western side was attempted but eventually given up. Grant's third try was to open up the old Yazoo Pass system east of the Mississippi, get above Vicksburg, and come down on the inland side. Slow but steady progress was made, but the effort was halted in March by the guns of Confederate Fort Pemberton at the head of the Yazoo River. The fourth and final fruitless attempt was made when the gunboat fleet under Commodore David Porter tried to use Steele's Bayou to steam to the upper reaches of the Yazoo and thereby reach central Mississippi. Although none of these schemes worked, Grant was not completely dissatisfied because he kept the troops busy and the enemy guessing at his intentions.[32]

After three months of maneuvering and exhausting all classic military approaches, in mid-April 1863 Grant worked out an overland route down the west bank of the Mississippi to a place where he could safely cross to the east side. On April 16 Commodore Porter's gunboats ran the batteries at Vicksburg, followed shortly by transports and barges. The navy's losses were minimal. Reunited downstream, the combined force landed at Bruinsburg, Mississippi, on April 30, 1863. Grant had taken a big gamble by leaving his base. Further, he had committed himself to action south of Vicksburg because Porter's gunboats were too weakly powered to run the batteries safely upstream against the current. But Grant had achieved his goal: he was on dry land in open country in the interior of Mississippi.[33]

On May 1 Grant advanced to Port Gibson, where he met and defeated three Confederate brigades thrown forward from Grand Gulf, the nearest Southern position. On May 2 Grand Gulf was evacuated. Grant was now free to move as he pleased in pursuit of the Rebel army or to an investment of Vicksburg. He had under his command at that time about forty-three thousand men in three army corps. Major General John McClernand, an Illinois Democratic politician, led the XIII Corps. The XVII Corps was commanded by Major General James B. McPherson, a young regular army engineer officer who had risen meteorically under Grant's command in Tennessee and Mississippi. Still west of the Mississippi at Grant's base but hastening forward was the XV Corps under Major General William Tecumseh Sherman, Grant's principal lieutenant and confidant.[34]

General John Pemberton, the Confederate commander in Mississippi and Walker's West Point classmate, at this point was able to match in manpower the number of men Grant had east of the Mississippi, about twenty-five thousand, but he could not contend with the numbers he knew the Union general had coming up. Pemberton was in a quandary. First, he was not sure where Grant's main effort would fall. Second, he was receiving conflicting instructions from his superiors. President Davis, from Richmond, was ordering Pemberton to hold on to Vicksburg, Grand Gulf, and every inch of Mississippi, the president's home state. Pemberton's nominal commander, General Joseph E. Johnston, who from Chattanooga supervised the Department of Tennessee (Bragg's command), as well as Pemberton's Department of Mississippi and East Louisiana, wanted him to give up the static positions, take to the field, and defeat Grant with his united forces. The cities and towns would be safe if Grant was thus occupied and Pemberton would be carrying out the true task of any military commander: seek out and destroy the enemy's army.[35]

By early May Pemberton was asking Richmond for additional troops so that he could meet Grant's army in the field as well as maintain the vital bastion. Additional troops were hard to come by. Lee's army in Virginia was preparing for its spring campaign. Bragg in Tennessee faced uncertainty in front of the Union army of William Rosecrans. Johnston could have ordered troops from Bragg to Pemberton but was reticent to do so without War Department sanction. Secretary of War Seddon, with

President Davis's approval, ordered three thousand men sent from Bragg's army, and two brigades were brought from Port Hudson. After the attack on Sumter had been repelled, the War Department asked Beauregard for troops for other theaters. Two brigades went to North Carolina to release two others for Lee's army; the department asked for ten thousand men for Mississippi. Beauregard protested that he could spare only half that number. Initially this was accepted; two brigades were designated for Pemberton. Later, a third brigade, that of Nathan G. Evans, an additional regiment for Walker's brigade, the 47th Georgia, and two more batteries were sent to Mississippi. On May 27, Beauregard was able to report to Adjutant General Cooper that he had dispatched more than ninety-seven hundred effectives to Mississippi.[36]

As early as April 17, it had been rumored in camp that Walker's brigade would be sent to another theater as soon as the situation on the coast settled. On May 5, Walker was informed that his brigade was to move to Jackson, Mississippi. A brigade from South Carolina to be commanded by General S. R. Gist would be sent also. The two brigades, five thousand men with two batteries of artillery, under the command of Gist, the senior brigadier, were to move by train to Mississippi as quickly as possible.[37]

Walker's brigade was composed of his three regiments, the 25th, 29th, and 30th Georgia. To these were added the 4th Louisiana Battalion from Taliaferro's brigade, the 1st Georgia Sharpshooter Battalion from the Savannah River defenses, and Captain Robert Martin's Georgia Battery. The commander of the Louisiana battalion was Lieutenant Colonel John McEnery, a future governor of Louisiana. The Georgia Sharpshooter Battalion was led by Major Arthur Shaaf, a former U.S. Army lieutenant. Captain Martin, the commander of the four-gun battery, had been in charge of the mortar battery at Fort McAllister during the gunboat attacks in the winter.

Gist's brigade was formed from several elements of the coastal Carolina defenses. From his own James Island subdistrict he had the 24th South Carolina under Colonel Clement H. Stevens. The lieutenant colonel of the 24th was the redoubtable Ellison Capers, younger brother of General Frank Capers of the Georgia State Troops, graduate of the South Carolina Military College (the Citadel), future historian, and future bishop of the Episcopal church in South Carolina. Also from the Charleston area came the 46th Georgia, Colonel Peyton H. Colquitt, the 8th Georgia Battalion, Lieutenant Colonel Leroy Napier, and Captain Thomas Ferguson's South Carolina Battery. Serving as lieutenant in Ferguson's battery was

René T. Beauregard, the general's son. To round out Gist's brigade the 16th South Carolina, Colonel James McCullough, was brought from the Second Military District.[38]

Walker's departure was scheduled for May 6, although his brigade did not actually leave until the eighth. General Mercer, the district commander, gave Walker the option, for personal reasons, of going with the brigade or staying behind. Walker chose to go with his men. The personal grounds for which Mercer showed such solicitous concern was the death of nine-month-old Adam Johnston Walker on April 22. It is not known whether Walker returned home for the funeral of his child. This was the fourth and final Walker son to be interred in the family burial ground at the arsenal.

Although Walker sympathized with his officers' wishes, he allowed almost no one to go home on leave before the departure of the brigade. He denied himself the privilege and felt that the officers should not go either. An exception was Cumming, who was permitted to escort his wife and infant son back to Augusta. As a result, Cumming and Lamar, also left behind, traveled with Gist's brigade and missed the first two actions in Mississippi.[39]

Walker's willingness to go to Mississippi was an apparent contradiction of his own terms for returning to service. He had informed his daughter that he was on active duty "at least during the emergency." He had been appointed since March 2 but did not return his acceptance to the adjutant and inspector general until April 21. During the intervening seven weeks he must have been doing some serious soul-searching about his future. But having made up his mind to accept the commission, when the call came for field duty in another department, he responded positively. He may have been "a well broken cart horse," pulling in the traces "with an even, steady pace," or perhaps "the pride and rank of command" had not been "entirely lost." Active field duty, the chance for real campaigning after so much training and administration, were irresistible magnets. Rather than a cart horse, the old war horse was responding to the sound of the bugle and the guns.[40]

Walker's brigade presumably traveled by rail from Savannah via Macon, Columbus, and Montgomery. Gist's brigade, coming a somewhat greater distance, left Charleston and rode by train to Augusta, where Cumming and Lamar must have joined them, then to Atlanta and on to Alabama and Mississippi. The two brigades had grown soft and lazy in the relatively easy duty of coastal garrisons. The alarms of the winter and early spring had been scant preparation for the extended field duty that faced them. This complacency, coupled with the natural desire of the men to visit their families before leaving, with or without official permission, led to very bad straggling. General Thomas Jordan, Beauregard's chief of staff, reported to the War Department on May 27, almost three weeks after the brigades had left, that straggling was "disgraceful" and one regiment had left fully five hundred men behind. George A. Mercer commented on the straggling in his diary. He attributed it to the "subordinate officers [who] set a bad example and exercise little authority over [the men]." In North Carolina another officer set the blame somewhat higher, at least for one regiment. Lieutenant Colonel John G. Pressley of the 25th South Carolina had found his regiment brigaded with the 46th Georgia in early 1863. Pressley recorded in his diary that Colonel Colquitt "was a brave man but lax disciplinarian. His regiment was a very fine body of men but in point of discipline was hardly up to the standard. Their way of doing things became somewhat contagious and the effect of the example was felt in the 25th." Presumably, the effects of Colquitt's discipline were also felt in the other units of Gist's brigade.[41]

Their arrival in the hot, humid Mississippi area was also a shock to the troops. Colonel Arthur Fremantle, a British observer, commented in his diary on May 19 on the condition of the troops and the laxity of their officers: "The troops were roughly but efficiently clothed; their boots were in good order, and all were armed with Enfield rifles. The straggling of the Georgians was on the grandest scale imaginable. The men fell out by dozens, and seemed to suit their own convenience in that respect, without interference on the part of the officers. But I was told that these regiments had never done any marching before, having hitherto been quartered in forts and transported by railroad." Fremantle added, "The horses were fine animals, and were in wonderful good condition, considering that they had been ten days on the railroad coming from South Carolina."[42]

Besides sending troops to Mississippi, President Davis ordered Johnston to go there from Chattanooga and take direct command. Johnston had been ill, but he obeyed forthwith, leaving Tennessee on May 10 and arriving in Jackson on the thirteenth, on the same train with the lead elements of Gist's brigade. Walker's first two regiments had arrived a day or two earlier, in time to support the Confederate troops falling back from Grant's advance toward Jackson.[43]

By May 7 Grant had his whole army together and had decided on a course of action. He would advance toward Jackson, seeking Pemberton's army in the field. McClernand's XIII Corps and McPherson's XVII Corps accordingly advanced in parallel to the northeast, maneuvering toward the important Mississippi Southern Railroad which connected Jackson and Vicksburg, the two cities being about forty-five miles apart. Sherman's corps was in reserve. Pemberton was east of Vicksburg near Edwards Station. Jackson had been selected as the assembly point for the forces being collected to support Pemberton.[44]

The brigade of General John Gregg, brought from Port Hudson, was about two miles east of Jackson on May 11 when word was received of the Federal advance. Gregg's brigade, about 2,500 strong, was marched out along the Port Gibson road. At 10:00 A.M. on May 12 Gregg encountered the advance of McPherson's corps, Major General John Logan's division, at Raymond. The Union army took several hours to prepare, then launched an attack with one full division, Logan's, and another in reserve. Gregg was easily dislodged. He suffered casualties of a little over 500 while the Union loss was about 450. As Gregg withdrew toward Jackson, he was met on the road by the 3d Kentucky Mounted Infantry and W. H. T. Walker at the head of 1,000 men of his brigade, newly arrived in Jackson, apparently only that day. The combined force fell back five miles to Mississippi Springs.

McPherson greatly exaggerated the size of Gregg's force and the importance of the engagement, a theme that was picked up and repeated by Grant. Grant went so far as to say that Gregg was sent "flying from the field not to appear against our front again until we met at Jackson." This happened only two days later so the effect could not have been too great. Johnston felt that the affair had a "trifling" effect on Gregg's brigade.[45]

After Gregg reported to Johnston in Jackson on the estimated size of the Union force, the latter officer decided to evacuate the city. To buy time to save the precious stores that had been accumulated, he ordered Gregg to take command of whatever forces were available and hold the roads leading into Jackson as long as he could. Besides his own brigade, Gregg now had part of Walker's and the advance party of Gist's under Colonel Colquitt. Johnston ordered the brigade of General Samuel B. Maxey, coming from Port Hudson, and the balance of Gist's brigade to fall back from Jackson forty or fifty miles to the east so as not to be caught unawares when they arrived.[46]

Early in the morning of May 14, Gregg deployed his small force, about six thousand men with three batteries, to check the advance of two army corps, Sherman's and McPherson's. On the Clinton road he posted Colquitt with the nine hundred men of Gist's brigade near Wright's farm. Walker was to support Colquitt. Gregg's own brigade was put on the Livingston road about two and a half miles to Colquitt's right. On the Mississippi Springs or Raymond road, on Colquitt's left, he placed the 3d Kentucky Mounted Infantry, 1st Georgia Sharpshooter Battalion, and Martin's Georgia Battery, the last two from Walker's brigade. At 9:00 A.M. McPherson's column came up the Clinton road and Sherman's force showed itself on the Mississippi Springs road soon thereafter. For about five hours the battle, conducted in a heavy rainstorm, was carried on, mostly an affair of skirmishes and dueling batteries. At two o'clock, the Union advance finally drove in the Rebel lines. Hearing that Johnston had gotten his trains safely away, Gregg withdrew into Jackson and then followed Johnston north along the Canton road. Gregg reported his loss as two hundred, almost all in Colquitt's small brigade. He estimated that Walker had suffered a few casualties but was not sure because the latter "has declined to make a report." Union estimates of Confederate losses were closer to four hundred. Grant later wrote that seventeen guns were captured from the defenders of both roads, but Gregg made no mention of artillery losses. Seventeen is obviously too high because there were only three batteries present with four guns each. Grant may have been counting pieces captured in the prepared defenses of Jackson. Union losses were three hundred.[47]

Walker's refusal to render a report after the battle at Jackson makes it difficult to know how he conducted himself in his first encounter with direct enemy fire since 1847. Gregg's comment on the small number of casualties in Walker's brigade suggests that it was not heavily engaged, except for the sharpshooters and Martin's battery, which would be natural for a support unit. Knowing Walker's personality, it may be supposed that he was unhappy with being in a subordinate role, unhappy with being in support, and unhappy with fighting a delaying action. Whatever the odds, he would probably have been happier taking the offensive against the advancing bluecoats. A week later, on May 20, Colonel Fremantle met Walker at Johnston's headquarters: "I also made the acquaintance of the Georgian General Walker, a fierce and very warlike fire-eater, who was furious at having been obliged to evacuate Jackson after having only destroyed four hundred Yankees. He told me, 'I know I couldn't hold the place, but I did want to kill a few more of the rascals.'"[48]

Following the withdrawal of Johnston's forces, Grant moved into Jackson and began the destruction of that important rail and manufacturing center. While at Jackson on the fourteenth, Grant received an intercepted copy of a message from Johnston to Pemberton ordering the union of the two wings of the Confederate army so that they might attack Grant in the rear while he was engaged at Jackson. Pemberton was fearful of leaving his riverside bastion undefended and, rather than join Johnston, he decided to turn south and place himself on Grant's line of communication to induce the Union general to attack him. Then, in the face of Grant's full force, which was moving to meet him, Pemberton, in response to a second order from Johnston, turned back to the north.[49]

On May 16, on a low rise along the Mississippi Railroad known as Champion's Hill, eight divisions of Grant's army, some forty thousand men, hurrying westward, collided with Pemberton moving north. The Confederate army had about seventeen thousand men in three divisions, although the Union estimate was twenty-five thousand. In a fight that began late in the morning and lasted five or six hours, Pemberton was routed. He lost about four thousand men and twenty-seven guns against a Union loss of just under twenty-five hundred. His army was badly demoralized and forced to retreat back toward Vicksburg, completely cut off from Johnston at Canton. Worse yet, one of his three divisions, that of Major General William W. Loring, a one-armed former U.S. Army colonel of mounted riflemen, was separated from Pemberton's main force and went off on its own, eventually winding up with Johnston's army. Despite Johnston's pleas for a union of their forces, Pemberton retreated all the way back to Vicksburg, where he was soon to be shut in by Grant. En route his army suffered one more indignity when at the crossing of the Big Black River its rear guard was beset by McClernand's corps and sent flying with a loss of seventeen hundred prisoners and eighteen more guns.[50]

Grant completed his encirclement of the city on May 19. After two unsuccessful assaults on May 19 and 22, he elected to begin regular siege operations. With more troops coming to him from the East and from within his own department, including the IX Corps under Major General John G. Parke, Grant's effective strength now approached seventy-one thousand men. In Vicksburg Pemberton had some thirty thousand men in four divisions. One major command change was made in Grant's army during the siege. On June 18 he replaced the politician-general John McClernand at the head of the XIII Corps with the career soldier General E. O. C. Ord. Trouble between Grant and McClernand had been long brewing, but the publication in the press without Grant's approval of a congratulatory order from McClernand to his men was the culminating incident. McClernand protested all the way to President Lincoln, but Grant had his way.[51]

Johnston had moved his headquarters to Canton after abandoning Jackson. Loring's division had escaped the debacle at Champion's Hill and joined Johnston at this time. In addition, Gist arrived with the rest of his own brigade, Matthew D. Ector's Texas brigade, and Evander McNair's Arkansas brigade, the two latter from Bragg's Army of Tennessee. Also at this time, Evans's brigade, the third dispatched from Beauregard's department, came up. And from the defenses at Port Hudson, the brigades of Maxey and Albert Rust finally arrived. With the addition of John C. Breckinridge's division of infantry and William H. Jackson's of cavalry from Bragg's army, Johnston now had about twenty-four thousand effective infantry and two thousand cavalry. Even if Pemberton's thirty thousand had abandoned Vicksburg and taken to the field, they were still overmatched by Grant. Johnston says, incorrectly, that the troops coming from the East had brought with them neither wagons nor artillery. Actually Beauregard sent four full batteries to Mississippi, one of which had already fought at Jackson on May 14.[52]

In his motley collection of units Johnston had only two cohesive infantry divisions, Loring's and Breckinridge's, and a mass of unmatched brigades. To make the most efficient use of his force he needed competent professional officers to form and lead the divisions and make them into proficient organizations. One division was given to Major General Samuel G. French, like Pemberton a Northerner who had sided with the South and a West Point classmate of Grant's. For the other Johnston was looking for an aggressive leader who could inspire the men to special accomplishments. Colonel Fremantle had described William Walker as fierce and warlike. No doubt these were the very qualities Johnston was looking for. On May 21, he telegraphed to President Davis: "There is a division without a major general; the only officer competent to command it is W. H. T. Walker. Please appoint immediately. This officer is indispensable." On May 23, Davis telegraphed back giving authorization for the promotion. On May 30, Davis notified Johnston that Walker's promotion had been confirmed. In the eyes of Johnston and apparently even Davis, if any man could breathe life into the collection of troops in Mississippi, it was W. H. T. Walker. Walker's promotion must also have given Johnston particular relish following the incidents of September and October 1861. It would certainly have been in keeping with the Davis-Johnston relationship for that general to take advantage of the crisis situation to win a point previously lost.[53]

Walker's fire-eating propensities spilled over from his professional to his personal life. At Pensacola, Manassas, and on the coast, he had been

relatively sheltered from the ravages of war. Now, in Mississippi, he witnessed at first hand the destruction wrought by Grant's and Sherman's
men in their efforts to destroy the South's economic infrastructure. At the
same time, he received reports of the rumors of Federal raids on Augusta.
Any feelings of kinship he might have harbored for Mary's family were
wiped out by this devastation. Mary's brother Franklin was adjutant general of New York, raising and equipping the troops to be sent to subdue
the South. Frederick was a major in the regular U.S. Army. He had led a
battalion at Perryville, Corinth, and Stones River and was now officer in
charge of the draft in northern New York State. Robert had volunteered
to be recalled to active duty in the navy and was commander of a gunboat
in Commodore Porter's Mississippi flotilla.

Walker's thoughts were on the futures of his children and the fratricidal
nature of the war when he wrote to Mary that June:

> I am glad you have a realistic sense of the atrocious villainies of our Yankee
> brethren. We are right and they know they are acting like villains. Sooner
> would I contaminate my hands by touching gold that did not belong to me
> than to touch the hand of one of them and I wish my children to be educated
> in the same school. You will oblige me if you unteach them to say Uncle Fred,
> Frank, etc. I wish none of my blood to claim kindred with a race that have
> disgraced the very name of civilization. Don't speak to them of them. Let
> their names ever be forbidden in the presence of my children.

It is not likely that Mary followed this advice.[54]

Walker's new division was the largest aggregation of men he had ever
commanded. It consisted of five brigades of infantry, one of cavalry, and
additional contingents of cavalry and artillery. His infantry brigades were
his own, now commanded by Colonel C. C. Wilson of the 25th Georgia,
Gist's, Gregg's, Ector's, and McNair's. John Adams commanded a brigade of cavalry; Colonel Samuel Wragg Ferguson, a cadet when Walker
was commandant and whose brother had a battery of artillery in Gist's
brigade, led a separate cavalry command. There were eight batteries of
artillery. Walker had almost 12,000 men present of whom some 10,500
were fit for duty.[55]

Among the miscellaneous units of cavalry, Walker found the Georgia
company of Captain Thomas M. Nelson. Nelson was a thirty-year-old
physician from Albany, Georgia, and may have served in one of the companies of cavalry attached to Walker's brigade at Savannah early in 1862. After
the disbandment of the Georgia State Troops he had raised an independent

company of cavalry for Confederate service. At first they were assigned in east Tennessee. While en route to the Trans-Mississippi Department in May 1863, Nelson's company was stopped by General Johnston and attached to his department. When Walker found Nelson he immediately "adopted" him and made the company of Georgia "partisan rangers" his personal escort. They served as such for about two months.[56]

Although Walker was pleased with his promotion and his new command, not all of the units in the division met what he considered acceptable standards. He had long since accepted the need for a volunteer army to fight this vast war, but he insisted on as much drill and discipline as he could instill in his citizen soldiers. While reviewing the troops brought from the West, he was struck by what he thought were deplorable conditions in Ector's and McNair's brigades. Walker thought the discipline of the two brigades was so bad that they should be discharged. He kept the two units separated as much as possible and later, when the size of the division was pared down, he willingly gave up McNair's brigade to French's division.[57]

All of the brigadiers of Walker's new division had outranked him when he arrived in Mississippi; Beauregard had specified that Gist should be commander of the two brigades when they were detached from the coast. The change had been so rapid that it led to some confusion in command relationships. On May 25, Gist wrote to Beauregard, "I sent Walker to relieve Yazoo City yesterday." Gist had been the senior brigadier in the army and had issued the order to Walker in Johnston's name. By the time the units moved, however, word had been received from Richmond of Walker's promotion and Gist found himself under the Georgian's command. There is no evidence that there was ever any hard feeling over this reversal in status.[58]

With Pemberton locked up in Vicksburg, Johnston felt that his best course of action was to collect as much strength as he could and then make an attempt to penetrate Grant's lines from the outside while Pemberton struck from the inside. Johnston wanted Pemberton to abandon Vicksburg to save his army. Meanwhile, he had to look to other threats to the Confederate position in Mississippi. Johnston was worried about Federals advancing to take Yazoo City, an important crossing of the Yazoo River. On May 24 he had Gist order Walker off to hold that point and collect information about enemy intentions. By the time Walker got under way he was a major general and took his entire division with him. The division advanced slowly and occupied Yazoo on June 4. In a letter to his wife on

June 6 he explained his problems: "I have a load of care and responsibility upon me. The most of the departments in a new division need direction and independent of my being obliged to plan and contrive for about the movements of masses, and then there is much detail about supplies, wagons, etc., that keep me constantly on the go."[59]

To assist him with this burden, Walker had the staff he had brought with him from Georgia. Major Alfred C. Dearing, commissary of Gist's brigade, joined the division staff in the same capacity. Captain J. Robert Troup, regular aide, and Walker's cousin Captain Matthew H. Talbot, volunteer aide, joined him while in Mississippi. When the brigade moved to Mississippi, the younger Henry Jackson preferred to remain in Georgia. His place as ordnance officer was taken by Lieutenant Lawson W. Magruder from Pemberton's staff. After Walker's division was formed in May, Dr. James A. Bowers, surgeon of the 3d Tennessee Regiment, came from Port Hudson with Gregg's brigade and was appointed division surgeon. This was the nucleus of the official family that would remain substantially together until July 1864. Walker also tried to have Captain Robert Martin promoted and appointed division chief of artillery. The adjutant and inspector general's office replied that officially there was no such position and the senior artillery officer with the division would be considered the chief. The rank of the senior officer would depend on the number of guns assigned. Walker did succeed in getting Martin promoted to major later that summer.[60]

From Yazoo Walker kept up a steady stream of reports to Johnston on the conditions of the roads and bridges, the availability of drinking water, the state of the defenses in the town, the depth of the river, enemy movements, and Walker's own ideas about the relief of Vicksburg. Grant had sent a division out to scour the country between the Yazoo and Big Black rivers. Walker was constantly on the lookout for this force and, with the support of Loring's division at Benton, successfully held them away from Yazoo.[61]

By June 11 Johnston had decided that holding Yazoo City was futile and he ordered Walker to move to Vernon, on the Big Black and closer to Canton. On June 28 Johnston issued orders for the concentration of his army, now about twenty-two thousand effective infantry, plus cavalry, for an assault on Grant's lines and the relief of Vicksburg. This movement was completed on July 1. The planned attack was to take place on July 7, but reconnaissance on July 2 and 3 convinced Johnston that an attack on Grant's line north of the railroad would be unsuccessful and he would have to move around to the south. Vicksburg surrendered on July 4, making Johnston's maneuvering pointless.[62]

Walker had remained hopeful to the end. On July 5, the day after the surrender but apparently before he knew about it, he wrote to his wife, "Our garrison are holding their own." He had had another asthma attack while at Yazoo, but otherwise he was holding up well, as he usually did while on active service. He found campaigning conditions in Mississippi miserable. "The weather is very hot and the water very bad. It is the worst country to campaign in I ever knew on account of dust in dry weather, mud in wet, and the almost total absence of good water, and very often on the march from eight to ten miles [with] no water at all. It is [hard] on the troops." The miserable conditions in Mississippi were a constant theme of those who recorded their impressions during this campaign.[63]

Following the surrender at Vicksburg, Johnston fell back on Jackson. For the Confederacy to maintain a position in Mississippi he felt it essential to hold that city. Reaching there on July 7, his four divisions took up a semicircular defensive line in the works previously prepared by Pemberton on the west side of town. Beginning where the railroad entered the city from the north Johnston posted the division of W. W. Loring. On Loring's left, extending as far as the Clinton road, stood the four brigades of Walker's division. Walker's four brigades from right to left, or north to south, were Ector's, Gregg's, Gist's, and Wilson's. On Walker's left, south of the Clinton road, was French, and the left of the line, carried back around to where the railroad exited Jackson on the south, was occupied by the division of John C. Breckinridge. The cavalry division of W. H. Jackson, who had been a cadet at West Point during Walker's tenure, was posted to watch the fords of the Pearl River north and south of Jackson. Johnston's effective strength was about twenty-six thousand of all arms.[64]

Even before the surrender at Vicksburg had been completed, Grant had alerted Sherman to be prepared to move to drive Johnston out of Mississippi and complete the interrupted business of destroying the Rebel infrastructure. Sherman left Vicksburg on July 4 with three army corps, forty thousand men in nine divisions. He had his own XV Corps under Major General Fred Steele; XIII Corps, led since the displacement of McClernand by Major General E. O. C. Ord; and Major General John G. Parke's IX Corps, recently arrived from the East. The Union army approached Jackson on July 9 and by the tenth had dug into positions facing the Confederate defenses.[65]

Rather than advancing to the attack as Johnston expected, Sherman settled down to shell and skirmish with Johnston's outnumbered army. This continued for two days while the Union lines were extended and improved. On July 12, a weak and unsupported attack was made on Breckinridge but was easily repulsed. Ord reported to Sherman that the attack had been made by one of his division commanders without orders, without coordination, and without preparation. That division commander was relieved from duty. The attacking brigade lost almost 500 out of 880 engaged. Other small skirmishes occurred, including one on Walker's front on July 15. A line of skirmishers had been driven in and the 30th Georgia of Wilson's brigade was rushed forward to hold the position. In a letter of commendation he wrote to the troops involved, the Georgia general noted the gallant behavior of the 30th Georgia and 24th Texas, Ector's brigade, in repelling the attack.[66]

On July 14 Johnston learned that a large trainload of artillery ammunition had left Vicksburg en route to Jackson. W. H. Jackson's cavalry division was dispatched to intercept the train but was unsuccessful. In anticipation of the expected barrage and attack Johnston felt that defense would be futile, and he ordered the evacuation of Jackson. This was carried out in great secrecy on the night of July 16, the army withdrawing first some four miles to Brandon and then falling back to Morton, thirty miles east of Jackson, on July 19. Johnston reported a total loss of 600 during the seven-day siege. Union losses amounted to 1,122, the largest single cause being the botched attack on July 12. In Walker's division, the two most prominent casualties were Major John Lamb of the 29th Georgia, beheaded by an artillery round, and Captain Thomas Ferguson of Gist's artillery battery, shot seriously but not fatally through the lungs while carrying dispatches from Walker to Loring.[67]

Captain Cumming recorded a close call with a happier ending for several high-ranking officers during the siege. Walker's headquarters was in a dry streambed just behind his division lines. Behind the headquarters encampment stood a large oak tree. On one occasion, Johnston called a staff meeting with all of his division commanders at Walker's headquarters. They held their conference at the base of the oak. About three minutes after the meeting broke up, a solid round shot came over the creek bank and crashed into the oak exactly in the place where the generals had been sitting.[68]

Upon arrival in Morton, Walker wrote an account of the fighting to his wife:

After seven days irregular fighting in Jackson, it was necessary to evacuate. The Yankees came in their usual numbers and commenced throwing up their works all around us and opened with their numerous artillery. Our men bore themselves nobly during the several days, returning their fire, etc., but it was a mere matter of time and numbers. In a few more days the place would have been completely invested. We would have been surrounded by an army three or four times as large as our own with superior works all around us and with a large preponderance (perhaps 4 to 1) of artillery (of heavier metal than ours). Had we have remained we should have either been obliged to surrender after desperate fighting or compelled to cut our way through with what remnant might have been left of our band (I don't call it an army).

Walker gave a graphic account of the withdrawal:

A retreat was decided upon and it was conducted with such secrecy that the Yanks knew nothing of it until we were 12 or 15 miles off. The two armies were not over 600 yds. from each other and they had pushed some of their skirmishers up within 250 yds. of our line. At night in the darkness we had our artillery dragged away by hand and hitched the horses to it a half mile off so that no noise could be made. Our pickets and skirmishers were kept out in front of our line until 1 A.M. and the army moved at 10 P.M. noiselessly. The Yanks did not find out until 8 o'clock next morning but at daylight commenced their usual firing of artillery and small arms upon empty trenches, and so ended my *second retreat* from Jackson.[69]

During the siege Sherman had been busy destroying railroads, rolling stock, and means of production. Rails were torn up and cars destroyed as far as sixty miles north and south of Jackson. After Jackson fell, a large part of the city went up in flames. Sherman reported to Grant that Jackson was "one mass of charred ruins." The Yankee soldiers referred to the city as "Chimneyville."[70]

As Johnston retreated eastward Sherman followed only a few miles and then abandoned the chase. At Morton, Johnston took a stand to guard the railroads east to Selma, Alabama, and south to Mobile. President Davis was greatly concerned that Grant might move toward Mobile or go north to join Rosecrans in Tennessee. Johnston was held in a state of readiness to go to the defense of Mobile, but Grant's superior, Major General Henry W. Halleck, disapproved that operation. William J. Hardee, now a lieutenant general, arrived at Morton on July 23 from the Army of Tennessee to take temporary command of Johnston's army. Johnston, with Pemberton, who had been paroled, was summoned to a court of inquiry convened at Montgomery to look into the causes of the loss of Vicksburg.[71]

One of the problems facing the Confederate command in Mississippi was the disposition of the thirty-one thousand paroled prisoners from Vicksburg. Many had left for home as soon as they were paroled, but the government was anxious to try to keep some semblance of discipline in their ranks so that they could be integrated back into service after being exchanged. A camp for this purpose may have been proposed at Enterprise, Mississippi, on the Alabama border. On July 26, Hardee ordered Walker to Enterprise to take charge of the arriving troops. Whether Walker actually went there is not clear. Letters to his wife and daughter dated as late as August 24 were still addressed from Morton.[72]

Walker was disgusted with the course of events in Mississippi and, as was his custom, said so plainly. He was satisifed that his men had done all that was expected of them, but he saw no prospect for further offensive action against Grant and Sherman. Now he hoped that his division would be called to fight with Bragg in Tennessee or even with Lee in Virginia. The defense of Mobile was another prospect. Walker hoped, however, for offensive action, and he was soon to get his wish.[73]

12

CHICKAMAUGA

September–December 1863

WHILE JOSEPH JOHNSTON and his meager forces had been battling to save Mississippi for the South, Braxton Bragg had been losing Tennessee. Following the drawn battle at Murfreesboro (Stones River) in January 1863, the opposing armies had settled into a stalemate of five months' duration. Then, in June 1863, William Rosecrans, the idiosyncratic commander of the Union Army of the Cumberland, under the urging of the War Department in Washington, began a near flawless campaign of maneuver to capture Chattanooga, the vital rail center of the Southeast. A secondary Union goal was to prevent further reinforcements from Bragg's army being sent to Johnston in Mississippi. Bragg was completely deceived by Rosecrans's operations and retired behind the Tennessee River, holding only Chattanooga and the extreme southeast corner of the state, just above the Georgia border. By the end of August, finding his position untenable because of Union artillery fire from the heights north of the city and because of further encircling movements by Rosecrans, Bragg was faced with the possibility of having to fall back behind Missionary Ridge on the Georgia side of the state line.[1]

Chattanooga was too important for the South to concede without a fight. Through it ran the only rail line from Virginia to Alabama, and another, equally important for the sustenance of Bragg's army, ran south to Atlanta. Southern strategists believed it was imperative for Bragg to defeat Rosecrans's army and hold Chattanooga. To this end, another redistribution of the Confederacy's dwindling manpower was effected. First, Simon B. Buckner's corps from east Tennessee was brought under Bragg's command. From Mississippi, where the summer campaign had ground to a halt, Johnston sent Breckinridge's and W. H. T. Walker's divisions, about nine thousand infantry. From the Gulf Coast came a few brigades and from the Atlantic Coast, several more. Later, from the Army of Northern Virginia, where offensive action seemed to be over following the disappointing defeat at Gettysburg, would come James Longstreet with two of the divisions of his corps under Generals John B. Hood and Lafayette McLaws.[2]

When Walker received his orders to move to Chattanooga on August 23, he was delighted. He had been chafing at the enforced inaction in Mississippi and had predicted a change to another theater. His division at this time had the four brigades of Gist, Wilson, Gregg, and Ector. The former two had journeyed with Walker from Savannah in May; the other two had joined his division in Mississippi. His effective fighting strength was about sixty-six hundred infantry, with sixteen guns in four batteries of artillery. The division departed by train on August 24. Before he left, Walker had time to dash off a note to his daughter. "We are all rejoiced at the change for we have become heartily wearied of this country and of the inactivity of our present life. We will have sharp work, I presume, at Chattanooga, but we are wanted more there than we are here and, of course, I desire to be where I can render the best service to the country. Now is the time for every Southron to be at the post of duty."[3]

Moving by rail through Montgomery, Atlanta, and Rome, the lead elements of Walker's division reached Chattanooga on August 27, and the rear closed in by the thirty-first. Gregg's brigade was detached before arriving so Walker brought only three brigades to the Army of Tennessee, about 5,000 men. After the rigors of the Mississippi campaign, the division's equipment was in poor condition. Straggling was also a problem. The passage through Atlanta gave many men an opportunity for a quick, unauthorized visit home. George W. Brent, assistant adjutant general on Bragg's staff, wrote in his journal on August 31: "The division of Walker, which has now nearly come up, is poorly equipped. It has many absentees and stragglers. It will give but little help." A. P. Adamson of the 30th Georgia attested that his regiment had 450 effectives when they left Morton and barely half that number when they arrived at Chickamauga. Many of the men had availed themselves of an opportunity for a short home leave while passing through Georgia. Fortunately, most returned before the battle commenced.[4]

The division camped at Chickamauga Creek and with Breckinridge's formed an army corps under General D. H. Hill, who had been brought from North Carolina. The day Walker arrived, he was alerted to be prepared to support Buckner, who was moving toward Chattanooga from east Tennessee. A week later, on September 4, Walker's entire division was ordered to move to Rome, Georgia, to protect that city from the threat of Union forces advancing eastward through the mountains from Alabama. The next day the order was rescinded; only Gist's brigade was sent to Rome, and Walker was placed in charge of the Reserve Corps.[5]

The Federal movement toward Rome was a part of Rosecrans's continued effort to maneuver Bragg out of Chattanooga, which the latter still held in the first week of September. The city was too strong to be taken by assault, but Rosecrans planned another envelopment to win control of that important center. Rather than making his move on the east side of the town, that is, upstream along the Tennessee River, as Bragg expected, the Union army crossed the river downstream from Chattanooga and advanced into north Alabama and north Georgia. Then, operating on a forty-mile front, Rosecrans's three army corps moved laterally west to east through the mountain passes, menacing Bragg's rear and his line of communications to Atlanta.

On September 6, Bragg fell back from Chattanooga to concentrate his eight infantry divisions at Lafayette, Georgia. It was his intention to defeat the elements of the Union army separately as they emerged from the passes east of Lookout Mountain. Rosecrans had successfully maneuvered Bragg out of Chattanooga, but his tactical dispositions were poor and he was open to defeat in detail. In addition, he mistook Bragg's withdrawal for a retreat. Each commander suffered from a lack of intelligence about his opponent's positions and intentions.[6]

Rosecrans's Army of the Cumberland was composed of three army corps: the XIV under General George H. Thomas, an Old Army officer from Virginia who had stayed with the Union, the XX under Major General Alexander McCook, and the XXI, whose commander was General Thomas L. Crittenden. In addition, Rosecrans had a Reserve Corps of five thousand under Major General Gordon Granger. The effective infantry and artillery strength was fifty-seven thousand with nine thousand effective cavalry. Unique among Rosecrans's cavalry was the mounted infantry brigade of John T. Wilder, who had equipped themselves with Spencer repeating rifles at their own expense. To oppose Rosecrans, Bragg could muster at this time about forty-five thousand infantry and artillery and approximately fourteen thousand cavalrymen. The two armies were nearly evenly matched in strength.[7]

Following the arrival of the troops from Mississippi and elsewhere at Chattanooga, Bragg had arranged his army into four corps of two divisions each. Generals Hill, Buckner, and Leonidas Polk, the fighting bishop, commanded three of the four. Polk's two divisions were those of Benjamin F. Cheatham and Thomas C. Hindman. Hill's division commanders were John C. Breckinridge and Patrick R. Cleburne, and Buckner had his own division under Brigadier General William Preston and that of Major General Alexander P. Stewart. Bragg's large cavalry was divided into two separate corps under Generals Joseph Wheeler, Walker's fellow Augustan, and Nathan Bedford Forrest. Bragg's appointment of Walker on September 5 to command the other corps was an approbation not only of his ability but a sign that he was a welcome addition to the circle of Bragg supporters.

Walker's was not much of a corps, but it represented the apogee of his professional career. He continued in command of his own three brigades (including Gist's, detached at Rome), while the Arkansas-Louisiana brigade of General St. John R. Liddell was merged with another from Mississippi under General Edward C. Walthall to form an ad hoc division under Liddell.

Walker's acting chief of artillery was Major Joseph Palmer. Robert Martin, who was nominally Walker's artillery chief, had been promoted to major in August and was absent from the Chickamauga campaign. Liddell's division derived its artillery support from the Mississippi battery of Captain Charles Swett and Captain William H. Fowler's Alabama battery, both under Captain Swett's command. The Georgia battery of Captain Evan P. Howell, formerly Martin's battery, was attached to Walker's division. Thomas Ferguson's South Carolina battery was off in Rome with Gist's brigade. The Missouri battery of Captain Hiram Bledsoe, under Lieutenant R. L. Wood, was with John Gregg's brigade in Bushrod Johnson's division during the battle. In his after-action report, Walker listed Bledsoe's battery under Major Palmer's command but such was not the case.

The combined strength of the four brigades and three batteries present in the corps was only six thousand. It was termed the Reserve Corps, and Bragg used it as a mobile reserve, or "shuttlecock concern," as Walker phrased it. Each time Bragg ordered an attack, Walker's corps was sent to support the attacking units. Each time the attack was called off, Walker's men marched back to camp.[8]

If Walker was pleased with his new command, Liddell considered his assignment to serve under Walker a punishment for having offended Bragg during a council of war earlier in the summer. Years later he wrote in his memoirs that Walker was a "crackbrained fire-eater, always captious or cavilling about something, whimsical and changeable and hardly reliable. . . . His orders were often destitute of common sense." Liddell's comments appear whimsical and changeable themselves because in the same memoir he noted of Walker on the occasion of his own departure from the Army of Tennessee, "I had never before appreciated Walker's kindly feelings. Under a rough exterior and brusque mannerism there was a large heart; a truer man and brave existed not in the army. He loved his state and died by its cause. I knew the man more thoroughly in those few moments of feeling than I had ever been able to learn in all my former associations." E. T. Sykes, the acerbic commentator on events in the Army of Tennessee, wrote of Liddell, "[He] was an officer illy-fitted, by reason of undue excitability, to personally command troops in time of action." Perhaps Liddell's excitability extended to his assessment of character.[9]

The army to which Walker had come was in a strange situation. It was engaged in two simultaneous campaigns, one against the Northern foe advancing from middle Tennessee and the other internal, between a stubborn, indecisive commander, Braxton Bragg, who was not trusted by the central government, against a coterie of dissatisfied, unhappy, and rebellious subordinate generals of whom Liddell might have been representative.

Walker and Bragg had been classmates at West Point. Although Walker resented Bragg's appointment before his own as a Confederate brigadier in 1861, he seems not to have held it against him personally. Sent to Pensacola as Bragg's second, Walker pined for more active fields and Bragg sympathetically let him escape. Soon after his arrival in Chattanooga, Walker wrote to his wife solicitously, "Genl. Bragg's health is quite delicate but he is improving. He has responsibilities and cares enough to break down a hearty man. He has been very kind and friendly to me." If by cares Walker meant problems with the command of the army, he was right.[10]

The factionalism in the Army of Tennessee had its genesis in the failed Kentucky campaign of 1862. Bragg had blamed his problems on his subordinates, who in turn had faulted Bragg for poor leadership. Both charges were true. Bragg was a better organizer and disciplinarian than he was a field commander. Cold and stubborn, he did not get along well with the men who worked for him. Kirby Smith, who was supposed to cooperate with Bragg in Kentucky, acted completely independently. Leonidas Polk, Bragg's principal subordinate, openly disobeyed orders, in Kentucky and later, and took every opportunity to undermine his superior. Polk had a direct line to his former West Point contemporary Jefferson Davis and took advantage of it frequently to denounce Bragg both publicly and privately.

The indecisive battle at Stones River at the end of 1862 did nothing for Bragg's reputation or for the tranquillity of the high command of his army. Bragg seriously weakened his own position by offering to resign if he no longer had the confidence of the army and then reneged on his offer when the lack of confidence became manifest. Polk's web of intrigue spread to include others. Hardee, who had a high reputation based on his service in the Old Army, also worked against Bragg, bringing with him his own followers, Cheatham and Cleburne. The Kentucky generals, Buckner, Breckinridge, Preston, and the like, smarting over the failed attempt to bring their state into the Confederacy, were another faction of the anti-Bragg cabal. Aware of Bragg's shortcomings, Davis tried to get Joseph Johnston to relieve him, but Johnston refused. Bragg continued in command throughout 1863, despite increasing evidence of a mental breakdown.[11]

On September 10, as part of Bragg's plan to defeat the Union forces in detail, the divisions of Hindman and Cleburne were directed to strike the corps of George H. Thomas emerging from the mountains into McLemore's Cove. Walker was to support Cleburne. The plan was good, but execution was faulty. Hindman was slow off the mark and Thomas withdrew. Bragg next turned on September 12 on Crittenden's corps, which was advancing on Ringgold, Georgia. Polk's corps was given the execution of the attack with Walker again in support. This time the Union commander was able to bring his forces together before Polk was ready so Bragg withdrew. These two failed attempts were to have strong repercussions on the high command in the weeks to come.[12]

The failure to coordinate the attack on Crittenden was the occasion for another of Liddell's anecdotes about Walker. As Liddell remembered it, Polk called a council of war at Rock Spring Church of the commanders of the units assembled to strike Crittenden. Walker found fault with Polk's dispositions and with his explanation of them. Polk tried over and over again to explain his plans but Walker was not satisfied. Liddell managed to draw Walker away temporarily, but he returned to Polk soon again. Finally, Cheatham intervened. But he, too, left after a few minutes, saying to Liddell that "he would not serve two hours under Walker to save his life." At last, Walker, "having exhausted rhetoric and expletives," left Polk alone.[13]

Walker's behavior toward his senior may have been less than respect-ful, but the reason is clear. Polk had four divisions assembled and the enemy (Crittenden) was thought to be advancing in detail, that is, with his divisions separated. Yet Polk maintained that he was not ready and would not be until Bragg sent him reinforcements. Despite Bragg's urg-ings for an attack and Walker's "rhetoric and expletives," Polk thought he would not be ready until the next morning. As events turned out, Critten-den's divisions were not separated, but Polk did not know that because he had not performed a reconnaissance. Based on the information avail-able at Polk's headquarters on September 12, Walker's probable desire for offensive action was more in keeping with Bragg's wishes than Polk's was.[14]

Having lost two opportunities to defeat Rosecrans in detail, Bragg de-cided at a council of war with his four corps commanders on September 15 to go over to the general offensive and advance on Rosecrans's army, which was concentrating around Chattanooga. The individual brigades that had been detached from the army to be stationed all across north Georgia were collected to support the advance. Bragg also was aware that help was on the way from Virginia. He enjoyed the prospect of having a real numerical advantage over his adversary. Despite this, Brent thought the plan a bad one which Bragg had devised while in a sickened and enfeebled state, but as Walker noted in a letter to his wife the same day, "It is impossible that this farce can continue much longer."[15]

The decision to send two divisions of Longstreet's corps from Virginia had been made in consultations between President Davis and General Lee in late August. The germ of the idea may have come from Longstreet himself, who says he suggested it to Lee. Certainly, some action had to be taken to bolster Bragg before he let Chattanooga slip away. Despite the high-level direction, it was not until September 9, days after Bragg had evacuated Chattanooga, that the first troop trains left Lee's lines on the Rapidan for north Georgia. Nine brigades of infantry in the divisions of Lafayette McLaws and John Bell Hood went first. The artillery battalion of Colonel E. Porter Alexander did not get off until September 17, the day after the first of Longstreet's units began arriving at the Confederate railhead at Catoosa.[16]

By September 17 Rosecrans had felt out the general position of Bragg's army and had also learned of the reinforcements from other theaters. He concluded that he should assume a defensive position across the LaFayette-Chattanooga road to cover the approaches to the latter city. The position he chose was along Chickamauga Creek. For the first time in two weeks all of his corps were together and within supporting distance of each other. Crittenden's XXI Corps was on Rosecrans's left or north flank, Thomas's XIV Corps in the center, and the XX Corps of Alexander McCook on the south or right.

Bragg planned an attack on Crittenden on the left flank (Bragg's right) on the eighteenth to cut Rosecrans off from his base at Chattanooga. Once having crossed Chickamauga Creek and outflanked Crittenden, the Confederate troops would wheel to their left and drive south along the west bank, pushing the other two Federal corps before them. Meanwhile, other forces facing the Federal center and right would wait for the troops in front of them to become engaged and then cross the creek and join in the fight. The enveloping force was composed of the four divisions of the corps of Buckner and Walker, plus Bushrod Johnson's separate division and Forrest's cavalry. Johnson's division, organized on the field, included his own brigade, those of Evander McNair and John Gregg from Mississippi, and the first three brigades of Longstreet's corps from Virginia, those of Henry "Rock" Benning, E. M. Law, and Jerome Robertson. Despite the large number of units under his command, Johnson could only muster thirty-six hundred muskets.

Bragg's line from right to left (north to south) had Johnson crossing Chickamauga Creek at Reed's Bridge, Walker at Alexander's Bridge, and Buckner's two divisions at Thetford's Ford. Forrest's cavalry supported Johnson and Walker. Polk's corps was next to the left, facing the Union center. Hill's corps held Bragg's left flank, and on his left was Wheeler's cavalry.[17]

The attack did not go as planned. Forrest's cavalry was delayed and did not participate until later in the day. Colonel Robert G. Minty's Federal cavalry brigade effectively blocked the advance of Johnson's division until the middle of the afternoon. Although the attack had been ordered for dawn, Walker's corps did not approach its objective, Alexander's Bridge, until near noon. Along part of the route, only a single road was available for both Walker's and Buckner's corps, and both were delayed. Upon arrival, Walker ordered Liddell to have Walthall's brigade attack and take the bridge. They attained their objective in less than an hour but suffered heavy casualties from the Spencer repeating rifles of Wilder's mounted infantry brigade on the other side. In addition, the Union troops had destroyed the bridge before retreating, making a crossing extremely difficult at this point. Walker moved his men further down the creek to Byram's Ford, crossed over, and moved back up to Alexander's Bridge on the west side. This movement took the rest of the day and most of the night because the wheeled vehicles of the corps became bogged down while negotiating the steep banks of the creek. Upon arrival at their objective, the troops bivouacked. After crossing, Johnson's division moved south along the creek and passed to Walker's left. Buckner did not cross Chickamauga Creek that day. Polk's and Hill's corps stood motionless throughout the day, waiting for a signal from the right flank to begin their advance. The difficulties in movement and the aggressive action by two mounted Federal brigades had frustrated the entire right wing of Bragg's army.[18]

All day Bragg sent a stream of messages to Walker urging him to hurry to attain his position. On the morning of the eighteenth, Bragg, through his assistant adjutant general, George W. Brent, urged Walker in writing to cross Chickamauga Creek "without delay." During the afternoon, after Bushrod Johnson had made his lodgment on the west bank of the creek, Bragg told Walker, "Your junction with General Johnson tonight is of vital importance." Later, after Walker had given up at Alexander's Bridge and was moving to Byram's Ford, Bragg told him that he must "effect a junction with [Johnson] tonight which [Bragg] entertains no doubt that you have already done." Finally, at 7:30 P.M., Brent wrote to Walker and Buckner, in Bragg's name, "The Commanding General, learning that you did not get your force across the river before dark, directs that you effect the passage in force at daylight tomorrow morning." The last message was based on faulty information; Walker was already crossing, Buckner was not.[19]

The struggle to get into position on September 18 was only a prelude to the two days of fighting formally known as the battle of Chickamauga. During the night of the eighteenth, both sides made more adjustments to their lines and to their organization. Rosecrans shifted the XIV Corps under Thomas from his center to his left to face Bragg's right wing, now on the west bank of Chickamauga Creek. Crittenden's corps now was the center and McCook remained on the right. Bushrod Johnson's division had moved to Walker's left, leaving the latter on the extreme right of the Confederate line. General Hood had arrived on the field and by virtue of seniority took command of his own three brigades and Johnson's division. Hill's corps was brought from the left to a position behind Polk's, and Cheatham's division from Polk's corps was started for the right. Bragg now had seven divisions on or moving to his right: Walker's demi-corps, Johnson and Hood, Stewart and Preston under Buckner, with Cheatham on the way, plus Forrest's cavalry. Bragg's left was held by Hindman's lone division of Polk's corps and Hill's corps.[20]

On the morning of September 19, the action was precipitated by a strong

Union reconnaissance from Thomas's corps on Bragg's right. Thomas had received intelligence that a lone Southern brigade was on the road near Reed's bridge. Instead, Forrest's cavalry, on Walker's right, was the first obstacle Thomas encountered. Under heavy attack from two divisions, Forrest called for infantry support and Bragg ordered Walker to send in Wilson's brigade. As the intensity of the fighting increased, Walker asked Bragg for permission to go himself. Bragg told Walker to go and take the rest of his corps with him. When Walker arrived at the line he found that Forrest had already committed Wilson's brigade and Ector's as well. All were now falling back before the superior Union numbers. Walker took command and ordered Liddell's division into the action. This advance broke through two Union lines, but upon the arrival of a third blue division Walker's force withdrew a mile and a half. For four hours, this slender force of four infantry brigades and some dismounted cavalry held back the advance of an entire army corps.[21]

As the battle on his left developed, Rosecrans gradually sideslipped more divisions to that flank, first the remaining two divisions of the XIV Corps, then others. As each new division came on line, it overlapped the Confederate position. On the Southern side, Cheatham's division arrived first to relieve Walker's tired brigades. For most of the day Hood's and Buckner's men stood idly by while Walker was fighting for his life. Later, Cleburne and Stewart were also shifted to the right. The attack by Stewart late in the afternoon nearly split the Union line, but he too was forced to retire. The last attack of the day was made by Cleburne's fresh troops. As they moved to the advance, they passed through Liddell's exhausted men who were lying in a field. Liddell's troops recognized their former comrades in the dark and cheered them as they went forward. By dark, command of this part of the front had been taken over by Lieutenant General Leonidas Polk, the senior corps commander in Bragg's army.[22]

At the end of the first day's combat Bragg was in a worse position than when he had started. Walker's corps and Stewart's and Cleburne's divisions had suffered heavy losses. The Army of Tennessee was now concentrated with Chickamauga Creek at its rear as a barrier to withdrawal. Also, the element of surprise had been lost and the battle was reduced to a knockdown fight between two almost equally matched opponents. The elements of Bragg's army were in a jumble as a result of having been committed piecemeal during the day as need dictated.

Bragg's plan for the second day was a continuation of his attempt to get around Thomas's right and cut the Union army off from Chattanooga.

The second day's battle was delayed by a series of bizarre communications mishaps which ultimately would cost Bragg his command.

First, Bragg decided to reorganize his troops. The right wing now consisted of Cleburne's division on the far right with Cheatham on his left. Walker's two small divisions lay behind Cheatham. En route to the right but not yet arrived was Breckinridge, whose division would complete Hill's corps on that flank. To Cheatham's left, in order north to south, were the divisions of Stewart, Bushrod Johnson, Hood, Joseph Kershaw commanding McLaws's division, Hindman, and Preston. Leonidas Polk had overall command of the right wing with Hill leading the divisions of Breckinridge and Cleburne under him. For the left wing, Bragg designated James Longstreet from Virginia as commander, though that general did not arrive on the battlefield until eleven o'clock that night. Longstreet brought with him the brigades of Joseph Kershaw and Benjamin Humphreys of McLaws's division. McLaws was not up yet, and Kershaw was in temporary command of his division. With Longstreet named as wing commander, Hood was assigned to lead the two divisions from Virginia and E. M. Law took command of Hood's division. Buckner was still nominally in command of Stewart's and Preston's divisions, but they were separated on the field by Hood's corps and Bushrod Johnson's division. As before, Forrest's cavalry covered the right flank and Wheeler's the left. Hill later estimated Polk's infantry strength at nineteen thousand and Longstreet's at twenty-three thousand. He thought Union infantry strength was about forty-five thousand. Most historians agree, however, that Bragg had a numerical advantage. The Union army lay facing the Confederates with Thomas's four divisions on their left, Crittenden in the center, and McCook on the right.[23]

At 9:00 P.M. on September 19, Bragg informed Polk in person of his plans for the next day and that he wanted the divisions beginning on the far right to attack at first daylight. As each division became engaged, the one next on its left would move forward until Bragg's whole army was at grips with Rosecrans's. Polk received no written instructions. When Longstreet arrived two hours later, Bragg briefed him on his assignment and the next day's plan. Longstreet then went to his front. Hill, the third lieutenant general in the Army of Tennessee, never received orders for the twentieth that night. First, he rode to where he thought Bragg's headquarters should be but could not find Bragg. Then Hill met one of his own staff officers, Colonel Archer Anderson, who had had a chance encounter with Polk in the road. Polk told Anderson that Hill was now under his, Polk's, command, but he did not mention the impending attack. Anderson informed

Hill that he was wanted at Polk's headquarters that night to receive orders, but Hill never found Polk and couriers and guides dispatched by Polk did not find Hill. Polk did send written instructions to Cheatham. Walker, that punctilious old soldier, went to Polk's headquarters where he received his written instructions in person.

Breckinridge, on the march from the left to the extreme right, met Polk as his division crossed the Chickamauga. Polk gave Breckinridge permission to rest by the creek rather than move directly to his battle position as he should have done and as Hill intended that he should. Breckinridge spent most of the night at Polk's headquarters. There Polk told him of the morning attack but told him to start as soon as practicable, not at daylight as Bragg had specified.

As a result of this confusion, when dawn broke on September 20, of the principal commanders only Polk, Walker, and Cheatham knew an attack was expected at daylight. Breckinridge, not yet in position, knew an attack was planned but not the prescribed time. Hill and Cleburne were ignorant of Bragg's plan.[24]

Just before daylight Hill rode to the front to confer with Cleburne and Breckinridge. On arrival, he found that the two divisions were not properly aligned, that Breckinridge was just moving into position, and that the men needed breakfast, many of them not having been fed since the day before. Meanwhile, Polk arose at daybreak and dispatched written instructions directly to Cleburne and Breckinridge to commence their attack. In addition, he renewed his fruitless search for Hill. About 7:00 A.M., while Hill was meeting with the two major generals, Polk's messenger arrived. Cleburne and Breckinridge read the order for an attack as soon as possible, Cleburne for the first time, and then passed a copy of the document to Hill. Thus, some ten hours after Bragg had issued his orders to Polk, Hill learned that he was expected to lead off the Southern attack on September 20.

Hill remonstrated at once. He sent the courier back to Polk with the information that his men needed to eat, that their alignment was wrong for an attack to the west, and that he felt he had insufficient strength in a line only one division deep to overcome the barricaded Northern defenders. Hill stated that he could not be ready for at least an hour. He also asked Polk to come and inspect the line for himself. Hill foresaw no problem with a delay, except for the chance for the Federals to improve their defenses, because he was under the impression that the attack could be made "as soon as possible." When Polk received Hill's message, he sent information to Bragg concerning Hill's delay and then went to the front as Hill had requested. He met the three generals and asked why the attack was delayed. Cleburne replied that his men were still waiting for rations. Polk apparently expressed no objection and went off to talk to Walker in Cheatham's rear. Soon after Polk left Hill's location, Bragg arrived, demanding to know why the attack had not started at daylight as ordered. Hill was stunned; this was his first intimation of such an order. After expressing his anger at Hill and Polk, Bragg ordered the attack to begin at once.[25]

At once could not mean immediately, however much Hill wanted to comply. Problems in alignment still existed and had to be rectified before the attack could begin. Two of Breckinridge's brigades were shifted further to the right so they could overlap the north end of the Federal fortifications. Cavalry was arranged to protect Breckinridge's right flank. Cleburne's left brigade was at right angles to Cheatham's right brigade. An advance by Cleburne would take him across Cheatham's path. An advance by Cheatham would be into Cleburne's flank. When Cheatham was finally turned properly, he found that his left was behind Stewart's right. Cheatham had been ordered to attack with the right wing, Stewart had not. Cheatham was blocked from the front. Walker's corps, which Hill expected to be Breckinridge's reserve, was lined up behind Cheatham. It took more than an hour to straighten out this tangle.[26]

Shortly before ten o'clock, four hours late by Bragg's reckoning, the Confederate right wing began its attack. Longstreet's left wing stood immobile waiting for its turn. Because of the impending tangle between Cheatham and Cleburne, Bragg had pulled the former's division out of line. As a result, only Breckinridge and Cleburne made the advance, but with considerable initial success. Because of Hill's judicious placement of Breckinridge's right brigades, they were able to sweep completely around Thomas and cross the Chattanooga road. The brigade Thomas sent to oppose them had no entrenchments and was easily dislodged. Breckinridge's left brigade, under General Ben Harden Helm, whose wife was Mary Todd Lincoln's half-sister, had more difficulty. Helm's brigade struck on the Union fortifications and was repulsed with heavy loss, including the life of its commander. Breckinridge pulled the broken brigade out of line and sent it to the rear. This created a gap between his and Cleburne's divisions which Union soldiers began to infiltrate. Seeing this action, Hill asked Polk for some of Walker's troops to bolster the line. Cleburne's division also met heavy resistance from the protected Federals and had to withdraw. On that front Brigadier General James Deshler was killed and the brigade of General Lucius Polk, the wing commander's nephew, was placed in serious jeopardy.[27]

Despite the losses of the previous day, Walker's corps was somewhat stronger than it had been on September 19. During the general collection of troops from across north Georgia to reinforce Bragg's army, Gist's brigade at Rome had been alerted on September 17. Competing with the other brigades in the area and with Longstreet's men traveling from Atlanta, Gist had been unable to find sufficient rail transportation for his whole brigade, some 2,000 men, but he did get C. H. Stevens's 24th South Carolina, Lieutenant Colonel Leroy Napier's 8th Georgia Battalion, and three companies of Colonel Peyton Colquitt's 46th Georgia to Catoosa Station on the eighteenth. Delayed by orders to protect a provision train, Gist did not march to Chickamauga Creek until the night of the nineteenth, arriving on the battlefield just at sunrise on September 20. He brought with him only 980 effective infantry and no artillery. All of the 16th South Carolina and Ferguson's South Carolina battery were left behind. The remaining seven companies of the 46th Georgia came on a later train and arrived to bolster Walker's corps later in the day. When Gist arrived, Walker placed him in command of his own, Ector's, and Wilson's brigades, in other words, Walker's division. Ellison Capers estimated their strength at about 3,000 muskets, but Gist said Wilson's and Ector's brigades mustered only about 500 effectives each and Wilson stated that his strength on September 20 was not more than 450. St. John Liddell retained command of his two brigades under Colonel Daniel C. Govan and General Edward C. Walthall. Command of Gist's little brigade devolved on Colonel Colquitt.[28]

There is some conflict in the testimony of how Walker's Reserve Corps was introduced into the battle on September 20. In simplest terms, Hill used Gist's division to plug the hole that had developed between Breckinridge and Cleburne while Polk fragmented Liddell's division between Cleburne's support and Breckinridge's right where they crossed the Chattanooga road and assailed the left of Thomas's defenses. The details show some disparities.

Walker, in his after-action report, wrote that on the morning of September 20 his two divisions, the four brigades much depleted from the fighting on the eighteenth and nineteenth, were positioned behind Cheatham's division. About nine o'clock Walker was ordered to move to the right to support Breckinridge's attack. This must have been the purpose of Polk's visit to Walker after leaving his meeting with Hill, Breckinridge, and Cleburne. Polk accompanied Walker's corps to the right, probably to guide them to the desired location. It was while this movement was in progress that Hill sent to Walker for a brigade to fill the gap in his line. Almost simultaneously, Gist's brigade caught up with Walker and Gist was assigned to the division command.[29]

Upon receipt of Hill's request, Walker had formed his four brigades from column into line of battle and advanced his whole corps to Hill's support. This change of formation would account for the lapse of time that Hill later complained of. Polk went with Walker to Hill's position. Hill was much surprised to find that four brigades had arrived although he had asked for one. He repeated his request for a single brigade, and Walker told him there was one, unspecified, in line immediately behind him. Hill asked specifically for Gist's brigade, and Walker told him it was deployed further to the left and had just arrived on the field, probably suggesting it was in no condition for immediate action. Hill insisted and ordered Gist's brigade, under Colonel Colquitt, forward into the battle. Walker then told Gist to put his three small brigades at Hill's disposal.[30]

General Polk, superior in rank to both Hill and Walker, apparently watched impassively this reportedly spirited exchange between his two subordinate commanders. If St. John Liddell was an accurate reporter, the confrontation between the two generals bordered on the childish. According to Liddell, Walker complained loudly about Hill's plan, upon which Hill walked away. Walker called for Hill to come back, which the latter did, but Hill continued to sulk. Liddell attempted to strengthen his story by the observation that Walker "disliked Hill anyway." This observation was probably based on a rumored disagreement between Hill and Walker over a leave request by a soldier in the Georgian's division.

As the story was reported in the *Atlanta Intelligencer* and elsewhere, a soldier in Walker's division asked for a home leave. Walker recommended disapproval but dutifully forwarded the request to Hill's corps headquarters. Hill, who could be more caustic than Walker, approved the leave with the annotation that if soldiers were not granted home leave all the children born in Georgia during the war "and the usual period afterwards" would be the offspring of "cowards or [those] who are otherwise exempt." In the different versions of the story in circulation, either Walker cheerfully approved the request or he was infuriated by this impugning of the virtue of Georgia women and was cool toward Hill thereafter.

It is conceivable that Liddell, aware of the rumor, manufactured the dialogue of the meeting on the morning of September 20 after the fact. Such action would have been consistent with the character of both generals, but none of the others present ever mentioned any of Liddell's colorful details. The flaw in Liddell's recollection is that we have Walker's word that the leave controversy with Hill never took place. In a tersely worded letter to the editor of the *Intelligencer*, penned on October 9, Walker wrote, "Allow me, in the most positive and unequivocal manner, to deny that my name was ever connected, directly, or indirectly, with the case in point. Such a paper was never submitted to me and the sentiments could never by any possibility have met with my approbation." The editor wisely admitted that he regretted the mistake.[31]

To return to the field of Chickamauga, in compliance with Hill's request, Gist organized his division into a column of brigades with Colquitt in the first line and Wilson and Ector behind him. Colquitt's brigade advanced into the gap in Hill's line at about 11:00 A.M. without any opportunity for reconnaissance and without knowing exactly where the Union position was. As they moved forward through the woods they were taken by fire in enfilade from an angle in the Yankee line. Colonel Stevens of the 24th South Carolina ordered a change of front to the left to meet this threat, but he was shot from his horse while his men were executing the maneuver. While Colquitt was adjusting the rest of his line to conform to Stevens's change, he too was gunned down, in his case, mortally. Ellison Capers, who had succeeded to the command of the 24th South Carolina, was also wounded, and the atack collapsed. This brief but furious melee lasted no more than forty-five minutes, but the losses were heavy. The 24th South Carolina alone suffered 169 casualties. Command of the remnants of the brigade, which had lost about one-third of its strength, devolved onto Lieutenant Colonel Leroy Napier of the 8th Georgia Battalion, whom Walker had disciplined as a cadet at West Point in 1854 and who had commanded a battery under Walker in the Georgia State Troops in 1862. After Gist's little brigade had advanced and been repulsed, Gist received Hill's approval to send in Wilson and Ector to cover their withdrawal. Polk then ordered the entire line back to the position held before the attack.[32]

While Gist's division was being committed to support Breckinridge, Lieutenant General Polk detached Walthall's brigade from Liddell's division to shore up Cleburne's line. They advanced in a fruitless attack on the well-fortified Union defenses. Eventually Walthall's Mississippians also were forced to fall back. On the far right, Govan's brigade under Liddell's direction advanced to and across the Chattanooga road on Thomas's left. According to Govan's report, he was ordered by Polk to circle to his left, behind Thomas's line, to support Gist's attack. Govan could not find Gist, who had been repulsed, and became separated from the rest of the Confederate army. In imminent danger of capture of his entire brigade, he made a fighting withdrawal to his line of departure, where he linked up with the rest of Walker's corps. Archer Anderson, Hill's staff officer, later called this attack "ill planned and ill conducted," a slap at Polk and Liddell.[33]

During the hour or more of combat Walker was a general without a command, but when his men were forced to retire he reformed them as an entity and prepared for further action. His criticism of his superiors, Polk and Hill, for their misuse of his corps is apparent in his remark, "My command being thus disposed of, brigades being sent in to take the place of divisions, my only occupation was to help form the detached portions of my command as they came out from a position I felt certain they would have to leave when they were sent in."[34]

A lull in the fighting now descended on the right of Bragg's army. The attacks of the Confederate right on Thomas's breastworks had not, however, been without benefit. Rosecrans had been constantly shifting units from his right to bolster Thomas. About 10:30 A.M., through a staff blunder, a division was pulled out of the Union line and ordered to its left. No action was taken to plug the hole in the line. By a stroke of good fortune, a few minutes later Bragg ordered Longstreet to launch an attack right at the place where the gap existed. Hood's veterans poured through the opening, and Bragg moved to exploit his advantage. The Federal right and center disintegrated as Crittenden's and McCook's troops fled toward Chattanooga. Only Thomas, reinforced by James Steedman's division of Gordon Granger's Reserve Corps, which had "marched to the sound of the guns," held his position on the field.[35]

Walker, who by now had been "compelled to insist on having something to do with my own command," found his corps behind but facing the place in the line where Cleburne's division had been posted. About one o'clock the report was received that a Federal column was advancing from Chattanooga. This was Granger with Steedman's division coming to reinforce Thomas. The Southern commanders were concerned about their weakened right flank. Walker favored withdrawing several hundred yards to concentrate forces for a strong attack on the enemy. Instead, Hill, who remembered the incident occurring about 3:00 P.M., changed Breckinridge's front to face north toward Chattanooga, while Walker remained aligned toward the west. In addition, Cheatham's division was sent to the right to oppose Granger if needed. Years later Hill criticized Walker's proposal as impractical, saying that two of the Reserve Corps brigades had been detached for other purposes and that a withdrawal in the face of Steedman's advance would have invited attack. Hill must have confused the time of Steedman's advance because by one or two o'clock Walker should have had all five brigades reassembled. In his battle report Hill wrote only that "preparations" were made to meet the advance of Steedman's division.[36]

Later in the afternoon Bragg and Polk ordered a general advance on the right. Walker's corps was placed on the extreme right of the Army of Tennessee with Liddell's two brigades on the right of the line and Gist's three on their left. Gist's brigade, still under Lieutenant Colonel Napier, had been increased to a strength of fourteen hundred by the arrival of the last seven companies of the 46th Georgia. Cleburne formed on Walker's left while Breckinridge and Cheatham advanced in a second line. Liddell and Gist advanced across the Chattanooga road on Thomas's left against little opposition. Circling to the left as Govan had done in the morning, they came up against the rear of Thomas, advancing upon his position from a northwesterly direction. Gist had no difficulty in continuing his forward movement, but Liddell encountered heavy rifle and artillery fire from both flanks and from the front. Liddell ordered his men to lie down in the field while he brought up his batteries to silence the enemy's guns. Just at this time the Union brigade of Brigadier General John Turchin charged up the Chattanooga-Lafayette road in a fighting withdrawal. They caught Govan's left flank, breaking his brigade. Walthall's soon followed. Once they were back across the Chattanooga road, order was restored and the two brigades advanced again. The Union troops had withdrawn toward Chattanooga in the interval so no opposition was encountered in the second attempt. The Reserve Corps camped on the field that night.[37]

Walker's corps, although not used in accordance with its commander's wishes during part of the battle, had rendered distinguished service. Despite serious delay and strong opposition, Walker had managed to get his four brigades across Chickamauga Creek on September 18. On the nineteenth, his little force held the Confederate right against Thomas's advance for hours before help arrived. They had taken part in the attacks on Thomas on September 20, thus attracting reinforcements from Rosecrans's right wing and making Longstreet's breakthrough possible. Finally, they had participated in the last assault on the night of the twentieth. So impressed was he with the valor of their troops that after the battle Walker went to Evander McNair (and presumably Matthew Ector) to offer his commendation and his apology for the earlier insult in Mississippi.[38]

Walker's official report was full of praise for his men and officers. Of the fighting on the nineteenth, he wrote, "The unequal contest of four brigades against such overwhelming odds is unparalleled in this revolution, and the troops deserve immortal honor for the part borne in the action. Only soldiers fighting for all that is dear to free men could attack, be driven, rally and attack again such superior forces."

As for the overall performance of his corps, he said:

In the three days' fighting I had the honor to command the gallant Reserve Corps, I witnessed nothing but a heroism that was worthy of men battling for their freedom. To the division and brigade commanders . . . I have only to say that the brigadier generals fought with a gallantry that entitles them to division commands, and the colonels commanding brigades with an obstinacy and courage that entitle them to the rank of brigadier general. The conduct of colonels, commanders of batteries, line officers, and privates is recorded by their respective commanders. I may be permitted in my own division, which was commanded on Sunday by General Gist, to state that Colonel Wilson, who commanded a brigade on both Saturday and Sunday, and acted with great distinction, and who is the oldest colonel from Georgia, is entitled, from long service with the brigade and from gallant conduct, to the command of the Georgia brigade he now commands in the capacity of brigadier general, and that the gallant Stevens, of Gist's brigade, who was severely wounded, from what I know of his capacity as an officer, from his gallantry on the field, and from his devotion to the cause, would grace any position that might be conferred.

To my staff . . . I am also indebted for distinguished and gallant service on the field. From the character of the fighting on both Saturday and Sunday they were greatly exposed, and bore themselves as became gentlemen and soldiers fighting for all that is dear. For the gallant dead we can but mourn. The noble, brave, and chivalrous Colquitt, who fell in command of Gist's brigade, was a soldier, a gentleman, a Christian, and a friend. I hope I will be excused for paying in my report a tribute to his worth.[39]

Walker felt, however, that he had been cheated out of his rightful command by his superiors. In his comments on his reaction to Granger's advance from Chattanooga, Walker's criticism was subdued, mentioning only that General Hill "differed" with him. His comments on the opening of the action on September 20 were more straightforward.

I owe it to myself and to the gallant command under me to state that when I reported to General Hill, had he permitted me to fight my Reserve Corps according to my own judgement, and had not disintegrated it, as he did, by sending it in by detachments, I would have formed my five batteries on the left flank of the enemy, toward the Chattanooga road, and opened fire upon the enemy's flanks, and would have either pushed them forward, supported by infantry, or have marched passed them with my combined force; and I feel satisfied that the enemy's left would have been carried much easier than it was, and many a gallant man been saved, and his [Thomas] retreat been intercepted.[40]

It is very doubtful that Walker's plan of action could have achieved the results desired against the strongly posted Union left flank, but it was a tactic in keeping with the spirit of the man who proposed it. Walker's opinion notwithstanding, Polk's and Hill's use of the Reserve Corps on September 20 should not be too harshly criticized. If they took the name of the corps literally, they had every right to expect that its components would be available for emergencies during the battle. In military parlance, a reserve is a commander's insurance, available to prevent disaster or to exploit opportunity. Hill, the astute veteran of the Army of Northern Virginia, looked on Walker's command as just such an asset. When crisis loomed on Breckinridge's and Cleburne's lines, Hill felt fully justified in expecting Walker to render whatever assistance Hill asked for. Just before his flare-up with Walker, Hill had received a stern rebuke from Bragg and probably was in no mood to bandy words with a subordinate over which brigade to employ in a crisis.

Judging the role of the Reserve Corps during the three days at Chickamauga, the adjutant of Walthall's brigade, E. T. Sykes, stated succinctly that, considering that Walker's corps opened the fighting on September 18 and was engaged almost continuously each day thereafter, "if names imply anything" it should have been called the "advanced corps."[41]

Walker reported casualties of 1,477 in Gist's division and 1,646 in Liddell's out of some 7,000 engaged in the three days. In Wilson's brigade, every field officer except two had been killed or wounded. William H. Reynolds of the 29th Georgia wrote to his sister that his regiment went into action with 200 men and lost 130 killed and wounded. In his own company Reynolds reported 5 men remaining out of 20. J. B. Cumming wrote to his wife, "We held our ground but suffered terribly." Captain Troup of Walker's staff had been severely wounded, and a few days after the battle Captain Crump's services were lost when his leg was broken by the kick of a horse. Returns for September 21 showed only 3,400 men present for duty in the five brigades. Of the four batteries assigned to the corps, three were in action with twelve guns. Three guns were disabled in the fight; three were lost but recovered.[42]

Reports were circulating that Walker had been killed. Immediately after the battle he telegraphed his wife to dispel that rumor. Governor Brown of Georgia came to camp to congratulate Bragg and the other officers. While there he made a special point of singling Walker out for praise before the Georgia troops, calling him "a distinguished chieftain." To his wife Walker confided, "He has, you know, always been a great friend of mine." [43]

The combat had been bloody on both sides. Although Bragg had won the advantage on the field, his losses were heavy, eighteen thousand. Rosecrans, who was the loser and was driven from the field, lost sixteen thousand men. [44]

Chickamauga has been called "the Great Battle of the West." In fact, it was a barren tactical victory. Bragg took no action to follow up on Rosecrans's retreat and on the night of September 20 went to bed not believing he had won the battle. The Union army was allowed to withdraw into Chattanooga and fortify itself there. Bragg's excuse was that his army was too exhausted to pursue. In addition, he felt he could capture Chattanooga without a fight. Some of his principal subordinates took issue with him, saying that he was unprepared for the victory he had won and had no plans to follow through. Not all the criticism was justified. Bragg did have some grounds to believe Rosecrans would evacuate Chattanooga. Beyond that, much of the criticism was written years after by those who were resentful about their treatment by Bragg during the war. Walker joined in the contemporary chorus of complaint, if not within army circles at least in his personal correspondence. On September 30 he wrote to his wife, "We gained a splendid victory, the fruits of which will be lost if we don't do something soon." [45]

While the army moved forward to occupy Missionary Ridge and Lookout Mountain overlooking Chattanooga, the Confederate camp broke out in squabbling between the pro-Bragg and anti-Bragg factions. Bragg relieved Polk and Hindman from command and had Polk arrested for his failure to act in a timely manner on September 12 and on the morning of September 20. Polk repaired to Atlanta and began a letter-writing campaign to vindicate himself. In his own defense, Polk blamed the delay of September 20 on his inability to find Hill the night of September 19. Polk wrote to his wife that Hill had accepted responsibility for the delay and that Walker sided with him (Polk) in the controversy. Hill's biographer points out that these comments by Polk conflict with Hill's version of events. Walker's support of Polk is more likely, at least on this issue. Polk opposed Bragg while Walker supported his classmate and commander, yet Walker's dislike of Hill was so great by this time that he probably took pleasure in the opportunity to lay blame on Hill. In Walker's opinion, Hill had proven his inability in his use of the reserve brigades on the morning of September 20 and had taken inappropriate action in response to the threat on the right flank that afternoon. Hence Hill was also at fault in not beginning the attack at the appointed hour. Walker had found his way to Polk's headquarters on the night of September 19; Hill had been derelict of his duty in not having done so himself.[46]

On September 22, the Reserve Corps was broken up and Walker was returned to the command of his division, first in Polk's corps, then in Longstreet's. The division consisted of the brigades of Wilson, still a colonel, Gist, and Gregg, reunited with Walker after the battle. Ector's brigade was returned to Mississippi.

S. R. Liddell made a cryptic comment on the breakup of Walker's command. In describing an interview he had with Bragg, Liddell wrote, "[Bragg] told me that Polk complained so much of being deprived of Walthall's brigade [in Liddell's temporary division], and Walker had annoyed him so much, that he [Bragg] had no other course to pursue." Who was the "he" who had been annoyed so much? If it was Polk, Bragg would not feel in the least constrained to accede to his wishes. Could it have been Bragg himself? There is nothing to suggest that Walker had a falling-out with Bragg except Bragg's disappointment that Walker had not been able to force the crossing of Chickamauga Creek on September 18. Yet it is difficult to understand why the army commander would have downgraded one of his few supporters unless some difference had risen between them. If Bragg felt that Walker's difficulties on September 18 had somehow contributed to the army's inability to achieve success in turning Rosecrans's left, then Walker would be out of favor. Bragg's most recent biographer, Judith Lee Hallock, has marshaled impressive evidence that Bragg "delighted in punishing those who were not his favorites."[47]

Walker had a definite opinion on this topic. William Mackall, the army's chief of staff, wrote to his wife about this time: "Bill Walker has just been here, much dissatisfied with everything and everybody. He never will forget that he ranked many of those now above him nor will he ever admit that opportunity or merit put them forward, and will see nothing but favoritism. I do not know a single contented General in this Army."[48]

If Walker was vocal about his removal when speaking with his fellow officers, he expressed relative equanimity and no ill-feeling toward Bragg to his wife. He wrote, "I have not rank enough *since* the battle to be called into the councils of the genls. and hence I am quietly awaiting orders." On November 9, writing to her again, Walker implied that he was still in Bragg's good graces: "We have had considerable shuffling of the cards here. It is said, in commotions the scum rises to the surface, so as I have not risen to the surface, I take it for granted I am made of some weightier matter." He added without elaboration, "I have been B[ragg]'s friend in his troubles." He also commented, "I send you a piece signed Historicus which gives a one sided account of the battle but it will give you some idea. His strictures on Bragg I don't endorse." Nevertheless, the Reserve Corps was dissolved, and Walker was henceforth excluded from the councils of the army commander.[49]

The trouble to which Walker alluded was the near-mutinous action of several of the senior generals of the army, including Buckner, Hill, and Longstreet. In a petition signed by them and by nine of the junior general officers of the army in October, they asked President Davis to remove Bragg from command. Among the malcontents, Cheatham and Breckinridge did not sign; Polk, of course, was away in Atlanta. The conspiracy must have been kept secret from Walker. Judging by his future actions, if he had known of it he would have informed Bragg. As it was, Bragg heard of the petition from S. R. Liddell, who, although not a Bragg supporter, apparently was more honest and forthright than his superiors.[50]

When Jefferson Davis learned of the conspiracy, he came immediately to Georgia, stopping to visit Polk in Atlanta on the way, and after long consultation with Bragg and the other principals determined to leave the besieged commander in his place. Davis and Bragg then undertook an extensive reorganization of the army. Polk was sent off to Mississippi in exchange for Hardee. Hill was demoted and went back to North Carolina. Buckner's department and corps were broken up and he became, like Walker, a division commander. Nathan B. Forrest, who had quarreled with Bragg, was deprived of his command and sent to Mississippi. Cheatham and W. W. Mackall, the army chief of staff, asked to be relieved. Cheatham withdrew to Atlanta for several weeks while Mackall joined Joseph E. Johnston in Mississippi.[51]

On November 12, possibly to further his aim of reducing dissidence, Bragg ordered yet another reorganization. Cheatham's Tennessee division was largely broken up. Gregg's brigade of Walker's division was disbanded, its regiments going to other brigades. John Gregg left for Virginia, where he was killed in action a year later. Walker inherited George A. Maney's brigade from Cheatham's division. Other shifts were made to fragment the cores of support which their anti-Bragg leaders had enjoyed. This was the "considerable shuffling of the cards" to which Walker had referred.

Walker's division now consisted of the brigades of Gist, Wilson, and

Maney. Wilson's brigade gave up the 4th Louisiana Battalion, which had been with it since Savannah, but gained the 66th Georgia Regiment and the 26th Georgia Battalion, en route from the interior of Georgia. Gist's brigade remained unchanged. On November 20, the artillery of the division was formalized in a battalion under Major Robert Martin, who returned to the army after Chickamauga. The three assigned units were Howell's Georgia battery, Ferguson's South Carolina battery under Lieutenant René T. Beauregard, and Bledsoe's Missouri battery. Bledsoe's men, who styled themselves the 1st Missouri Battery (Confederate) were proud of their four new three-inch rifled guns captured at Chickamauga by Gregg's brigade from the 1st Missouri Battery (U.S.). Howell's battery had four old six-pounder field guns, and the Carolinians boasted four brass twelve-pounder Napoleons. This battalion would remain assigned or attached to the division until Walker's death.[52]

Maney's brigade was composed of the 1st and 27th Tennessee, 4th Tennessee Confederate, 6th and 9th Tennessee, 24th Tennessee Sharpshooter Battalion, and 41st and 50th Tennessee regiments, recently part of Gregg's brigade. Maney's Tennesseans, formerly of Cheatham's division, were unhappy under Walker. They found the strict military discipline of their new commander not to their liking and very different from the easygoing ways of Frank Cheatham. Even when Walker was on leave they objected to the dictates of S. R. Gist. The only balm in being transferred to Walker was that they would not have to serve under John K. Jackson, Cheatham's senior brigadier and temporary replacement during the few weeks the senior Tennessee general was absent from the army.[53]

Walker was anxious to go home on leave now that the fighting was over, but Bragg delayed his departure. He was one of Bragg's few supporters left in camp, and Bragg wanted to keep him around. Walker spent the time preparing his positions on the Confederate left on Lookout Mountain. On November 9, he was given command of Cheatham's division, temporarily under John K. Jackson, as well as his own. Walker's division was posted at the base of the mountain while Jackson's held a line about halfway up. Stevenson's division, not under Walker's command, held the mountaintop. That same day Walker and Hardee took Jackson up the mountain and Walker made recommendations for Jackson to lay out his lines near the Craven house. Jackson had a contradictory opinion about the best defense of the area, but he was hesitant about differing with a man of so much greater experience so he kept his silence. The issue would become important later.[54]

Walker finally obtained a twenty-day leave for himself and his staff and departed on November 12, leaving his division in Gist's hands. The *Augusta Chronicle and Sentinel* of November 14 reported that Walker had arrived in the city the day before "in excellent health and spirits." [55]

Bragg's strategy for taking Chattanooga was simple. The city, although not surrounded, was confronted on the south by Confederate forces who could bombard it at will from Lookout Mountain and Missionary Ridge. Chattanooga was open to the north, but the mountainous terrain made contact between Rosecrans and other Union commanders extremely difficult. The only supply line available was a torturous track across the mountains. Both Southern and Northern soldiers suffered from a lack of provisions while the two armies faced each other.[56]

Bragg may have wanted to use U. S. Grant's Vicksburg strategy of starving his opponent into submission, but he was not facing a Pemberton. After Chickamauga, Grant had been made commander of all Union forces west of the Alleghenies, the Military Division of the Mississippi. Rosecrans came under Grant's command. Grant came to Chattanooga himself to take charge in October, riding over the mountain on horseback. First, he relieved Rosecrans and placed Thomas in charge of the Army of the Cumberland. Then he arranged for an improved supply line by opening up the route of the Tennessee River. He brought in Sherman with four divisions of the Army of the Tennessee from Mississippi, and the War Department sent the XI and XII Corps by rail from the East under Major General Joseph Hooker, another of Walker's and Bragg's West Point classmates.[57]

One way for the Union army to relieve its supply problem was to shorten the supply route. Grant approved the plan of his chief engineer, General William F. "Baldy" Smith, to drive the Confederate force from its western position at Raccoon Mountain so that supplies could move by way of Brown's Ferry. In a nighttime operation on October 27, troops of the IV Corps secured a base on the south side of the Tennessee River at Brown's Ferry. The Confederates were compelled to withdraw their left, thereby opening up the river. The bulk of Hooker's force began to march forward from Bridgeport to Brown's Ferry. A single division, John Geary's, was left to guard the flank at Wauhatchie.[58]

James Longstreet, who commanded on the Confederate left from Lookout Mountain, had been warned of such an eventuality by Bragg several times. At first he chose to ignore the warnings; later he sent a force too small to defend Brown's Ferry. Longstreet believed that Hooker's real intention was to ascend the southern end of Lookout Mountain at a place called Johnson's Crook and come up in the Confederate rear. Even after Brown's Ferry was taken he thought it was only a feint to mask Hooker's move. Bragg, however, directed Longstreet to take action to recover that important river crossing. Again, Longstreet was dilatory and wished to send a brigade of Walker's division to Johnson's Crook. At length, on Bragg's insistence, he agreed to assault Geary's isolated division. Bragg put at his disposal both of the divisions he had brought from Virginia plus Walker's division, which was also a part of his corps.[59]

Rather than taking advantage of all this manpower, in a remarkable display of truculence, Longstreet, on the night of October 28, launched an attack with the single division of Micah Jenkins (Hood's division). The subsequent fighting was so confused that the reports submitted by commanders on both sides are largely incoherent. Three brigades were posted to prevent Hooker's troops from coming to Geary's support while one brigade attacked Geary. Fighting was heavy, but Geary beat off all attacks. One of Hooker's divisions, en route to assist Geary, was fired on by the interposing force and diverted from its primary mission. Another of Hooker's divisions, ordered to the attack, never made it. The final result was that Longstreet's corps was forced to withdraw. Walker's division took no part in the fight.[60]

Longstreet blamed the failure on everyone but himself. He faulted his brigade commanders; he blamed jealousy among the generals for their lack of cooperation; he thought the cavalry had failed by providing insufficient reconnaissance; he later stated he felt that Bragg's order for a corps attack was discretionary. The entire episode reflected poorly on the leadership and morale in the Army of Tennessee.[61]

While Grant was strengthening his army, Bragg was weakening his. Against the advice of his subordinates but with the concurrence of President Davis, on November 4 he sent Longstreet with his two divisions to try to capture Knoxville, another important rail center in east Tennessee. This was as much a political move on Bragg's part as a military one, one more step in ridding the army of the fomenters of the cabal that opposed him. On November 20, Bragg sent Buckner's division to assist Longstreet. Bragg had now virtually cleansed himself of opposition in his own army, or so he thought. Hardee had been brought back from Mississippi to take over Polk's corps. Breckinridge, reinstated to favor with the commanding general, had command of Hill's corps. Cheatham and Hindman were absent for the time being. The only remaining foes were the bluecoats in Chattanooga.[62]

By late November Grant had collected over seventy thousand men to face Bragg's fifty thousand. On his right, Grant had Hooker with a heterogeneous force of three divisions from the various corps. They faced Hardee's Confederate left with the divisions of Carter Stevenson, Cheatham, under John K. Jackson, and Walker, under S. R. Gist, on Lookout Mountain and both sides of Chattanooga Creek. In the center, Thomas's Army of the Cumberland, and on the left, Sherman's detachment of the Army of the Tennessee were confronted by Breckinridge's corps with the divisions of Hindman, led by J. Patton Anderson, Breckinridge's own, under William B. Bate, and Alexander Stewart, on the crest of Missionary Ridge. Bragg's entire position was weak. Lookout Mountain was nearly indefensible because of the nature of the terrain. Bragg had put half of Breckinridge's men in rifle pits at the base of Missionary Ridge where they would block the fire of those on the crest. Beyond that, he had committed the great blunder of deploying those at the higher elevation along the top of the ridge rather than along the "military" crest, that is, the point where they would have an unimpeded view of the area below.[63]

Grant launched his attack to relieve the siege on November 23 by having Thomas make a reconnaissance toward a height known as Orchard Knob on the right of Bragg's position. Grant wanted to know the truth of rumors, probably based on the detachments to east Tennessee, that Bragg was withdrawing. He also wanted to test the mettle of the Army of the Cumberland. Thomas's troops performed well, not only conducting the reconnaissance but actually taking Orchard Knob. Besides having gained ground, Grant acquired two useful pieces of information: the veterans of Chickamauga would fight and Bragg had no intention of leaving.[64]

Bragg reacted to this probe by strengthening his right flank at the expense of his left. As a result, Gist's (Walker's) division was withdrawn from the base of Lookout Mountain and sent to Missionary Ridge. The defense of the Confederate left remained in the hands of the eight thousand men of Jackson's and Stevenson's divisions under the latter's overall command. Bragg also brought back Cleburne's division and Reynolds's brigade of Buckner's, which were preparing to entrain for Knoxville, to extend his line to the right. Hardee was moved to the right to command Cleburne's and Gist's divisions. The stage was set for the battle of Chattanooga.[65]

Walker's division had received modest reinforcements during November. Since Chickamauga, it had been able to muster no more than thirty-three hundred effectives after its heavy losses. Wilson's brigade had been down to a strength of less than eight hundred and Gregg's to eleven hundred. Sometime between November 3 and November 20, however, the 26th Georgia Battalion arrived, and just before the commencement of the action around Chattanooga the 66th Georgia under Colonel James C. Nisbet joined the division. Both units were assigned to Wilson's brigade. Nisbet became the acting brigade commander because of the illness of Colonel Wilson. Gregg's brigade had been broken up on November 12 and replaced by Maney's weaker unit, but the transfer of two of Gregg's regiments to Maney resulted in a small net gain. These additions gave Gist a strength of forty-four hundred on the eve of the battle.[66]

On November 24, in the celebrated "Battle Above the Clouds," Hooker's three divisions, ten thousand strong, wrested Lookout Mountain from a rather inept defense by Jackson and Stevenson. E. T. Sykes, the adjutant of Walthall's brigade, was especially critical of Jackson's behavior. In characterizing Jackson, Sykes said, "He was a splendid officer in camps, but was deficient in the necessary element of a good commander in time of action." Hooker's success opened up the Federal supply line via the Tennessee River and the railroad from Alabama. In addition, Bragg's line of communications became vulnerable because there was nothing to block Hooker from penetrating down Lookout Valley to Bragg's rear.[67]

Meanwhile, on the Union left, Grant had launched Sherman to what they thought was the north end of Missionary Ridge, Tunnel Hill. They were much chagrined to find that the small rise Sherman occupied was separated from the ridge by a dip in the terrain which reconnaissance had not disclosed. Nevertheless, Sherman decided to hold and fortify it.[68]

Overnight Bragg brought Stevenson and Jackson from his left to reinforce his right and center. On November 25, Sherman reopened the assault on the Rebel right while Grant unleashed Thomas in the center up the face of Missionary Ridge. The result was disaster for Bragg. Although he had lost his positions on the left, he, Breckinridge, and Hardee were confident they could hold in the center and on the right. No one, including Grant, had counted on the pluck and perseverance of Thomas's men. In a seemingly impossible advance, they scaled the heights and attacked the Confederate lines. First one unit and then another of the center of Bragg's army broke and scattered. Their success, of course, was much aided by Bragg's poor deployment of his troops.[69]

Cleburne held the extreme right with Gist, Stevenson, and Cheatham, who had returned to the army the night of November 24, in order to his left, where they were holding their own against Sherman. As the center of Bragg's army disintegrated, he and Hardee realized they must take measures to prevent the right from being rolled up. Cheatham, on his own or by order, changed front with his three brigades to face left along the crest. With some difficulty they held their line but had to be reinforced by some of Stevenson's troops. Cleburne formed his own and Gist's divisions into a second line to protect Cheatham's flank. Gist's men were preparing supper, thinking the day's fighting was over because of Sherman's lack of progress against their front. They were hustled away from their cooking fires by Colonel Nisbet and other officers and hurried to their left into battle.[70]

As dark fell, Hardee began to extricate his units from the ridge top in a driving rain. First, Cheatham was pulled out, then Gist, Stevenson, and finally Cleburne. The artillery pieces had already been lowered by hand down the precipitous mountain trails, Colonel Nisbet of the 66th Georgia providing an escort and lighted pine torches for Lieutenant René Beauregard commanding Ferguson's South Carolina battery. As the troops retreated across Chickamauga Creek, which they had struggled so valiantly to gain two months earlier, Gist's division protected the rear of Breckinridge's corps while Cleburne performed the same service for Hardee. Once the army was across the creek, the bridges were fired and the men stopped for the night. When the retreat to Ringgold, Georgia, resumed the next day, Cleburne, supported by Maney's brigade, beat back the pursuing Federals. In the last stage of the retreat, to Dalton, Cleburne held a pass in Taylor Ridge for five hours with Gist in support until the rest of the army got safely away. For his part in this rear-guard action, Patrick Cleburne received the thanks of the Confederate Congress. Gist was commended by Bragg in his official report.[71]

Bragg's army suffered 6,600 casualties in the battles of November 1863. More than 4,000 of these were men counted as missing. Straggling and desertion were serious problems in the days after Missionary Ridge. Possibly as many as 7,000 men left the army before reaching or while at Dalton. Union losses totaled some 5,800. In Gist's division, losses were relatively light, 14 killed, 118 wounded, and 190 missing. Artillery losses were more serious. Two guns of Howell's Georgia battery, shifted to Lookout Mountain to support Walthall's brigade, were left behind after the Battle Above the Clouds. Despite the efforts of Colonel Nisbet and Lieutenant Beauregard, Ferguson's battery lost all four guns with their horses and equipage, three caissons, and their colors, plus 26 men, in the retreat from Missionary Ridge. Only Bledsoe's Missouri battery jealously brought off its four new guns.[72]

In a letter of explanation written on December 9, Major Robert Martin described the loss of Beauregard's guns to the lieutenant's father. He noted that the Yankees had not been able to carry the four cannon off the field and that General Hardee had sent out an expedition to recover them. The recovery operation did not succeed, and Martin asked if General Beauregard could supply from his command four pieces in their place. Martin also lamented that twenty-one of the missing men had still not returned.[73]

When Walker left Chattanooga it was with the understanding that Bragg would summon him back when Sherman's troops arrived from Mississippi. Bragg had not done so. Walker was not informed of events at Chattanooga until the battle was already under way, and he arrived back with the army only in time to see it retreating through Chickamauga. On December 2 he wrote to his wife, "Our army behaved badly at Chattanooga," but on December 3 he reassured her: "My division had been transferred from the left to the right before the battle and behaved handsomely under its gallant leader, Genl. Gist. I am perfectly satisfied with its performance." In a general order to his troops upon resuming command on November 27 he reiterated that theme, commending the men for their conduct at Chattanooga and exhorting them to renewed efforts in the campaign to come.[74]

On November 29, Bragg offered his resignation, which was accepted by the government on December 2. Characteristically, while claiming to accept responsibility for the defeat, he sought to lay much of the blame on his subordinates. Cheatham and Breckinridge were accused of drunkenness, others of failure to do their duty. This time there was no way Davis could avoid relieving Bragg. Hardee was named to temporary command of the Army of Tennessee on November 30.[75]

Bragg's command behavior following his victory at Chickamauga was inexcusable and indefensible. He failed to follow up and push the Union army out of Chattanooga. He exhausted himself in political squabbling with his generals. He frittered away his strength to east Tennessee in the face of evidence of Grant's growing forces. His frequent changes in organization, shifting of units, and poor tactical dispositions led to bad morale, weak command relationships, and the loss of Lookout Mountain and Missionary Ridge. His attempts, after the battle, to save himself by blaming others for the loss added less than honorable conduct to his other transgressions. No wonder, then, that Grady McWhiney, author of the first volume of Bragg's latest biography, is alleged to have given up on his subject in disgust.[76]

Walker, having satisfied himself of the honor of his command, spoke of Bragg's departure. "It was sad for me to part with Bragg. He has worked hard for two years. His enemies did their work. I hope they are satisfied." If there were any hard feelings left over from Chickamauga, he had forgotten them. Walker's support of Bragg had been mainly moral. He came to the Army of Tennessee too late and was of too low rank to have a serious impact on its politics. By that time, the clique of Polk, Hardee, Buckner, and the others had closed their ranks against Bragg. Walker was one of a few who if not openly supportive were at least sympathetic to Bragg. Others were Generals John K. Jackson, Joseph Wheeler, Alexander Stewart, William B. Bate, J. Patton Anderson, Henry D. Clayton, and Walker's associate S. R. Gist.

Despite Bragg's shortcomings, Walker had shown him support as much by omission as by commission. His name had not appeared among those asking for Bragg's removal. In none of his extant correspondence did Walker ever hint that he was a party to the conspiracy against Bragg. True, he wrote several times of his concern over the failure to follow up on the victory at Chickamauga, but this was an observation of military fact, not a personal attack on his commander. By the fall of 1863, however, Bragg's bumbling leadership, his inability to admit mistakes, and his near complete mental breakdown had finished him as a field commander. Nonetheless, Walker subscribed to Bragg's own thesis that he owed his failure to his detractors: "His enemies have done their work."[77]

It has been suggested that Bragg's fall signaled the end of the anti-Bragg coalition, that once their object had been obtained, their reason for being had evaporated. Whether this was true will be analyzed in the light of events that transpired early in the winter of 1864. Walker maintained his relationship with Bragg after the latter left the Army of Tennessee and was only too happy to correspond with him the next spring. Walker certainly had personal motives in cultivating Bragg, but there is little doubt he felt genuine sympathy for his old chief.[78]

While in Dalton, Walker also became involved in the issue of Jackson's command at Lookout Mountain. When they wrote their official reports of the action in December, three brigade commanders, Generals Walthall, Edmund W. Pettus, and John C. Moore, who had been involved in the fight, criticized Jackson for being impossible to find during the battle. Carter Stevenson, commander on the left, blamed the loss of Lookout Mountain on the withdrawal of Gist's division on November 23. Stevenson exonerated Jackson, saying he had acted properly in coming to Stevenson for orders in person, making him temporarily inaccessible to his subordinates.

Jackson was wounded on Missionary Ridge on November 25 and was temporarily hospitalized in Atlanta. When he returned to the army in December he challenged his former subordinates' version of events. Walker took up a correspondence on Jackson's behalf, and Walthall's version was presented by one of his captains, John B. Sale, a Mississippi lawyer. None of the letters have been found, but Walker's bellicosity can be imagined. Walker would have felt a personal interest in the matter because of the role he had played in advising Jackson on his position. One strange twist to the controversy was the involvement of so many pro-Bragg men. Walthall, Jackson, and Walker had been Bragg supporters; Sale became Bragg's military secretary in Richmond. So low was morale in the Army of Tennessee and so stressful the loss at Chattanooga that these former loyalists of the deposed commander found themselves on the brink of violence. At one point it was feared in the army that the case might result in a resort to duels, with Walker urging Jackson to "Call them out, sir! Call them out!" But when the facts became known, cooler heads prevailed and the matter was allowed to drop. Christopher Losson, Cheatham's biographer, concludes that the criticism of Jackson was not well founded. Given the nature of the weather and terrain, the Union superiority in numbers, the frequent changes in command structure, and the unfamiliarity of the troops with each other and their commander, no one, including the veteran Cheatham, could have done a better job on Lookout Mountain.[79]

Walker had written earlier of his wish to have additional troops brought in from Beauregard's command and from Mississippi and expressed the desire to have General Johnston take over the army at Dalton. The first wish was brought true by the arrival of William E. Baldwin's and William A. Quarles's brigades from Mississippi in December. Despite losses of only three hundred at Chattanooga, Walker's division could muster no more than thirty-four hundred effectives by the time it arrived at Dalton. The disparity was caused by straggling and desertions. The temporary addition of Baldwin's brigade of some sixteen hundred and the return of nearly three hundred of the absentees swelled his ranks to over fifty-three hundred by December 20. There were still only six guns available in the three batteries of artillery.[80]

Joseph E. Johnston did come to Dalton as Walker had hoped, taking command on December 27. Walker greeted the news with exultation. "If I had a bottle of champagne, I would open it on the occasion. For our country's sake I am rejoiced that he has been sent. He is my choice of all of them." Walker's delight in having Johnston brought to Dalton was as much personal as professional. For one, Walker was an acquaintance of Johnston's family of twenty-five years' standing. As he was to write to his wife a few months later, "Johnston and I have always been friends. For over a quarter of a century we have known each other," and "I admire him and am fond of him." Walker had known Johnston's brother-in-law, Robert Milligan McLane, at West Point. Although McLane had left the service in 1843 to pursue a career in the law and in Maryland politics, eventually taking a seat in the U.S. House of Representatives, it is likely that the former classmates kept track of each other. Walker's interest for the well-being of Lydia Johnston may have been based on his connection with her brother. Lydia Johnston's solicitude for Walker's family following his death probably had a similar basis.

If Walker was happy to see an old friend, he was no doubt elated to be reunited with the commander who had given him preference twice before. Johnston had recommended Walker for promotion to major general in Virginia in 1861 and had won that grade for him in Mississippi the previous May. Walker might have hoped that if a vacancy for a lieutenant general should occur in the Army of Tennessee in the coming campaign, he would receive the same consideration that he had in Mississippi. The evidence of his own letters following just such a contingency in June 1864 suggests that he did.[81]

On a professional level, Walker was one of those who credited Johnston for the Fabian-like quality of his tactics. To Johnston loyalists the campaign in Mississippi had been a failure not of their idol but of the Confederate government. Sent too late, with too small an army, with an uncooperative subordinate (Pemberton), and with no support from Richmond, Johnston had done well to save his own army let alone relieve Vicksburg. Writing to his wife from Mississippi, Walker had said, "We have at our head an old and tried and shrewd soldier."[82]

Johnston also had the admiration of the troops. Morale had been destroyed under Bragg, first by the wrangling of the generals, later by the defeat at Chattanooga. In the coming months, Johnston's assumption of command would restore the strength, tone, and spirit of his army. Not only the troops but the generals themselves, though still divided into two camps, seemed to respond positively to Johnston's presence.[83]

Finally, Walker might have viewed Johnston as a political ally. Taking as his motto the adage "The enemy of my enemy is my friend," Walker could have seen in Johnston a kindred spirit in his never-ending feud with Jefferson Davis. If Walker felt badly treated by Davis, how much worse must Johnston feel. For all of these reasons, then, Walker was ready to welcome Johnston to Dalton.

To dim his pleasure at Johnston's arrival, Walker had to mourn the loss to camp fever, or typhoid, at Ringgold, Georgia, on November 27, of General C. C. Wilson, who had gallantly led Walker's brigade since May. Walker had repeatedly recommended him for advancement to the rank commensurate with his responsibility, but the promotion had been long delayed. While Walker was on home leave, President Davis finally appointed Wilson a brigadier general on November 16. Eleven days later, following the retreat from Missionary Ridge, Wilson succumbed to typhoid at the age of thirty-two. His promotion was posthumously confirmed by the Confederate Senate the following January. The brigade continued under the temporary command of Colonel Nisbet, who had had tactical command on Missionary Ridge because of Wilson's illness. In early 1864, Clement H. Stevens of the 24th South Carolina, senior colonel of the division, who had recently returned from nursing his wound at Chickamauga, was promoted to fill Wilson's vacancy.[84]

On Christmas Day 1863, Walker hosted dinner for his staff at his headquarters. Katherine Hubbell Cumming, wife of the division chief of staff, who had come to Dalton to visit her husband, was there and remembered the dinner in her memoirs. As the old year ended, Walker contented himself with optimistic thoughts of the future and with memories of warm family Christmases in the past.[85]

13

EMANCIPATION

January 1864

WALKER WELCOMED the New Year 1864 with a letter to his wife in which he expressed his hopes, fears, and aspirations.

> A happy new year to you and my little flock. May the 1st of Jany. of [18]65 find us a free, prosperous and happy people. Only the prescience of that omnipotent, omniscient Being can know what are to be the events of the year 64. We, though, with our finite knowledge and with our poor mole's eyes can only judge of the future by the past and we must feel assured that many of the scenes that have been enacted in the last three years will be reenacted. I am satisfied that the North is in earnest and that the whole energies of her people will be brought to bear to destroy us as a people, to enslave us, to desolate our fields, and put a yoke on our necks that will crush the proud spirit of the South. This is their object. Heaven and earth are raised to accomplish this object. Let us then buckle on our armor. Let us prove to them and the world that we are not the degenerate sons of a noble race but that we will dare everything, suffer everything but a loss of our honor and our liberty.[1]

The doldrums of the winter season had set in. As many officers and men as could be spared were away on leave. Gist had gone home for Christmas, and Walker was the only general on duty with his division. He looked forward, as soon as Gist returned, to completing the leave that had been interrupted in November. The army's new commander, General Joseph E. Johnston, was concentrating on restoring the physical strength and moral spirit of his men.[2]

The day following the dispatch of Walker's letter to his wife, a new and momentous issue was thrust upon the general officers of the Army of Tennessee. On January 2, the corps and division commanders of the army received an invitation from Lieutenant General Hardee to meet with him at Johnston's headquarters in Dalton at 7:00 P.M. At the appointed hour the several officers assembled in a large room in the house where General Johnston was in residence. Present were Hardee, the second senior officer of the army; Major Generals Walker, Stewart, Hindman, Stevenson, and Cleburne; and Brigadier Generals Anderson and Bate. General Frank Cheatham, acting corps commander, had been detained and could not attend.[3]

After all the officers were assembled, Johnston opened the meeting by asking Hardee to introduce the main topic. Hardee took the floor and told the group that General Cleburne had prepared a paper on an important subject and wished to read it to them. Cleburne then took over. By way of introduction, he stated that he had already circulated the paper among the general and field officers of his division; many approved of it and a dozen, including Generals Daniel C. Govan and Mark P. Lowrey, had endorsed it with their signatures. Several other general officers had expressed a willingness to sign it. These remarks indicated that some of the generals present had been aware of what was about to transpire before the meeting took place.[4]

Cleburne then began to read his document. The long preamble was a recitation of the plight of the South. Cleburne reviewed the losses of the past three years and predicted a worsening of circumstances if "some extraordinary change" did not take place. He laid heavy stress on the numerical superiority of the North with its large white population, the constant influx of European immigrants, and its latest source of manpower, former slaves who now wore the Union blue.

None of this was news to the assemblage. It was a problem they wrestled with every day. It was Cleburne's next paragraphs that riveted their attention. He proposed that the South should begin immediately to arm slaves and, further, to free those slaves who would fight for the South to the end of the war.

As arguments to support his radical proposal, Cleburne cited improved hopes for foreign recognition and aid, removal of emancipation as a war aim in the North, elimination of the slave population as a source of aid and of recruits to the invading Yankee armies, and, most important, a new source of manpower for the South. He noted that freedom for the armed slave and for his wife and children would be a necessary inducement to get him to fight. Anticipating the question "Would slaves fight?" Cleburne listed historical incidents when blacks had fought for their own freedom or slaves had fought at the sides of their masters. He concluded by saying that although there were problems with his proposal, it was the most likely solution to allow the South to continue the war.[5]

After Cleburne had finished, Hindman spoke up in favor of the proposal and mentioned ways black soldiers could be used. No one else present agreed with Cleburne and Hindman. Bate and Anderson spoke against the idea. One of Cleburne's own staff officers joined the meeting and read a paper in opposition to the plan. The harshest criticism came from W. H. T. Walker.[6]

As he phrased it later in a letter to Braxton Bragg, Walker "blew out denunciatory" of Cleburne's plan. He "honestly believe[d] that the propagation of such sentiments in [the Southern] army will ruin [its] cause," he told Jefferson Davis later. Walker made clear to Cleburne and the others that he would make the proposal known to the president and would send him a copy of the document. He told them he would ask for each officer's opinion in writing and would send the answers to Davis. Walker then subsided, and Hardee turned the discussion to ways other than arming that might make slaves useful to the army. Finally, the paper was tabled, Cleburne withdrew his proposal, all present (with the exception of Walker) agreed to keep the topic quiet, and the meeting adjourned.

Walker's reaction was not merely a grandstand play or an act of jealousy against Cleburne and the other anti-Bragg men. It was a heartfelt cry of revulsion against violation of an ingrained, lifelong belief, one of the tenets of plantation culture in the South. As he later wrote to Bragg, Cleburne's ideas were at odds with "all the teachings of my youth and the mature sentiments of my manhood."[7]

His place of birth and his upbringing ensured that Walker would have a less than flattering view of blacks. In his opinion, they were born to be subservient to whites. In a letter to his wife in 1855 he had written: "I don't want any more white servants about me. I go in for the darkies," and "I don't think white people were ever intended to perform menial duties. God almighty intended, when he made the darkies, that they should be servants and he so stated in the Bible." Whites who attempted to elevate the social status of blacks or who treated blacks as social equals were also contemptible. The treatment accorded Frederick Douglass in the North earned Walker's special scorn. When Douglass was invited to sit in the speaker's chair in the New York legislature in 1855, Walker wrote to Mary, "This is going it rather strong for our notions down this way." Walker's support for Franklin Pierce in the election of 1852 had been based on

Pierce's support for Southern values. Walker wrote in a letter on October 30, 1852, "I believe the prosperity of our institutions depends upon the success of the Democratic party." Of Pierce he wrote, "[He is] a candidate whose career shows 'a clean bill of health' [regarding the slavery issue]."[8]

Walker's sense of financial prosperity centered around the slave economy. From his childhood he had been buying, selling, and mortgaging slaves. The records of the Richmond County, Georgia, probate and superior courts document at least four instances of Walker's slave transactions in his own right, not to mention several others that he handled for his aunt or his sister. The acquisition of the Mobley Pond plantation was based on the mortgage of twenty-five of his mother's and aunts' slaves to secure the bank loan. The census of 1860 had shown one hundred slaves living at Mobley. Although Walker railed at how much they ate and how expensive it was to keep them, he could not operate without them. Also, when there was no work for the hands on the land they could be hired out for cash income, as they had been to work on the railroad in 1852 and again in Savannah in 1863. Freeing the slaves would not only offend his moral sense, it would ruin his family financially and destroy his plans for the future.[9]

Walker believed that as important as slave labor was on the farms, firm control of the blacks was equally important. He expressed his opinion early in the war in a letter to Henry Wayne asking for a draft exemption for his overseer:

The owners off in the war and the neighborhood will be left completely to the negroes which will end in the destruction of the property and the demoralization of the negroes. It does seem to me that as the country will require to be fed and as the agricultural popu[la]tion is the largest and the country actually requires that crops should be made, that overseers should be exempt in thickly populated slave communities. I am willing to make any sacrifice in the cause individually but the country will be ruined if our plantations are deprived of their overseers whilst the owners are off fighting the battles of the country.[10]

Walker also believed that blacks were lazy, lustful, and dependent. At different times he wrote to his wife, "Yesterday I was beset by all of Aunt Zemula's hands. They are hired on the railroad and Negro-like don't like hard work but want to get back in the piney woods where they can lay in the shade these hot summer days," and "Naught disturbs my silent, quiet meditations but the occasional Ha! ha! ha! Oh Lord, of some darkie in the yard (this being the day for all the family negroes to gather from the four quarters of the globe to see 'old Miss' and, of course, to ask some favor)." On another occasion he wrote, "I have long since come to the deliberate conviction that human nature and negro nature are as an Hyperion to a Satyr." [11]

He often displayed the callous yet paternal attitude toward blacks common among his peers. When Zemula Walker's slaves were hired out to the railroad being built from Waynesboro to Augusta he found their working conditions so intolerable that he interceded on their behalf with the executor of his uncle's estate. Although he explained this by saying that "[I] really feel attached to the negroes that I have known all my life," it could also be seen as an effort to conserve a valuable asset. Yet he was ready to dispose of those assets when they were not to his liking. When a slave girl apparently burned a roast turkey, he told Mary, "The first thing I will have done is to turkey her in gail [sic] or in my pocket [sold]." [12]

Although he recognized that blacks could have human emotions, Walker could be selfish about the consequences. During the war his servant, George [Talbot?], so pined for his sweetheart at home that Walker wrote to his daughter: "Tell Becky George is dying to know how she is. As I don't want to lose a nigger, please let Becky console the poor brokenhearted constant lover at least with one sigh of remembrance." The emphasis was on "lose a nigger." [13]

Walker never said that the war he was fighting was to defend slavery, but he did make a pronouncement early on that he would fight against abolition. In a letter to the editor of the *Augusta Chronicle and Sentinel* dated January 9, 1860 [1861], he wrote, "As God is my judge, I will raise 'with uplifted arm' against the rule of a renegade southern abolitionist (Lincoln), let Georgia go as she may in her convention," and in the same letter he said, "I war for the South to govern the South." Toward the end of his life he wrote, "No power except the Power above could keep me from marching to meet an enemy who has come to . . . make free men of our blacks and blacks of our free men." With expressions and sentiments like these, it is no wonder that he "blew out denunciatory." [14]

Walker wasted little time in following up on the January 2 meeting. As he wrote to his wife on the seventh, "I have been going night and day for at least a week. Matters of pressing importance have occupied me both day and night." Within days of the meeting Walker asked Cleburne for a copy of what he is alleged to have called the "incendiary" proposal, making very clear that he intended to send it to Richmond. Cleburne gladly acceded to the request, even signing the document, although he refused to divulge the names of the other officers who had signed previously. On January 7, Walker sought and obtained a personal interview with General Hardee, accompanying that officer to the railroad depot on the night of his departure for his wedding. Hardee was noncommittal, then and later. After Hardee left, Walker wrote to him in Alabama asking for his views on Cleburne's plan. As late as March 1864, Hardee had not answered or acknowledged the letter, even after his return to the army.[15]

Next Walker addressed a circular letter to the other general officers who had attended the meeting. He asked each to state in writing his own opinion of the issues raised by Cleburne and gave notice that he would forward the responses to Richmond. In answer to his circular, Walker received from Generals Anderson, Bate, Stevenson, and Stewart "just such answers as you would expect Southern gen'ls. to make." Anderson thought the plan "would shake our governments, both state and Confederate, to their very foundations." Bate called the proposal "hideous and objectionable." To Stewart the idea was "at war with my social, moral and political principles." Stevenson was more amenable to the plan. Although firmly opposed to arming slaves, he thought they might be used in the army in other capacities.[16]

Other responses were outright hostile to Walker or, at best, noncommittal. Hindman, who had supported Cleburne at the meeting, denied Walker's right to question him. He objected to Walker's violation of the agreement on privacy and complained to Johnston about the Georgia general's interrogation. Cheatham, who had not been at the meeting, also refused to answer Walker on the grounds that Cleburne's plan was unofficial. At some point Bate had informed Walker that Cheatham had been named as willing to sign his name to Cleburne's paper. This heightened Walker's suspicion.[17]

Though he had not been asked, Johnston also had an opinion. In letters to a friend written shortly after the meeting, Johnston had spoken in favor of using slaves to perform camp duties so that soldiers might be freed for the front lines. This opinion approximated Hindman's and Stevenson's. Johnston was not the only one violating the privacy agreement. Patton Anderson wrote to Leonidas Polk in Mississippi on January 14 informing him of the "monstrous proposition," and Mary Boykin Chesnut in Richmond heard of it, probably from General John C. Breckinridge, on January 19.[18]

By the tenth Walker had collected as many answers as he had time for. He asked Johnston to forward the package of correspondence to Richmond through official channels, but the commanding general refused. Walker then penned a personal note to President Davis and sent off the package by special messenger. The cover letter explained his actions:

> I feel it my duty as an officer of the Army to lay before the Chief Magistrate of the Southern Confederacy the within document, which was read on the night of the 2d of January 1864, at a meeting which I attended. . . . The gravity of the subject, the magnitude of the issues involved, my strong convictions that the further agitation of such sentiments and propositions would ruin the efficacy of our Army and involve our cause in ruin and disgrace constitute my reasons for bringing the document before the Executive.[19]

After Gist returned, Walker went to Augusta on the twelfth to complete his leave of absence. A few days after arriving back at Seclusaval, he sent another letter to Davis clarifying his actions and motives.

> My excuse for sending the communication of Genl. Cleburne direct to you is that the Commanding Genl. of the Army of Tennessee declined for reasons satisfactory to himself to permit me to forward it through the regular official channel. My excuse for sending it at all is that I honestly believe that the propagation of such sentiments in our army will ruin our cause and that it is my duty to lay the document before the Chief Magistrate of the country. I have written a note to the Hon. H. V. Johnson requesting him to hand the sealed package to you and requested him to inform me of its safe delivery. The contents of the package he is not acquainted with.

Whether Walker sent Cleburne's paper and the generals' responses together or separately and which of them was carried by Herschel Johnson are details that are unknown.[20]

Davis responded to Walker on January 23: "I have concluded that the best policy under the circumstances will be to avoid all publicity." He also ordered Secretary of War Seddon to have Johnston prevent the further dissemination of Cleburne's paper. Seddon wrote to Johnston on the twenty-fourth. He praised Walker's action in forwarding the paper to Davis but at the same time approved Johnston's decision not to send it through official channels, thereby reducing the publicity it might have received. Seddon further instructed Johnston to ensure that all officers under his command maintain a discreet silence on the topic. Johnston complied with Davis's wishes, Cleburne agreed to destroy all copies of the paper (except the one sent to Davis, which was endorsed back to Cleburne by him), and the matter was thankfully shelved by everyone involved except for one man in Richmond.[21]

Braxton Bragg, who by his own request had been relieved from duty with the Army of Tennessee, was now Davis's military adviser. He was still smarting from the acrimonious exchanges with his subordinates during his tenure in command. He remembered well the factional division of his generals. He had not forgotten who had been his supporters and who had not. The responses given to Walker's circular in support of Cleburne's proposal showed that the division still existed. Almost to a man, those who had opposed Bragg in 1863 supported Cleburne. No wonder that Breckinridge in Richmond knew so quickly of the suggestion; he had been a party to the proposal before the meeting of January 2 took place. By contrast, Bragg loyalists generally lined up in opposition to the proposal.[22]

S. R. Gist was numbered among those who felt that Bragg had been ill-treated while at the head of the Army of Tennessee. On February 27, 1864, Gist wrote to Bragg congratulating him on his new appointment as presidential adviser and asking for his good offices in winning for Gist command of Breckinridge's old division. Bragg responded quickly. Through Gist, he sent a message to Walker flatteringly praising "my old and true friend" on winning a great battle against the "Abolition party of the South." Further, he went on, "I should like to know as a matter of safety the secret history of the treason and the names of the traitors."[23]

Gist received the letter on March 8 and answered the next day. He assured Bragg that he had read the letter to Walker, who would respond on his own. Gist said, "It is really a rich affair and I am delighted beyond expression to know that the traitors will meet with their just deserts at the hands of the 'powers that be.'" He added, "You will see that Hindman is one of the chief offenders and is, I think, the most dangerous man of all." The pro- and anti-Bragg factionalism did not die in November 1863; the groups simply found other issues to divide them.[24]

Walker allowed not even a day to go by before answering Bragg. On March 8, he fired off a four-page letter explaining the convening of the meeting, the subject matter discussed, the names and arguments of the proponents and opponents, and his own actions in bringing the matter to the president's attention. He gave in detail the responses to his circular letter. Then he went on:

You may well imagine that the course I have thought proper to pursue has made me no friends amongst the advocates of such overtures and I am happy to [report], as far as I can learn, the Army is sound, and if I have made some enemies, I have the proud satisfaction of knowing that these gentlemen reformers who have gone ahead of the Government, the People and the Army, are in a most glorious minority. As my duties throw me in contact with these gentlemen (Hardee, Cleburne and Cheatham are all in the Corps I am attached to), my first impulse was to apply to be transferred to some other army, but matters were so threatening here that I felt it my duty to *remain* as disgusted as I was and am with the whole affair.[25]

All of the "gentlemen reformers" were members of the anti-Bragg faction. This was exactly the information to discredit his detractors Bragg was fishing for when he wrote to Walker. Also, despite Johnston's admonition to his senior officers to maintain silence, Walker thought enough of his friendship with Bragg to give all the particulars asked for, ignoring Johnston, of whom he also thought highly. What motivated Walker?[26]

Describing Walker's motives as a petty desire to undo Cleburne (or Cheatham) in an attempt to advance his own ambitions, or jealousy of those two fine officers, is overstating the case. Cleburne and Cheatham both outranked Walker as major generals. There was no doubt that Cleburne was the best division commander in the western army. Cheatham, by virtue of longer service, had a Civil War combat record superior to Walker's. But the Georgia general had one distinct advantage over his two potential rivals, an advantage that was important in the estimation of the Confederate president and the commander of the Army of Tennessee: he was an academy-trained, regular army officer. Cleburne, whatever his leadership skills, had only negligible military experience before the war and was foreign-born besides. Cheatham had been a combat officer in the Mexican War but could claim no formal military training.

With only three exceptions, no Confederate officer ever rose to the rank of general or lieutenant general who was not a West Point graduate. Two of these, Nathan Bedford Forrest and Wade Hampton, were cavalry officers who were promoted in the last months of the war. Although Cheatham, Hindman, Breckinridge, and other nongraduates from time to time exercised temporary corps command, none of them was ever officially promoted to that grade. As far as unofficial promotion policy was concerned, Walker had little to worry about from his putative rivals. Indeed, those promoted to the rank of lieutenant general of infantry in the Army of Tennessee in 1864 and 1865 were all former regular officers: John Bell Hood, A. P. Stewart, and Stephen Dill Lee.[27]

Another factor Walker might have considered was favoritism. He had already voiced his complaint on that topic to W. W. Mackall in October 1863. Walker's own promotion to major general and his appointment as commander of Bragg's Reserve Corps were both marks of favoritism. The other non–West Point lieutenant general was Richard Taylor. His whole career, despite his outstanding qualities, was suspect of favoritism. Favoritism would play a part in the selection of a corps commander for the Army of Tennessee in July 1864. Favoritism plays a part in the politics of every organization. Even a successful officer needs a sponsor to get ahead. There was nothing Walker could do about this except to stay in favor with his patrons, Johnston and Bragg, an activity he practiced assiduously.

Finally, there was the matter of Walker's relations with Jefferson Davis, the ultimate patron in the Confederacy. Walker's resignation in 1861 was notorious. He was reinstated in 1863 because of the exigencies of the situation. In May 1863, Davis would have accepted anyone Johnston nominated for major general if it would help save Vicksburg. Johnston probably delighted in using that leverage to rectify the contretemps of 1861. But promotion to lieutenant general was a much more selective process. It would take some outstanding event or unusual crisis to overcome Davis's prejudice and allow him to consider Walker favorably for further promotion. In corresponding with the president on the emancipation issue Walker took advantage of just such an event. The proof of his missive's favorable reception was in the president's courteous response and Secretary Seddon's kind words of appreciation: "The motives of zeal and patriotism which have prompted General Walker's actions are . . . fully appreciated."[28]

In summary, in January 1864, Walker could feel fairly confident about his chances for promotion. He was junior by date of rank and had less Civil War combat service than Cleburne or Cheatham, but to offset these disadvantages, he was a West Point graduate with an extensive history of gallantry in the U.S. Army. As to favoritism, Walker could not hope that his handling of his corps in the small opportunities given him at Chickamauga could counterbalance the enviable reputation won by Cleburne at Missionary Ridge and Taylor Ridge. He also knew that Cleburne stood high in the estimation of William J. Hardee, their mutual corps commander. But Walker's long-standing social intimacy with the Johnston family, his close association with Bragg, Johnston's and Bragg's previous marks of approbation, and the fact that Hardee, Cleburne, and Cheatham were all in the anti-Bragg camp could cancel out the advantages of the other major generals.

The one unknown in Walker's promotion equation was Jefferson Davis. By 1864, had Davis "got his revenge out" as Walker was to remark at a later date? Only time would tell. Walker could help by giving Davis a nudge on the emancipation issue. Davis liked Bragg. Bragg was appreciative of Walker's activities in uncovering the "treason," therefore Bragg would have good words to say to Davis on Walker's behalf. Of course, Davis and Johnston hated each other, but Bragg stood at the president's elbow. Walker's action in sending his emancipation package directly to the president could well have been a ploy to impress Davis with his loyalty and reliability. As Walker had said of Franklin Pierce in 1852, so he hoped would be said of him in 1864: "He shows a clean bill of health." Walker did not need to undo Cleburne and Cheatham, he needed only to maintain or improve his own case.[29]

The theory of jealousy or pettiness is offset by all the actions and statements of Walker's adult life. There can be no denying that he acted with complete integrity, given the cultural values by which he lived, when he spoke out at the January 2 meeting. The thought of making black slaves the equal of free white men for any reason was anathema to him and he so reacted. Nonetheless, whatever the political overtones of Walker's letters to Davis and Bragg, and however Davis felt about Walker, no more was heard on the matter as the army turned to other pursuits.

Walker returned from home leave about February 12. He engaged at once in a round of brigade inspections and reviews to renew his acquaintance with the conditions of his men and probably to welcome some new units to the division. When he went on leave in January, the division was still composed of Gist's Georgia–South Carolina brigade, Wilson's, formerly Walker's, Georgia brigade, still under Colonel Nisbet, Maney's Tennessee brigade, and Baldwin's Mississippi brigade.[30]

Baldwin's brigade returned to Mississippi while Walker was away. Just about the time Walker returned, General Johnston effected one of the measures designed to improve the morale of the army. Johnston and Cheatham had taken to each other quickly after the former arrived in Dalton. Cheatham's veterans had been agitating for some time to be reunited under their chief. Those who were in Walker's division were especially unhappy under the strict discipline he imposed. Johnston decided to please Cheatham and his men by allowing the reformation of the Tennessee division. Maney's brigade was removed from Walker's division and exchanged for the Georgia brigade of John K. Jackson. Either by design or by accident, by so doing Johnston also created a Georgia division. From mid-February 1864 to his death, Walker frequently signed himself as "Major General, Commanding Georgia Division."[31]

Jackson was an Augusta lawyer who had commanded a brigade under Bragg at Pensacola. He had followed Bragg to Shiloh, into Kentucky, Murfreesboro, Tullahoma, Chickamauga, and Chattanooga. His tribulations on Lookout Mountain were recounted in the last chapter. He brought to the Georgia division the 5th, 47th, and 65th Georgia, 2d Georgia Sharpshooter Battalion, a battalion of the 1st Georgia Confederate, and the 5th and 8th Mississippi.[32]

The division was camped three or four miles east of Dalton, probably along Mill Creek on the Spring Place road. Richard Irvine Manning, an officer on General Johnston's staff, described Walker's camp. "Their camp is a beautiful one, very nice, snug houses—wide streets regularly laid off and looking like a village—the men well clothed and shod—in excellent discipline and well drilled." Johnston complimented Gist, acting division commander, on the appearance of his troops and camp, calling his brigade "the best in the army." Without taking anything away from Gist and his fine brigade, one perceives the hand of the old regular in camp layout and unit discipline.[33]

By the return of February 20, 1864, division strength was 4,723 effectives, 5,134 present for duty, and 6,119 aggregate present. This was all infantry strength, the artillery battalion having been detached and assigned to a regiment of corps artillery. Robert Martin was still artillery commander, and the composition of the battalion remained unchanged.[34]

Consolidation of organizations was not Joseph Johnston's only move to improve morale. The army he had inherited was in terrible condition, physically as well as psychologically. During Hardee's brief tenure of command in December, he had painted an overly rosy picture of the Army of Tennessee for the authorities in Richmond, but when Johnston took command, he set about the business of putting his army back on its feet.[35]

He began by providing the basic necessities of life. Shelter was already available in huts built by the soldiers themselves. This was fortunate in the unusually harsh winter of 1863–64. Food and clothing were lacking, principally because of the uncertainty of the supply line from Atlanta. Johnston addressed this issue personally. In addition, Walker, either by direction or voluntarily, opened up a correspondence with Georgia governor Joseph Brown on the army's use of the state-owned Western and Atlantic Railroad from Atlanta to Dalton.[36]

Besides acquiring food and clothing, Johnston took measures to increase army strength by declaring a general amnesty for deserters and absentees. The returns had already begun to show an increase in December, which continued throughout the winter. Walker's division showed an effective strength of some thirty-four hundred on December 10, 1863. By January 20, 1864, he had almost thirty-eight hundred effectives, and by February 20, over forty-seven hundred. For the rest of the winter, the number of effectives in the division never fell below forty-five hundred and stood at fifty-two hundred by the end of April.[37]

A system of home leaves for whole units was begun, officers were allowed to bring their families to camp, and steps were taken to improve arms and equipment. On their own, the soldiers turned to religious revivals, took up hunting to supplement their rations, and engaged in healthful outdoor activities. Discipline was strengthened by constant drilling, and officers attended schools of instruction conducted by their seniors.[38]

Reenlistments were encouraged with gratifying results. By the winter of 1864, the three-year enlistments of the men who had joined the ranks in 1861 were near expiration. Johnston's army stood fair to lose its corps of experienced veterans. A majority of those eligible did sign up for another term, sometimes encouraged by slightly questionable means but always with a justifiable end. In Hardee's corps of four divisions and an artillery regiment, 17,471 had extended their term of service by March 10. In Walker's division, more than 4,400 men reenlisted. His present for duty strength in enlisted men that day was 4,800, meaning that 90 percent of the men present were reenlisted veterans.[39]

Besides infantry strength, another serious deficiency in Johnston's new army was in artillery. Forty pieces of ordnance had been lost in the battles of November 1863. Walker's division alone lost six of its twelve cannon. Sufficiency of horses and draft animals for artillery, cavalry, and the army's trains was also a problem. Johnston addressed both issues. Large numbers of the army's animals were sent behind the lines where better forage was available. The artillery losses were made up, although not always with the most desirable types of guns. A comprehensive review of the artillery situation was carried out by General William N. Pendleton, chief of artillery in the Army of Northern Virginia, in March. Pendleton found that only about half of the guns in the Army of Tennessee could be considered reliable: the rest were ranked from serviceable to useless. He concluded that the horses were on a par with those found throughout the Confederate armies. Martin's battalion, in a concurrent rating by the artillery regimental commander, Major Melancthon Smith, was found to have all three batteries in generally good condition. Bledsoe's battery had four 12-pounder Napoleons, Ferguson was equipped with two 12-pounder Napoleons and two 6-pounder guns, and Howell had four 12-pounder howitzers. Fifty horses were needed to bring the battalion up to draft requirements.[40]

Walker worked diligently to drill and discipline his men. He also devoted much energy to providing for their physical well-being. Next to Johnston and Hardee, Walker was the senior officer in the army in length of professional service, and he could be counted on to keep his troops in fighting trim and high morale. Hardee's biographer, Nathaniel C. Hughes, comments that "Walker knew the business of war thoroughly and at Dalton brought his division around with startling rapidity." During this time, according to one source, Walker also took up a letter-writing campaign to his friends in Augusta extolling the morale and fighting spirit of the Army of Tennessee. Some of these letters found their way into the Augusta newspapers but, to prevent embarrassment to their author, were printed over a pseudonym and cannot now be identified.[41]

When Walker had first come to Dalton in December he found a residence about three miles from camp in a private home, the Morris house. He was the sole occupant of the house other than an ancient housekeeper and her husband. Although he was allotted a large room for his office and another for a bedroom, he preferred sleeping in his stove-heated double tent, which he pitched close to the side of the house.[42]

Officers' morale was improved by the visits of friends and family members. Walker's cousin and volunteer aide Captain Matthew H. Talbot took advantage of his leave to get married. Another aide, Lieutenant G. DeRosset "Derry" Lamar, brought his bride of the previous summer, Maria Cumming, to Dalton. Walker graciously gave up his room in the house to Mrs. Lamar, who described it thus: "The house is very comfortable and pleasantly situated. I can stick my hand out and touch General Walker's tent out the window. There is no furniture in the room, just three big windows without blinds or curtains. The general's office is just across the hall. There is an old couple here in charge of the house."[43]

The division chief of staff, Major Joseph B. Cumming, was Mrs. Lamar's brother. Later in the winter he went on home leave and brought his wife, Kate, back to Dalton, and she found quarters for herself. Other members of the official family were Major Nathaniel Tilton, quartermaster, Major A. C. Dearing, commissary, Dr. James Bowers, surgeon, Lieutenant Thomas H. Kenan, aide, and Lieutenant Lawson W. Magruder, ordnance officer. Captain J. Robert Troup, who had been badly wounded at Chickamauga, returned as Cumming's assistant during the winter. As a result of a ruling by the adjutant and inspector general's office that Walker could have only two staff officers for adjutant and inspector duties, Captain Samuel H. Crump, formerly division inspector, left the staff to rejoin his unit, the 12th Georgia Artillery Battalion, in Virginia. After Crump left, Walker assigned Captain William Henry Ross of Macon, a company commander in the 1st Georgia Sharpshooter Battalion, as his unofficial division inspector general.[44]

Just before Walker's return from home leave, the prospect of action in the field surfaced once again. Early in February, Sherman, who had returned to Mississippi after the victory at Chattanooga, launched an offensive toward the rail facilities at Meridian. Polk's army of three divisions was too small to intervene effectively. Cleburne's and Cheatham's divisions from Dalton were moved to Demopolis, Alabama, by rail. Walker was alerted to follow them. His baggage and supplies were loaded on the cars, but the crisis passed when Sherman withdrew, and Walker's orders were rescinded. During this episode, Thomas with the Army of the Cumberland moved forward in force from Ringgold toward Dalton on the suspicion that Johnston's army had been weakened to support Polk. This time Walker did leave camp in command of his own and Patton Anderson's divisions to protect the Tunnel Hill–Cleveland road. Again the Federals withdrew and the Southern troops returned to Dalton.[45]

Walker saw in these moves and an unassociated advance from the coast into interior Florida a coordinated Federal offensive. The Confederate victory at Olustee, Florida, on February 20, and the withdrawal of Sherman and Thomas, enabled Walker to report to Mary that the offensive had been defeated. Before leaving camp on February 24, Walker had penned a poignant note to his wife and left it in his portfolio to be sent to her in the event of his death. In it he wrote: "I fear not for my cause is just and the great God always protects a man in the discharge of his duty. Kiss my dear little ones for me and say to them how much their papa loves each and all of them and as for yourself, eighteen years marriage perhaps may have caused you to have discovered that I have always loved you." Even, perhaps especially, amid military crisis, Walker never forgot two of the principles for which he was fighting, devotion to duty and devotion to family.[46]

Suddenly a personal crisis erupted in Walker's life. His ordnance officer, Lawson Magruder, had visited Augusta in the late summer of 1863 while on a leave of absence. While there he was introduced into local society with the families of General Walker, Major Cumming, and Doctor

James B. Walker, the general's business agent. In the course of these social rounds, Magruder met young Molly, age sixteen, fell in love, and decided she was the girl he would marry. Molly, apparently, was equally infatuated. Magruder was well received by Mrs. Walker, but all involved feared the response of the father when "what had passed should be laid before Genl. Walker whom we all dreaded knowing his notorious fastidiousness about [Molly's], I may say foolishness." [47]

The young captain was much taken with "Mrs. Genl. Walker [who is] a most excellent and elegant lady. . . . She is a woman of *superior* intellect and one of the *best* women in the world (much too good for the General)." Describing Molly, he wrote: "She is tall and slender, of brown hair and a dark bright full eye. . . . She has been most rigidly raised never goes out without her mother, and never enters the parlor without her. . . . She is *anything* but worldly minded or giddy. . . . She is for her age remarkably dignified, sensible and quite intelligent." [48]

Although Magruder had been in the army for nearly three years, he was only twenty-one or twenty-two years old. A student at Princeton College when the war began, he had enlisted as a private in 1861 and served at Manassas before obtaining a commission. He had been on Walker's staff since the latter's arrival in Mississippi and was a veteran of the Chattanooga campaign, where he had been commended for his attentiveness to duty at Chickamauga. Later, Walker had recommended him for promotion to captain. [49]

Magruder apparently went to Augusta to visit Molly again in March. Walker was alerted to the situation by a letter from his wife, Mary, and by Magruder's straightforward approach in asking for Molly's hand. The young suitor told the father that he was aware that the girl was underage and was willing to wait for her, but with or without the general's approval he meant to marry her.

Walker's outrage was predictable in its violence. Apparently he saw no parallel between his courtship of seventeen-year-old Mary Townsend over the objections of her family in 1846 and Magruder's attentions to his sixteen-year-old daughter in 1864. He demanded to know by what right Magruder had "made love to my daughter," apparently in the romantic, not the sexual, sense. Magruder replied that he had had the girl's mother's permission to call on her. This response drew a blast to the young lieutenant that he was never to see Molly again and another one, in writing, to Mary about her responsibilities as a mother. [50]

The parents thought this interview had settled the matter but were soon horrified to learn that the two young people had been corresponding through an intermediary, the daughter of Dr. James B. Walker. What is more, apparently a plan was afoot for Molly and her friend to visit Atlanta for a secret rendezvous with Magruder. Walker's rage knew no bounds, but he had the good sense to take it out on Mary rather than Molly. He must have realized that his peremptory orders would be met with stubborn disobedience.[51]

Walker began to find many faults in Magruder. Despite the commendations and recommendations of the previous year, he was an indifferent ordnance officer. He was the outcast of the officers' mess, where others dealt with him only on official business. His father in Mississippi was a drunkard and his mother the hardest of hard cases. When the army had been in Mississippi, Magruder had been so ashamed of his parents that he had never invited the other officers of the staff to visit, even while they were camped in his hometown.[52]

When Mary came to visit Walker at Dalton in April, she picked up the litany. She wrote from camp to Molly that the things her father had told them were only one-tenth of what was wrong with Magruder. All the officers in camp knew his reputation as a liar and a scoundrel. So lost to conscience was he that he had tried to read one of Molly's letters aloud for the enjoyment of the mess until Derry Lamar stopped him. Walker and his wife wrote jointly to Molly urging her to ask for her letters back, to return to him all the letters and poetry she had received from him, to return future mail from him unopened, and to put him out of her mind forever. Perhaps she did, for his name never came up again. Walker had Magruder shifted to the division of William Bate posthaste and had no further association with him to the day of his death.[53]

At this distance in time and without more information, the facts of the case cannot be known. The disapproving parents would certainly look for any discrediting reports they could find. In fairness to Magruder, it must be said that he served faithfully to the end of the war, surrendering as ordnance officer of William F. Brantley's Mississippi brigade in North Carolina in May 1865. In later years he had a career, if not distinguished, at least successful, as a lawyer and politician in Jackson and Vicksburg. He served on various boards and commissions and was an officer in the United Confederate Veterans. E. T. Sykes, writing about 1902, called him a "noble fellow" and mentioned that "his many, many friends, who are legion, deplore his [recent] affliction." After the war he married and fathered seven sons, several of whom had distinguished military careers. Two became flag officers in the U.S. Navy. Later generations, including the present one, have also produced outstanding military officers. It is hard to understand what the Walkers could have found so objectionable in the young officer of 1864. Only one clue did Captain Magruder leave us. Writing to his father about his relationship, he admitted that he had been "foolish" and "indiscreet" in his attitude about women in the past. Perhaps this was indicative of the indiscretion of which the Walkers complained so loudly later.[54]

This incident is most important for its portrayal of Walker as a man defending his family honor. If he believed everything he wrote about Magruder, that young man was certainly not an acceptable suitor for Molly. As Magruder phrased it, Walker was "fastidious" about Molly's behavior and associations. In addition, Magruder did the family dishonor by persisting. Under the code of Southern honor, Walker was perfectly justified in the harshness of his reaction because he was protecting not only his family's name but also his own reputation as a respectable patriarch. If the women of his family could be sullied without his reproach, then he was subject to opprobrium as an unfit father.[55]

Mary came to Dalton in April. Walker had been asking her to pay him a visit all winter long. When she finally made the trip, she regretted not having done so sooner. She was delighted with the attention paid to her although taken aback by what she heard about Lawson Magruder. Mrs. Lamar made way for her in the general's quarters, and she made herself comfortable. The Walker, Cumming, and Lamar wives made a striking social set for a time. Kate Cumming was a New Yorker like Mary, and all three had roots in Augusta. For some reason, there was later a falling-out between Mary and Maria Lamar, and Walker felt that Kate took her sister-in-law's part. Kate Cumming noted in her memoirs, however, that "Maria and I had had some differences at Dalton, and our relations were strained." As a result of those strained relations, Derry Lamar asked for a transfer, and in early July he moved to the staff of his brother-in-law Alfred Cumming. But in the early days at least, there was harmony on the distaff side in the Georgia division.[56]

When the full facts of the Magruder affair became known, Walker and Mary instructed Molly and Willie, Jr., to join their parents in Dalton, leaving the two younger children with their aunts. Molly was courted, although circumspectly, by many of the young officers of the division. Willie, Jr., eight years old, had a lifelong memory of wearing a Confederate uniform, riding a white pony around camp, and being introduced to General Johnston.[57]

Brigadier General William W. Mackall, chief of staff to General Johnston, had some definite and amusing impressions of the Walker family visit in Dalton, which give some indication of what life must have been like in the Walker household.

Late in April, Mackall commented facetiously in a letter to his wife, "About half past 1. o'clock William H. Walker came in and he only talked till 15 minutes of four, at this hour, thanks to the fates, he was obliged to go to the cars to meet his daughter." Three days later, Mackall wrote, "Yesterday the Genl. [Johnston] and myself went over to see Mrs. Walker, where I suppose we spent an hour. William was sick a little and therefore not in a condition for his best talking but his wife filled the space very well." Finally, on May 2, Mackall observed: "Yesterday, Genl. Joe and I went over to see Walker's daughter. She is a pretty girl, very talkative and self-possessed, but I much prefer my own daughters manners. I do hate this eternal chattering whether it proceeds from a desire to display or the mere habit of letting your jaws wag." Life with the Walkers must have been lively indeed.[58]

The Walkers and Johnstons were close. Correspondence passed back and forth between the husbands and wives. Walker had earlier told Mary to invite Lydia Johnston to come and stay at Seclusaval if she could find no other home in Georgia. She never did, instead spending her time away from the army in Atlanta or Macon. She was usually seen with her companion, Mrs. A. P. Mason, the wife of the army's assistant adjutant general and the daughter of Confederate assistant secretary of war John A. Campbell. Campbell, a Georgian by birth, was a former associate justice of the U.S. Supreme Court, and Walker referred to him as a friend. Other wives in camp who helped to make up the social circle were the new Mrs. Hardee and Mrs. S. R. Gist.[59]

One other arrival in Dalton that winter was the new commander of the corps temporarily led by Thomas C. Hindman. After D. H. Hill had been relieved by Bragg in October 1863, his corps had been commanded by Breckinridge at Missionary Ridge. When that general left the army in December, Hindman acted as commander pending the appointment of a new lieutenant general. President Davis never sent Hill's name to the Senate for confirmation; consequently, his commission as lieutenant general was vacated when Congress reconvened. Seeking a commander who would bring verve and aggressiveness to the Army of Tennessee, Davis chose John Bell Hood, West Point class of 1853, and a stellar brigade and division commander in the Army of Northern Virginia. Hood had lost the use of

an arm at Gettysburg and had lost one leg at Chickamauga when he led
Longstreet's corps in that battle in September 1863. Despite his physical
handicaps, he had an outstanding reputation as a bold fighter. He was also
socially intimate with the Davis family while convalescing in Richmond.

Davis nominated Hood for promotion, and he was confirmed to rank
from September 20, 1863. Some officers senior to him as major general were unhappy over his appointment, but Hill, whom he superseded,
thought that Hood had won the promotion fairly. Hood arrived at Dalton
on February 25 and took command of his corps on the twenty-eighth.[60]

Before the arrival of the wives, social life had been grim in Dalton. On
one occasion, about the time of Thomas's reconnaissance in February,
Walker had tried to arrange a ball. It never occurred, for as he wrote, he
"could not drum up enough females about here now for a game of soli-
taire." With the ladies in camp, and with the end of winter, the different
corps of the army spent some of their energy on sham battles. Walker was
glad that one scheduled for his division for April 1 did not happen, but
another one was dramatically conducted later in April, no doubt much to
the delight of the guests.[61]

Of all the events and personages in Dalton that last hopeful winter of
the Confederacy, nothing evoked more comment in after years than the
celebrated snowball battles. The winter of 1864 was extraordinarily cold
and was marked by frequent and enduring snowfall. Early in the winter,
the men, few of whom had ever seen more than a dusting of snow, turned
to snowball fighting for recreation and for relief from boredom. Some of
the fights involved whole units and some turned into brawls and vandalism
when the outcome of the sport was not to the liking of one side or another.
Frequently, men not satisfied with the impact of mere snow would lace
their ammunition with stones, leading to broken heads and teeth. Some,
however, did not know how to make a snowball. When one group overran
another's camp, they were prone to looting or downright stealing. When
Walker returned from leave in February, he formally protested the "dis-
orders" committed by Otho Strahl's brigade of Tennesseans in Cheatham's
division against John K. Jackson's brigade.[62]

Late in March, after a snowfall of five or six inches, snow fighting broke
out generally in the army. Two brigades of William B. Bate's division
fought against each other, then united to stave off an attack by Alexander P.
Stewart's entire division. Two of the brigades in Cleburne's division were
pitted against each other in a staged match. Cleburne led his old brigade
himself and was captured and paroled. When he saw that his brigade was

Lithograph of the "snowball battle," which involved several Confederate divisions, including Walker's. From Joseph M. Brown, *The Mountain Campaigns in Georgia; or, War Scenes On the W. & A.* 5th ed. Buffalo, N.Y.: Art-Printing Works of Matthews, Northrup & Co., 1890.

still getting the worst of the fight, he violated his mock parole to rejoin the fun. Once more he was captured and threatened with dire punishments, but he was finally pardoned by the men to whom he had never before broken his word.[63]

None of the snow battles excited more interest than that between the Tennessee and Georgia divisions. The two divisions were camped close to each other, separated only by a creek bed, probably Mill Creek. Rivalry between the two was intense. Maney's and Jackson's brigades had been exchanged between the divisions only a month before. The Tennesseans had not liked the discipline in Walker's division, and some bad feeling may have lingered over the incident involving Strahl's men.

After some desultory fighting during the morning, one side or the other issued a challenge, which was quickly accepted. Lines possibly a mile long were drawn up on each side. Estimates of the total number of combatants run to five thousand or more. Snow ammunition was stockpiled. The affray began when Cheatham's men charged across the creek and up the hill against the Georgians. They had not brought enough ammunition with them and were driven back. The Georgia division counterattacked, and charges and countercharges continued for hours. Finally, when both sides were exhausted, the battle came to a temporary halt.

The first combat had been led by enlisted soldiers acting as officers. Now a bona fide field grade officer appeared to lead each side. For the Tennesseans, it was Colonel George W. Gordon of the 11th Tennessee; for the men of Walker's division, an unidentified major. Seizing a make-shift banner, Gordon rode right into the Georgia lines. Following their colonel's lead, the Tennessee men sprang forward and routed their opponents, even capturing the Georgia camp and looting it. At least one source says Walker took part in this combat and personally demanded the return of his men's provisions, which was refused. Colonel James Nisbet claimed that he was captured and paroled during the fighting.[64]

When most of the Georgians refused to renew the fight, two of the Tennessee brigades turned on each other and continued for the rest of the afternoon. Not all of the Georgians, however, gave up so easily. Perhaps still harboring resentment from the February incident, the men of John K. Jackson's brigade turned against those of Otho Strahl. It was an ill-conceived move. Summoning help from other brigades, Strahl's men counterattacked and captured Jackson. In response to a demand from his captors, the general praised their prowess and wished them as much success against the Yankees as they had had against his Georgians. Cheers were given for Georgia and Tennessee, and the men retired to their huts.[65]

Warmer weather brought back the reality of the impending spring campaign. In anticipation of the Yankee offensive, General Johnston informed the ladies on May 1 that it was time to leave, and the dependents were shipped off to Atlanta about May 6. The ladies were serenaded at Walker's headquarters before their departure. Gist's brigade held a dress review for their general and his wife on their first wedding anniversary, May 6, before she left. Many years later Kate Cumming remembered that she and Mary Walker and their children had ridden in two ambulances over a corduroy road to Dalton to catch the train to Atlanta. They spent the night at a house in Dalton while soldiers dug up the garden outside for trenches. The guests left just in time for Sherman had begun his forward movement on May 4.[66]

14

THE LAST CAMPAIGN

February–July 1864

ON MARCH 9, 1864, U. S. Grant was elevated to the rank of lieutenant general and given the chief command of all the Union armies in the field. His successor as head of the Military Division of the Mississippi was William T. Sherman. Grant moved his headquarters to Virginia, the better to coordinate his strategy of involving the Confederacy on all fronts. Whereas in 1863 there had been cooperation between theaters, in 1864 the Federal offensive would be totally integrated. Under Grant's general instructions, Sherman was left largely to his own devices to "break up" Johnston's army and "inflict all the damage you can against [the South's] war resources." This meant getting to Atlanta, the rail hub of the Deep South and the second most important city in the Confederacy. The coordinated spring campaign was to begin the first week in May.[1]

Sherman indicated his understanding of the grand design and his role in two letters. To Grant he replied, "I will not let side issues draw me off from your main plan, in which I am to knock Joe Johnston, and do as much damage to the resources of the enemy as I can." In another letter to Grant's aide, Cyrus B. Comstock, Sherman put it even more succinctly: "Concurrent action is the thing," and "We saw the beauty of time in the battle of Chattanooga and there is no reason why the same harmony of action should not pervade a continent."[2]

If the strategy of the Union forces for 1864 was clear to the principals concerned, the same could not be said for the Confederate side. Even before Johnston had formally taken command of the Army of Tennessee, he had been besieged by the authorities in Richmond with plans for a spring offensive. President Davis, Secretary of War Seddon, and, later, military adviser Braxton Bragg, had urged Johnston to take the initiative by advancing into Tennessee. All winter long the drumbeat of appeals and urgings was kept up. Although Johnston was cautious by nature, he was fully justified in refusing to attempt such an effort with the resources he had. While Davis and Seddon constantly magnified the strength of Johnston's army, that general continually played down his capabilities. That Bragg joined the chorus for offensive action was almost ludicrous. He, better than anyone, should have known the weaknesses of the army he had recently commanded. Even Robert E. Lee urged Johnston to advance to prevent Federal reinforcements being sent to Virginia. Despite all these blandishments, Johnston proposed a strategy of waiting defensively at Dalton for a Union advance, defeating the Northern army, and then moving into Tennessee. Hood was probably sent to command a corps in his army in part to bolster Johnston's offensive spirit. The issue was decided, not by any harmony in Confederate command circles but by the unfolding events of Grant's and Sherman's plan.[3]

By May 1864, Sherman had over one hundred thousand men arranged in three armies. There were seven infantry corps, a cavalry corps, and lines of communications troops. In the Army of the Cumberland, commanded by George H. Thomas, the IV, XIV, and XX corps contained seventy-two thousand men. This was Sherman's strongest army and made up the center of his position around Chattanooga. Thomas's three corps commanders were Major Generals Oliver Otis Howard, a one-armed regular army veteran of Chancellorsville, Gettysburg, and Chattanooga; John M. Palmer, a militant antislavery politician-soldier from Illinois; and Joseph Hooker, Walker's West Point classmate, former commander of the Army of the Potomac, and victor at Lookout Mountain the preceding November. Thomas also had three cavalry divisions grouped in a corps led by Brigadier General Washington L. Elliot.[4]

Next in size was the Army of the Tennessee, Grant's and Sherman's old command from Vicksburg and Chattanooga. Only five divisions of the army were present with Sherman, some having been sent off on an expedition up the Red River in Louisiana in March and others still en route from west Tennessee. The new army commander was Major General James B. McPherson, whose rise in the western armies, under Grant's and Sherman's patronage, had been phenomenal, from lieutenant of engineers to major general commanding an army in two years. In the XV Corps under Major General John A. Logan, the fiery Ohio radical Republican, there were three divisions; Major General Grenville M. Dodge led two divisions in the part of the XVI Corps in east Tennessee. McPherson had twenty-five thousand men present for duty.[5]

The smallest contingent in Sherman's horde was the Army of the Ohio, a single army corps, the XXIII, with an attached cavalry division. Major General John M. Schofield, a West Pointer who had been a philosophy instructor there when Walker was commandant of cadets, commanded both the corps and the army. The commander of the cavalry was Major General George Stoneman. McPherson's army was deployed on Thomas's right and Schofield was on his left.[6]

Against this massive force Johnston could field an effective strength of only forty-four thousand of all arms. His army was still divided into two corps. William J. Hardee, the senior lieutenant general, commanded the divisions of Patrick R. Cleburne, Benjamin F. Cheatham, William B. Bate, and W. H. T. Walker. John Bell Hood, who had arrived in the army in February, was at the head of the three divisions of Thomas C. Hindman, Carter L. Stevenson and Alexander P. Stewart. Major General Joseph Wheeler continued as commander of the cavalry corps. The artillery of the army had been taken away from the individual divisions and brigades and massed in corps-level regiments. The army's chief of artillery was Brigadier General Francis Shoup. Colonel Melancthon Smith commanded the artillery in Hardee's corps. Hardee and Hood each counted twenty thousand infantry and artillery in his corps, Wheeler commanded only about twenty-five hundred cavalry, and there was a small artillery reserve. Brigadier General James Cantey's brigade from the Gulf area was included on the return for April 30 but had not arrived.[7]

Walker's division was as strong as it had been at any time since he had joined the Army of Tennessee in the summer of 1863. He now had four brigades and could truly call his the Georgia Division. To the brigades of Gist, Stevens, and J. K. Jackson on May 2 had been added that of Hugh Mercer, composed initially of the 54th and 63d Georgia regiments, brought from Beauregard's coastal department to reinforce Johnston's army on May 2. Mercer's brigade was intended to be exchanged for two regiments from John K. Jackson's, but Johnston did not release Jackson's until several months later. Mercer had been Walker's superior when the latter was brought back to active duty in March 1863; the two seem to have achieved a comfortable relationship in their new roles.

Another addition to the division was the balance of the 1st Georgia Confederate, which arrived from Mobile to join the battalion already in Jackson's brigade. Walker's escort was a company of the 53d Alabama. The division's assigned artillery support was the same battalion of twelve guns in three batteries under Major Robert Martin. The strength of the division at the outset of the campaign was about fifty-two hundred effective infantry, and Mercer brought another fourteen hundred. A Tennessee veteran who saw the new regiments arriving in camp was awed by their size as well as their lack of experience. Robert D. Smith wrote in his diary, "This morning I saw a regiment [sic] 1400 strong just from Savannah. It has been in service nearly three years but has never been in a fight." Private Samuel McKittrick of the 16th South Carolina was equally awed by the division's size. In a letter to his wife on May 4 he estimated Walker's strength at six thousand infantry and noted that the division formed a column more than two miles long when on the march, excluding wagons and ambulances.[8]

Much has been made of the relative strengths of the two armies at the outset of the Atlanta campaign and of the different ways the Northern and Southern armies counted their soldiers. In the Union forces, strength was usually given as "present for duty," meaning the number of officers and men available for duty in each unit. The Confederacy had several different yardsticks for preparing unit returns. First was "present for duty," the number of officers and men present in each unit. Next was "effective strength," which counted only the number of enlisted soldiers standing in line with muskets in their hands. Officers, some noncommissioned officers, and men on sick call or on detail were excluded. Finally, a count was taken of "aggregate present," what in modern wars has been referred to as the "ration strength," the total number of souls under command. Sometimes the return also included "aggregate present and absent," the sum total of all names carried on the unit rosters. This last item included those who were absent on detached duty, absent with leave, absent without leave, absent sick, prisoners of war, every category of unit member who was still borne on the rolls but was not present, as well as those actually in camp.[9]

Southern commanders, notably Joseph E. Johnston, preferred to give their effective strength. Their critics, political or military, usually pointed to their present for duty strength. Johnston, like many commanders, always minimized his own strength while magnifying that of the enemy. During the offensive-defensive debate in the winter of 1864, he used this stratagem to argue for defensive action, while the Richmond authorities always pointed to the number of men present for duty as a measure of his ability to fight offensively. The same had been true during the Mississippi campaign of 1863 and would be later when he was in front of Atlanta in July.[10]

Johnston always claimed he was outnumbered more than two to one when Sherman began to advance on Dalton. Some Northern authorities have calculated the strength of the Army of Tennessee differently. Jacob Cox, E. C. Dawes, and others have used the present for duty strength to show that Johnston had 60,000 men available on May 4, 1864. Some of their calculations are erroneous and possibly contain duplications, but it is safe to say that using the Northern method of figuring strength, Johnston had between 55,000 and 60,000 men in his army when the campaign began. Using this method of computing strength, Hardee had 23,000 and Hood had over 21,000 on April 30. Wheeler's cavalry jumped from 2,500 effective to 8,000 present, mostly made up of men whose horses were in the rear but were brought forward in time for the opening of the action. Walker counted 5,750 present for duty on April 30, and Hugh Mercer probably brought another 1,600. Estimating the artillery battalion at 250 would bring the total number of men assigned or attached to the Georgia division to more than 7,500.[11]

Whether his strength stood at sixty thousand or forty-five thousand, Johnston was still seriously outnumbered, but he was sufficiently strong that Sherman could not break through merely by frontal assaults. The Northern plan, then, was a series of holding actions on the front while other forces attempted to get around one of Johnston's flanks. The campaign opened with just such a move. While Thomas's Army of the Cumberland advanced along the railroad directly in Johnston's front and Schofield's Army of the Ohio threatened the right, McPherson's Army of the Tennessee tried to turn (get around) Johnston's left or southern flank.[12]

Johnston had his army arrayed north to south along Rocky Face Ridge west of and protecting Dalton, with part of his right wing thrown across Crow Valley to the north. Hood was on the northern flank, which Johnston considered the most threatened. His divisions, from the right, were those of Hindman, Stevenson, and Stewart. Hardee's corps was on the left, or south, with Bate, Cheatham, and Cleburne. Walker was in army reserve behind Hood's corps.[13]

Johnston's position behind Rocky Face Ridge was not as strong as he supposed. The ridge was cut by three gaps. On the north was Mill Creek Gap or Buzzards Roost. Through it ran the rail line and road from Chattanooga to Atlanta. Several miles south was Dug Gap. At the far southern end of the ridge was Snake Creek Gap, which opened onto Resaca, a village on the railroad. Johnston was ready to defend Mill Creek Gap, and

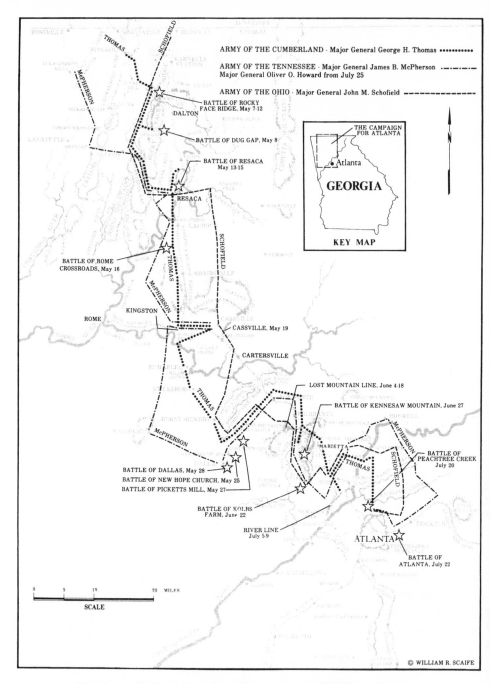

The Campaign for Atlanta from May 7, 1864, until Walker's death
on July 22, 1864

he had Dug Gap screened with cavalry, but from ignorance, carelessness, or confidence in his perception of Union plans, he left Snake Creek Gap undefended, an unfortunate oversight.[14]

Long before the campaign had started, Thomas had suggested that he move south along the western side of Rocky Face, pass through Snake Creek Gap, and debouch into the open at Resaca. In one swoop he could get in Johnston's rear and cut the line of communications to Atlanta. Sherman did not immediately approve Thomas's suggestion, but when he finalized his plan of action he made use of Thomas's idea, instead sending McPherson's smaller and presumably more maneuverable army. Sherman may have felt that Thomas moved too slowly and that McPherson would be more aggressive in his approach. Perhaps he also wanted to keep his largest army in the center of his advance. At any rate, while Thomas and Schofield advanced straight down Crow Valley toward Dalton from the north, McPherson would make the end run around Johnston's left.[15]

In the first two days of the action Johnston was completely taken in by Thomas's advance and shifted two more divisions, those of Bate and Cheatham, from Hardee's corps to Hood's flank to strengthen the right. Meantime, McPherson had felt his way down the west side of the ridge. He found Mill Creek Gap hotly defended, Dug Gap covered only by cavalry, and Snake Creek Gap, further south, defended not at all. The Western and Atlantic Railroad, Johnston's supply line to Atlanta, ran through Resaca only five miles east of Snake Creek Gap. Resaca was held by James Cantey's division, his own brigade, and that of Daniel H. Reynolds that had arrived from Mobile, about five thousand men.[16]

Throughout these maneuvers, Walker's division was held in reserve and was relatively uninvolved. Mercer's and Gist's brigades were ordered to the north end of Rocky Face on May 8. During the ninth they came under fire from enemy artillery and repulsed a strong advance by Yankee skirmishers. Only a few casualties were suffered in this short engagement.[17]

On May 8, McPherson advanced through Dug Gap. He was beaten off by the small infantry and cavalry force there, backed by two of Cleburne's brigades that were rushed to the field. On May 9, he pushed unopposed through Snake Creek Gap toward the railroad at Resaca. The fierce resistance put up by Cantey's two brigades made McPherson think it was more strongly held than was the case. He withdrew toward the gap toward nightfall, but that night Johnston sent Hood with Walker's, Hindman's, and Cleburne's divisions to Resaca in response to the threat. Hood decided Resaca was safe, and he returned to Dalton with Hindman's troops.

Walker and Cleburne were posted three miles north of Resaca at Tilton and waited to strike McPherson should he advance again. As more and more Federal troops pushed through Snake Creek Gap, however, Johnston realized that the Dalton position was untenable, and he abandoned it on May 12, concentrating his two army corps around Resaca. There he was joined by the first of Leonidas Polk's two divisions, that of William W. Loring, coming from Alabama and Mississippi with another five thousand men. The strength of Johnston's army was now increased to about sixty-five thousand.[18]

The march of Walker's division to Resaca was an unpleasant one. The weather was rainy, the roads were slippery, and the troops were tired and unfed. During the night of the tenth a strong wind came up; those who were so fortunate as to have tents saw them blown away. The marching was especially hard on the troops newly arrived from Savannah. William W. Mackall, Johnston's chief of staff, wrote to his wife, "Mercer's troops have had one hard march; it broke many of them down. They are not yet used to it." One of the new arrivals, Lieutenant Hamilton Branch of the 54th Georgia, however, was proud of the accomplishments of his division. He wrote to his mother, "We, Walker's Foot Cavalry, have been doing all of the strategy for Gen. Johnston." Another soldier, in the 29th Georgia, wrote his family, "It looks like our Division is all ways put in the deanges place. I dount Know what any them do it without, it is becase old Johnson thinks we are the best Troops that is in his Command."[19]

Although the Georgia division had been little involved in fighting as yet, Walker was constantly on the alert, moving about ceaselessly and getting little sleep. He had received a slight injury when his horse slipped off the road in the dark and fell on him. On May 12, in the first letter he found time to write since the campaign started, Walker told Mary: "I have not had time to say my life was my own since you left. Have been moving night and day and this is the first leisure moment (and I am now expecting orders any moment) I have had. I am quite well with the exception of a stiff neck and bruised leg. [My horse], in a night march, whilst I was passing a column of troops, stepped into a ditch and fell on my leg. My head struck the bank and I was knocked senseless for a moment. I soon revived and am all right except I feel a little sore." In a letter to his wife on May 13, J. B. Cumming wrote, "There has been constant skirmishing, but this division has had little part."[20]

While the two armies were concentrating between Snake Creek Gap and Resaca on May 12 and 13, Sherman ordered McPherson to dispatch one division further south to cross the Oostanaula River below Resaca and threaten Johnston's rear once more. General Thomas Sweeny's division of the XVI Corps was assigned this mission. Earlier, elements of Judson Kilpatrick's cavalry division had threatened the crossings of the Oostanaula below Resaca, but no Union troops had made it over the river. Lay's Ferry on the north side was picketed by the Yankees on the thirteenth, and demonstrations were made at Gideon's, Calhoun, and Lay's ferries on the fourteenth.[21]

Contrary to the impressions given in many accounts of this phase of the campaign, Johnston had not been unmindful of the threat posed by possible crossings of the Oostanaula downstream from Resaca. Winfield S. Featherston's brigade of French's division coming from Rome had been ordered to wait at Calhoun. On May 12, General Polk, commanding at Resaca, ordered Walker's division to the vicinity of Calhoun in exchange for Featherston. Sometime during the day on May 13, Walker forwarded to Polk at Resaca a message from the cavalry pickets that the enemy had occupied a bridge on the far side of the river about two miles downstream from Resaca. Walker was at Calhoun at the time. On his own initiative he personally took forward a battery of artillery to back up the cavalry. Polk and Johnston, who had arrived at Resaca, responded quickly, approving the dispatch of the artillery and directing Walker to send a brigade of infantry also "to prevent the enemy from crossing." It must have been the Union cavalry approach to the ferries to which Walker responded, but the main arena of action was still in front of Resaca.[22]

After heavy skirmishing on May 12 and 13, the combat for control of Resaca commenced in earnest on the fourteenth. The two armies faced each other from the opposite sides of Camp Creek. Johnston had his army aligned south to north from the Oostanaula crossings south of Resaca, west and then north of the town. On the south or left flank were the two divisions of Cantey and Loring under Lieutenant General Polk. Hardee's corps was deployed in the center of the line with three divisions, and Hood held the right, bent back to protect the Dalton road, with his three. Opposed to them were McPherson on the Federal right with two corps, less Sweeny's division, Thomas in the center with the XIV and XX corps of the massive Army of the Cumberland, and Schofield's lone corps on the left facing Hood's right. Later, Howard's IV Corps of the Army of the Cumberland, advancing from Dalton in Johnston's wake, formed on Schofield's left.[23]

The Union army spent most of the morning of the fourteenth negotiating the difficult terrain west of Camp Creek. By 11:30, the troops were in position and Thomas and Schofield were launched against the right center of Johnston's line. Hood's corps bore the brunt of the attack but held up well, repulsing the enemy with considerable loss. Howard's corps entered the combat on Schofield's left and Hood was driven back several hundred yards. During this action Howard's left flank was in the air, that is, without a firm anchoring point. Sherman and Johnston detected this weakness simultaneously. Sherman sent Hooker's XX Corps around to Howard's left while Johnston ordered Hood to attack with Stewart's and Stevenson's divisions, supported by Featherston's brigade from Polk's reserve and two of Walker's brigades. Hood's attack began about 6:00 P.M. and met with good success, advancing about two miles until stopped by the arrival of the first of Hooker's divisions.

While the fierce fighting was taking place on the northern flank, McPherson rolled forward against Johnston's left. Polk had occupied a series of hills on the west side of Camp Creek that were difficult to support from the main line. McPherson took them easily, and Polk's counterattacks were to no avail. Featherston's brigade was brought back to Polk's front and was put in line to Cantey's right. Yankee batteries were quickly able to bring the town and the river crossing to the south under fire from this position. Johnston was forced to build another bridge further upstream out of range of the Federal gunners.[24]

At 5:30 in the morning of the fourteenth, Walker was ordered to move his command closer to Resaca and to keep the cavalry informed of his new position. At 3:00 P.M. he was moved up just south of the Oostanaula bridge with orders to remain there out of sight. Finally, late in the afternoon he brought the brigades of Gist, Jackson, and Mercer up behind Johnston's main line. Only Stevens was left to watch the river to the south. A. P. Adamson of the 30th Georgia later recalled that his regiment was just across the river in plain view and came under fire but did not participate in the battle.

The rest of the Georgia division was obliged to cross the pontoon bridge over the Oostanaula under fire and suffered some casualties. Walker dashed across at the head of the division and then reviewed the men, head bared in salute as they passed, while General Polk nearby urged, "Double quick your men, double quick your men!" to reduce casualties. Lieutenant T. B. Mackall met Walker coming up the road from the bridge about 5:00 P.M. General Johnston personally posted Mercer's brigade behind Hood's corps, where it joined Hardee's, while another brigade, certainly

Jackson's, was sent to Hood's extreme right. Gist was held in reserve behind Cheatham's division of Hardee's corps left, probably to replace Featherston, who had gone to the right. Walker's troops supported but did not participate in Hood's advance.[25]

Meanwhile, Thomas Sweeny's division had moved on May 14 to Lay's Ferry, where Snake Creek flows into the Oostanaula, and made one attempt late that day to cross to the south bank near the confluence of the river with Snake Creek. The brigade of Colonel Patrick Burke was crossed, but while some of the boats were still in the water General Sweeny received a report of a large Rebel force crossing to the north bank above them. Fearing for his communications with Sherman, Sweeny retreated to the north side of the river.[26]

At Resaca, Johnston wanted Hood to renew his advance on May 15, but reports of Federal crossings lower down the Oostanaula during the fourteenth caused him to delay. That same night Walker was ordered to return to Calhoun to determine the situation. Walker's troops left Resaca about 9:00 P.M. and arrived back near Calhoun in the early morning darkness of May 15 after an all-night march. Daylight revealed no sign of Yankees, and Walker sent a message to Johnston to that effect. Johnston was encouraged enough by this report to order Hood to resume his advance. While he had been waiting, Sherman threw Hooker's corps against Hood, but the fighting ended in a standoff. Before Hood's attack could get under way, however, Walker sent another report that the Federals had crossed the river successfully that morning and were now in force on the south bank. Johnston hastily called off the attack. Stewart's division did not get the word and attacked, supported only by Maney's brigade of Cheatham's division. They were easily beaten back.[27]

Having determined that the reports of Rebel crossings above him were exaggerations based on construction of fortifications on the south side of the Oostanaula, early in the morning on May 15 Sweeny set out to cross the river again. This time, Colonel Elliot Rice's brigade was selected to go first. A heavy rifle and artillery fire from the north bank drove the Confederate defenders from their rifle pits, after which Rice's brigade crossed, followed by the brigade of Colonel Burke. They quickly entrenched. Rice sent one regiment forward into a wood on his right and sent skirmishers upstream along the south bank to search for Rebels. By early afternoon Rice felt he was prepared to defend his bridgehead.[28]

The best Southern account of the affair of May 15 can be gleaned from the letters of several members of Jackson's brigade who transmitted their experiences to the editor of the *Augusta Constitutionalist.* Using such pen names as "William M.," "Mignonne," and "5th Mississippi," they provided versions of events that while differing in details give us the true flavor of what really happened at Lay's Ferry.

After marching back from Resaca on the night of May 14, the brigade was posted close to the river near the ferry. The 8th Mississippi had been detached for provost duty while the army was still in Dalton and had not yet returned. The 2d Georgia Sharpshooters were sent to watch a ford upstream from Lay's. Consequently, Jackson had available only about nine hundred muskets in the 5th, 47th, and 65th Georgia, and the 5th Mississippi. Two companies of the 5th Georgia were detailed as skirmishers to search out the enemy and the rest of that regiment formed the brigade picket line. The other three regiments settled down in line of battle behind a meager barricade of fence rails to wait for word from their skirmishers. The battle, which one of the correspondents described as "the hottest fight [our brigade] ever yet participated in," was not long in coming.

Rice's skirmishers and the companies of the 5th Georgia must have discovered each other simultaneously. The Rebels were driven back upon their own lines and the first intimation the main line had of the enemy's advance was the sound of the approaching fire fight. Jackson ordered his men to hold their fire until the enemy came within good range. Advancing to the crest of a hill to succor their own, they found not an advancing enemy force but a view of the blue skirmishers turning tail toward their own position at the sight of the Southern battle line.

Here Jackson erred seriously. Apparently without notifying division headquarters and without waiting for support, even though Mercer's brigade was in the vicinity, he threw his slim brigade against Rice's breastworks. The combat lasted only fifteen minutes during which 150 to 175 of his brigade were shot down or captured. Jackson, his staff, and the regimental commanders showed great coolness and bravery in urging their men to advance within two-hundred yards of the Northern entrenchments, but they were forced to withdraw to prevent further "useless sacrifice," leaving their dead and wounded on the field. The Yankees made no attempt to follow immediately. Although praise for Jackson was universal, one veteran wryly commented, "I cannot divine the object of this charge against such fearful odds. . . . The rascals swarmed the banks of the river as far as the eye could see."[29]

Lieutenant Hamilton Branch wrote that Jackson's brigade had "foolishly charged the enemy's breastworks without support." Private Helms of the

Lithograph of the Battle of Lay's Ferry, May 15, 1864. In the foreground Jackson's Confederate brigade is depicted assaulting Sweeney's division of Dodge's corps. From Brown, *The Mountain Campaigns in Georgia.*

63d Georgia wrote that he had heard that 'the 5th Georgia got about half of them killed." Rice reported recovering 36 Confederate bodies, capturing 23 prisoners and one stand of colors. Total Southern loss was estimated by Northern commanders at 250 while their own casualties amounted to 100. Official Confederate casualty reports do not match Northern claims. Captain William G. Foster, commanding the 65th Georgia, reported that his regiment lost 4 killed, 26 wounded, and 4 missing on May 15. The killed and wounded reported for Jackson's brigade for all of May 7 to May 20 was 13 and 113, respectively. This is yet another example of problems in assessing Confederate strength and losses. Some prisoners were certainly taken because General John Corse, Sherman's inspector general, through interrogation, was able to identify accurately all but one of the regiments in Jackson's brigade. Corse also reported members of the 8th Georgia Battalion, Gist's brigade, among the prisoners, but he may have meant the 8th Mississippi, some individual members of which might have been present.[30]

Professor Albert Castel, in *Decision in the West*, says that the Federal com-

manders believed Walker's full division was present in their front, which
explains Sweeny's brigades assuming a defensive rather than an offensive
posture after crossing the river. Castel, however, concluded that only Jackson's brigade was available because Stevens and Gist were both north of
the river on May 15. Castel does not mention Mercer's brigade at Lay's
Ferry.[31]

The Federal commanders were correct. Rice had appropriately established a bridgehead for his two brigades while he felt out his enemy's
strength and position. Walker's whole division was in his front. The only
evidence found to suggest that any of Walker's division had gone back
to Resaca on May 15 is the report of Ellison Capers of the 24th South
Carolina, Gist's brigade. Capers wrote that in conjunction with the 16th
South Carolina, on May 14 he met a Federal force crossing at McGinnis's
[Calhoun] Ferry and drove them back across the river. He further says
that after this action he returned to his previous position at Gideon Ferry
between Calhoun and Resaca until he was ordered with his brigade to
Resaca on the fifteenth. Actually, Gist's brigade returned to Resaca on the
fourteenth with the rest of Walker's division and was posted in the rear
of Cheatham's division. After the battle Capers's brother Frank wrote him
a letter about his appearance as he crossed the Oostanaula with General
Walker on May 14. It is clear that Walker did not personally lead any of his
division back to the north bank on May 15. The chronology of Capers's
report therefore appears to be in error on this point.[32]

Accounts by other members of Gist's brigade do not support Capers's
version. Captain John H. Steinmeyer of the 24th South Carolina wrote:
"The command was transferred hurriedly to Resaca to meet the flank
movement threatening there and near there engaged the enemy in crossing
the river [Oostanaula]. The battle of Resaca coming on, Walker's division was ordered back, had to cross the river, led by Company A of the
24th Regiment, under fire (on pontoon bridge) of the enemy's artillery.
How well I remember the dead that were left there over who we had to
march. We gained the position, recovered some entrenchments that had
been taken by the enemy, with little seeming resistance, but were withdrawn during the night." This statement indicates that the 24th crossed to
Resaca on May 14, was involved in the fighting on Polk's front, and withdrew that night. Lieutenant Mackall noted in his journal for May 15, "Our
skirmishers last night occupied original position on extreme left . . . ," that
is, the west side of Camp Creek.[33]

Private Samuel McKittrick of the 16th South Carolina, however, commented: "On last Saturday morning [May 14] the Yanks attacked Resaca. Our division was ordered [south of the river?]. We . . . marched within some three miles of the battlefield where several companies had to go on picket duty. We stayed nearly a day and a night on the river bank [Oostanaula] in sight of the Yanks. . . . In the meantime, the battle was raging at Resaca. Our Regiment were ordered to it but were not in the fight. We left on Sunday morning [May 15] as the Yanks were about to bag us." This statement can also be read to mean the regiment went back to Resaca on May 14 and left early in the morning of the fifteenth.[34]

The force the 16th and 24th South Carolina faced at McGinnis's Ferry on May 14 was Burke's brigade. Capers reported that his two regiments drove the enemy back to and across the river. Reports covering the action of Sweeny's division on May 14, its first crossing, say it withdrew under orders. Colonel Elliot Rice did report, however, that he was ordered to support Burke's brigade, which was under heavy Rebel fire, and later detailed men to help that brigade recross to the north bank. This was the encounter Capers wrote of as seen from a different perspective. Therefore, Capers and McCullough must have marched directly from McGinnis's Ferry to Resaca with Gist. Most likely, Capers was posted back at Gideon's Ferry when the division crossed back to Calhoun on the night of May 14. Walker's division crossed the river to Johnston's support sometime after 2:30 on the afternoon of the fourteenth. Sweeny's brigades began their river crossings late that afternoon. Capers and McCullough must have faced Burke right after he landed, driven him back to his boats, and then marched to Resaca.[35]

Walker had fumbled his mission of protecting the crossings of the Oostanaula and, by extension, Johnston's line of communications. In his first independent role in the campaign, he used the brigade of the brave but inept John K. Jackson, supported by the inexperienced regiments of Hugh Mercer. The troops advanced without reconnaissance and were easily repulsed by the well-organized Union defense. Why Mercer was not brought forward immediately and why the veterans of Stevens and Gist were not used at all are questions that may never have been asked and that Walker never answered. Walker's messages to W. W. Mackall only add to the puzzle. At 2:45 P.M. from Lay's or Tanner's Ferry, Walker telegraphed that he would "do all I can with my force" without mentioning the attack by Jackson's brigade. At 10:00 P.M. he compounded the mystery by wiring, "I did not attack the force in my front today." Either Walker did not want to admit his failure or he was not in control of the activities on his front.[36]

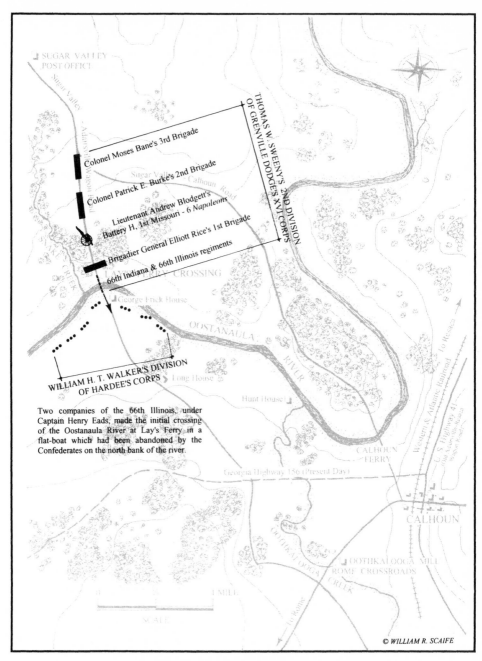

Lay's Ferry Crossing, May 15, 1864

While staying in Calhoun Walker involved himself in a trivial incident that showed his weakness for a woman as well as his asperity when faced with an affront to his authority or dignity. The anecdote, as related by Captain John Steinmeyer, is long and involved. Walker had issued orders that no one was to be allowed to cross the Oostanaula from north to south without a permit from division headquarters. Two young women in a buggy approached a crossing point on the north bank, which was picketed on the south side by a detachment from Steinmeyer's company of the 24th South Carolina. They said they wanted to visit their uncle who lived in Calhoun. They were refused passage at first, but upon their importunings Steinmeyer was summoned to listen to their tale. His compromise solution was not to give them permission but to place them under arrest and carry them to the general's quarters for a decision. As it happened, Walker had established his headquarters at the residence of the uncle, a Mr. Bunting. When they arrived there the general immediately released them from arrest and allowed them to stay the night.

The next day he gave them a permit to travel further south, but the army's provost guard refused to honor the permit because it had not been countersigned at General Johnston's headquarters. When he heard of this rebuff to his authority, Walker placed Steinmeyer under arrest for having allowed the women into the lines in the first place. Naturally, Steinmeyer protested. Walker endorsed his application for release from arrest, "Orders should be always obeyed, this is not the first time a good man has been gotten into trouble by the feminines." Steinmeyer was released from arrest, but for some time he was the butt of many jokes in Gist's brigade.[37]

Whatever the details of Walker's action at Lay's Ferry, Johnston was forced to withdraw once more. Pressed on the west and north by Sherman and with Sweeny threatening his line of communications, the Southern commander had again been outsmarted by his Northern counterpart. That night Polk and Hardee withdrew across the bridges at Resaca and Hood crossed on the new bridge upstream. After the crossing the railroad bridge was torched and the pontoon bridges taken up. The regular road bridge was overlooked. Colonel Nisbet of the 66th Georgia claimed that his regiment was assigned to perform this detail and so deserved both the credit and the blame.[38]

Casualties on each side at Resaca are not easy to determine. Estimates range from close to two thousand to close to six thousand for each army. Thomas L. Connelly believed that Johnston lost his best chance of the campaign to take a stand against Sherman in the few days after the battle at Resaca. With Sherman's army divided, some on the north bank of the Oostanaula near Resaca, some on the south side of Calhoun, and some diverted to Rome, the Federal army was at its most vulnerable.[39]

Walker, in turn, had lost his best opportunity for glory and advancement in the north Georgia campaign. If he had been able to dislodge Sweeny from the south bank of the Oostanaula on May 15, Johnston's line of communications to Atlanta would have been secure and that general would have been free to pursue vigorously his offensive against Sherman's left. A Southern victory at Resaca, though not decisive in turning back the Union army, would have dislodged Sherman's plan of campaign and could have delayed the fall of Atlanta for months, perhaps even past the November election in the North, the political goal of all Southern effort in 1864.

While Hardee's corps lay around Calhoun on May 16, Federal skirmishers from Sweeny's bridgehead advanced so close to the encampment that Hardee ordered Walker with his own and Bate's divisions to drive them off. Cleburne was deployed to protect Walker's right. Colonel Capers was sent out with the 24th South Carolina and Major Arthur Shaaf's 1st Georgia Sharpshooters from Stevens's brigade to handle the mission. With Mercer's brigade in support, Capers advanced smartly, drove back the skirmishers, and nearly captured their supporting battery. In this action, the 24th South Carolina lost forty-one killed, wounded, and missing.[40]

From Calhoun Johnston fell back to Adairsville, where he hoped to make another stand. Walker joined Hardee's rear guard as they passed through Calhoun. By Colonel Nisbet's account, his regiment and the 26th Georgia Battalion were assigned to support Wheeler's cavalry in protecting the wagon trains. When Wheeler attempted to retain control of Nisbet's troops to hold more defensive positions farther south along the road, Nisbet refused and returned to Stevens's brigade.[41]

Finding the topography at Adairsville unsuitable for his need, Johnston next moved to Cassville. Hardee wanted to stand and fight at Adairsville, but Johnston overruled him. Hood's and Polk's corps moved directly overland southeast to Cassville while Hardee and the baggage trains followed the more circuitous route of the rail line south to Kingston and then east to Cassville. Johnston hoped to lead Sherman to believe that the entire Army of Tennessee had gone to Kingston. If one wing of Sherman's army went to Cassville while another pursued Hardee to Kingston, Johnston would unite his force and fall on the detachment at Cassville. Sherman did divide his army, sending McPherson's army and Thomas with two corps after Hardee, while Hooker's XX Corps and Schofield's Army of the

Ohio followed Hood and Polk. Skirmishing continued on a daily basis, but Sherman took his time advancing, repairing the railroad as he came forward.[42]

The troops greeted Johnston's announcement that they would stand and fight at Cassville with great joy. A line of battle was formed on May 18 just north of Cassville with Polk on the left and Hood on the right. Hardee was still approaching from Kingston. Hood was to advance to his front on the morning of the nineteenth and outflank and attack the oncoming Union XX Corps. But while Hood was moving into position, reports, later confirmed, of large bodies of Yankees to the northeast caused him to abort his attack. Johnston approved Hood's decision and moved his line to a new position southeast of Cassville, where he would stand on the defensive again and await Sherman's attack.[43]

Meanwhile, Hardee's corps, followed by the two corps of Thomas's army, had come up from the west and formed on Polk's left. Polk's other division, Major General Samuel G. French's, had arrived from Mississippi to fill out his corps. Confederate cavalry was strengthened by the addition of W. H. Jackson's division, also assigned to Polk. Estimated strength of the Confederate army present for duty was now close to eighty thousand, less losses suffered since leaving Dalton. A statement of casualties for May 6 to 20 showed some thirty-four hundred killed and wounded. There was no accounting for sick and missing. At Cassville, Johnston fielded an army of seventy to seventy-five thousand men.[44]

Extricating Hardee's corps and especially Walker's division from before the enemy at the first position was a delicate operation. The Georgia division was unprotected in an open field and under heavy artillery fire. Mercer's brigade was in advance of the rest of the division with the 63d Georgia's Major Joseph V. H. Allen of Augusta in command of the skirmish line. During the withdrawal the 63d was nearly surrounded and was brought off the field only by the skillful action of its commander, Lieutenant Colonel George R. Black. The withdrawal was successfully carried out and the new line was taken up. Although several units had been engaged and some casualties suffered, Walker's division as an entity had still not been committed to battle. Through May 20, the Georgia division lost 28 killed and 269 wounded, second only to Cheatham in Hardee's corps, but far fewer than Hood's losses.[45]

Losses were heaviest in Jackson's brigade, 13 killed and 113 wounded, a result of their engagement near Lay's Ferry on May 16. Gist had 7 killed and 62 wounded, Stevens 4 killed and 53 wounded, and Mercer 4 killed and

41 wounded during the first two weeks of the campaign. The numbers of prisoners and missing are not available.[46]

Johnston reformed his army along a low ridge just southeast of Cassville with a northeast to southwest axis. Hood remained on the right with Polk in the center. Hardee's corps was the left of the line on low ground at the south end of the ridge with Walker's division between Cheatham's and Cleburne's athwart the rail line. Sherman's troops took position on an equal or slightly higher ridge north of the town. In a review of positions before the battle was expected to begin, Johnston's chief of artillery, General Francis Shoup, pointed out that Union artillery could enfilade part of Polk's line, making it untenable. Johnston dismissed this advice with the comment that the troops could shelter on the reverse slope until they were needed to repel attackers.[47]

Johnston confidently waited for a Federal attack on the morning of May 20, but an artillery bombardment of Hood's and Polk's front on the evening of the nineteenth convinced those two generals that Shoup had been right and they could not maintain their positions. In a hurried late night meeting, Johnston, Hood, Polk, Mackall, and others huddled together to discuss their courses of action. Although Hardee was for standing, Johnston felt that the attitude displayed by his other two corps commanders would lead to a dispirited defense if an attack came the next day. Reluctantly, he ordered another withdrawal across the Etowah, the next to last river line before Atlanta. The sudden and unexpected change of plan led to some demoralization among the troops, and the evacuation of Cassville was accompanied by considerable confusion, units being mixed together, trains mixed in with marching troops, and so on.[48]

Richard McMurry says that May 19 was "one of the strangest days of the war" and for the troops "one of the most frustrating." Johnston had lost two favorable opportunities to strike a blow at Sherman, first at an unsupported detachment and then from a prepared position. Worse, a sense of acrimony began to develop between Johnston and the principal subordinate to whom he had recently looked so frequently for aggressive action. Twice on May 19 Hood counseled caution in the face of, at most, uncertain circumstances, or so Johnston remembered. Hood, however, remembered that, far from urging Johnston to withdraw, he spoke out in favor of taking the offensive. Only Johnston's defensive mind-set caused another retreat. The controversy resulting from that day would separate the two for the rest of their lives. The continued retreat was most damaging to the private soldiers. Writing to his wife from Cassville on May 18, Sergeant John

Hagan of the 29th Georgia, Stevens's brigade, said, "The truth is we have run until I am getting out of heart and we must make a stand soon or the army will be demoralized." Lieutenant Thomas B. Mackall, aide and nephew to Johnston's chief of staff, recorded in his diary that the troops were "dispirited and fagged" upon arriving south of the Etowah.[49]

William Walker left no record of his reaction to this fiasco, but his sentiments must have been similar to those of his brother officers. Irving Buck says that Cleburne "expressed his disappointment and surprise" to General Hardee. General French, whose line was supposed to be the most threatened, later said he thought Johnston would fight and was surprised at the order to retreat. Hardee himself argued with Johnston, but to no avail. Surely the Georgia fire-eater agreed with these offensive-minded opinions.[50]

After crossing the Etowah at Cartersville on May 20, Johnston broke off all contact with the Federals and withdrew back to Allatoona Pass, a strong position on the railroad, where his army rested for two days. During the night of May 20–21 Sherman advanced to the north side of the river and skirmished across the water with John K. Jackson's brigade, which had advanced post duty. But, Sherman now gave up the direct advance and attempted another turning movement, this time westward toward Dallas, a small town about fourteen miles south of the Etowah River and about the same distance east of the all-important railroad. Carrying twenty days' rations in wagons, Sherman cut loose from his supply line and moved off cross-country. Learning of this movement, Johnston moved Hardee's corps to Dallas and took up strong positions there beginning on May 23. Hood remained at Allatoona for the time being, and Polk was posted between Hardee and Hood in the Lost Mountain area.[51]

At Allatoona Walker's division was strengthened on May 20 by the arrival of the 57th Georgia Regiment, which was assigned to Mercer's small brigade. The 57th was composed of men who had been captured at Vicksburg and exchanged. Before joining the Army of Tennessee the regiment had spent several months guarding prisoners at Andersonville. Its strength probably was not great and its morale questionable.[52]

Hardee moved eight miles toward Dallas on May 23 and closed in on the town the next day. As Johnston's information on Sherman's movements improved, he shifted Hood to a position about four miles northeast of Dallas. Polk was placed between Hood and Hardee. On May 25, Hood was moved to New Hope Church at a country crossroads and Polk and Hardee shifted to their right to close on Hood.

In its usual fashion, Sherman's army was advancing with McPherson on the right, or west, Thomas in the center, and Schofield on the left. Hooker's XX Corps was in the van of Thomas's Army of the Cumberland. Early on May 25, as they neared Dallas, the lead division, Geary's, came to a fork in the road. Turning southeast, Geary continued his advance and in a few hours stumbled into Hood's deployed troops, in this case Alexander P. Stewart's reinforced division. A fierce fight drove back the advanced Confederate detachments, but Geary halted to build barricades while Hooker summoned help from his other two divisions.[53]

Sherman, who had come up, thought that he was on Johnston's left and disbelieved the reports of his generals that they had encountered a large body of Rebels. Nevertheless, he allowed Hooker to align his corps and the three-division attack went in through tangled underbrush and under threatening skies about 4:00 P.M. The result was disaster. Each division advanced on only a brigade front, and Stewart's riflemen and artillery were able to concentrate their fire accordingly. Federal losses were enormous. A heavy rain only made the scene more gloomy. The attack was abandoned, and Hooker's men fell back to construct more log breastworks. Stewart was so confident of success that he refused further reinforcement.[54]

While the battle between Hooker and Stewart had been raging, the rest of the Union army was closing on the battlefield. McPherson moved to within a mile of Hooker's right, the IV and XIV corps came up in support, and Schofield's army was still somewhere to the rear. Sherman spent all of May 26 adjusting his lines in the woods. Hooker held the center of the line with McPherson's two corps stretched to his right, the IV Corps and Schofield on his left, and the XIV Corps in support.[55]

Hood had originally aligned his three divisions with Stewart in the center, Hindman on the left, and Stevenson on the right. Late on May 25 and during the day on May 26, the Confederate army also made some adjustments. Hindman was sent to Hood's right and Polk shifted to his right to close up on Stewart, now on Hood's left. Cleburne's division of Hardee's corps was brought around to the far right and put under Hood's command. Cheatham held Hardee's right and Bate was on the left, but there was a gap of over a mile between them. Walker's division was in reserve behind Stewart, where it suffered a few casualties during Hooker's attack but was not actively engaged. Cleburne had originally been ordered to the right on the night on May 25, but his van became entangled with Walker's rear in the dark woods and the movement was postponed until the next morning.[56]

For May 27, Sherman opted for a turning movement around Johnston's right followed by an attack on the flank or rear. General Oliver O. Howard of the IV Corps was directed to form a miscellaneous command of two divisions and one brigade from three different corps, in modern parlance a task force, to effect this maneuver. While Howard was getting into position, demonstrations were to be made along other parts of the line. Early in the morning Walker was sent to Bate's left and, with the cavalry on his left, had some sharp skirmishing during the day. Howard got under way late in the morning and, after one false attempt, turned near Pickett's Mill at what he hoped was a point past Johnston's right flank. As he put it in a message to Thomas, "I am turning the enemy's right flank, I think." [57]

Unfortunately for Howard, he had turned right into Cleburne's massed infantry. As the Union divisions crashed through the underbrush, they came to a small ravine. At the top of the slope on the far side stood the Confederate infantry. Bravely the Yankee infantry charged up the slope, but the battle was a repetition of Hooker's failure two days before. After the attacks petered out in the dark, the Confederates discovered many Federals concealed in the ravine. A quick counterattack captured several hundred while the rest withdrew to their own lines. [58]

While Howard was marching across Hood's front, more action was taking place before Hardee. Cheatham was ordered to clear the enemy from Ellsberry Ridge, a rise south of New Hope Church. Mercer's brigade was committed on Cheatham's right. The attack was strongly resisted, and once Cheatham cleared the ridge he had trouble sustaining his position. Hardee sent more troops to help the Tennessee division hold its thin line connecting Polk's corps and Bate's division on the left. Despite this help, the Tennesseans and Georgians on Ellsberry Ridge suffered mounting casualties from blue-coated sharpshooters both that day and the next. [59]

Following the twin debacles of May 25 and 27, Sherman determined to shift back to the east and occupy Allatoona Pass. The movement began on May 28. Johnston guessed that this would be Sherman's tactic, and he ordered Hardee to probe his front for the presence or absence of Federal troops. Bate's division was pushed forward and ran into McPherson's men still in their trenches. The attack was driven back, but it had the effect of holding Sherman back from implementing his plan. Johnston continued his attacks on May 29, 30, and 31, but Sherman gradually disengaged. Staff officers of Mercer's brigade posted on Ellsberry Ridge could see the Federal columns moving eastward. By June 3, Sherman had returned to the rail line at Acworth, well south of Allatoona. Once more he had maneuvered Johnston out of position, this time, though, at considerable loss of life.[60]

The Northern army rested for a few days while Sherman continued to improve the railroad in his rear. Up to now the campaign had not gained the Union forces their first objective, breaking up Johnston's army, but Sherman was considerably nearer to Atlanta than he had been and had captured the important industrial city of Rome. On the Southern side casualties had been severe.

Confederate casualties in the New Hope Church–Dallas portion of the campaign were approximately 2,200 killed and wounded with the heaviest losses in Cleburne's and Bate's divisions, 458 and 401, respectively. Walker's losses were relatively light, emphasizing the secondary role his division played. Mercer had 14 wounded, Gist 3 killed and 39 wounded, Jackson 10 killed and 71 wounded, and Stevens 2 killed and 38 wounded. Excluding prisoners and missing, the division's total loss was only 177. Captain Foster of the 65th Georgia, Jackson's brigade, reported his losses for May 28 and 29 as 7 killed and 20 wounded.[61]

During the lull in the fighting Walker took the opportunity to write home. On June 2 he addressed letters to both his wife and daughter. To Molly he wrote of the conditions of the campaign: "I have no time to write letters. Night and day I am on the move and every leisure hour has to be passed in rest and sleep. You can form no conception of the hardships and fatigues we have passed through since leaving Dalton. Night marches, irregular meals, heat and dust, etc. For a day or two we have had a respite but it is the only [sic, only the] clouds collecting together to hurl their flashes of destruction." The recriminations of the previous winter were forgotten, and he could give her fatherly advice on self-improvement. After listing romantic novels she could read, he counseled: "Now is the time to improve your mind and your manners. Your age is one of physical and mental development. Don't idle now. Exercise both body and mind and when you shall have arrived at woman's age, you will be a woman, not a foolish, silly girl." As in his defense of his daughter against Lawson Magruder three months earlier, Walker was exhibiting the normal characteristics of the Southern patriarch in advising his daughter on her behavior and her education.[62]

To his wife, Walker gave practical advice and reassurance. Concerning a report in the *Augusta Chronicle and Sentinel* that he had been wounded at New Hope Church on May 26, he wrote, "I again caution you not to take newspaper rumors about me. You will be informed if anything occurs. If I am alive, I will inform you. If not, some of my staff will." He had already had Major Nathaniel Tilton, the division quartermaster, telegraph the editor to refute the unconfirmed rumor. Despite his personal and public disclaimers, as late as June 21 the *Augusta Constitutionalist* was still reporting that Walker had been "shot through the foot" near Dallas.[63]

During this time Walker had a visitor from home. His older brother, Beverly, whose only military service had been in the Charleston defenses in 1863, came to camp to enlist the aid of Generals Johnston and Hardee in securing a position for his oldest son, John P. K. "King" Walker, at the Augusta Powder Works. Walker took Beverly up to the lines to observe the Union movement to the right. At least one Augusta soldier recognized him there. William O. Norrell asked him to carry a letter home to his wife. Beverly not only agreed but promised to call on Mrs. Norrell when he arrived home. Beverly's white shirt caused a sensation in camp, and he was the butt of much soldier humor as a result.[64]

Other new arrivals in camp were the 1st Georgia Volunteers, who arrived on May 27 with six hundred men under Colonel Charles H. Olmstead, brought from Savannah to reinforce Mercer's brigade. Olmstead, writing many years later, remembered that "Walker's was a reserve division which meant that as a rule it had no fixed place in the line of battle but was moved about from point to point as occasion might require to strengthen any weak places in the line when threatened by the enemy. These changes were generally made at night and they involved much loss of sleep marching and countermarching while other commands were resting." Another addition to the army at this time was Quarles's brigade from Mobile, twenty-two hundred effectives, added to Cantey's division. Despite continued losses, Johnston was able to hold his strength at close to seventy thousand men.[65]

Sherman had also received reinforcements. On June 8 the two veteran divisions of Frank Blair's XVII Corps, 10,000 men, finally caught up with the army and were joined to McPherson's Army of the Tennessee. Returns for Sherman's army for May 31, 1864, showed a strength of 112,000, very close to what it had been at the start of the campaign.[66]

The Federals were ready to resume their advance on June 10. Johnston had positioned his army on a range of mountains north of Marietta. After some adjustments, the line stretched across Lost, Pine, and Brush mountains, west to east, and was protected by cavalry on both flanks. Polk lay on the right, Hardee in the center, and Hood on the left. Walker was posted first at Gilgal Church east of Lost Mountain, with Mercer's brigade pushed out on the Burnt Hickory road; later the division was moved to the rear of Pine Mountain. Bate's division of Hardee's corps was in a salient on Pine Mountain with two batteries for support. One of those was the South Carolina battery of Captain René Beauregard from Martin's battalion. Sherman probed Johnston's lines for two weeks. As usual, skirmishing took place constantly. The 29th Georgia of Stevens's brigade suffered casualties in an affair of charge and countercharge on June 15. Heavy rains severely hampered operations, but Sherman's threatened envelopments forced Johnston gradually to give up his position and retire to Kennesaw Mountain about June 18.[67]

Hardee was so concerned about the salient on Pine Mountain that on June 14 he asked Johnston to go to the summit with him to estimate the danger. Johnston, Hardee, and Lieutenant General Polk, with their staffs, went to the mountaintop, where Johnston agreed that the position should be evacuated. The presence of this large group soon drew Union artillery fire. Johnston and Hardee quickly sought cover, but Polk, moving more slowly, from dignity or from physical deficiency, was struck by the third shell. A Parrott round passed laterally through Polk's body, breaking both arms and smashing his chest, killing him almost instantly. Although Polk's death was mourned by his friends, it was not seen as a great deficit to army command. His corps was taken over temporarily by the senior division commander, Major General Loring.[68]

The move from the Pine Mountain line was not without incident. On June 15, a strong advance by Hooker's XX Corps against Hardee's lines near Gilgal Church drove in Confederate cavalry and forced Cleburne to retire Lowrey's and Mercer's brigades from their advanced positions. The fighting continued on the sixteenth with heavy local attacks. Again, Mercer's brigade gave up some ground. Casualties for the two days in that brigade were almost one hundred, of which more than seventy occurred in the 1st Georgia Volunteers. The 29th Georgia of Stevens's brigade lost forty-two men on June 16.[69]

On June 18, near Mud Creek, the division picket line and skirmishers were driven in by a determined Federal thrust. The sudden withdrawal allowed a Federal unit to get behind the skirmishers of French's division on Walker's right. French was unable to dislodge his enemy and claimed a loss that day of 215 men as a result. Of the same incident, however, George A. Mercer recorded that his father's brigade "[held] their ground nobly with heavy loss, both Gen. Walker and Gen. Hardee compliment[ed] our picket on their good conduct." Walter Clark reported that the 63d

Georgia of Mercer's brigade fought for twelve hours that day and suffered 29 casualties. That evening the division fell back two miles.[70]

That same night or soon after, another embarrassment occurred when part of a company of the 1st Georgia Volunteers failed to receive an order to withdraw from the picket line and was captured. A detail of companies from all the regiments of Mercer's brigade was on picket duty as the division prepared to pull back to Kennesaw. After the brigade had withdrawn, the pickets were to be collected by their commander, Major J. V. H. Allen of the 63d Georgia, and brought off. When Allen came to get his men he could not find the company of the 1st Volunteers, left without them, and they were captured.[71]

The stress and constant fighting took other tolls. Sergeant Hagan of the 29th Georgia told his wife that his regiment had lost eighty-three men killed, wounded, or missing between June 14 and 21. There were no field officers with the regiment, which Hagan called "very much diminished," and only two captains on duty, the senior of whom was commanding the regiment. Hagan was acting commander of his own company because the company officer, a lieutenant, had been feigning sickness for three days.[72]

The ensuing battle at Kennesaw Mountain was the severest of the long campaign from Dalton to Atlanta. By June 19, Johnston had taken his chosen position. Once again he was aligned across three crests, Big Kennesaw, Little Kennesaw, and Pigeon Hill. Hood was on the right, Loring in the center, and Hardee on the left.

Sherman moved up against the new positions as soon as they were occupied. The constant, grinding warfare in the midst of bad weather continued. Shelling went on constantly. Hamilton Branch, who had a knack for a neat phrase, wrote his mother, "There have been constant rains, both of water and minnie balls." On June 22, Captain Mercer recorded losses in his brigade from May 6 to that date as 435: 29 killed, 224 wounded, 182 missing. Corporal Blanton B. Fortson of the 63d Georgia wrote to his father that his regiment had lost 130 killed, wounded, and missing up to June 24. Charles L. Thiot of the 1st Georgia Volunteers wrote that his regiment had been reduced to a little over 300 effectives in the four weeks they had been with the army. As a further indication of difficulty in keeping track of casualties, Dr. A. J. Foard's records show that Mercer's brigade lost 4 killed and 255 wounded from May 7 to July 4. The casualties affected morale. Calathiel Helms wrote that "the men is going to the Yankees, a swarm at a time."[73]

A particularly fierce night action developed on Walker's front on June

20. His division held the army's left flank at that time, before the transfer of Hood's corps from the right. About 4:00 P.M. the brigade of General Walter C. Whitaker in David S. Stanley's division, IV Corps, Army of the Cumberland, made a demonstration with a strong line of skirmishers along its whole front. The demonstration turned into a charge against a hill, which they captured, driving in Gist's and Jackson's pickets, taking prisoners, and making a lodgment in Gist's line. Major C. C. O'Neill of the 16th South Carolina, commanding Gist's picket line, was killed. The 24th South Carolina and 46th Georgia counterattacked and drove the Federals out of Gist's position but could not retake the hill.

Whitaker reported that between nightfall and 11:00 P.M. three Confederate brigades tried to retake the hill but were beaten back after each charge. Union losses were about 270, including one regimental commander killed and two wounded. Lieutenant Colonel James Watson of the 40th Ohio was called away from his cooking fire to repel the last attack and was captured when he got lost in the dark. Whitaker claimed to have captured 26 Rebels, killed 200, and wounded another 400.

The slaughter in the 46th Georgia was especially heavy. Veteran J. H. Booker remembered this fight, including the capture of an officer whom he identified as "Colonel Watts" of the 40th Ohio. Booker recalled losses of 147 killed and wounded in his regiment alone, including 6 killed in his own company. Booker was himself wounded. Lillian Henderson identifies by name 76 casualties in the 46th, including 27 killed or mortally wounded and 49 wounded, captured, or missing. The *Augusta Chronicle and Sentinel* reported that only 11 officers of the regiment escaped injury that night.

Captain J. H. Steinmeyer of the 24th South Carolina recorded the fight in his diary and mentioned that he met an unnamed Union colonel who was captured when he got lost in the dark that night. General Gist later commended the 46th Georgia for their action on June 20.[74]

As before, Sherman chose to find his way around Johnston's left, always reaching for the railroad and, by now, the Chattahoochee River. McPherson's Army of the Tennessee faced the Confederate right; Thomas, with the Army of the Cumberland, was in the center; and Schofield's Army of the Ohio had been brought around to Sherman's right to make the flanking movement.[75]

As Sherman reached to his right, Johnston extended to the left, eventually bringing Hood's corps of three divisions to the left flank. The new alignment left Loring across Kennesaw and Little Kennesaw. Loring's division, under its senior brigadier, Winfield Scott Featherston, was on the right of the line, just east of the mountain. Next was Edward C. Walthall's, formerly Cantey's, division, across the peak of Kennesaw. To the left lay French's division on Little Kennesaw and Pigeon Hill. Hardee's corps was posted on Loring's left. Walker was on the right from the base of Little Kennesaw with Bate, Cleburne, and Cheatham to his left. Hood held the far left with Hindman, Stevenson, and Stewart. Cavalry covered both flanks. The position described an arc of about ninety degrees.[76]

Sherman had several choices. He might remain in position and continue to wear Johnston down. He could try to extend farther past Johnston's left. Or he could try an assault on the Rebel lines, looking for a breakthrough and the chance to destroy part of the enemy army. For a variety of reasons, not the least of which was that he believed his troops wanted a real fight, Sherman decided on the frontal assault.[77]

The attack, scheduled for June 27, would be multipronged. McPherson's army would attack against the south end of Kennesaw Mountain. Thomas would strike against the left of Hardee's corps, and Schofield would either attack or feint against Hood's left. None of the three army commanders had much confidence in the effort, but all three planned their actions carefully. McPherson chose John A. Logan's XV Corps to make the attack at the junction between French and Walker. Walker had in line the brigades of Mercer, Gist, and Jackson. Stevens had been detached on June 26 to support Hindman or Stewart in Hood's corps as needed. Thomas hoped to launch three attacks with the IV and XIV corps against Cheatham's and Cleburne's positions. Schofield began his demonstration on June 26.[78]

McPherson's attack began with about fifty-five hundred men of Morgan L. Smith's division. Their advance could be easily seen from Kennesaw, and French's men were ready for them. Their forward progress was slowed by the terrain, but they eventually emerged into the open and rushed the Southern trenches. General Johnston described the action: "[The Federals] advanced from the west [sic]. Their right dashed through the skirmishers of Walker's right before they could be reinforced and took in reverse those on their right and left while they were attacked in front. In a few minutes, about 80 of Walker's men had been bayoneted or captured in their rifle pits."[79]

Eight companies of the 63d Georgia were posted in the rifle pits on Walker's right. A dense forest growth obscured the field in front from most of the men. Only the company on the extreme right, next to French's skirmishers, had a clear view. As French's men fell back, so did the lone company of the 63d. The commander of the 63d, Major Allen, led his

reserve company into the gap in the line, just in time to be met by the
onrushing Federals from front and flank where they had already occupied French's pits. Seeing his company about to be overrun, the company
commander gave the order, "Save yourselves, boys." According to Private William O. Norrell of B Company, the men "went off like a flock of
sheep." The men ran pell-mell up the slope of Kennesaw, but it was too
late. A Company of the 63d Georgia had taken 47 men into action and
only 23 or 24 returned. The regiment lost 88 in all out of 265 engaged,
and estimates for total loss in the brief melee ran as high as 150.[80]

Having cleared the first hurdle, the Northern troops next charged up-
ward against French's main line. This attack was doomed to failure. Only
a few small groups reached their goal and were easily driven back. The
survivors huddled on the mountainside or retreated to the abandoned rifle
pits. They were driven from the pits in front of Walker's division by a
counterattack led by Major James Williams, Mercer's brigade inspector.[81]

Walker commended the 63d Georgia for gallantry though he commented adversely on their discretion, but he blamed his losses on French
for not covering his (Walker's) right flank. In successive messages on
June 27 and 28 he wrote to French: "My skirmishers are about 250 yards
in my front now. I think, general, from a communication I have just read
from you to General Loring about my skirmishers, that you are laboring
under a great misapprehension. I understand your skirmishers are in your
intrenchments; mine are 250 yards in front of mine."[82]

Later, he wrote: "I have just sent a staff officer, Major Williams (of
Mercer's staff), to General Cockrell [French's leftmost brigade com-
mander]. To advance my skirmishers now, who are 250 yards in front of
my line, yours being in your intrenchments (if I am correctly informed),
exposes them to an open fire in a field, which after they have crossed they
meet a line of battle which they gallantly fought with today, being clubbed
and bayoneted in the pits, owing, they say, to the enemy having passed
their right flank, where your skirmishers were supposed to be."[83]

On June 28 he reminded French one more time: "I lost over 100 of my
skirmishers yesterday; they were flanked and attacked by a line of battle.
They were butted and bayoneted from the pits." When Walker had a
grievance, he did not quickly forget it. Johnston, however, set the record
straight when he showed how French did support Walker after the initial shock: "The Federals approaching Walker's line on the south of the
road were driven back by the fire of artillery directed against their left
flank by Major General French." The reports of French and his chief of

artillery, Major George Storrs, emphatically stated their ability to clear Walker's front with artillery fire. For the rest of the battle Walker's sector was quiet.[84]

If Walker thought the travails of the 63d Georgia were owing to short-comings of French's picket line, one member of that battered regiment had his own opinion. Private Calathiel Helms of E Company wrote home on June 28: "I learn that this loss [in his regiment] would not have been very much if it had not been for the mager [J. V. H. Allen] he made them charge on the yankeys. I recon the mager wanted to get a repertashion and I expect that he will get his wants but I think it will come contrery to his expectashion or at least the privets will not think any the more of him for his bravrey and not so mutch of the bravrey as fool." [85]

The correspondent of the *Augusta Chronicle and Sentinel*, "Aristides," received a different opinion when he visited the army. From Smyrna Church on July 3 he wrote, "In [Jackson's] brigade as well as Mercer's the Augusta boys who escaped on the 27th [June] were all safe and well. I heard much praise of the gallant conduct of Major Allen on that occasion. Colonel Gordon and Lieutenant Colonel Black were both absent, sick, and he was in command. The men like him and stand square up to him. He is kind, affable, and thoughtful of his men and a good soldier. He has been in all the active skirmishers in which his command has been engaged and never leaves his post." [86]

Elsewhere on the field Sherman's planned attacks were equally abortive. On Cheatham's front at the "Dead Angle," no attack was expected but the story was the same. Cheatham had fretted over the salient, or angle, in his line, but he need not have worried. The first Yankee rush overcame the Southern pickets. The main line was more than they could manage. Those who charged against Cleburne's lines fared no better. The attacks of both the IV and XIV corps were failures. Cleburne's division lost only eleven men.[87]

Only on his far right did Sherman achieve a degree of success. Schofield's demonstrations on June 26 and 27 pushed several infantry brigades across Olley Creek, south of Hood's position. From there they were able to move southward, behind Johnston's lines. It was this small action and not the fierce fighting in the other sectors on June 27 which caused the further displacement of the Southern army for from where Schofield now stood he was closer to the Chattahoochee than Johnston was.[88]

Losses at Kennesaw for the Union army range from Sherman's low estimate of 3,000 to the Confederate guess of 7,500. Johnston reported losses

in Hardee's and Loring's corps of 500, but this is certainly too low. Walter
Clark gave his estimate as 630 for the Confederate army of whom more
than one-eighth came from his regiment. Hardee's adjutant general reported losses of slightly over 200 in Cleburne's and Cheatham's divisions
combined. He gave no total for Walker. Walker's estimate of a loss of 100
is about right. In addition to the 88 reported for Mercer's brigade, Ellison
Capers said 11 pickets of the 24th South Carolina were captured in the
rifle pits. French reported his division losses at 186.[89]

Confederate records do not give separate figures for the action at Kennesaw Mountain. Instead, a total is shown for the period June 4 to July 4,
that is, from the withdrawal from Dallas to the withdrawal to the Chattahoochee. These numbers, as usual for killed and wounded only, signify
the intensifying nature of the campaign, especially in losses to sniper fire.
Mercer's brigade suffered 200 wounded in that thirty-day period according to the official returns. Gist had 41 killed and 216 wounded, Jackson
lost 15 killed and 81 wounded, and Stevens's losses were 22 killed and 204
wounded. Overall, the division lost 78 men killed and 679 wounded for a
total of 757. This was a 50 percent increase over the losses from Dalton
through Dallas.[90]

The *Augusta Chronicle and Sentinel* printed casualty reports from three
of the regiments of Mercer's brigade on July 2. For the 54th Georgia for
May 19 to June 30 there were 10 killed, 42 wounded, and 27 missing, totaling 79. From May 7 [?] to June 22, the 57th Georgia reported 2 killed and
28 wounded, totaling 30. The 63d Georgia, which suffered the worst, had
8 killed or mortally wounded, 63 other wounded, and 22 missing, totaling
93, for June 15 to 19 alone. In addition, there was the loss of 88 on June 27
and 5 killed and 30 wounded before the fifteenth. For some unaccountable
reason, none of those killed in Mercer's brigade during this period were
listed in army casualty reports. On June 24, the *Constitutionalist* had listed
names of 11 killed or mortally wounded, 39 wounded and 14 missing in
the 2d Georgia Sharpshooter Battalion through June 20. The battalion
had entered the campaign with 171 effectives.[91]

In a letter to his daughter, apparently written before the opening of the
assault on June 27, Walker described conditions on Kennesaw Mountain:

> For nine days now, our army and the Yankee army have been four or five
> hundred yds. apart, both behind breastworks (and in some places we are only
> one hundred and fifty yds. apart). Our skirmishers are thrown out in front of
> each of our lines and a continuous sharpshooting is kept up. Our batteries,

in sight of each other, are thundering away all the time and, between the minnies [sic] and the shell, soft places are rare. Many of our men and officers are killed and wounded every day. Of course, it must all end in a grand battle to which we are surely but gradually approaching. One hundred and fifty or 200,000 men can't be calling to each other from their respective breastworks without an effort on the part of one or the other to shorten the distance. For instance, Lt. Butler of Genl. Gist's staff was waking up some of the men in the trenches who had from exhaustion fallen asleep. The Yankee skirmisher was near enough to hear him, he was speaking in a loud tone. The Yank yelled out, "That's right. Wake up the d——d rebel. Don't let him sleep." Yesterday another amazing affair occurred. A Yank in front of our works was putting up a bush harbor and one of our men commenced firing at him. "Stop that, Reb, I am only want to get a shady place to go to sleep in. Your sun is too hot for me." "Ah, you rascal, you would not let me sleep last night and I am paying you off," the Reb replied. These kinds of scenes are constantly occuring so you may know in some places we are very close.[92]

Major J. B. Cumming provided a colorful account of the domestic scene:

General Walker and staff, bivouacked a short distance behind the line of his Division, protected, to some extent by the slope of the ground, but there was no safety except under cover. The General had thrown up, for his occupation, a little earth "lunette." I established myself behind a big oak tree and the rest of the staff made a similar provision for themselves. Thus we were pretty safe except on occasions when we had to go up to the lines for one purpose or another. Most of my time was spent behind my tree, reading, writing, sleeping, eating or doing nothing. Our horses were sheltered somewhat lower down the slope. Lucius was with our wagons some distance in the rear, where the cooking was done. He brought me my meals, and every night he came up with a bucket of water, a sponge, and a gourd of country soap and scoured me down behind my tree. This bath was very refreshing but neutralized in a great measure at the end of it by my having to slip back into my dirty and hot old Confederate uniform. I dared not lie down to sleep unless fully dressed, even to my boots. To add to my discomfort I was tortured with "camp itch," otherwise I was well and slept well except when I was disturbed to receive or send out orders.[93]

On July 1 Sherman, reverting to form, began to expand his envelopment of Johnston's left, and on the second the Confederate army, fearing for its line of communications, fell back, first to Smyrna and then to the north bank of the Chattahoochee River.[94]

At Smyrna, General Mercer was taken ill and Colonel Olmstead temporarily assumed command of his brigade. Walker's division had a well-fortified, commanding position except for one hill in their front which would give the enemy a superior location if they occupied it. Hardee ordered Walker to have the hill fortified and defended. Walker relayed the order to Olmstead, who demurred. Walker required that the order be carried out, and Olmstead reluctantly obeyed, sending forward a battery and two hundred infantry. As Olmstead had foreseen, the post did come under Union artillery fire; ten men were killed and wounded before it was evacuated the next day. Forty men were killed and wounded in two days as a result of this incident.[95]

While at Smyrna on July 2, Walker's Georgia Division underwent a modification of its organization. On that day the brigade of John K. Jackson was broken up. Jackson was sent to Florida and the 5th and 47th Georgia Regiments went to Savannah and Charleston. The 5th and 8th Mississippi, 65th Georgia, and 2nd Georgia Sharpshooter Battalion were attached to Gist's brigade. When Mercer's brigade had been sent to the army in April, it had been intended as a replacement for Jackson's depleted regiments. Now the dissolution could be put off no longer. The loss of the two regiments to Savannah cost the division about six-hundred effective men. Walker's division, which had had fifty-five hundred present for duty on June 30, was reduced to forty-five hundred by the return of July 10. Private William Hurst of the 66th Georgia wrote on July 4 that his company had only half the men it had when it left Dalton two months earlier. Walker's was still the largest division in Hardee's corps.[96]

A month before the breakup of Jackson's brigade, Colonel George Smith's 1st Georgia Confederate Regiment had been transferred from it to Stevens's brigade. Major John Nisbet's 26th Georgia Battalion had been detached from the army in June to escort Yankee prisoners to Andersonville and remained on prisoner escort duty to the end of the war. The transfer of Smith's regiment made up for the loss of strength in Stevens's brigade.[97]

One other change in the division in June was the substitution of a Georgia company as escort. Company F, 10th Confederate Cavalry, formerly Company A, 19th Georgia Cavalry Battalion, was led by Captain Thaddeus G. Holt. Holt was familiar to Walker from Savannah days in the winter of 1862 when he had commanded a company of Georgia state cavalry attached to Walker's brigade.[98]

Johnston had long since had defensive positions prepared on the south bank of the Chattahoochee in the unlikely event that he might be driven that far back. More recently, General Francis Shoup, the army's chief of artillery, had constructed another line on the north side of the river. Shoup's field fortifications, or "Shoupades" as they were known, were the objects of much derision by the troops who were asked to occupy them. William Norrell called them "ridiculous pens" and said, "The man who put up such works . . . deserved eternal disgrace as an army engineer." Patrick Cleburne made a personal appeal to his men to use them, to which they agreed, but Walker's men tore them down and dug the earthworks to which they had become accustomed. Hamilton Branch wrote that "after dark we were ordered to pull down the stockade and build a breastwork instead," indicating that the order came from higher headquarters than the regiment. Branch could not resist a pun, calling the Shoupades "a wall between the cornfeds and the wheatfeds." [99]

As Johnston's men filed into the works on the north side, there was a general feeling of dissatisfaction with the way the campaign was developing. Morale and fighting spirit were still high for the most part, but there were some soldiers who felt that the crossing of the Chattahoochee marked a low point in their personal war. On July 10, William Adams of the 30th Georgia wrote to his sister from "this side of Chattahoochee" that "I am worse out of hart than ever," and "Well, it looks like we are gone up the spout." William L. Dickey of G. W. Smith's Georgia militia division noted that a great many men from Tennessee and the northern counties of Georgia were leaving the army to go home. [100]

Sergeant John M. Davis of the 66th Georgia wrote his wife, "Some think [the Yankees] can't flank us from the river where we are now but that is all a mistake they will do it if they try it was said they never would drive us from Dalton Gap the best position we ever had but they did if we could not hold them there we can't hold them no where. . . . We are a gone people without healp soon." Calathiel Helms had a similar opinion: "When we went to Dalton [Dallas?] the word was that the Yankees could not flank Johnson any more but they soon flanked him there. . . . The men is all out of heart and say that Georgia will soon have to go under and they are going to the Yankees by the tens and twenties and hundreds a most every night." Even Hamilton Branch noted, "We do want this falling back to stop." [101]

The soldiers were not alone in their discontent. In Richmond the Davis administration was questioning Johnston on his plans for future operations. To Confederate political leaders visiting his headquarters Johnston expressed the opinion that he could hold Sherman on the north side of the Chattahoochee for at least two months. There must have been great chagrin in Richmond when word was received that Johnston had fallen back behind the river on July 9 and taken up a position along Peach Tree Creek, seven miles from Atlanta.[102]

This move was prompted, like so many others, by another of Sherman's skillful envelopments. Finding the Southern position in the prepared fortifications too strong to assault, the far larger Northern army had crossed the river upstream and established a firm bridgehead on the south bank. Johnston, who had looked for a crossing downstream, lost contact with Sherman's army for several days and was completely taken in. Unless Johnston was to allow Sherman's army to get between his and Atlanta, he had no choice but to retire.[103]

In fact, Hardee's corps headquarters had given a warning order to withdraw to the division commanders two nights before they actually pulled back, that is, on July 7. When the withdrawal took place on the ninth, Walker's division evacuated its positions around Bolton Station and crossed to the south bank on a pontoon bridge prepared for the purpose. After the crossings, the bridges were destroyed. This event brought to a head the issue of Johnston's continued leadership.[104]

Walker, too, was approaching another crossroad in his career, as Polk's death in June had created a vacancy for a lieutenant general. The senior major general in the army was Loring, who was temporarily in command of Polk's corps. Next after him, the infantry major generals in order were Cheatham, Hindman, French, Stevenson, Cleburne, Walker, Stewart, and Bate. Hindman, gravely wounded at Kennesaw Mountain, was out of the running. Loring, French, and Stevenson seem not to have been seriously considered. Cheatham had fallen in Bragg's bad graces after Chickamauga, and Cleburne, despite his fighting record, had drawn disfavor with his abolition proposal. He was not a professional soldier, and was foreign-born besides. That left the three junior generals, of whom Bate also was not a professional. Stewart received the promotion on July 7.[105]

We can only speculate on why Walker was not promoted. He was certainly a Bragg man and probably counted on that weighing heavily in the advice given to the president (Bragg was still military adviser to the president). He had taken a strong position during the abolition controversy for which Davis had thanked him. He looked to Johnston, with whom he was also on good terms, for support as a friend and as another professional officer. Also in his favor was Davis's inclination to give weight to West Point officers when making promotions.

To counter those assets, Walker was in chronic bad health. Although his health had not been a factor during most of the time he had been with the Army of Tennessee, he had suffered an attack and been ill during part of June and July. He was known to have a mercurial disposition, to be difficult to get along with, and to be quick and sharp in his criticism of others, as in the case of French at Kennesaw Mountain. Johnston might appreciate Walker's fighting qualities, but there was a limit to how highly he would reward them. If Walker had shone brilliantly on the field at Chickamauga or Chattanooga or during the long retreat from Dalton, he might have been advanced. But his performance had been merely competent and his feeble effort at Lay's Ferry perhaps less than that and was not enough to outweigh his other characteristics. Johnston may have thought Walker was the most competent division commander in the army in May 1863, but evidently he had reevaluated his performance by July 1864. After the performance of Stewart and his division at New Hope Church in May, that general's stock had soared in the army's estimation. Besides, Johnston's opinion counted for little with Jefferson Davis. Even if Johnston had recommended Walker, Davis most likely would have chosen another.

Walker took the promotion more philosophically than might have been expected. In a letter to young Molly on July 2, he wrote:

> I have just learned that Major Genl. Stewart of this army has been appointed a Lt. Genl. to fill Genl. Polk's place. He served in the old army for a short time and afterwards was a professor in a college. He is a very worthy, modest gentleman and, being my junior in years and in rank as a Major Genl., I would under ordinary circumstances feel somewhat overslaughed and slighted but I have been so accustomed to those little mementoes from His Excellency that they have ceased to have any effect on me. Under the trying circumstances we are in, it is my duty to serve in the position that has been assigned me and what I would not stand (being overslaughed) in time of peace I have in these times to calmly submit to. . . . I have the honor of having been *deliberately slighted* from the commencement of the revolution without trial. . . . I shall calmly tread the path of duty feeling that my position is above the shafts of malice and revenge.[106]

Later, Walker found out just how much support he received from his old army friends. On July 12 he informed his wife:

> I have . . . learned something of that recent appointment that has been made. My friends did not recommend me for it. I have understood that one of the Lt. Genls. recommended Stewart and the other Cleburne, and that the

Commdg. Genl. recommended a Virginia Lt. Genl. to take the place who already had the commission. So I don't think friend Jeff is responsible for all the sins that are committed. If my Lt. Genl. [Hardee] had recommended me and the Commanding Genl., backed by Genl. Bragg, had have endorsed it, I think it quite likely Mr. D. would have thought that he had his revenge out and would have appointed me. But here are 3 of my old army acquaintances, men I have served with for over a quarter of a century, two of the 3 professing great friendship, who sit quietly and see me overslaughed.[107]

Hardee had recommended Cleburne and Hood preferred Stewart, a general in his own corps. Johnston wanted to bring to the army Richard S. Ewell, a surplus lieutenant general in the Army of Northern Virginia. Balancing these recommendations, Davis and Bragg found that the most acceptable course was to promote Stewart. Hood was already Davis's favorite, and his recommendation probably carried the most weight with the president. Hardee was tainted as an anti-Bragg man. Johnston's recommendation would have been for nought. Walker's last chance for promotion had gone aglimmering. He must have thought back bitterly to his cooperation with Bragg and Davis over the abolition issue the previous winter and regarded it as wasted effort. Henry D. Clayton, who had been colonel of the 1st Alabama in Walker's brigade at Pensacola, was promoted to lead Stewart's division, and the army prepared for the defense of Atlanta.[108]

15

DEATH OF A GENERAL

July 1864

WHILE WALKER WAS wrestling with his emotions over the promotion of Alexander Stewart, the Army of Tennessee was holding its position on the Peach Tree Creek line. Sherman continued crossing to the south bank of the Chattahoochee until he had his whole army over by July 17. But the real struggle before Atlanta at this point was over the future leadership and operations of the Confederate army defending the city. The army and the Davis administration were dissatisfied with Johnston's tactics. Even so staunch a friend of the commanding general as Walker could write, "I have grown very wearied of this eternal retrograde. When it is to stop I don't know." Now, with Atlanta threatened, some positive action had to be taken.[1]

President Davis dispatched Braxton Bragg to Atlanta to confer with Johnston. Bragg arrived on July 13 and began a round of meetings with the army and corps commanders. Walker was aware that Bragg was in camp but did not know the precise purpose of his visit. As a division commander he was not privy to the confidential discussions. The purpose of Bragg's arrival was not clear at army headquarters either. On July 13, Mackall wrote his wife that Bragg would pay a visit that morning but "with what purpose we know not." Mackall thought Bragg might have been sent by Davis to infuse discontent into the army and then use that as an excuse to relieve Johnston. Mackall said that if Bragg were to be Johnston's replacement Mackall would leave the army. On July 14 Mackall informed his wife that he thought Bragg's visit had no special purpose and on the fifteenth he wrote further that he felt that Davis had sent Bragg into "honorable exile."[2]

Bragg did have a purpose. He was there to evaluate Johnston's plans for the defense of Atlanta and to make a change in army command if warranted. On July 16 Davis sent Johnston a telegram demanding that he state his intentions. Johnston refused to commit himself to an offensive other than to say that he was watching for an opportunity to fight to advantage. Later, Johnston claimed that he was ready to go over to the offensive when Sherman tried to cross Peach Tree Creek and he had told Senator Louis Wigfall of this strategy in June.[3]

It was too late. Johnston's reply to Davis's telegram had sealed his fate. Bragg had already recommended that Hood be given command of the army. Hood would be jumped over Hardee, who outranked him, but Bragg, perhaps in connivance with Hood, convinced Davis that Hardee was too closely associated with Johnston's withdrawal policy. Too, Hardee was still identified as an anti-Bragg man. Late on July 17 Davis had the adjutant and inspector general send Johnston a telegram relieving him from command and appointing Hood in his place.[4]

Hood's first reaction was to telegraph Richmond asking that the order be countermanded on the grounds that a change in the face of the enemy would be harmful to the army. In this request he was joined by Hardee and Stewart. Davis refused. Johnston turned command of the army over to Hood on the afternoon of the eighteenth and went into Atlanta. He left for Macon the next day. When Walker moved his division along the Marietta road on July 18, he had his men shoulder arms while the officers saluted as they passed Johnston's quarters in tribute to the old commander. Many of the officers and men removed their hats. General Clement H. Stevens wrote Johnston a personal note of condolence. Walker wanted to have the division halt and give a cheer for "Old Joe" but Johnston asked that they not do so. According to a letter written by Mrs. Johnston ten days later, Walker accompanied the Johnstons to the train on the day of their departure. "His was the last face we saw in Atlanta, his generous hand was the last that clasped my husband's, his the last affectionate voice that bade farewell and offered his home as a home with his soldier's face covered with tears. I shall never forget him, never cease remembering that last grasp of the hand, that last look of his face as the cars moved off, and the two faithful soldiers, now parted forever on this earth."[5]

The news of the change of command was announced to the army early in the morning of the eighteenth. Hamilton Branch reflected the feelings of the army when he wrote, "Everyone seemed to feel as if they had lost their best friend and the general remark was, well this army is lost, and everyone seemed whipped. As for myself, I have never felt so downhearted in my life as I did yesterday and if we had not been ordered off, I know that I could not have helped crying."[6]

Walker explained how he heard the news and his reaction:

I was handed early this morning before I got out of blanket (I won't say bed) an order of Genl. Johnston turning over the command of the army to Lt. Genl. Hood. I thought when I saw Bragg come that he had come to relieve him but I knew he had something on hand. I have feared this all along. Now that it is all over, I tell you . . . that I never have approved of our falling back but have been in favor of a fight and I have felt satisfied in my own mind that if Johnston fell back behind the Chattahoochee he would be relieved and when I saw Bragg I jumped at the conclusion that he had come to relieve him. Johnston and I have always been friends. For over a quarter of a century we have known each other and though . . . I do not think officially he has stood up for me as I expected from our past friendship, yet I admire him and am fond of him and dislike exceedingly to see him leave us. Hood has "gone up like a rocket." It is to be hoped . . . that "he will not come down like the stick." He is brave. Whether he has the capacity to command armies (for it requires a high order of talent) time will develop. I will express no opinion. A fight now is obliged to come off for if Johnston has been relieved for falling back (as I take it for granted he was), it is as much as to say to Hood, don't you try the same game.[7]

Walker's remarks were prescient. He was not the only one to doubt Hood's abilities at the highest level of command. In Virginia, when queried about Hood's capacities by President Davis, Robert E. Lee had responded, "Hood is a bold fighter. I am doubtful as to other qualities necessary." When further pressed by Davis, Lee had answered, "Hood is a bold fighter, very industrious on the battlefield, careless off." As for a fight being "obliged to come off," Walker would only have to wait two days to find out.[8]

After Hood's promotion was confirmed, Hardee asked for a transfer from the Army of Tennessee, saying he had no confidence in Hood's leadership. Bragg supported Hardee's removal, even suggesting that he be exchanged with General Dick Taylor in the Trans-Mississippi, but Davis ordered Hardee to remain at his post for the good of the country. Walker compared Hardee's being passed over for promotion to his own problems:

Hardee ranks Hood. "The poisoned chalice is commended to his own lips" now. I wonder how he fancies this *overslaughing* business. His star has always been in the *ascendant* and his always the most daz[z]ling light around the

throne. I wonder how he likes to have it obscured and suffer an eclipse by
the passage of this new planet between him and the sun. He ought to revolve
around my headqrs. awhile and get a little consolation from one who has
suffered so many similar eclipses as to have lost all light. It might be some
consolation to him since his light is somewhat obscured to see that mine has
been entirely extinguished.[9]

On Hardee's recommendation, Hood appointed Cheatham to the temporary command of his own corps. This was a questionable assignment.
Cheatham had no prior experience commanding a corps in battle. He was
clearly an anti-Bragg man, which made him an unusual choice for Hood,
the Bragg supporter. Although Hardee had recommended Cheatham for
the vacancy created by Polk's death in June, he had not been selected,
almost certainly because of army politics. His appointment gave Hood two
out of three corps commanders who were his political opponents at a time
critical to the needs of the Army of Tennessee. But it would be Cheatham's
inexperience more than his politics that would detract from the army's
ability to carry out Hood's wishes. Cheatham's senior brigadier, George
Maney, took command of the Tennessee division.[10]

About the time of the change of command, Walker was interviewed by a
correspondent of the *Atlanta Intelligencer* and asked his opinion about the
defense of Atlanta. Echoing the fire-breathing sentiments voiced at Savannah two years earlier, Walker said he "had rather receive the death wound
than see Atlanta surrendered without contesting every inch of ground for
its possession," and, he went on, he "would hang his head in shame to
see Georgia overrun by the enemy, and her men failing in their duty."
His new commander would soon adopt a policy that would meet with his
approbation.[11]

In the midst of the changes taking place in the Confederate high command, Sherman continued his inexorable advance on Atlanta. Thomas
faced Hood across Peach Tree Creek directly north of the city while Schofield and McPherson were further to the east, in the direction of Decatur.
A gap of about two miles had opened up, separating Thomas's left from
Schofield's right. On the morning of July 19 Thomas secured a lodgment
on the south side of the creek and rapidly passed four divisions over while
the rest of his army remained on the north bank. His army was spread
along a six-mile front, and with Schofield and McPherson miles away
Thomas might be vulnerable. This was the opportunity for which Johnston claimed he had been waiting, and Hood now moved to take advantage
of it.[12]

The question arises as to whether or not Johnston ever announced to the army his intention to attack Sherman while the latter was astride Peach Tree Creek. Ellison Capers stated unequivocally in his report that Johnston published an address on July 17 announcing his intention to make an attack. Capers also wrote that the change of command order was read to the troops on July 18. Thomas L. Connelly concluded that Johnston's plans were never sufficiently formalized to have been announced and were mainly described after his removal or after the war. It is possible that Capers combined the two announcements into one in his memory.[13]

Under Hood's command, Cheatham (commanding Hood's corps), the Georgia militia under General G. W. Smith, and Wheeler's cavalry were deployed to the east against Schofield and McPherson. Hood's plan of action was for an attack of two corps on the exposed Union front, Hardee on the right and Stewart on the left. Hardee's divisions right to left were those of Bate, Walker, and Maney (commanding Cheatham's division), with Cleburne in reserve. Stewart formed with Loring and Walthall on line and French in reserve. Each division would attack on its front in turn, that is, in echelon, beginning on the right. The object was to isolate Thomas's divided army, break it up, and pin it against the Chattahoochee.[14]

The action was disjointed, poorly coordinated, and poorly executed. To begin with, Hood ordered Cheatham to shift to his right, south, so as not to be overlapped by McPherson's left. Cheatham fumbled the assignment and moved so far that his left lost contact with Hardee's right. In compensation, Hardee and Stewart were also ordered to move laterally to the right, but the move occurred in sporadic shifts and jerks to keep up with Cheatham's erratic movement. As a result of those delays, the attack, which had been ordered for 1:00 P.M. on July 20, did not get under way until 4:00 P.M. Stewart's corps actually preceded Hardee in the attack. After initial success, the attack was repulsed with terrible loss, partly because of lack of support on its right.[15]

While the Confederate army was shuffling into position, Thomas passed the rest of his army across the river and even had time for some of his men, notably John Newton's division of IV Corps, to build field fortifications. Newton formed his division with the brigades of General Nathan Kimball and Colonel John Blake on line. Colonel Luther P. Bradley's third brigade was in support, as was a single four-gun battery of artillery. Newton's left flank was in the air, covered only by a thicket of heavy underbrush. On the right, William T. Ward's division of Hooker's XX Corps was in line several hundred yards to Newton's rear. Thus both Newton's right and left flanks were exposed.

Bate led off the attack against Newton first, between three and four o'clock in the afternoon. His division passed the Federal left flank and floundered through the woods for hours. An attempt was made late in the day to have him turn inward against Newton's left, but it did not happen. Walker's troops, aligned with the brigades of Mercer, Stevens, and Gist right to left, stepped off soon after Bate. The Georgia division swept forward "with a rapidity and absence of confusion I have never seen equaled," General Kimball later reported. Colonel Joseph Conrad of the 15th Missouri in Kimball's brigade said the Rebels advanced "firing and yelling, demanding [us] to surrender," so confident were they of success.[16]

The three advancing brigades rolled up to Newton's barricades and lapped around both ends. Some of Mercer's men wandered into the thickets where Bate's division was enmeshed. Gist's left passed Newton's right, penetrating as far as Ward's front. In so doing, they exposed themselves to an enfilading fire from Newton's flank and fell back. Some of them were captured by Ward's troops before they could retire.

While Newton's two flanks were being threatened, his barricaded front line was more than holding its own. In the face of withering musket and artillery fire the Confederate troops slowed, began to waver, and then came to a standstill. They continued to fire "heavily but wildly" into the Union lines as their confusion increased. Numerous Southern color-bearers attempting to rally the men were shot down. Despite the exhortations of their officers the Confederate infantry finally gave way.[17]

Hamilton Branch gave a somewhat different version of the battle. According to the account in a letter written to his mother the next day, Walker's division formed in two lines with Stevens's brigade on the left and half of Mercer's on the right in the front line, and Gist on the left and the other half of Mercer on the right in the second line. The front line went forward and Stevens made good progress on his right but his left was repulsed. After Stevens was wounded and his brigade driven back the second line advanced. The 54th Georgia formed on the right of Gist's brigade and three of its companies acted as brigade skirmishers.[18]

On Walker's left, Cheatham's division under Maney enjoyed partial success. Driving first into the gap between Newton and Ward, the Tennesseans approached within two hundred yards of the XX Corps position where they also came under concentrated artillery and rifle fire. They were able to hold on in place by digging in behind the crest of a hill but withdrew after nightfall. All along Hardee's front the fighting continued until about 6:00 P.M., when the attack was called off. Orders were given for Cleburne to replace Walker in line but were countermanded before they could be carried out and Cleburne was sent off to another crisis point.[19]

Hood praised Stewart for his conduct but implied that Hardee had done little more than conduct a skirmish. He also blamed Hardee for delaying the start of the action. Hardee's biographer concedes that the delay was the corps commander's fault. The real fault lay with both Hood, who had exercised virtually no supervision over his corps commanders, and Hardee, whose sulkiness in complying with the orders of his former junior was unforgivable in a man of his maturity and experience. Confederate losses were estimated at twenty-five hundred to five thousand.[20]

The Georgia division was so badly cut up that later, in his report, Hardee referred to it as "Walker's beaten troops." Complete casualty figures are not available for any except Mercer's brigade, which reported losses of three killed, fifteen wounded, and three missing. This was the brigade that partially bypassed Newton's left and went off into the woods. Returns prepared after the war for the two South Carolina regiments of Gist's brigade identify fifteen killed, eleven wounded, and one killed or captured at Peach Tree Creek.[21]

Colonel Nisbet recorded that the 66th Georgia of Stevens's brigade lost one-fourth of its strength. Lieutenant William R. Ross of the 66th Georgia told his sister in a letter that his regiment went into action with 190 men and lost 74. Among them was Private William R. Hurst of Company C, killed in action. In his own company Ross lost 7 out of 12 men. The *Augusta Chronicle and Sentinel* of July 26 listed the names of 14 officers of the 66th Georgia wounded, 1 mortally, at Peach Tree Creek. Sergeant Hagan of the 29th Georgia, same brigade, told his wife that his regiment had "suffered considerably," although not as badly as some other regiments in the brigade. The most serious loss was that of Brigadier General Clement H. Stevens, who had his horse shot out from under him. As he stepped off the fallen animal, Stevens received a mortal shot in the head, just behind the left ear. He died in Macon on July 25.[22]

William Napier, younger brother of Lieutenant Colonel Leroy Napier, formerly of the 8th Georgia Battalion, wrote to his sister-in-law, Mrs. Briggs H. Napier, on July 25 to tell her that her husband, a captain in the 66th Georgia, had lost a leg at Peach Tree Creek. In the same letter he told her that General Stevens had been "shot in the temple," and that he had carried Stevens off the field. Command of the brigade devolved temporarily on Colonel George A. Smith of the 1st Georgia Confederate.[23]

The attack by Hardee and Stewart was not the only combat taking place on July 20. To the east, McPherson and Schofield continued to press Cheatham and Wheeler's cavalry from the east. A fierce struggle developed over an eminence called Bald Hill, later known as Leggett's Hill, which dominated the southern end of the lines of the contesting armies. Wheeler was struggling to prevent Frank Blair's XVII Corps from taking the height, and late in the day called for help. Hood ordered Hardee to send his freshest division, Cleburne's, to Wheeler's assistance. By the evening of July 20 and all the next day, Cleburne was closely engaged with McPherson in the fight to protect Hood's right flank.[24]

The unsuccessful action at Peach Tree Creek and fears for his right flank caused Hood to withdraw from the north into the inner defenses of the city. Nevertheless, he was determined to strike an offensive blow to break Sherman's chokehold. Hood feared that Sherman might swing McPherson further to the south to sever the Macon rail line. Union cavalry was raiding as far east as Covington, tearing up railroad track. A large Union artillery and wagon park was encamped in the town square at Decatur. Hood's next blow would be against this left wing of Sherman's army.[25]

Hood's plan was sound. Cheatham's corps, supported by the Georgia militia, would continue to hold Atlanta's eastern defenses. Stewart and Hardee faced Thomas on the north. Hood would leave Stewart in the lines, send Hardee and Wheeler on a wide sweep to the south and east, strike in behind McPherson's left, unleash Wheeler's cavalry in the Union rear, and roll up the Union line from left to right. When Hardee's action proved successful, Cheatham would strike against McPherson's front and drive the whole Union force back behind Peach Tree Creek. Hood's original plan was to send both Hardee and Wheeler all the way to Decatur, but he later modified that for Hardee only to get behind McPherson's left flank. Hardee's corps was picked for the turning movement because in Hood's view it was fresher than Stewart's after its relative lack of exertion on the twentieth. Also, it was the largest corps in the army and had the only experienced corps commander and two of the most experienced division commanders, Cleburne and Walker. The movement was to begin on the night of July 21 and the attack to start early the next morning.[26]

Hardee was still fuming over Hood's criticism at Peach Tree Creek. He was just beginning to taste the "poisoned chalice." The weather was extremely hot and humid. The troops were weary from the battle of July 20 and from a day of digging entrenchments on July 21. On the night of the twenty-first the lucky ones got three hours sleep, some as few as an hour. Several officers, including Major Cumming, later commented on how many men fell out of ranks during the march because of exhaustion. Nevertheless, in the darkness the divisions of Bate, Walker, and Maney filed out of their entrenchments near where West Peachtree now joins

Peachtree Street and began the long slog down to the McDonough road. The distance to be covered that night has been estimated at fifteen to eighteen miles. Hood later repeated several times in his own defense that the distance from Atlanta was only six miles. In doing so, he deliberately ignored the roundabout route taken by Hardee.[27]

As they moved down Peachtree and passed Hood's headquarters in the Leyden house, Walker pulled out of line and entered, leaving Major Cumming waiting in the street. A curious interview between Hood and Walker followed. In Hood's words: "[Walker] called me aside, and with characteristic frankness expressed his appreciation of the grave responsibility attached to the position in which I had been placed; assured me he well understood the condition of the Army after our retreat from Dalton, and wished me to know before he entered the battle that he was with me in heart and purpose and intended to abide by me in all emergencies." According to Major Cumming, when Walker came out from his meeting with Hood he was "full of serious enthusiasm." Walker told Cumming that Hood had said that the next day's battle was necessary to save Atlanta. Cumming wrote that Walker "was aglow with martial fire from that moment."[28]

Certainly the prospect of combat always animated Walker, but what had prompted him to call on Hood? No doubt he saw in the "bold fighter" a kindred offensive spirit. No doubt, as he had said earlier, he was tired of the "eternal retrograde." The policy of an aggressive defense of the city was in consonance with his own expressed opinion. But it is possible to look at this late night meeting from another perspective. Bragg, who had been Walker's first patron, had failed him in the matter of promotion. Johnston had also let him down. Now Johnston, though lamented, was gone and Hood was in charge. Hood seemed to be in favor with Bragg. Hardee was out of favor with Bragg and now, apparently, with Hood. Walker's ambition, though dampened from what it had been three years before, led him once again to seek out the source of power and promotion in the Army of Tennessee. In the letter three days previously, Walker had indicated his doubts about Hood's ability to command an army. Now he was signaling his intention to "abide by" the commander about whom he entertained such doubts.

Having completed his fence-mending, Walker again took up the march around McPherson's left flank. The route was south down Peachtree and Piedmont streets to the location of the present state capitol, then down Capitol Avenue (the McDonough road) out of the city. The trek continued in a southerly direction for about five more miles to the Fayetteville road, near the crossing of the South River. Here the straggling column made its first change of direction, to the east. Somewhere in this area Cleburne's division disengaged from McPherson's front and fell in column behind Walker's. Proceeding in a northeasterly direction, the troops made their way along the Fayetteville road to the crossing of Intrenchment Creek. William Cobb's mill was located here. About half a mile further east the column turned north on Middle McDonough road. Another half mile to the north and the column halted near dawn at William Cobb's house. The troops rested for an hour while Hardee, Cleburne, and Walker conferred with Cobb, who agreed to act as guide for Cleburne. A local resident, Case Turner, a sometime employee of Cobb's, volunteered or was pressed into service as guide for Walker's division. In answer to questions about obstacles in the path, Cobb and Turner agreed there was only one, Terry's millpond, a wide span of water on Sugar Creek, just northwest of where the creek was crossed by the Fayetteville road.[29]

A private in the 5th Company of the Washington Artillery, Slocomb's Battery, in another battalion, saw Walker about this time and later gave a vivid picture of the General's appearance.

> When on this march behind our men, we passed close by Gen. W. H. T. Walker and his staff. There were his men in front on the other side of a clearing. We could see the long line of them, standing, waiting "to go in." We passed close to Walker himself, "Fighting Billy," as he was called, a hero of the Mexican War.
>
> One of the thinnest men I ever saw. Imagine a fence rail, dressed in complete uniform, closely buttoned up warm as it was, topped by a long pale face, almost hidden, however, by a bushy black beard, and above all a huge black felt hat with a big black feather curling around it. I saw him "full front" as we went by, and there seemed hardly space enough on his attenuated body for the double row of buttons of his general's uniform coat. Long and tall [!] as he looked, as he sat on his horse, straight as a ram rod, evidently waiting with his staff around him to "go in."[30]

The weary column resumed its forward movement for something less than a mile. Here Cleburne's division branched off to the northwest along Flat Shoals road. Hardee, with the divisions of Bate and Walker, continued on up the Fayetteville road to the northeast. The initial role of Maney's division is unclear. Some say he was first deployed to Bate's right and later moved around to the left, some that he was in reserve and then moved to the left, and others that he was put in line on Cleburne's left from the outset. Bate said that Maney's brigade of Cheatham's division was assigned to him as support but was taken away before going into action. Wheeler's cavalry also took the Fayetteville road on the way to the Decatur town square and the Union wagon park. After another three or four miles the infantry divisions began their deployment by facing to their left, or northwest, and advanced parallel to the flow of Sugar Creek. In his report, Daniel Govan of Cleburne's division said his brigade formed the left of the line and the rest of the corps was to dress to his right. Bate reported that his division formed the right of the line and originally all other divisions were to dress on him but later he was ordered to dress to the left. Bate may have been on the east side of the creek; Walker was on the west side with Cleburne off in the woods to his left.[31]

The area along the banks of Sugar Creek was densely overgrown. The troops advancing in line of battle had great difficulty maintaining their alignment and keeping contact with their flank formations. Walker was trying to keep in touch with Bate on his right on the other side of the creek and was groping for Cleburne off to his left somewhere in the woods. As the line approached the widow Terry's house, Walker proposed to Hardee a change in the advance to get free of the entanglement. Hardee responded quickly and hotly with a retort that the attack had been delayed enough already and he would brook no more setbacks. Walker was infuriated by the answer and by Hardee's curt manner. He vowed to Cumming that he would make Hardee pay for the insult. Walker, of course, was not taking into account Hardee's state of mind over Hood's promotion and Hood's criticism of Hardee's delay two days earlier or of the mental weariness of both Hardee and himself.[32]

About 11:00 A.M. the division came within sight of the millpond. The advice had been right. It was a formidable obstacle. The pond was about half a mile long, ten feet deep, and filled the entire width of the narrow creek valley. The ground around its banks was damp and muddy, causing horses to mire almost up to their bellies. A detour to higher ground on the west bank of the creek was required. Now the worst came to light. An arm of the pond ran off to the left, or west, of the creek valley for some distance requiring an even wider detour and loss of contact with Bate's division.

Walker flew into a rage. The long night march, his own physical discomfort, the rebuff from Hardee, the delay in the attack, and now this obstacle were too much for his volatile temper. He vented his wrath on Case Turner, the guide, accusing him of deliberately leading the division astray. In vain did Turner protest that he had warned of the pond earlier.

Walker became so incensed that he drew his pistol and threatened to shoot the guide. Only the intercession of Major Cumming, or so the guide thought, prevented Walker from carrying out his threat. Just about this time, a courier arrived from Hardee apologizing for the exchange that had taken place between them. Walker was somewhat mollified but promised Cumming that he would still settle with Hardee later.[33]

Nevertheless, the advance must continue and it did. Stevens's and Gist's brigades were on line right to left with Mercer's behind them. The maneuver around the west arm of the pond was completed and Walker pushed on ahead, crossing Sugar Creek to the east bank at the head of the pond. The three brigades moved farther upstream before crossing, but soon the entire division had shifted direction to the northeast. Here the division commander sent three of his staff officers, Major Cumming, Captain Troup, and Captain Ross, to the three brigades with messages on their alignment. He continued forward accompanied by Captain Talbot, his cousin and volunteer aide, the guide Case Turner, his orderly, Private J. T. Collier of the 10th Confederate Cavalry, and his personal escort, Company F of the 10th Confederate under Lieutenant J. F. Bass. As they pushed up the slope from the creek line, Walker stopped to raise his field glasses to his eyes. One or two shots rang out. Walker slumped forward. He may have fallen from his horse or he may have been propped up in the saddle by an aide. It was just about noon and he was only a few feet northeast of where present-day Glenwood Avenue crosses Sugar Creek.[34]

There are no clear accounts of what happened next. Case Turner claimed that he fled immediately. Whether Walker was still alive when his aides reached him is unclear. According to Wilbur Kurtz, he was carried to the widow Terry's house, possibly still alive. A 1973 book on the Atlanta campaign cited an eyewitness report that the body was left where it fell and recovered from a pile of dead after the battle, but this is unlikely. The tale that Walker was shot laterally through one or both thighs, fell from his horse, and bled to death in a few minutes also appears to be without merit. This story was supposed to have been given to Wilbur Kurtz as part of the Case Turner file, but there is no evidence of it in Kurtz's notes. In another version of the story, Walker was stopped by a courier with a dispatch and paused to ask for his portfolio to write a response when he was shot.[35]

So far, the story of Walker's death has been told as it was written by Wilbur Kurtz in 1930. Kurtz based his account on the story of Case Turner as it had been told to J. W. McWilliams years earlier and then repeated to Kurtz. In succeeding years Kurtz's rendition gained acceptance and is now widely believed because of his stature as a historian of the Atlanta campaign. But there was another version of Walker's death that had currency in the late nineteenth century, especially among the officers and men of his division. It first appeared in print only a few weeks after the general's death, and will be described in due course.

In spite of Hood's later claims to the contrary, Hardee, at the end of his long march, had managed to turn the extreme left of McPherson's Army of the Tennessee. The left of Hardee's line of four divisions, Maney, Cleburne, Walker, and Bate, from left to right, just fronted on McPherson's extreme left. The rest of the Confederate corps would have lapped completely around the Union left flank but for one fortuitous event.[36]

As Sherman's grip closed in to the east of Atlanta, the two divisions of Grenville M. Dodge's XVI Corps were squeezed out of the line between Schofield's Army of the Ohio on the right or north and McPherson's Army of the Tennessee, to which they belonged, on the left or south. This happened on July 21. One of them, John W. Fuller's two-brigade Fourth Division, sent one brigade to protect the wagon park in Decatur. The other brigade with division headquarters marched to the immediate rear of the far left of McPherson's line, where it was expected to extend the line the next day. There it camped on the night of the twenty-first. On the morning of the twenty-second the other division, Thomas Sweeny's Second, brought its two brigades on line with the Fourth. These three brigades with their supporting artillery formed an accidental but vital left flank guard for Sherman's entire command, facing to the southeast while the main line at this point faced west.[37]

When the advancing divisions of Hardee's corps broke from the cover of the underbrush into the open that afternoon, they found themselves confronting across a ravine the lines of Fuller's and Sweeny's three brigades and three batteries, about five thousand men. Bate's division advanced against Sweeny, Walker struck Sweeny's right and Fuller's left, and Cleburne's attack fell on Fuller's right and into the gap between Fuller's right and the rear of Frank Blair's XVII Corps around Leggett's Hill. Maney's division apparently did not participate in this first charge.[38]

Although taken by surprise, the veteran Union troops and their commanders reacted quickly. Their concentrated rifle and artillery fire mowed down the attackers. Several lines of blue-coated skirmishers were overrun, but the Rebel masses could not penetrate Dodge's main line. Two separate charges were made against the XVI Corps without effect and with great loss before Hardee shifted the weight of his attacks. Only on the left was there success when Cleburne's brigades got into the gap between Dodge's right and the rear of Frank Blair's XVII Corps.[39]

About 1:00 P.M. that day Dodge was having lunch at Fuller's headquarters when the sound of heavy firing broke out to the southeast. Hardee's corps, after its hours of blundering through the underbrush, had finally come in contact with McPherson's army. Dodge, Fuller, and Sweeny quickly aligned their men and guns to meet this unexpected threat. In the position they took, any attackers would have to advance against them across an open field. And so the Confederate divisions did.[40]

While Cleburne advanced successfully on the left, in the gap between Blair's left and the XVI Corps, Bate and Walker had to contend with Dodge's brigades on Hardee's right. With or without Walker at its head, the Georgia division had formed in line of battle just before noon along with the rest of Hardee's corps. Each division had one brigade in reserve behind the front line. Walker's division was ordered to pivot to its right and along with Bate's division attack the hill on which Sweeny and Fuller were posted.[41]

Stevens's brigade on the right, under Colonel George A. Smith, made the turn successfully, but Gist, on the left, having to cover a greater distance, fell behind. Smith's men crossed a field covered with underbrush, forded a marshy stream waist deep, and then advanced up a sloping field into the teeth of Fuller's rifles and artillery. Twice they reached the blue line and twice they were driven back. Worse, with their left flank unguarded because of Gist having fallen behind, they came under enemy fire from that quarter and were driven back to their starting point in confusion. Among the wounded was Colonel Smith, who received flesh wounds in both arms and had his horse shot from under him. Command of the brigade passed to Colonel Nisbet of the 66th Georgia.[42]

Then it was the turn of Gist's men. Again a lone Confederate brigade swept forward. The Georgians and South Carolinians found themselves in the same predicament as their predecessors a few minutes before. With both flanks exposed they were subject to murderous fire. If this version of the battle is to be believed, there was one difference: Walker placed himself at the head of Gist's brigade and waving his hat urged them on. Gist was wounded, but pushed forward; his aide was mortally wounded. Once again the fire was too much. Though they pressed within forty yards of the Federal line, they could not stand the withering blast from three sides. They fell back, their trail marked by the bodies of the dead and wounded. It was at the beginning of the advance that Walker was allegedly killed by a Union volley.[43]

Meanwhile, Mercer's brigade waited in reserve, partially sheltered in the woods. Here Colonel Olmstead of the 1st Georgia Volunteers was struck in the head by a shell fragment while he was adjusting his line. When Walker was killed, General Mercer was called to lead the division. With Olmstead wounded, the command of the brigade fell to Colonel William Barkuloo of the 57th Georgia. Mercer ordered Barkuloo to attempt where Gist and Stevens had failed. Barkuloo got as far as the marshy stream, but after losing twenty to thirty men from artillery fire, he prudently retired back to the wood. Captain George Mercer seconded Barkuloo's report of his actions, saying that after Gist's and Stevens's brigades "became badly scattered" his brigade advanced for a charge but withdrew when success appeared impossible.[44]

General Mercer then ordered the fragments of Smith's brigade to form on Barkuloo's right and the balance of Gist's on his left. A second assault by the whole division in concert with Bate's division was contemplated, but just then Mercer's brigade was ordered off to the left to support Cleburne's successful attack. As a result, what was left of Smith's brigade, under Colonel Nisbet, after waiting vainly for Gist to join them, advanced on Bate's left. After crossing the same low ground as before, Nisbet and his brigade encountered the single brigade of Fuller's division. Nisbet and two officers and several men of the 66th Georgia were surrounded by men of the 39th Ohio and captured. The colors of the 25th Georgia were captured by the 64th Illinois at the same time, one of only two sets of colors lost by any unit of Walker's commands during the war.[45]

All that afternoon the Confederate troops hurled themselves against the Union lines. Bate reported that his division was reduced to twelve hundred effectives. With Maney's brigade of Cheatham's division and Robert C. Tyler's brigade of his own sent to the left to support Cleburne's success, his men could do no more than hold their ground. Guns and colors were captured on both sides, the battle ebbed back and forth, and McPherson was killed in the woods by Cleburne's men. At 3:00 P.M. Hood, who had been watching from Atlanta, finally launched Cheatham's corps and G. W. Smith's Georgia militia division against McPherson's front. The pressure was great, but the Union line held. About five o'clock Maney's (Cheatham's) division got into action against the south end of Blair's line. Their attack was resolute but fruitless. They too were driven back. Large parts of the Union line were occupied but had to be abandoned that night.[46]

At the end of the day Mercer's brigade, by now commanded by Lieutenant Colonel Morgan Rawls of the 54th Georgia, was attached to Lowrey's brigade of Cleburne's division for one more attempt. Lowrey's, Maney's,

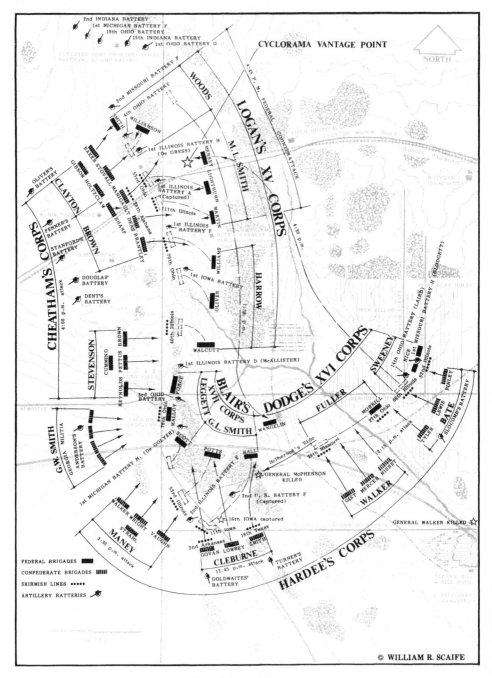

The Battle of Atlanta, July 22, 1864

and Mercer's brigades were aligned to overcome the last line of defenses in the rear of Blair's XVII Corps. The brigade organization was badly confused with regiments mixed together and even men of the three brigades intermingled. Rawls was severely wounded in the face, and the command of Mercer's brigade fell on Lieutenant Colonel Cincinnatus Guyton of the 57th Georgia. The initial rush was full of enthusiasm but soon ran out of steam. When some of Maney's troops were ordered to halt and lie down the others followed suit. Despite his utmost exhortations, Guyton could not get the men to advance any farther. For this brigade, at least, the battle of Atlanta was over. Hamilton Branch believed that the Rebel commanders erred in halting after overrunning two Union lines but it was obvious to most that the men could do no more.[47]

By evening each side claimed a partial victory. Hood claimed fourteen guns and eighteen colors as trophies and could boast that Hardee held his position in close proximity to the Federal left. Sherman's triumph was that his grip had not been dislodged. He estimated that Hood had suffered 8,000 casualties he could ill afford. John A. Logan, who had succeeded to the temporary command after McPherson's death, reported that the Army of the Tennessee captured 1,017 prisoners and buried or returned to Confederate lines 1,822 dead. Logan's estimate of total Confederate losses was 10,000. Federal losses were about 3,700.[48]

To support the second version of Walker's death there are several contemporary stories of him being shot from the saddle while charging the Union lines or rallying his troops. The first of these was reported on August 2 by Brigadier General John W. Fuller, commanding one of the two divisions of XVI Corps. Fuller wrote that sometime after 2:00 P.M. that hot July afternoon, "A general officer (supposed to be General Walker) rode out from the woods, and swinging his hat made a great effort to urge forward his troops. The next moment his horse went back riderless, and so sharp was the fire of our men that nobody seemed to heed the cry of their officers to 'bring off the general.'"[49]

Two Confederate generals besides Walker were hit by enemy fire on July 22. S. R. Gist received a painful but not debilitating wound in the hand. He continued to lead his brigade until he fainted two hours later. James Argyle Smith, commanding Hiram Granbury's brigade of Cleburne's division, was gravely wounded but not in front of Fuller's division. While the incident Fuller witnessed could have been Gist falling from his saddle in a dead faint, it could also have been Walker receiving his death wound.[50]

Some of Walker's officers gave similar accounts of his death years after the battle. In a letter written to a newspaper in 1867, Theo. H. Winn of the 25th Georgia wrote that Walker had been killed while urging on the 24th South Carolina. By Winn's account, Walker's horse was shot and, as the general stepped off, he too was gunned down. This detail sounds suspiciously like the mortal wounding of C. H. Stevens on July 20 and Winn may have confused the two incidents, but it was a confusion common among veterans of Walker's division. Captain John H. Steinmeyer of the 24th South Carolina gave a similar story in a letter to Ellison Capers in 1880. Steinmeyer's report was secondhand because he was absent from the regiment on July 22. Steinmeyer wrote that during the approach to the battlefield Gist halted at one point to get a better feel for the lay of the land. Walker rode up and ordered "in strong terms" that the advance be continued. Then "with his usual impetuosity, [he] dashed forward" and was killed. This could well have been the incident construed to be Walker "rallying" Gist's brigade.[51]

Colonel James C. Nisbet of the 66th Georgia also reported that Walker was killed while rallying the South Carolinians. In Nisbet's version, the left flank of his brigade was exposed because Gist's brigade became separated from the rest of the division. Walker went personally to find Gist and was shot while leading that brigade back into line. Nisbet, however, was not a particularly reliable reporter. In his letter to Joseph B. Cumming in 1951, Wilbur Kurtz said that Nisbet only heard about Walker being killed while rallying Gist's brigade in front of Fuller's division, but this does not mean it was not true.[52]

More substance is given to these reports by the accounts carried in contemporary newspapers, which stated that Walker had been killed about 3:00 P.M. If the time was recorded accurately, Walker could have been engaged in the battle that afternoon and led his troops against the Federal lines. Colonel Barkuloo, in his report of the battle, wrote that he succeeded to the command of Mercer's brigade during the morning of the twenty-second, soon after the latter was called to command the division as Walker's replacement and before they were engaged.[53]

Barkuloo's testimony is not without contradictions, however. The senior colonel of Mercer's brigade was Charles Olmstead of the 1st Georgia. Normally, he would have succeeded Mercer when the latter took over Walker's division, but Olmstead had been wounded himself. If Barkuloo's time was correct, then Olmstead would have had to have been wounded in the morning during the advance to battle, but as Olmstead recalled it, he was hit in the head by a shell fragment while leading his regiment across an open field "late in the day." If Olmstead was wounded during the attack on Dodge's line in the afternoon, and Barkuloo took over from Mercer thereafter, then one would conclude that Walker was, indeed, shot during that afternoon's battle.[54]

Further muddying this evidence, a seniority dispute was going on between Olmstead and Barkuloo. Olmstead's commission as a Confederate colonel dated from December 26, 1861. Barkuloo had been a Confederate colonel only since February 1862, but before that he had been a colonel of Georgia State Troops ranking from October 14, 1861. Apparently Barkuloo claimed seniority on the basis of his Georgia commission. Whose seniority Mercer recognized is unknown but it is certain that he tapped Barkuloo to lead the brigade when he himself was suddenly called to division command. Also contradicting Olmstead's account, Captain George Mercer of the brigade staff said the colonel of the 1st Georgia Volunteers was wounded in the morning.[55]

One other item of question was the number of times the general was shot. Most accounts mention his wound, or the "fatal ball," or use other terminology to indicate he was shot once. However, a eulogy printed in the *Augusta Chronicle and Sentinel* on July 24, the date of his funeral, spoke of "two balls." Cumming also mentioned "the bullets that pierced [his] heart" and his "recent wounds." "Pierced his heart" may have been an exaggeration, but if Walker was struck in the breast by two shots he probably died instantly. John Steinmeyer told Ellison Capers he had heard that Walker was shot three times in the heart.[56]

A major difficulty in reconstructing the last minutes of Walker's life lies in the absence of written reports by officers of the Georgia division. The division was broken up two days after the battle. As a result, the usual system of collecting after-action reports from unit commanders, always weak in the Confederate army, broke down completely. In a span of five days two of the generals of the division were killed, a third wounded, and the fourth reassigned. One colonel commanding a brigade was wounded, one was captured, and a third got sick. Unit cohesion was destroyed. Major Cumming, the chief of staff, who would normally have been responsible for collecting the brigade reports and preparing one for the division, was reassigned to Hardee's staff and immediately went on ten days' leave. The temporary brigade commanders were busy adjusting to their new divisions. Few officers, if not pressed to do so, bothered to write reports. Cleburne's adjutant, Irving Buck, had two of the Georgia regimental commanders who were assigned to his division turn in documentation on their roles on

July 22. Ellison Capers's report for the 24th South Carolina did not cover the battles of July 20 and 22. About July 18 he departed the army to escort his family back to South Carolina and did not return until mid-August. Mercer never wrote a report for his brigade before he left for Savannah. All the rest of the immediate post-battlefield memory was also lost.[57]

One of the most articulate witnesses was not present when Walker was shot. Major Cumming had been dispatched by Walker to carry an order to Colonel Smith of Stevens's brigade. In his speech at the dedication of the Walker Monument in East Atlanta in 1902, Cumming recounted some of the details he remembered from that fateful July 22. Significantly, Cumming said that upon hearing of Walker being shot "before the battle was fairly begun" he reported directly to Hugh Mercer, the replacement commander of the division. He also noted that he never again laid eyes on the general, "in life or in death," and that the body was on its way to its final resting place before the end of the day. A reasonable interpretation of these remarks is that Walker was killed at the Terry millpond, not mortally wounded. If Walker had been alive, one might suppose that the faithful chief of staff would have reported to him to check on his condition and to find out what orders he might have for his successor. Cumming did not do this. We may conclude that Cumming had been informed Walker was already dead. Nor was there an opportunity for Cumming to view the body after the battle. This indicates that Walker's remains had already been moved to the rear for shipment back to Augusta before the end of the fighting on the twenty-second, a contradiction of the story the body was found in a pile of dead.[58]

The best evidence of the immediate death and quick removal of the body is the eyewitness testimony of Lieutenant William R. Ross, 66th Georgia, and Private Peter Lastinger of the 29th Georgia. Ross wrote to his sister on July 25, 1864, that as the dead body was carried from the field he covered the face with the general's own handkerchief. Lastinger reported years later that he had driven the four-mule wagon bearing the general's body into Atlanta to be shipped to Augusta. Ross's testimony refutes the rumor that Walker was killed on Gist's front and Fuller's report that the retreating troops left the body on the field. If the body was carried through the lines of the 66th Georgia the death probably occurred in front of Stevens's (Smith's/Nisbet's) brigade.[59]

The evidence, which is persuasive on both sides, and the real and potential contradictions, indicate that Walker was killed, or died within a few minutes of being shot, on the banks of Sugar Creek before the battle was fairly started, that his body was removed to the widow Terry's house for safety, and that it was carried into Atlanta that same afternoon.

The issue of Walker's mental condition on July 22 must also be addressed. Allegations have been made that he might have been drinking or under the influence of alcohol on the march to the east of Atlanta. Wilbur Kurtz, whose research has influenced many writers on the Atlanta campaign, relied on an interview he conducted with J. W. McWilliams in 1930 for the story of the guide Case Turner and Walker's behavior that day. McWilliams, an ancient veteran by 1930, had worked with Turner after the war, had listened to many of his stories, and repeated them, replete with details, for Kurtz's benefit. McWilliams had served in the 42nd Georgia, not in Walker's division, and had no personal knowledge of events.[60]

One of Turner's colorful details, as relayed by McWilliams, was that after Walker threatened to shoot Turner for leading the division astray, he holstered his revolver and produced a canteen of peach brandy from which he drank. It defies the imagination how Turner, even if correct, could have known the contents of the canteen. Surely Walker did not tell the guide what he was drinking or offer to share it with him. More likely, Walker had filled his canteen at William Cobb's well earlier that morning, but on this flimsy allegation is built the contention that Walker may not have had control of himself that day because of the influence of alcohol.

Kurtz himself said that although he accepted the truth of the body of Turner's story he disbelieved many of the details because of the old man's natural proclivity "to figure as a sort of hero." Yet, when Kurtz retold the story in 1955 he repeated the canard and by that time had promoted the canteen to a "demijohn of peach brandy that General Walker is alleged to have carried."[61]

Walker was not a stranger to strong drink. From Mexico in 1847 he had written to his wife that her brother Robert was the only man there who drank nothing stronger than water. During one of his illnesses in the 1850s, his doctor had prescribed red pepper and brandy or whiskey as an antidote. From Pensacola he had asked for Catawba wine, and since being with the Army of Tennessee he had shared wine with Braxton Bragg and had offered to toast Joseph E. Johnston's arrival with champagne. The Civil War period was a time of hard-drinking generals on both sides, and Walker drank his share, but there is no hint in any contemporary writing that his sometimes erratic behavior was caused by alcohol.[62]

Mary Chesnut was a plain-spoken diarist who recounted Walker's outburst at a dinner party in Richmond in 1861, but she never mentioned alcohol. Cary Eggleston was amazed by Walker's behavior in the Savannah hotel in 1862 but again did not ascribe the event to alcoholic fervor. Bragg had no timidity about labeling John Breckinridge and Frank Cheatham as drinkers but never said the same of Walker. Richard I. Manning, a member of Johnston's staff, wrote to his parents from Mississippi about the drinking habits of Breckinridge and Nathan G. Evans but had no such comment about Walker. W. W. Mackall informed his wife of the adverse consequences of Hugh Mercer's good living but never hinted at such a complaint in Walker. In short, the only evidence that Walker's faculties were influenced by alcohol was the secondhand tale of a man who desired "to figure as a sort of hero."[63]

The real cause of Walker's behavioral problems was his health. Beset by asthma, racked by old wounds, he had recently undegone another bout of sickness. Walker's inability to control or understand events at Lay's Ferry may be attributed to this cause. Tired, sick, perhaps affected by the quaint, even harmful, remedies prescribed by his doctors, on July 22 Walker was surely not at his best and may have been drinking brandy for medicinal or sedative purposes, but it is difficult to understand how Case Turner could know that or to conclude that he was not in control of himself as a result.

A greater concern is Walker's inability to better control the actions of Gist's and Smith's brigades in the first attack, if he was still alive at that time. Surely, an experienced and careful commander would have had Smith's brigade halt and wait for Gist's to catch up before allowing the two to advance in tandem. Instead, each brigade seems to have been left to its own devices in the timing of its attack. It appears that rather than going to Gist's front to urge him forward, Walker would better have spent his time, and perhaps saved his life, by going to Smith and having him wait until Gist came up. In his report of the battle, Bate said that he was supposed to align himself on the division on his left (Walker). When he received the first order to move forward, however, he advanced before the line on his left (Smith's brigade) was adjusted. Undoubtedly, the need to dress on Bate's movement forced the precipitate rush of Smith's regiments. In retrospect, Walker's performance at Atlanta was not unlike his behavior at Lay's Ferry and markedly different from the precision of his advance at Peach Tree Creek. However, if Walker was already dead, the confusion can be attributed to Mercer's inexperience.[64]

Sherman's first claim of Confederate losses on July 22 is certainly exaggerated. Even he must have realized that because when he wrote his memoirs ten years later he cited the same numbers as aggregate Confederate losses for the month of July. There has been a great deal of misunderstanding about Confederate casualties. Christopher Losson, in Cheatham's biography, gives total Confederate losses that terrible day as at least 10,000. Dr. A. J. Foard, medical director of the Army of Tennessee, in 1866 gave 3,297 as the loss in killed and wounded for Hardee's corps for the period July 4 to July 31, 1864. That would include the retreat from Marietta, Peach Tree Creek, and Ezra Church on July 28, as well as the casualties for July 22. Foard's figures for killed and wounded for the whole army for the same period is 8,800 which approximates Sherman's number for the losses on July 22.[65]

For Hardee's corps in July, Dr. Foard reported 317 casualties in Bate's division, 925 in Cheatham's, 902 in Walker's, and 1,153 in Cleburne's, which makes up the total of 3,297. These figures were killed and wounded only and take no account of missing or captured. Sherman's three armies reported 3,932 prisoners taken and deserters received in July.[66]

Actual losses in Hardee's corps for July 22 alone are hard to pin down in the absence of so many unit reports. In 1880, Colonel T. B. Roy, Hardee's son-in-law and former adjutant, wrote a lengthy vindication of Hardee's actions at Atlanta in 1864. Roy cited a letter that Hardee wrote on July 24, 1864, as his source for saying that Hardee's corps lost 3,299 killed, wounded and missing on July 22. This number is so suspiciously like the medical director's figures for losses in killed and wounded for the corps for the whole month of July that one must question it. It also approximates the number of Confederate dead John A. Logan mentioned in his report. Perhaps Roy misinterpreted what Hardee wrote. The cited letter seems not to be available for examination.[67]

As for the known losses, Cleburne's division suffered 1,388 in killed, wounded, and missing. Cheatham's division under Maney lost 619 killed and wounded. The only number available for Bate's division is the 135 killed and wounded in Lewis's Kentucky brigade. These partial returns add up to 2,142. The three brigade commanders of Dodge's corps reported capturing some 750 prisoners from Walker's and Bate's divisions. In addition, General Elliot Rice of Sweeny's division said he buried 79 Rebel dead on the battlefield and left another 40 bodies unburied because they were too far in front of the line to be retrieved.[68]

Losses for Walker's division in killed and wounded for the month of July were reported by the army's medical director as 902. This included 57 killed and 243 wounded in Stevens's brigade, 46 killed and 320 wounded in

Gist's, and 38 killed and 198 wounded in Mercer's. Only Mercer's brigade of Walker's division reported its losses for July 22. They were 168 killed, wounded, and missing. William O'Neal of the 54th Georgia wrote that his regiment lost 40 men. His own Company G went into battle with an effective strength of 11 and lost 6 killed and wounded. Lieutenant Ross of the 66th Georgia gave his regiment's casualties as 54 out of 110 who went into action.[69]

A page by page examination of Lillian Henderson's *Roster of Confederate Soldiers of Georgia* for the units of Walker's division gives some information about casualties on July 22, 1864. Many of the individual entries are fragmentary or incomplete. Some bear only notations such as "killed 1864," "killed at Atlanta," "wounded, date and place unknown," or "listed as wounded on the rolls for July and August 1864." Counting only the men who are clearly identified as casualties on July 22, Henderson lists 34 killed, 80 wounded, and 70 captured in Stevens's brigade, for a loss of 186. In the two Georgia regiments of Gist's brigade, 46th and 65th, Henderson shows 15 killed, 61 wounded, and 11 captured, for a total of 87. In addition, the South Carolina "Memory Rolls" for the 16th and 24th Regiments show 10 killed and 17 wounded at Decatur on July 22, making Gist's total 114.[70]

Mercer's brigade losses are found in *Official Records* and show 32 killed, 122 wounded, and 14 missing, only one of the latter from the 1st Georgia Volunteers. Henderson identifies from the four regiments of Mercer's brigade 22 killed, 59 wounded, and 17 missing, 10 from the 1st Georgia Volunteers. It is obvious not all casualties were reported to higher headquarters.[71]

Figures derived from Henderson encompass only the numbered Georgia regiments. The three separate Georgia battalions in Walker's division are not included. Nevertheless, using Henderson's numbers, Mercer's report, and the "Memory Roll," it is possible to conclude that losses in the Georgia division on July 22 were at least 477, plus one general killed and one wounded.

If Gist's and Stevens's two brigades suffered actual casualties of 500 each, and if Bate's division lost another 1,000, the estimated total for the day would be about 4,500 in Hardee's corps. The combined losses of Hood's old corps, under Cheatham on July 22, and Wheeler's cavalry were under 3,000 killed and wounded for the whole month of July. If 1,500 of those were lost on July 22, a generous estimate, plus a few in the Georgia militia, then total casualties for that day for Hood's army should be in the neighborhood of 6,000.[72]

Impressions of Confederate casualties by participants on the battlefield were in line with conclusions drawn by modern historians. The correspondents of the *New York Tribune* and the *Cincinnati Commercial* both reported to their readers a few days after the battle that Confederate casualties amounted to about five thousand.[73]

The most grievous loss to the army was in officers. Cheatham's division lost eighteen officers killed, including three regimental commanders. One of these was Colonel Francis M. Walker of the 19th Tennessee, who was leading Maney's brigade while Maney commanded the division. In Cleburne's division, at least fifteen field officers were killed, wounded, or captured. General James A. Smith, commander of the Texas brigade, was wounded, and by battle's end the brigade was led by a lieutenant colonel. One of the regiments was commanded by a lieutenant. Sometime between July 10 and 20 the 5th and 8th Mississippi regiments had been transferred from Gist's brigade to Lowrey's. Colonel John Wilkinson of the 8th Mississippi, who had served under Walker from February to July, was killed while charging with Lowrey on July 22.[74]

The losses of Walker's division were led by the death of the division commander. General Gist and Colonel Smith, commanding brigades, had been wounded. In Smith's, formerly Stevens's, brigade, Colonel Nisbet of the 66th Georgia was captured, Colonel William J. Winn, 25th Georgia, wounded, and Lieutenant Colonel James S. Boynton, 30th Georgia, wounded. Colonel Barkuloo of Mercer's brigade reported himself sick, turned command of the brigade over to Lieutenant Colonel Rawls, who was wounded, and Lieutenant Colonel Guyton succeeded to the command. Major William H. Mann of the 54th Georgia was killed when Colonel Rawls was wounded and Colonel Olmstead of the 1st Georgia Volunteers had been wounded earlier in the day. In Gist's brigade, besides the general himself, Major Samuel J. C. Dunlap, commanding the 46th Georgia, and Major Edward F. Morgan of the 8th Georgia Battalion, were wounded.

By the end of the day the division commander was Brigadier General Mercer. Gist's brigade was led by Colonel James McCullough of the 16th South Carolina, Mercer's by Lieutenant Colonel Guyton, and Stevens's probably by Colonel William D. Mitchell of the 29th Georgia. In all, Hardee's corps lost about sixty field officers. Walker's division lost two generals and nine field officers on July 22, and three generals and ten field officers July 20–22. By July 31, nine of the regiments and battalions in the former division were commanded by captains, four by majors, and three by lieutenant colonels. Only two of the units were headed by their nominal commanders.[75]

Sergeant Hagan of the 29th Georgia was captured and wrote to his wife from Nashville on July 28 to tell her. Samuel McKittrick had been elected third lieutenant of his company on June 28. On the evening of July 22 he was separated from his company when Gist's brigade fell back, but he went forward with Govan's brigade in their last attack and was wounded either in the lungs or in the groin. He died in hospital on the morning of the twenty-third. The official report of his death identified him as a private.[76]

Hood was quick to blame Hardee for not achieving the complete victory desired. As he had on July 20, Hood accused Hardee of being too slow and attacking late. He added the charge of not having gone far enough to get completely around the left of the Army of the Tennessee. Hardee may not have been completely blameless in his handling of the operation, but an astute Union observer later wrote: "The facts do not justify [Hood's] complaint. Hardee . . . could not have wished for a change in his line if he had known exactly where it stood. The attack was to the full . . . vigorous and persistent . . . and it was made as early as could have been expected." Possibly Hardee's worst error, as pointed out by his biographer, was in deploying from column into line too far in advance of his objective. The corps blundered needlessly through the brush for two miles as a result. The most comprehensive defense of Hardee's actions was made by Colonel Roy after Hardee and Hood had died.[77]

Hood also deserves criticism for his delay in supporting Hardee's attack. The sounds of battle from east of Atlanta could be distinctly heard for at least three hours before Hood launched Cheatham at Blair's front. A more astute commander would have made better use of his coordinating attacks. Even Sherman came in for criticism after the battle. Many felt that he had erred in allowing the Army of Tennessee to fight by itself all day while Thomas and Schofield stood by. Sherman's excuse that McPherson's army would have been jealous of assistance is weak. He lost a chance to roll over Hood's divided army.[78]

Might the results have been different if Walker had lived? Might his personal bravery and empathy with the troops have led his division to greater efforts to pierce the thin Federal line? The evidence suggests not. The men were too tired to give their best effort. They had been badly used on the afternoon of July 20, sweltered in the heat and humidity of July 21, and marched eighteen miles all night almost without rest before coming to the battlefield. The last two miles of this advance they had struggled through a wilderness fully as dense as the more famous one in Virginia. The weather on the twenty-second was as sultry as it had been on the twenty-first. It was simply too much to ask these men to do more than they had already. No individual feat or display of courage could have elicited from these physically used up veterans effort enough to carry the Union lines. General M. P. Lowrey was speaking for all of Hardee's corps when he described the condition of his men on the afternoon of July 22, 1864: "My men had had neither sleep nor rest for two days and nights, and under the rapid marching [to advance into battle], and under the oppressive heat, many good men fell completely exhausted and could go no farther." [79]

These factors, compounded by the murky politics and bad feelings in the high command of the Army of Tennessee, preordained that "Hood's second sortie" would be a failure for Southern arms.

16

POSTLUDE

WALKER'S BODY was sent by train to Augusta under escort of Captain Matthew Talbot, the general's cousin and volunteer aide, and old George Talbot, his body servant. Because Federal cavalry had broken the Georgia Railroad line east of Decatur, the melancholy route was by way of Macon, Millen, and Waynesboro. The body arrived in Augusta Sunday morning, July 24, at the same time news of his death was received, and was laid out in the home Mary rented from Major J. V. H. Allen of the 63d Georgia. Somewhere en route from Atlanta, probably at the depot at Millen, Walker's sword and scabbard went astray from the body. They were advertised for in the newspapers and later recovered.[1]

The funeral was conducted that same Sunday evening with burial in the arsenal cemetery. Walker was laid to rest among his children, his siblings, and his forebears. The editors of the *Constitutionalist* and the *Chronicle and Sentinel* described the interment ceremonies. The *Chronicle* said: "General Walker's funeral obsequies were fittingly observed Sunday afternoon, the remains having arrived by the Augusta and Savannah Road Sunday morning. A portion of the military followed by a long line of carriages, the whole headed by the Palmetto Band, marched to the Sand Hills where the honored soldier was interred."[2]

Two days later an editorial in the *Chronicle* entitled "The Pride of Georgia" spoke the feelings of the residents of Augusta.

Upon last Sabbath evening we left the sweetly singing children of St. James, to attend the funeral of him known on the rolls of the grand Army of the West as William Henry Walker, Major General. The public will perhaps pardon one who knew him, and greatly loved him, for talking for a while on paper of this old Colonel. A commission of Major General in the Provisional Army sent him to the front. His presence there made history. In the memorable battle of July 22d at Atlanta, amid that carnival of blood in which human heroism was unnoticed, Walker shone in the fullest light of his own red planet, Mars. At last the long baffled energies of fate sent two balls upon a mortal mission. We lost the battle of a thousand lives when Walker died. No effort was made to have a grand funeral, for his beautiful home by the amber river was too sad to wish for show and ostentation. By the old walk of the Arsenal, in the old home grounds, in the shadow of the drooping folds of his country's flag, his burial case draped in the colors, the presented arms of the Arsenal guard, and the thunder of its cannon, tell of the wish of all hearts to honor him to the last; thus and there he was buried. There, where the dew falls softly and the angels set up the tapers of the stars to keep watch and ward forever, there they laid all of Walker that could die.[3]

In the following days and weeks many articles appeared in both newspapers in honor of the dead hero. Mary and the children were the objects of an outpouring of condolence. Letters were received from across the South. One of the most poignant was that of Lydia McLane (Mrs. Joseph E.) Johnston, who wrote: "You have been so incessantly on my mind for the last week and I have wept so many bitter tears with you and for you, since the loss of our glorious, brave hero, that I can keep silent no longer. Pardon me, my dear friend, for intruding in an hour like this upon such affliction as yours, but your dear, noble husband was our dear friend, his country's glorious defender, and we all weep for him, and as I dearly loved him, honored soldier, I ask to weep with you."[4]

Numerous officials commented on Walker's service after his death. Samuel Wragg Ferguson, commanding a brigade of Wheeler's cavalry and a cadet when Walker was commandant at West Point, said, "He was of the bravest of the brave and as guileless as a child." Noted John Bell Hood, his erstwhile commander, "I am certain that those officers and men who came within the sphere of his genial presence will unite in the verdict that no truer or braver man ever fell upon the field of battle." Forty years after the war, E. Porter Alexander, Longstreet's artillery commander and another of Walker's former cadets, commented on the death of Walker, "whose frail thin body had survived" wounds in two wars.[5]

The same day as the funeral Walker's division was broken up. Hood proposed, Hardee concurred, and Bragg, who was visiting the army, approved the dissolution of the division because of the heavy casualties it had

received on July 20 and 22 and the unavailability of a suitable division commander. General Mercer, the acting commander, was sent to Savannah for
his health. Mercer's brigade went to Cleburne's division, Gist's to Cheatham's, and Stevens's to Bate's. Henry R. Jackson was brought from Savannah to take over Stevens's brigade, and Charles Olmstead, after recovering
from his slight wound, led Mercer's but without promotion to general.
Later that brigade passed to the command of General James A. Smith.[6]

The siege of Atlanta continued until September. After Sherman captured the city and then moved on toward Savannah, Hood took the much
depleted Army of Tennessee on the ill-conceived winter campaign of 1864–
65. At Franklin, Tennessee, on November 30, 1864, in one of the most
pointless and fruitless battles of the war, States Rights Gist and Pat Cleburne were among the six Confederate generals who gave up their lives
before the Union breastworks. Hood was replaced by Joseph E. Johnston
following the ignominious defeat at Nashville in December. The remnants
of Walker's division played out their roles in the drama to the final cur-
tain, finally surrendering to Sherman in North Carolina in April 1865. So
worn down was the army by that time that in March 1865 Walker's old
brigade could muster only seventy-six effectives. The brigade was reduced
at the end to a single consolidated battalion. J. B. Cumming was offered
command of the battalion but stayed with the staff of General Johnston to
the finish.[7]

In September 1864 Walker's older brother, Beverly, died suddenly. Mary
and the children, with Walker's aunts Betsy Cresswell and Zemula Walker,
had moved to Mobley Pond in the summer of 1864. The advance of a
wing of Sherman's army through that fertile region caused them to return to Augusta, evacuating their livestock with them. What little of value
remained on the property was commandeered for the sustenance of the
Kentucky "Orphan Brigade" under General Joseph Lewis, which was the
Confederate defense force in the area. The farm was left in the hands of
the overseer. After the war the property was leased out for quarrying for
about five years and was finally sold in 1874. In 1871, the body of John
David Walker was brought back from Virginia for burial in the family plot.[8]

The war had no sooner ended than Mary was ready to return to the
North. By July 1865 she was already back in Albany from where Molly
kept up a steady correspondence with her fiancé, Charles Cunningham
Schley. Charles or "Charlie" had been a surgeon with Evans's brigade in
the Army of Northern Virginia. Molly returned to Savannah in late 1865 to

marry Charlie. She lived there with him the rest of her life, bearing three children, W. H. T. Walker Schley, Charles C., Jr., and Mary Townsend, who died at the age of eighteen months in 1876. Charlie died in Savannah in 1908 and Molly in 1910. They are buried side by side in Laurel Grove Cemetery in Savannah.[9]

Mary Walker survived her husband by only four years. In increasingly poor health, she remained in Albany tended by her Townsend relations and her four children. She died of a heart condition in December 1868, and her remains were brought to Augusta to be buried next to Walker.[10]

Mary's will set up a trust for the care and education of her children and for the support of their old nurse, Sally Byrnes. The trust ran until the youngest child was twenty-one. Franklin and Frederick Townsend served in turn as administrators. The three minor children were Willie, Jr., aged twelve, Hannah, ten, and Freeman Valentine, eight. Molly took Sally and the two younger children to Savannah with her when she married. Willie was left in school in Cornwall, New York, in the care of his uncle Frederick.[11]

Willie hated it. In a tearful letter he begged his sister to bring him to Savannah. "Won't you please bring me home in the family. Don't exile me for I love to be home with all. Don't keep me of[f] from all." Molly refused, telling him she was complying with their mother's wishes. Obviously under great emotional stress, Willie began to act out his insecurities and was dismissed from school for conduct problems just after his fifteenth birthday. He moved to Savannah, then to Augusta, living at Seclusaval and caring for his impoverished aunt and uncle, Ann Eliza and Adam Johnston. Eventually he found employment as a clerk at King Mill, one of the new textile mills in Augusta. He remained there for all of his adult working life. In 1880, Willie married Carolyn Fowle of Covington, Georgia, and had four children. His grandson and great-grandson, respectively Hugh McLean Walker, Jr. and III, are the last of the name in the Augusta area. His great-granddaughter, Karen Allmond, is the daughter of Hugh Walker, Jr.'s, sister Martha Walker Mitchell.[12]

After the deaths of Ann Eliza in 1881 and Adam Johnston in 1891, Willie inherited the Seclusaval property. In 1907 he formed a partnership with George M. Clark to operate the Windsor Spring Water Company. Later, Clark bought the entire property from Walker and the latter retired to his home, Jasmine Hill. This house had been built by C. C. Schley's grandfather Governor John Schley but apparently passed to Willie, Jr., through his wife's family, the Fowles. He died there in 1948 and was buried in the arsenal cemetery. The water company is still operated by Clark's daughter, Ella Nuite, who occupies the house formerly known as Seclusaval.[13]

Hannah T. Walker married Clifford Wayne Anderson of Savannah. They moved to Albany, where she died in 1904 leaving two daughters. She is buried in the Townsend section of the Albany Rural Cemetery. Freeman V. Walker attended Virginia Military Institute, obtained a medical degree, and served as a surgeon in the U.S. Army from 1886 to 1895. He married Mary Ellen McAlpin of Savannah, retired to private practice in Bluffton, South Carolina, and died there childless in 1933. Sally Byrnes, the longtime family nurse, died in 1888 at the age of seventy-four. She is buried in the arsenal cemetery among the children she loved.[14]

Of the Townsend family, Robert, after a successful career as naval officer in the Civil War, died on active duty in China in 1866. His body was brought back to Albany. Howard died in 1867 and is interred in the Rural Cemetery. Franklin and Frederick lived on into their seventies. Frederick died in Albany in September 1897, Franklin a year later in September 1898. Anna Townsend Martin also died in 1866. Her son Bradley T. Martin added to his father's fortune, married the daughter of another wealthy New York family, and lived out his days on an estate in Scotland.[15]

John K. Jackson returned to Augusta after the war but died in Milledgeville in 1866. Henry R. Jackson went on to a distinguished career in the law, the foreign service, and as president of the Georgia Historical Society, before his death in 1898. Ellison Capers was promoted to brigadier general in March 1865. After the war he entered the clergy and became Episcopal bishop of South Carolina. He was the author of much of the South Carolina volume of *Confederate Military History*. Robert H. Anderson finished the war as a brigadier general of cavalry. Before his death in 1888 he was chief of police in Savannah for twenty years. Henry C. Wayne went into the lumber business and died in 1883. William J. Hardee retired to his wife's plantation in Alabama before his death in 1873. Hugh Mercer died in 1877 in Baden-Baden, Germany, where he had gone for his health. John Bell Hood and his wife died in New Orleans of yellow fever in 1879, leaving a large family of orphans. Joseph E. Johnston caught cold at the funeral of William T. Sherman, where he had marched bareheaded in the procession, and died in 1891. Braxton Bragg, contentious to the last, fell dead while walking in the street in Galveston, Texas, in 1876. Walker's cousin and volunteer aide, Matthew Talbot, served with the Georgia State Line until the end of the war. He suffered an early death in 1876. Joseph B. Cumming lived a long and successful life in Augusta before his death in 1922.[16]

In 1955 the U.S. government closed the Augusta Arsenal. In contravention of the terms of Freeman Walker's sale, the land was deeded to the county Board of Education and eventually passed into the hands of the state. The property is now occupied by Augusta College. One acre is reserved for the Walker family cemetery, and the house Bellevue, where Freeman and Mary were married, is preserved as an administration building.[17]

When the Confederate Monument Association of Augusta was planning its memorial to the war dead, its members wished to select suitable figures to represent the different elements involved. Robert E. Lee and Stonewall Jackson were chosen to represent the South and Virginia. Thomas R. R. Cobb was selected as Georgia's representative. Richmond County is represented by the life-size figure of W. H. T. Walker. Surmounting the four is the figure of a Confederate private soldier for whom the model was Berry Benson, a local veteran. The monument was dedicated in 1878.[18]

A group of admirers in Atlanta also wished to memorialize the fallen hero. Subscriptions and donations were collected to erect five upright cannon on concrete bases on Glenwood Avenue. Because the environs were still wild, the monument was placed about half a mile from where Walker actually fell. It was dedicated on July 22, 1902, with veterans of both North and South present. Joseph B. Cumming gave the memorial address, and Janet Walker, Willie, Jr.'s, daughter, unveiled the monument. In 1936, after urban development, the monument was moved to its present location at Wilkinson Circle and Glenwood, closer to where Walker received his mortal wound. When it was rededicated in 1937, it was reduced to a single cannon.[19]

Today, from his plinth above Broad Street in Augusta, 125 years after his death, William H. T. Walker gazes with unblinking stare across Richmond County, in death as in life in the posture of a soldier "to the manner born."[20]

17

THE SOLDIER AND THE MAN

W. H. T. WALKER left no tangible legacy by which he can be remembered. His death during the war forestalled a memoir, explanatory or exculpatory. The reputation he enjoyed as military hero and Southern beau ideal died with his contemporaries. Those who looked into his life in later years found only a few vignettes of youthful valor and prideful bad temper from later life.

Walker's early Civil War career was as an organizer and administrator. His return to service in 1863 brought him the field duty he craved, but it turned out to be not much to his liking. Although his presence may have raised troop morale and heartened the citizens of Savannah, there was nothing outstanding about his two-month tenure there.

For him, the Vicksburg campaign was an affair of "march and countermarch." At Jackson, Mississippi, on May 14, 1863, Walker faced hostile infantry fire for the first time in the Civil War and for the first time since 1847. The occasion lent itself neither to a display of valor nor to one of tactical genius. Joseph Johnston's little brigades were deployed against Union divisions and even army corps. Johnston professed to recognize in Walker the ability to pull together the heterogeneous units of his command and had him promoted to major general, telling Richmond he was the only officer competent to command a division. Politics aside, this may have been as much a comment on the lack of credentials of the other brigade commanders as it was on Walker's talents. Only at the siege of Jackson in July 1863 did he have an opportunity to show some flashes of his youthful leadership qualities.[1]

Walker's greatest chance for personal glory came in September 1863 at

William H. T. Walker
(courtesy of Hugh M.
Walker, Jr., and
Karen Allmond)

Chickamauga in north Georgia. Whether through cronyism or recognition of ability, his old classmate Bragg created for Walker a separate corps composed of two thrown-together divisions. The glory never materialized. Although he was given the potential for a leading role in the drama that unfolded, Walker's troops were snatched away from him by other, more senior commanders. He was forced to fight his brigades piecemeal, seldom was his corps ever wholly assembled, and his advice was ignored by his superiors. He put the best face he could on events in his official report, but the battle's progress must have been a sore disappointment to him. The praise of Governor Brown was insufficient balm for the wounds of being deprived of leading his corps in combat and then having his command broken up because of army politics.

Walker escaped the debacle and the denunciations of Chattanooga. He had kind words for the behavior of his division there under Gist and even

gave a passing thought to the hard treatment Bragg received. Through the
winter at Dalton Walker was engaged in keeping up the morale of his men,
seeing to their needs, and bolstering the spirits of the citizens at home.
He never lost faith in the fighting ability of the soldiers of the Army of
Tennessee.

Johnston's retrograde tactics in the spring campaign of 1864 tried
Walker's patience, but he remained faithfully at his post. As before, there
was scant opportunity for brilliant generalship during the long, grinding
retreat from Dalton to Atlanta. Although the division was available for
every task it was asked to perform and participated fully in every phase of
the campaign, at no time was its service outstanding. The fumbled attack
at Lay's Ferry and the fiascoes of the pickets and skirmishers at Mud Creek
and Kennesaw reflected poorly on division leadership and small unit commanders alike. Hardee and Walker might praise their men for gallantry,
but the rest of the army could see the shortcomings of the Georgians.

In the final scenes around Atlanta, Walker had one last opportunity to
stand out. He seemed to be a different person, more philosophical than
before. He took the promotion of Stewart almost stoically and professed
allegiance to the new army commander, Hood. On the battlefield his men
took heavy casualties at Peach Tree Creek on July 20. On the fateful day,
July 22, Walker, certainly tired and in a black mood, moved at the head of
his division to the death at least one source claimed he had foreseen some
days earlier.[2]

Twenty-five years after Walker's death, Marcellus Stovall wrote, "I think
no man of information can truly say that Walker was ever placed in a position [in the Civil War] in which results could be harvested." Throughout his career as a senior commander he was destined to play secondary
roles. On the few occasions when he was on the verge of dramatic tactical
results, opportunity was snatched away by events or by his own perverse
nature.[3]

Despite his desire for glory, Walker's greatest contribution to the Southern cause was in training, disciplining, and organizing troops. His reputation from earlier wars and his long experience as a regular officer made him
the ideal commander and model for the volunteer troops he led. His men
always spoke highly of his concern for their welfare. Veterans remembered
that Walker's division was always well fed, which was of vast importance
to the experienced soldier. Even his critic E. T. Sykes said that Walker
treated his staff "with the utmost consideration and deferential courtesy,"
as if they were "superior to the ordinary subaltern." Although quick to

criticize misconduct, he was equally prone to praise valor on the battlefield or outstanding appearance in camp. He was a stickler for military protocol and for strict obedience of orders. When young Derry Lamar left camp in Dalton to escort his wife from Augusta, he neglected to call on the general before his departure. When Lamar returned, he feared he might be arrested for his lapse in courtesy. He was not.[4]

One failing of the Georgia general was his claim to strategic acumen. Early in the war, in a letter to his wife, he suggested that had his plan been accepted the South would have been successful in gaining paramountcy over the North in only a few months. Later, he thought he perceived a grand design in the concurrent Federal attacks in Mississippi, Georgia, and Florida in the winter of 1864. In the first case, he offered no evidence to support his claim. In the second, he misread a set of coincidental reconnaissances and raids.[5]

Walker's strict adherence to the orders of his superiors is a matter of record. In the famous march around Sherman's left on July 22, 1864, the question of a slight deviation from orders led to the black confrontation between Walker and Hardee. As Cumming points out, another officer might have merely made the required adjustment, but Walker felt bound to consult Hardee first. The rebuke Hardee gave him led to the flaring of temper. Colonel Olmstead wrote of the losses of the 1st Georgia Volunteers at Smyrna.

If Walker sometimes seemed to be a martinet, he could also be what in later wars was referred to as a "soldier's general." Isaac Hermann wrote that Walker offered him one of his own shirts so that he would be suitably attired for a home leave after Hermann had volunteered for a dangerous mission.[6]

The common soldiers were delighted when Walker shared hazards with them. Walter Clark, the Richmond County historian who had been a first sergeant in the 63d Georgia, related an incident illustrative both of Walker's empathy with his troops and of his disregard for personal danger. When the Georgia division was recalled to the battlefield at Resaca on the afternoon of May 14, 1864, it crossed the Oostanaula River on a bridge being shelled by a Union battery. According to Clark, "Crossing the river, Gen. W. H. T. Walker passed us going to the front and as he rode by, another shot from the battery struck immediately behind him, barely missing his horse. Glancing around at the dust it had raised and turning to us with a smile on his face, he said, 'Go it, boots,' and galloped on to the head of the division. On this, as well as on every other occasion when under fire, he seemed not only absolutely indifferent to danger, but really to enjoy its presence."[7]

With few exceptions, no officer with whom Walker served ever had occasion to complain of his professional conduct. Richard Taylor wrote, "No enterprise was too rash to awaken his ardor if it necessitated daring courage and self devotion." And John Bell Hood said, "I am certain that those officers and men who came within the sphere of his genial influence will unite in the verdict that no truer or braver man ever fell upon the field of battle." Even Sykes acknowledged that "he was brave as Julius Caesar."[8]

Joseph B. Cumming, who also served on the staffs of Generals Johnston, Hood, Hardee, and J. K. Jackson, said of Walker that "membership of [his] staff was in itself a certificate that such member was performing his full soldierly duty." Marcellus Stovall called him the "personation of integrity, of unerring truth [and] of directness of all actions."[9]

Several veterans remembered Walker as a rough-tongued campaigner. Sam Watkins of celebrated "Company Aytch" related an anecdote of Walker returning to Ringgold the night after the debacle at Missionary Ridge. The exhausted Watkins had fallen asleep by his camp fire. He was awakened by a rough hand. When Watkins demanded to know who the intruder was, he was "politely and pleasantly, but profanely told [that] he was General Walker and that I had better get further [to the rear]." During the siege of Jackson, Mississippi, in July 1863, Private Isaac Hermann observed an incident in which his battery commander questioned Walker about what infantry support was available in the event of a Union attack. Walker erupted. "Support, Hell! If they charge you, fight them with the handspikes, don't you never leave this post." The grammar might have been Hermann's, but the sentiment was Walker's.[10]

Among more senior contemporaries, Marcellus P. Stovall remembered, "As a frank soldier, [Walker] always aimed to his opinions." S. R. Liddell's comment on Walker's personality bears repeating: "Under a rough exterior and brusque mannerism there was a large heart. A truer man and brave, existed not in the army. He loved his state and died by its cause."[11]

In his life of John Bell Hood, Richard McMurry identified his subject as having all of the characteristics of a military officer of the post-1830 South: "physical bravery; aggressiveness; superb combat leadership; intuitiveness; emotionalism; impatience; lack of attention to obstacles, planning, and detail." A good part of McMurry's evaluation could have been applied to the Augusta general. Physically brave and aggressive, emotional and impatient, Walker was far more the nineteenth-century military officer than he was the Southern gentleman he ascribed to be. His ambition and pride gave him more in common with men like Joseph Hooker or Thomas Sweeny than with Richard Taylor or J. Johnston Pettigrew, two officers recently held up as examples of the chivalric Southerner. Walker's similarities to Joseph E. Johnston have already been discussed.[12]

After the death of James B. McPherson on July 22, 1864, Sherman selected Oliver O. Howard to be new commander of the Army of the Tennessee. Several other generals in Sherman's armies were miffed at being overlooked. One, the politician-soldier John A. Logan, bore his disappointment manfully and continued to serve. Another, XX Corps commander Joseph Hooker, was outraged. Hooker, Walker's West Point classmate from 1837, was second only to Sherman and George A. Thomas as senior general in the Military Division of the Mississippi. In the regular army he was senior to both Sherman and Thomas because his date of rank as brigadier general was earlier than either of theirs. Hooker felt that by his seniority and service he was entitled to an army command. Sherman did not like Hooker and let his prejudices rule his decision.

Hooker responded as Walker would have. In a letter to George Thomas, he wrote: "I have just learned that Major General Howard, my junior, has been assigned to the command of the Army of the Tennessee. If this is the case I request that I may be relieved from duty with this army. Justice and self-respect alike require my removal from an army in which rank and service are ignored." To Logan, who had commanded the army for a few days after McPherson's death, Hooker wrote, "I asked to be relieved from duty with the army, it [the promotion of Howard] being an insult to my rank and service." The incident is reminiscent of Walker's resignation in 1861 and is instructive in understanding the quest for place and promotion among professional soldiers.[13]

Although Walker had previously expressed his disdain for Irish-born officers, he might have approved of the actions of Thomas Sweeny, his adversary at Lay's Ferry and Atlanta. On July 22, Sweeny's division had stood beside Fuller's in repelling the assault of Hardee's corps. On July 25 Sweeny accused the English-born Fuller of cowardice during the battle and "assisted Fuller with the toe of his boot in leaving his (Sweeny's) tent." Grenville Dodge, their corps commander, came to Fuller's defense and Sweeny shifted his attack to Dodge, accusing him of mismanagement. When Dodge defended himself against Sweeny, the Irishman called him a liar and an "inefficient son of a bitch." Dodge slapped Sweeny's face, Sweeny punched Dodge in the nose, and Fuller wrestled Sweeny to the ground. The three generals had to be pulled apart. Sweeny was arrested and relieved from command. When informed of the fight, Sherman sided with Sweeny the regular against Dodge the volunteer.[14]

Dodge was lucky he got off with a punch in the nose. In September 1862, Major General William Nelson, commanding Union troops in Kentucky, slapped the face of Brigadier General Jefferson C. Davis, a regular army man who had been an officer in the garrison at Fort Sumter in April 1861. Davis went and got a pistol and shot Nelson dead as the latter descended the stairs in a hotel where they were staying. No legal action was ever taken against Davis, but although he eventually rose to be a corps commander under Sherman, he was forever denied promotion to full major general.[15]

These were Walker's contemporaries and brothers in arms from the Old Army. His own outbursts and reactions seem much less bizarre when viewed in the context of the atmosphere in which he had spent his adult life. One old soldier whom Walker had known since his childhood was David E. Twiggs, also of Richmond County. Twiggs was famous throughout the army for years for his coarse language, vile temper, and enduring ability to remember slights and bear grudges. If Walker used Twiggs as a role model, then the behavior of the younger officer appears mild by comparison.[16]

Disputatiousness was a way of life in the Old Army. A small officer corps, slow promotion, and heavy reliance on political and family influence for advancement made all officers rivals for the few vacancies that existed. Walker's efforts to pull strings to be named inspector general in 1849 are an example. As Edward Coffman summarized the period, "Men closely watched and interpreted to their own interests everything, no matter how seemingly trivial, that could affect their careers and, indeed, their very lives." Braxton Bragg had the reputation of being cantankerous in the extreme. Walker, his classmate, sometime messmate, and temperamental soul mate, was cast from the same mold.[17]

Walker the person is more elusive than Walker the soldier. He was a product of the class and region into which he was born. His weak early education led him to rely on intuition and emotion rather than reason when facing new or unforeseen situations. His belief in the superiority of the Southern white male bordered on fanaticism. The emotional upheavals of his youth resulting from the death of his father and the near destitution of his family bred an insecurity that compelled him to spend his adult life seeking financial prosperity which he was ill-prepared by training or inclination to achieve. The code of Southern "chivalry," which he cited so often, was the basis of his behavior as a combat officer and as a gentleman.

Walker quarreled with anyone over anything. Extremely sensitive to insult, he allowed no challenge to his opinions or inference of dishonor to go unnoticed. His exchange of letters with Secretary of War Judah P. Benjamin in 1861 is mentioned in every recitation of his career. His resignations from the army in 1838 and from West Point in 1856 are further examples. His inclination to argument upset office routines and dinner parties alike. His belligerent tendencies sometimes led him to comic extremes. Writing to his wife from shipboard in December 1846, Walker said:

> At the south, if young men were to act toward married ladies as they do in New York City, there would be at least a dozen men shot every day, and the consequence is that gentlemen are very particular how they become intimate and devoted with other men's wives for death is certainly their portion and it is the best custom that ever was to keep up a high and chivalric feeling toward the female sex and to preserve friendship from all suspicion. The finest social intercourse exists. Gentlemen go and stay days at each others' houses, but as soon as a *just* suspicion crosses the husband's mind that his friend is *too fond* of his wife, he is a candidate for eternity.[18]

Walker's love of his wife and fondness for his children, often expressed, did not prevent his from quarreling with other members of his family. Usually money or property was the cause. Bad feeling between Walker and Mary's brothers dated from the couple's wedding in 1846. Although his heroism in the Mexican War partially assuaged their dislike, the Townsends remained distrustful of his motives and saw to it that he could never lay claim to Mary's share of the family wealth. The apportionment of her father's estate in 1852 led to an eruption of outrage on Walker's part which probably was never resolved. The dissolution of the Union in 1861 and the resultant separation of the family led to his diatribes about no more "uncling or cousining."

His own family was not immune from Walker's wrath. At different times during the Civil War he accused his sister Ann Eliza and her husband, Adam Johnston, and his brother George Beverly and his wife, Arabella Pearson, of attempting to fleece or deprive him of his just share of the Mobley Pond profits. Only his younger brother, John David, seems to have held Walker's complete loyalty. During John's short life, William nursed him through sickness and war wounds, provided him employment, and sought to use his own influence to win for John government appointments. Strangely, though, after John's death Walker never mentioned his name again. Perhaps he felt guilty for not having kept the younger man under his military wing. Perhaps the topic was too painful.[19]

If Walker could quarrel with his family, his prominent military position sometimes allowed him to play extended paterfamilias, a role he probably enjoyed. In October 1863 he had his cousin Samuel Cresswell transferred from a company of an Alabama regiment to a safer and more comfortable billet in the divisional commissariat staff. When the skirmishers of the 63d Georgia were overrun at Kennesaw on June 27, 1864, Walker's distant kinsman Lawrence Regail Reab was among those captured. Walker took the time from his responsibilities during the retreat to the Chattahoochee to inquire about Reab and to tell Mary to assure other family members that he was looking into the case.[20]

Walker's volatile personality sometimes prompted him to intrude into situations where there was no need or no quarrel. After Lookout Mountain, he interjected himself gratuitously into the correspondence between John K. Jackson and his accusers. He could not restrain himself from replying in writing to criticism of his actions at the Richmond County secession convention in December 1860. When his wife quarreled with Mrs. Cumming and Mrs. Lamar at Dalton, he made it a point to involve himself in the dispute. He overreacted to the attentions of Lawson Magruder to Molly Walker. Walker seemed congenitally unable to refrain from disputatious wrangling, but he was not unaware of this propensity. Shortly before his death he wrote, "Rarely do I see a man or a woman who comes up to my standard of what they should be. Perhaps I suit other people as little as they suit me."[21]

Walker's lack of patience was as well-known as his bad temper, but he was able to recognize the quality and sometimes laugh at himself. When his doctor prescribed whiskey and hot pepper as an asthma cure, Walker noted, "One would have supposed that I was fiery enough without the addition of so much steam." Writing from Augusta in 1852, he related another self-revealing anecdote:

> I brought Clyde [his dog] to Seclusaval and to make him accustomed to me I put him in my room when I went to bed. At first he was very quiet but after awhile he commenced scratching himself and his knee would strike against the floor. Then he would wag his tail and strike that on the floor and about

a dozen times he woke me and the noise sounded as if someone was in the room. I bore it with all that Christian fortitude and *patience so characteristic of me* until endurance ceased to be a virtue when at last I jumped up and pitched Mr. Clyde head foremost out of the window and did not care at the time if I never saw him again.[22]

Walker's chauvinism toward foreigners and other lesser beings has been amply demonstrated. One rare exception was his attitude toward Sally Byrnes, the family nurse. Irish though she might be, he recognized her devotion to his children. In a letter to his wife from Dalton in 1864, he wrote, "If anything should happen to me, always keep Sally with you."[23]

In social life Walker was usually a pleasant companion. He enjoyed good conversation, overmuch in William Mackall's opinion, he liked to dance, he played billiards, he attended parties and balls, he rode and hunted. His wide circle of friends and acquaintances included doctors and lawyers, judges and clergymen, planters and newspaper publishers, at least two U.S. Supreme Court justices, and politicians too numerous to mention. He was known personally to President Zachary Taylor, General Winfield Scott, Jefferson Davis, Governor Joseph E. Brown, and other luminaries of prewar and Civil War America.

The biographer is hard-pressed to reconcile this brave, congenial, warmhearted gentleman with the ill-tempered, volatile hothead portrayed in other situations. How can Sykes's "irritable dyspeptic" be the same man as Cumming's "soul of honor and generosity"?

Walker's lifetime ambition was twofold. First, he wished to gain glory and honor for himself in the army. He had already accomplished this objective as a young man in two wars and hoped for more renown in Confederate service. As W. L. Cabell said, "The breath of battle always brought an unusual glitter to his eye." His second goal was to restore the family fortunes to the level achieved by his father and his uncles. To this end he pursued his various business ventures. The success of Mobley Pond plantation seemed well on the way to satisfying that ambition, but its fruition was cut short by the war and his death. Up to July 22, 1864, William Walker may fairly be characterized as a man frustrated by events and personality from achieving fully either of his life's goals.[24]

Besides his ambitions, one central theme of Walker's life was his devotion to his family. Some months before his death, he wrote to his wife, "Kiss my dear little ones for me and say to them how much their papa loves each and all of them and as for yourself, eighteen years marriage perhaps may have caused you to have discovered that I have always loved you." This was no onetime expression of affection. Over and over through the years he reverted to the theme of family love. In the early years of their marriage, his adoration of his young wife was couched in clumsy terms of endearment. As the children were born and grew older, his attention turned more and more to them and his aspirations for them. Never did he neglect his four "dear lost boys," the little ones who did not survive the ravages of nineteenth-century childhood disease. In the final years of his life he wrote of his pride in his children's accomplishments and renewed affection for his wife.[25]

Health was an important factor in the makeup of this complex man. Many of those who knew him spoke of his frail constitution. Cursed from birth with asthma, he labored under its burden all his life. In times of mental or emotional stress and during periods of boredom he seemed to suffer especially. Only occasionally was he able to shake off its oppressive weight. So seriously was he afflicted, Richard Taylor wrote, that Walker could sleep only in the sitting position. Sykes called Walker irritable. Anyone who suffers from chronic illness or chronic lack of sleep tends to be irritable. The wonder is that Walker could function at all. The combined effect of the asthma and the wounds of two wars must have disposed him to frequent fits of ill temper purely from his own physical agony. The variety of remedies he took to combat his pain may have been as detrimental to his health as the malady itself. One combination in particular, ingesting laudanum and inhaling ether, surely clouded his judgment and affected his behavior when under its influence. How often he resorted to this form of pain killer is not known. If he used it with any frequency it might explain some of his sudden mood changes.[26]

Walker was not alone among Southern generals in his egocentricity. Many others exhibited characteristics that might be questioned in modern society. Stonewall Jackson's behavior was eccentric in the extreme. It was an age of individualism nationally and of an exaggerated sense of honor, especially in but not confined to the South. These national and regional traits, combined with his vaulting ambition, his desire to restore the luster of his family name, and the unfortunate psychological effects of his physical disabilities, produced in W. H. T. Walker a self-defeating personality that thwarted him in the achievement of some of his goals. Marcellus Stovall laid the blame for lack of military success on lack of opportunity. The rest of the responsibility was Walker's alone.

If Walker's life was not the success he had hoped for, to his contemporaries he was a model for Southern manhood. An extract from a lengthy biographical sketch printed a month after his funeral reads:

> There was no limit to the warmth of his heart, to the strength of his faithful friendship, to his filial and fraternal affections, his careful and parental duties. His love of truth, of directness of purpose, of honesty, and uprightness of conduct, was as unbounded as was his scorn for low and mean and sordid actions. There was nothing like selfishness in his nature. His contempt for petty vanities was excessive, and there are many of our citizens who have been often charmed by the modesty and simplicity with which he carried himself when, from time to time, he returned to his friends and home, bearing with him the sheaves of the hero's honor and the hero's fame. Deeply did these gentler traits, these noble qualities, endear this remarkable man to a wide circle of friends, both in civil life and in the army.[27]

The final word is left to Joseph B. Cumming, who summed up his former chief's character in his eulogy at the unveiling of the Walker Monument in 1902: "He was the bravest of the brave, the soul of honor and generosity, the incarnation of truth, the mirror of chivalry, the devotee, I had almost said the fanatic, of duty. . . . For nothing, not whistling bullet, nor shrieking cannon ball, nor bursting shell, nor gleaming bayonet, had he any fear — for nothing except one thing — failure to obey orders to the letter and do his soldierly duty to the uttermost."[28]

For what better epitaph could a soldier hope?

APPENDIX I

W. H. T. Walker's Military Staff

WALKER'S MILITARY CAREER can be conveniently divided into five phases for the purposes of identifying the units that served under him and the members of his personal staff: major general of Georgia Volunteers, March–April 1861; commander, 2d Brigade, Pensacola, June–August 1861; commander, 8th Brigade, Army of the Potomac, September–October 1861; commander, 3d Brigade, Georgia State Troops, December 1861–April 1862; and successively, commander, Walker's Brigade; commander, Walker's Division; commander, Reserve Corps; and commander, Walker's or the Georgia division, all the latter between March 1863 and July 1864. Not all officers who served in various capacities have been identified.

1. Major general, Georgia Volunteers, March–April 1861.

The officers named here are those for whom Walker asked Governor Joseph Brown to provide commissions. It is not known whether the commissions were forthcoming or if other staff vacancies were ever filled.

Inspector general	Lt. Col. W. P. White
Quartermaster	Major A. V. Brumley
Judge advocate	Major William Schley
Aide-de-camp	James R. Brown
Aide-de-camp	W. J. Mealing

2. Commander, 2d Brigade, Confederate States Troops, Pensacola, June–August 1861.

Little is available in the official or unofficial records concerning Walker's tenure at Pensacola. Only one staff officer has been identified although there may have been others.

Aide-de-camp (& AAG?)	Lt. Robert H. Anderson

3. Commander, Eighth Brigade, Army of the Potomac, September–October 1861.

Assistant adjutant general	Major Robert H. Anderson
Assistant adjutant general	Lt. (Capt.?) Eustace Surget
Quartermaster	Major Thomas R. Heard
Commissary of subsistance	Capt. Aaron Davis
Surgeon	Surgeon Stokes A. Smith
Volunteer aide	Cmdr. Henry Hartstene, CSN

While in Virginia, Walker asked repeatedly to have Lieutenant Joseph Wheeler brought from Pensacola to be his aide, but Wheeler had already been commissioned colonel of the 19th Alabama Infantry.

4. Commander, 3d Brigade, Georgia State Troops, December 1861–April 1862.

Assistant adjutant general	Major Octavius C. Myers
Quartermaster	Major John W. Walker
Ordnance officer	Major E. R. Harden (resigned)
	Lt. Col. Randolph Spalding
Aide-de-camp	W. J. Mealing

5. Commander, Walker's Brigade, March–May 1863; Walker's Division, May 1863–July 1864; Reserve Corps, Army of Tennessee, September 5–24, 1863.

Assistant adjutant general (later chief of staff)	Capt. (later Major) Joseph B. Cumming
Assistant adjutant general	Capt. J. Robert Troup
Assistant inspector general (1863)	Capt. Samuel H. Crump
Acting assistant inspector general (1864)	Capt. William H. Ross
Quartermaster	Major Nathaniel O. Tilton
Commissary of subsistance	Major Alfred C. Dearing
Surgeon	Dr. James Bowers
Ordnance officer (Savannah)	Cadet Henry R. Jackson
Ordnance officer (Mississippi and Georgia)	Capt. Lawson W. Magruder
Aide-de-camp	Capt. Thomas H. Kenan
Aide-de-camp	Lt. G. De Rosset Lamar (transferred)
Volunteer aide	Capt. Matthew H. Talbot

APPENDIX II

Military Commands of W. H. T. Walker

AS WITH HIS STAFF, the military units under Walker's command can be grouped into five periods. Following his first military appointment as colonel of the Second Georgia Regiment, Walker became major general of Georgia Volunteers. His division consisted of two brigades, commanded by generals. The designations of the units in these brigades has not been researched. Details of his commands subsequent to his appointment in the Provisional Army of the Confederate States in May 1861 are as follows.

1. Second Brigade, Confederate States Troops, Pensacola (June–August 1861)
   1st Alabama Regiment
   7th Alabama Regiment
   1st Georgia Battalion
   Washington Artillery Company (only one gun)
   one other company not identified

2. Eighth Brigade, Army of the Potomac (September–October 1861)
   6th Louisiana
   7th Louisiana
   8th Louisiana
   9th Louisiana
   1st Louisiana Special Battalion
   Bowyer's Virginia Battery (joined October 1861)
   Latham's Virginia Battery (attached)
   Whitehead's company Virginia cavalry (attached)

3. Third Brigade, Georgia State Troops (December 1861–April 1862)
   8th Regiment
   9th Regiment

10th Regiment
3rd Battalion
(attached)

Macon German Artillery Battery
Macon Light Artillery Battery
Bibb Cavalry Company
Thomas County Dragoons
Tattnall Guards cavalry company (sixty-day volunteers)

4. a. Walker's Brigade (March–May 1863)
25th Georgia Regiment
29th Georgia Regiment
30th Georgia Regiment
1st Georgia Sharpshooter Battalion
4th Louisiana Battalion

(attached for defense of Charleston)
1st Regiment, Georgia State Line
2d Regiment, Georgia State Line
South Carolina Volunteer Battalion (including Augusta Volunteer Company)

(attached for movement to Mississippi)
Martin's Georgia Battery

4. b. Walker's Division (May–September 1863)
Escort (Capt. Thomas M. Nelson)
Nelson's Georgia Rangers (June–July only)

Walker's Brigade (Col. Claudius C. Wilson)
25th Georgia
29th Georgia
30th Georgia
1st Georgia Sharpshooter Battalion
4th Louisiana Battalion
Martin's Georgia Battery

Gist's Brigade (Brig. Gen. States Rights Gist)
16th South Carolina
24th South Carolina
46th Georgia
8th Georgia Battalion
Ferguson's South Carolina Battery

Gregg's Brigade (Brig. Gen. John Gregg)
   3d Tennessee
   10th Tennessee
   30th Tennessee
   41st Tennessee
   50th Tennessee
   1st Tennessee Battalion
   7th Texas
   Bledsoe's Missouri Battery

Ector's Brigade (Brig. Gen. Matthew D. Ector)
   9th Texas
   10th Texas Cavalry*
   14th Texas Cavalry*
   32d Texas Cavalry*
   Stone's Alabama Battalion
   Pound's Mississippi Battalion
   McNally's Arkansas Battery

McNair's Brigade (Brig. Gen. Evander McNair)
(Mississippi, May–June 1863 only)
   1st Arkansas Mounted Rifles (Dismounted)
   2d Arkansas Mounted Rifles (Dismounted)
   4th Arkansas
   25th/31st Arkansas
   39th North Carolina
   Culpeper's South Carolina Battery

Adams's Cavalry Brigade (Brig. Gen. John Adams)
(Mississippi, May–June 1863 only)
   3d Kentucky (Mounted Infantry)
   4th Mississippi (two companies)
   20th Mississippi
   Adams's Mississippi Regiment
   18th Mississippi Battalion
   Hall's Cavalry Company
   Nelson's (Georgia) Rangers
   Red's Cavalry Company (Mississippi State Troops)
   Hoskins's Brookhaven Mississippi Battery

Ferguson's Command (Col. Samuel W. Ferguson)
(Mississippi, May–June 1863 only)

*Dismounted

Alabama Sharpshooter Battalion
Bridges's Cavalry Battalion
Mississippi Sharpshooter Battalion

Louisiana Siege Battery
Bledsoe's Missouri Battery (later transferred to Gregg's brigade)

4. c. Reserve Corps, Army of Tennessee (September 5–22, 1863)

Walker's Division   (Maj. Gen. W. H. T. Walker)
                     (Brig. Gen. S. R. Gist [September 19–20])

Walker's Brigade   (Col. C. C. Wilson)
    25th Georgia
    29th Georgia
    30th Georgia
    1st Georgia Sharpshooter Battalion
    4th Louisiana Battalion

Gist's Brigade*   (Brig. Gen. S. R. Gist [September 5–19])
                   (Col. Peyton Colquitt [September 20])
    16th South Carolina (left at Rome)
    24th South Carolina
    46th Georgia
    8th Georgia Battalion
    South Carolina Battery (en route to battlefield September 20)

Ector's Brigade (Brig. Gen. Matthew D. Ector)
    9th Texas
    10th Texas Cavalry†
    14th Texas Cavalry†
    32d Texas Cavalry†
    Stone's Alabama Battalion
    Pound's Mississippi Battalion

Division Artillery (Maj. Joseph Palmer)
    Howell's (formerly Martin's) Georgia Battery

Liddell's Division (Brig. Gen. St. John R. Liddell)
    Liddell's Brigade (Col. Daniel C. Govan)
        2d/15th Arkansas
        5th/13th Arkansas
        6th/7th Arkansas

*At Rome, Ga., until September 18.

†Dismounted

8th Arkansas
1st Louisiana

Walthall's Brigade (Brig. Gen. Edward C. Walthall)
24th Mississippi
27th Mississippi
29th Mississippi
30th Mississippi
34th Mississippi

Division Artillery (Capt. Charles Swett)
Fowler's Alabama Battery
Warren Light Artillery (Mississippi) Battery

4. d. Walker's Division (September 1863–January 1864)
(Commanded by Brig. Gen. S.R. Gist, November 12–28, 1863, and January 12–
February 10, 1864.
Escort (Lt. James M. Boydstun; shown on the roll for December 31, 1863)
Detachment, 4th Georgia Cavalry
Wilson's Brigade   (Col. [Brig. Gen.] Claudius C. Wilson)
                    (died November 27, 1863)
                    (Col. James C. Nisbet [November 1863–January 1864])
                    (Brig. Gen. Clement H. Stevens)
25th Georgia
29th Georgia
30th Georgia
66th Georgia*
1st Georgia Sharpshooter Battalion
26th Georgia Battalion*

Gist's Brigade (Brig. Gen. S. R. Gist)
16th South Carolina
24th South Carolina
46th Georgia
8th Georgia Battalion

Gregg's Brigade (Brig. Gen. John Gregg)
(September–November 1863; brigade broken up November 1863)
3d Tennessee
10th Tennessee
30th Tennessee
50th Tennessee
1st Tennessee Battalion

*Joined November 1863.

7th Texas
41st Tennessee

Maney's Brigade (Brig. Gen. George Maney)
(November 1863–February 1864)
  1st/27th Tennessee
  6th/9th Tennessee
  34th Tennessee
  41st Tennessee
  50th Tennessee
  Maney's Tennessee Battalion

Baldwin's Brigade (Brig. Gen. William E. Baldwin)
(December 1863–January 1864 only)
  4th Mississippi
  35th Mississippi
  40th Mississippi
  46th Mississippi

Division Artillery   (Maj. Joseph Palmer)
                      (Maj. Robert Martin)
  Howell's Georgia Battery
  Beauregard's (formerly Ferguson's) South Carolina Battery
  Bledsoe's Missouri Battery

4. e. Walker's Georgia Division (February–July 1864)
Escort
  Company G, 53d Alabama (Capt. P. B. Mastin, Jr.)
  (April–May 1864)
  Company F, 10th Confederate Cavalry   (Capt. Thaddeus G. Holt)
  (June–July 1864)   (Lt. James Bass)
  Stevens's Brigade   (Brig. Gen. Clement H. Stevens
                                           [died of wounds July 25, 1864])
                                         (Col. George A. Smith
                                           [July 20–22, 1864])
                                         (Col. James C. Nesbit
                                           [July 22, 1864, captured])

    25th Georgia
    29th Georgia
    30th Georgia
    66th Georgia
    1st Georgia Sharpshooter Battalion
    26th Georgia Battalion (to June 1864)
    1st Georgia Confederate (joined June 1864)

Gist's Brigade (Brig. Gen. S. R. Gist)
 16th South Carolina
 24th South Carolina
 46th Georgia
 65th Georgia (after July 2)
 8th Georgia Battalion
 2d Georgia Sharpshooter Battalion (after July 2)
 5th Mississippi (July 2–10)
 8th Mississippi (July 2–10)

Jackson's Brigade (Brig. Gen. John K. Jackson)
(Disbanded July 2, 1864)*
 5th Georgia
 47th Georgia
 65th Georgia
 2d Georgia Sharpshooter Battalion
 1st Georgia Confederate (transferred to Stevens's brigade June 1864)
 5th Mississippi
 8th Mississippi

Mercer's Brigade (Brig. Gen. Hugh W. Mercer)
(Joined May 2, 1864)
 54th Georgia
 57th Georgia (joined May 20, 1864)
 63d Georgia
 1st Georgia Volunteers (joined May 27, 1864)

Division artillery support
 Martin's Artillery Battalion (Maj. Robert Martin)
   (assigned to Corps Artillery Regiment)
 Howell's Georgia Battery
 Beuaregard's South Carolina Battery
 Bledsoe's Missouri Battery

* 5th and 47th Georgia sent to Savannah; other regiments attached to Gist's brigade; 5th and 8th Mississippi reassigned to Lowrey's brigade; Cleburne's division from Gist's brigade about July 10.

ABBREVIATIONS

AAG	Assistant Adjutant General
AG	Adjutant General
AGO	Adjutant General's Office
AOG	Association of Graduates, U.S. Military Academy
B&L	Robert V. Johnson and Clarence C. Buel, *Battles and Leaders of the Civil War*
CCSC	Chatham County Superior Court
CRG	Allen D. Candler, comp., *The Confederate Records of the State of Georgia*
DAB	*Dictionary of American Biography*
DGB	*Dictionary of Georgia Biography*
GDAH	Georgia Department of Archives and History
GHQ	*Georgia Historical Quarterly*
GO	General Orders
HQA	Headquarters of the Army
HQCC	Headquarters, Corps of Cadets
KMNP	Kennesaw Mountain National Battlefield Park
LR	Letters Received
LS	Letters Sent
Mxxx	National Archives Microcopy, as in M258
NA	National Archives
ORN	U.S. Navy Department *Official Records of the Union and Confederate Navies in the War of the Rebellion*
OR	U.S. War Department, *The War of the Rebellion: A Compilation of the Official Records of the Union and Confederate Armies*
RCPC	Richmond County Probate Court
RCSC	Richmond County Superior Court

RG	Record Group
SHSP	*Southern Historical Society Papers*
SO	Special Orders
USMA	United States Military Academy
WHTW	William H. T. Walker

NOTES

CHAPTER 1. PREPARATION OF A SOLDIER, 1816–1837

1. *DAB*, 10:365; William J. Northern, *Men of Mark in Georgia*, 7 vols. (1907; reprint, Spartanburg, S.C.: Reprint Co., 1973), 3:200; and Patricia L. Faust, ed., *The Historical Times Illustrated Encyclopedia of the Civil War* (New York: Harper & Row, 1986), 798–99. Stewart Sifakis, *Who Was Who in the Civil War* (New York: Facts on File Publications, 1988), 686–87, outlines Walker's life but gives some factually erroneous information. Steve Davis, "A Georgia Firebrand: Major General W. H. T. Walker, C.S.A.," *Georgia Historical Quarterly* 63 (Winter 1979): 447–60, provides an interesting but narrow analysis of Walker's character. The most complete biographical sketch of Walker is Paul M. McCain, "The Military Career of William Henry Talbot Walker" (M.A. thesis, Duke University, 1948). Walter A. Clark, *A Lost Arcadia, or the Story of My Old Community* (Augusta: Chronicle Job Printer, 1909), 64–77, describes the Walkers of Richmond County, Georgia. A comprehensive published genealogical source for the Walker family is Mary Meadows, *The Genealogy of the Families Foremon-Boisclair, Walker, Beers, Lacy* (Easley, S.C.: Southern Historical Press, 1980), 150–212.

2. Joseph Mellichamp, *Senators from Georgia* (Huntsville, Ala.: Stroud, 1976), 85–90.

3. Meadows, *Walker Genealogy*, 158–64, 187–91. Frances G. Satterfield, *Madame LeVert: A Biography of Octavia Walton LeVert* (Edisto Island, S.C.: Edisto Press, 1987), records the life of Walker's famous second cousin.

4. Meadows, *Walker Genealogy*, 164; Walker family collections of Adele Shearer and Laurie Wolfe; Eliza A. Bowen, *The Story of Wilkes County, Georgia* (Marietta, Ga.: Continental Book Publishing Co., 1950), 53–54, 155, 157–58; F. M. Newsome and Nell H. Newsome, *Wilkes County Cemeteries* (Washington, Ga.: Wilkes Publishing Co., 1970), 90; *"Ceded Lands": Records of St. Paul's Parish and Early*

Wilkes County, Georgia (Albany, Ga.: Delwyn Associates, 1964[?]), 152; Robert S. Davis, Jr., comp., *The Wilkes County Papers, 1773–1833* (Easley, S.C.: Southern Historical Press, 1979), 167, 190–91, 224; WHTW to wife, August 29, 1846, and October [13?], 1852, W. H. T. Walker Papers, Duke University, Durham, N.C. Despite Walker's obviously firsthand information, there is no documented evidence that John Talbot had a son named William Henry.

5. Meadows, *Walker Genealogy*, 164, 167; Mellichamp, *Senators from Georgia*, 85–90.

6. *Augusta Chronicle and Sentinel*, May 25, 1850; *Kennesaw Gazette*, September 15, 1889; WHTW to wife, October 2, 1852, Walker Papers; Clark, *Lost Arcadia*, 126. The *Kennesaw Gazette* was the house newspaper of the Western and Atlantic Railroad. I believe that the sketch of Walker's life which appeared in the *Gazette* in 1889, although unsigned, was written by General Marcellus A. Stovall.

7. Meadows, *Walker Genealogy*, 167–68; Mellichamp, *Senators from Georgia*, 85–90; WHTW to John David Walker, September 1853, Walker Papers; RCPC, Will Book A (1798–1839), 268–69; RCPC, Court of Ordinary Minute Book C (1822–36), 138, 144, 157, 165, 206; RCSC, Deed Book 2A, 458; interview with Ella Nuite, owner and resident of Seclusaval, now known as Windsor Spring, and her son-in-law, Kenneth Kitchens, December 6, 1989. Windsor Spring is on the National Historic Register.

8. Information from Laurie Wolfe and Adele Shearer; WHTW to wife, August 29, 1846, Walker Papers. George A. B. Walker's diary of some of the years he spent in Alabama is at Georgia Southern University, Statesboro, Ga. A microfilm copy of the diary is on file at the Georgia Department of Archives and History, Atlanta, microfilm records drawer 19, box 77.

9. Sidney Forman, *West Point: A History of the United States Military Academy* (New York: Columbia University Press, 1950), 68–69; Stephen E. Ambrose, *Duty, Honor, Country: A History of West Point* (Baltimore: Johns Hopkins Press, 1966), 83, 127; John Forsyth et al. to Lewis Cass, January 4, 1831, and George A. B. Walker to Cass, April 23, 1832, NA Microfilm Publication M688, U.S. Military Academy Cadet Application Papers, 1805–66, file 1831/96.

10. Forman, *West Point*, 51–60, 94–95, 98–99; Ambrose, *Duty, Honor, Country*, 71, 92–102, 128–30, 134–35. Individual class members can be identified in George W. Cullum, *Biographical Register of the Officers and Graduates of the United States Military Academy at West Point, New York*, 3d ed. (Boston: Houghton Mifflin, 1891), and U.S. Military Academy AOG, *Register of Graduates and Former Cadets* (1970 ed.). Identifications herein will be by graduation number.

11. Ambrose, *Duty, Honor, Country*, 129; William K. Scarborough, "Science on the Plantation," in *Science and Medicine in the Old South* ed. Ronald L. Numbers and Todd L. Savitt (Baton Rouge: Louisiana State University Press, 1989), 86.

12. RG 14, Proceedings of the Academic Board (Staff Records), 1818–1968, Vol. 1 (1818–35), 505, 519, USMA Archives; *Kennesaw Gazette*, September 15, 1889.

13. RG 14, 1:533, 541, USMA Archives.

14. Ibid., 551; ibid., Vol. 2 (1835–42), 14; RG 96, Bimonthly and Semi-Annual Muster Rolls, Vol. 4 (October 1817–April 1839), bimonthly returns for September 1834 to March 1835, USMA Archives.

15. Cullum, *Biographical Register;* AOG, *Register of Graduates and Former Cadets.*

16. RG 14, 2:32, 76, USMA Archives.

17. RG 167, Post Orders, Vol. 6 (1832–37), 457, 459, 473, 482, 505–6, 526, ibid., Records of the Office of the Judge Advocate General (Army), RG 153, Records of the Proceedings of General Courts-Martial, 1809–90, Case CC193, NA.

18. Edward M. Coffman, *The Old Army: A Portrait of the American Army in Peacetime, 1784–1898* (New York: Oxford University Press, 1986), 49.

19. Cullum, *Biographical Register,* 936; Walker to Secretary of War Joel Poinsett, NA Microfilm Publication M567, Letters Received by the Adjutant General of the Army, Main Series, 1822–60, Roll 155, Item W283.

CHAPTER 2. GLORY AND AGONY, 1837–1844

1. The origin and course of the conflict with the Seminole are fully discussed in John K. Mahon, *History of the Second Seminole War, 1835–1842* (Gainesville: University of Florida Press, 1967). For a contemporaneous account see John T. Sprague, *The Origin, Progress, and Conclusion of the Florida War* (1848; facsimile ed., Gainesville: University of Florida Press, 1964). A good summary is in Francis P. Prucha, *The Sword of the Republic: The United States Army on the Frontier, 1783–1846* (New York: Macmillan, 1969), 269–306.

2. Details of the death of Wiley Thompson can be found in Russell K. Brown, *Fallen in Battle: American General Officer Combat Fatalities from 1775* (Westport, Conn.: Greenwood Press, 1988), 139–40.

3. Zachary Taylor's Okeechobee campaign is described in Brainard Dyer, *Zachary Taylor* (Baton Rouge: Louisiana State University Press, 1946), 100–127; Mahon, *Second Seminole War,* 227–30; Sprague, *Florida War,* 203–14; and Prucha, *Sword of the Republic,* 291–93.

4. Taylor's report of the battle, including casualty lists, is in *American State Papers, Military Affairs,* Vol. 7 (Washington, D.C.: Gales and Seaton, 1860), 986–89. It is also printed as U.S. Congress, Senate, *Official Report of Action of 25th December, 1837, with the Seminole Indians,* Senate Document 227, 25th Cong., 2d sess.

5. *Augusta Constitutionalist,* March 13, 1861, and August 25, 1864 (biographical sketches of WHTW); Civil War Miscellany-Personal Papers, W. H. T. Walker Biographical Sketch, GDAH.

6. *American State Papers, Military Affairs,* 7:988.

7. Ibid., Appendix, 990–91; Prucha, *Sword of the Republic,* 292; Cullum, *Biographical Register,* 936.

8. WHTW biographical sketch, GDAH; Richard Taylor, *Destruction and Recon-struction* (New York: D. Appleton, 1879), 22.

9. WHTW to Roger Jones, May 31, 1838, NA M567, Roll 178, Item W243.

10. WHTW to Roger Jones, October 10, 1838, NA M567, Roll 179, Item W460; Jones to Commanding General Alexander Macomb, December 27, 1839, enclo-sure to M567, Roll 200, Items W448 and W449, explaining the circumstances of Walker's resignation; NA Microfilm Publication M1094, General Orders, Spe-cial Orders, and Circulars Issued by the Adjutant General of the Army, NA, Roll 4, Vol. 9 (October 1837–December 1841), p. 176, GO 45, October 31, 1838, resignation accepted; p. 179, GO 46, November 1, 1838, resignation announced.

11. WHTW biographical sketches, GDAH and *Augusta Constitutionalist*, March 13, 1861, and August 25, 1864; *Catalog of the Officers and Students in Yale College, 1839–1840* (New Haven, 1840), 8, 33–34.

12. Zachary Taylor to Roger Jones, December 12, 1839, John Forsyth to Joel Poinsett, April 15, 1840, petition of fourteen officers of the 6th Infantry and other documents, NA M567, Roll 200, Items W448 and W449; WHTW to Poinsett, August 12, 1840, M567, Roll 221, Item W405; GO 51, November 18, 1840, re-appointment of WHTW as first lieutenant, M1094, Roll 4, Vol. 9, p. 358; NA Microfilm Publication M127, Letters sent to the President by the Secretary of War, 1800–1863, Roll 2, December 11, 1840, List of Officers for Promotion and Persons for Appointment to Be Transmitted to the Senate; NA Microfilm Pub-lication M665, Returns from Regular Infantry Regiments, Roll 65, 6th Infantry, 1837–43, return for December 1840.

13. NA M665, Roll 65, return for March 1841; Francis B. Heitman, *Biographical Register and Dictionary of the United States Army, 1789–1903*, 2 vols. (Washington, D.C.: U.S. Government Printing Office, 1903), 1:643, Charles S. Lovell; RG153, Judge Advocate General of the Army, Records of the Proceedings of General Courts-Martial of the U.S. Army, Case DD25, NA.

14. W. W. Bliss to Gustavus Loomis, April 10, 1841, to Jacob Brown, April 14, 1841, to W. Hoffman, April 22, 1841, Records of the Adjutant General's Office, 1780s–1917 (RG 94), Records of the Army in Florida, LS, 1841–42, NA; Walker K. Armistead to Roger Jones, April 30, May 3, 1842, M567, Roll 222, Items A141 and A142; WHTW to Roger Jones, April 9, 1841, NA Microfilm Publication M711, Register of Letters Received by Office of the Adjutant General, 1812–89, Roll 14 (1840–41), Item W140/1841.

15. RG 153, Records of the Proceedings of General Courts-Martial, Case DD25, NA.

16. WHTW to wife, October 21, 1852, Walker Papers.

17. Bertram Wyatt-Brown, *Southern Honor: Ethics and Behavior in the Old South* (New York: Oxford University Press, 1982), 156.

18. Ibid., 44, 191–92; WHTW to wife, April 30, 1847, Walker Papers.

19. Wyatt-Brown, *Southern Honor*, 48.

20. WHTW to wife, undated [July 1856?], Walker Papers.

21. Justin H. Smith, *The War with Mexico*, 2 vols. (New York: Macmillan, 1919), 1:144, 158, 211; K. Jack Bauer, *The Mexican War* (New York: Macmillan, 1974), 35; Robert Selph Henry, *The Story of the Mexican War*, 2d ed. (New York: Frederick Ungar, 1961), 45, 52–53; *DAB*, 20:536.

22. NA M665, Roll 65, 6th Infantry returns for April 1841 to February 1842; Sprague, *Florida War*, 360, describes one patrol in which WHTW commanded the mounted detachment; U.S. Congress, House of Representatives, *Correspondence, Secretary of War and Commanding General in Florida*, House Executive Document 262, 27th Cong., 2d sess., 25.

23. Cullum, *Biographical Register*, 936; WHTW to Lt. James Belger, Adjutant, 6th Infantry, July 31, and to Roger Jones, August 31, September 30, October 31, November 25, December 6, 1842, NA M567, Roll 263, Items W435, W443, W491, W558, and W602, and NA M711, Roll 15, Item W553; No. 1582, Jones to WHTW, December 3, 1842, and No. 1593, Jones to WHTW, December 9, 1842, NA Microfilm Publication M565, Letters Sent by the Adjutant General (Main Series), 1800–1890, Roll 13, Vol. 19 (November 1842–October 1843); NA Microfilm Publication M617, Returns from United States Military Posts, 1800–1916, Roll 1287, Fort Towson, May to November 1842, Roll 404, Fort Gibson, November 1842 to May 1844; NA M665, Roll 65, 6th Infantry returns for March 1842 to December 1843, Roll 66, 6th Infantry returns for January to May 1844; WHTW to Jones, January 31, 184[3], NA M567, Roll 278, Item W69; Coffman, *Old Army*, 185.

24. Information from Adele Shearer and Laurie Wolfe; *Augusta City Directory 1841*; RCPC, Marriage Book B (1839–55).

CHAPTER 3. HIGH SOCIETY, 1844–1846

1. Coffman, *Old Army*, 137–48; Newman S. Clarke to Roger Jones, June 17, 1844, NA M567, Roll 283, Item C135.

2. WHTW to Jones, June 16, 1844, Clarke to Jones, June 17, 1844, NA M711, Roll 17, Item W219; Jones to Clarke, June 19, 1844, RG 94, Recruiting Service LS, 4:339, No. 68, NA; WHTW to Jones, July 4, 1844, NA M567, Roll 293, Item W239; Jones to Clarke, July 10, 1844, Recruiting Service LS, 4:343, No. 79.

3. WHTW to Jones, November 4, 1844, NA M567, Roll 293, Item W388; January 22, 1845, M567, Roll 306, Item W31; and September 27, 1845, M567, Roll 307, Item W423.

4. RG 94, Register of Recruits, Vol. 5 (1839–46), 113, NA. The life and character of Stephen Van Rensselaer are sketched in *Appleton's Cyclopedia of American Biography*, 6 vols. (New York: D. Appleton, 1888), 6:252; WHTW to wife, September 4, 1846, Walker Papers.

5. WHTW to "Teeny," undated [1845?], Hargrett Rare Book and Manuscript Library, University of Georgia, Athens, Ga.

6. Cuyler Reynolds, ed., *Genealogical and Family History of Southern New York*

and the Hudson River Valley, 3 vols. (New York: Lewis Historical Publishing Company, 1914), 3:1098–1120, 1005–7; George Rogers Howell and Jonathan Tenney, *History of the County of Albany, N.Y.* (New York: W. W. Munsell, 1886), 524, 526, 572. Family notes can be found at the Albany Institute of History and Art in the Franklin Townsend Family Papers, especially Franklin Townsend, "Family Records" (1839), and Annie Townsend Lawrence, "Family Record 1635" (1869); Frederick Townsend Papers; and Isaiah Townsend Papers. A sketch of the life of Franklin Townsend is in Cuyler Reynolds, ed., *Albany Chronicles* (Albany, N.Y.: J. B. Lyon, 1906), 602; of Frederick in *The National Cyclopedia of American Biography*, 43 vols. (New York: James T. White, 1891–1961), 4:458–59, and David A. Harsha, *Noted Living Albanians* (Albany: Weed, Parsons and Co., 1891), 408–16; and of Robert in *Appleton's Cyclopedia of American Biography*, 6:149, and Joel Munsell, *Collections on the History of Albany*, 3 vols. (Albany, N.Y.: J. Munsell, 1870), 3:325. Robert's obituary appeared in the *New York Times*, November 15, 1866. The records of the Register, Albany Rural Cemetery, for Section 45, Lot 4, also contain much useful information. Other information on family events through the years can be obtained from the Walker Papers. See particularly the letters of Hannah Townsend to her daughter, Mary Townsend Walker, November 27, December 17, 1853, February 16, March 29, May 10, 1854; Hannah Townsend to her brother, Solomon Townsend, March 1, 1849; and Hannah to her daughter, Anne Townsend Martin, September 9, 1851. In the same collection are Anne T. Martin to Mary T. Walker, November 30, 1852, December 4, 1853; Justine Van Rensselaer to Mary, November 30, 1852; Howard Townsend to Anne T. Martin, December 5, 1853 [?]; Justine V. R. Townsend to Mary, April 6, [1854?], October 27, [1854?]; Howard Townsend to Mary, April 22, 1854; and Robert Townsend to Mary, June 6, 1854.

7. GO 1, January 13, 1846, NA M1094, Roll 5, Vol. 10 (1842–46), 366; WHTW to Clarke and Jones, February 3, 1846, NA M567, Roll 329, Item W45; Jones to Clarke, February 11, 1846, RG 94, Recruiting Service LS, Vol. 4, p. 435, No. 13, NA; WHTW to Jones, April 16, 21, 1846, M567, Roll 329, Items W136 and W145.

8. WHTW to wife, August 29, 1846, Walker Papers.

9. Bauer, *Mexican War*, 32–46; *Augusta Constitutionalist*, August 25, 1864.

10. Jones to WHTW, April 24, 1846, NA M565, Roll 14, Vol. 22, p. 209, No. 555; Church Register, First Presbyterian Church, Albany, N.Y.; *Daily Albany Argus*, May 11, 1846.

11. Bauer, *Mexican War*, 48–70; Jones to WHTW, May 14, 1846, RG 94, Recruiting Service LS, Vol. 4, p. 454, No. 83, NA; Jones to Gustavus Loomis, May 15, 1846, RG 94, Recruiting Service LS, Vol. 5, p. 1, No. 84, NA; WHTW to Jones, May 15, 1846, NA M567, Roll 329, Item W180.

12. Jones to Francis Belton, Ft. McHenry, June 5, 9, 1846, RG 94, Recruiting Service LS, Vol. 5, p. 13, No. 119, and p. 14, No. 126, NA; WHTW to Jones, June 7, 1846, NA M711, Roll 19, Item W240; Belton to Jones, June 7, 1846, NA M567, Roll 309, Item B284; WHTW to Jones, June 19, 1846, M567, Roll 329,

Item W270; WHTW to Jones, July 21, 28, 1846, M567, Roll 330, Items W343 and W368; WHTW to wife, July 13, 1846, Walker Papers.

13. WHTW to wife, August 27, 28, 29, 30, September 1, 2, 3, 4, 6, 7, 8, 9, 10, 11, 1846, Walker Papers; RG 94, Register of Recruits, 5:167, NA.

14. WHTW to Jones, July 21, 28, 1846, NA M567, Roll 330, Items W343 and W368; WHTW to Jones, October 14, 1846, with endorsement by Col. R. B. Mason, Superintendent of Recruiting, NA M567, Roll 330, Item W535; Jones to Mason, October 31, 1846, RG 94, Recruiting Service LS, Vol. 5, p. 86, No. 368, NA; WHTW to Jones, November 9, 18, 1846, NA M711, Roll 19, Items W568, 569, and 583; WHTW to wife, November 24, 27[?], 29[?], 30, 1846, Walker Papers; WHTW to Jones, January 3, 184[7], M567, Roll 364, Item W48; RG 94, Muster Rolls, F Company, 6th Infantry, November 17 to December 31, 1846, NA; NA M665, Roll 66 (1844–48), return for December 1846. See Erna Risch, *Quartermaster Support of the Army, 1775–1939* (Washington, D.C.: Center of Military History, 1989), 258–62, for problems in arranging shipping from East Coast ports to Mexico in 1846.

CHAPTER 4. A NEW ADVENTURE, 1846–1847

1. WHTW to wife, December 1, 2, 16, 1846, Walker Papers; RG 94, Muster Rolls, F Company, 6th Infantry, November 17–December 31, 1846, NA; NA M665, Roll 66, 6th Infantry return for December 1846.

2. Risch, *Quartermaster Support of the Army*, 262–63.

3. WHTW to wife, "Half past one P.M." [December 2?], December 2, 6, 1846, Walker Papers.

4. WHTW to wife, "Half past one P.M.," December 1, 6, 12, 16, 18, 1846, ibid.

5. WHTW to wife, December 9, 12[?], 21, 23, 1846, ibid.

6. WHTW to wife, December 12[?], 14, 16, 1846, ibid.

7. WHTW to wife, December 16, 18, 1846, ibid.

8. WHTW to wife, December 21, 23, 1846, ibid.

9. WHTW to wife, December 27, 29 (with a postscript for December 30), 1846, ibid.

10. Roger Jones to Rudolph Ernst, Chillicothe, Ohio, November 13, 1846, RG 94, Recruiting Service LS, Vol. 5, p. 89, No. 384, NA; AOG, *Register of Graduates and Former Cadets.*

11. Bauer, *Mexican War*, 232–40; WHTW to wife, February 12, 1847, Walker Papers.

12. WHTW to wife, February 1, 1847, ibid.

13. WHTW to wife, January 2, 1846 [1847], January 22, February 16, 18, 1846, ibid.

14. WHTW to wife, January 22, February 12, 1847, ibid.

15. WHTW to wife, February 12, 19, March 2, 5, 7, 1847, ibid.; *New Orleans Daily Picayune*, March 26, 1847. See Charles Byrne, "The Sixth Regiment of Infantry," in *The Army of the United States*, ed. Theophilus F. Rodenbough and William L. Haskins (New York: Maynard, Merrill, 1896), 485–86, for the assembling of the companies of the 6th Infantry in Mexico.

16. Bauer, *Mexican War*, 241–42.

CHAPTER 5. TO THE HALLS OF MONTEZUMA, 1847–1848

1. The siege and capture of Vera Cruz are described in Bauer, *Mexican War*, 241–53; Smith, *War with Mexico*, 2:17–36; Roswell S. Ripley, *The War with Mexico*, 2 vols. (New York: Harper and Brothers, 1849), 2:9–52; and Douglas S. Freeman, *R. E. Lee: A Biography*, 4 vols. (New York: Charles Scribner's Sons, 1948), 1:224–35. Walker briefly described the unopposed landing in his letter to his wife, March 11, 1847, Walker Papers.

2. Bauer, *Mexican War*, 247; WHTW to wife, March 13, 21, 25, 27, 1847, Walker Papers.

3. Bauer, *Mexican War*, 245.

4. WHTW to wife, March 21, 1847, Walker Papers.

5. Emma Jerome Blackwood, ed., *To Mexico with Scott: Letters of Captain E. Kirby Smith to His Wife* (Cambridge, Mass.: Harvard University Press, 1917), 118–20; WHTW to wife, March 21, 1847, Walker Papers.

6. Bauer, *Mexican War*, 252–53; WHTW to wife, March 27, April 1, 1847, Walker Papers.

7. WHTW to wife, February 1, 1847, Walker Papers.

8. WHTW to wife, March 30, February 1, 1847, ibid.

9. Bauer, *Mexican War*, 259–63; WHTW to wife, April 1, 1847, Walker Papers.

10. NA M665, Roll 66, 6th Infantry returns, December 1846 to April 1847; Byrne, "Sixth Regiment of Infantry," 485–86; Smith, *War with Mexico*, 1:509, 2:343; Cadmus M. Wilcox, *History of the Mexican War*, ed. Mary Rachel Wilcox (Washington, D.C.: Church News Publishing Co., 1892), 636–37; *Savannah Daily Morning News*, January 8, 1863.

11. Bauer, *Mexican War*, 263–64; WHTW to wife, April 15, 1847, Walker Papers. See also George Ballentine, *Autobiography of an English Soldier in the United States Army* (New York: Stringer and Townsend, 1853), 167–73; J. Jacob Oswandal, *Notes of the Mexican War, 1846–47–48* (Philadelphia: N.p., 1885), 108–12; and Wilcox, *Mexican War*, 271–81, for a description of conditions on the march from Vera Cruz.

12. WHTW to wife, April 15, 1847, Walker Papers.

13. Bauer, *Mexican War*, 264–68; Smith, *War with Mexico*, 2:37–60; Ripley, *War with Mexico*, 2:64–75; Wilcox, *Mexican War*, 283–92; Freeman, *R. E. Lee*, 1:237–48; WHTW to wife, April 22, 27, 1847, Walker Papers.

14. WHTW to wife, April 26, 8, 1847, Walker Papers.

15. WHTW to wife, April 30, 1847, ibid.

16. RG 94, Muster Rolls for F Company, 6th Infantry, March 1–April 30, 1847, NA; WHTW to wife, September 4, 1846, Walker Papers.

17. WHTW to Roger Jones, May 14, 1847, NA M567, Roll 365, Item W369; RG 94; Muster Rolls for F Company, 6th Infantry, May 1–June 30, July 1–August 31, 1847, NA.

18. Ralph W. Kirkham, *The Mexican War Journal and Letters of Ralph W. Kirkham*, ed. Robert R. Miller (College Station, Tex.: Texas A&M Press, 1991), xii, 3, 11.

19. Bauer, *Mexican War*, 269–71; Smith, *War with Mexico*, 2:60–78; Henry, *Story of the Mexican War*, 291–310; WHTW to wife, [May?] 19, 1847, Walker Papers.

20. WHTW to wife, May 26, 1847, Walker Papers; Coffman, *Old Army*, 107–8.

21. See Bauer, *Mexican War*, 279–301; Ripley, *War with Mexico*, 2:205–85; Smith, *War with Mexico*, 2:99–119; and Wilcox, *Mexican War*, 358–409, for the battles at Contreras and Churubusco.

22. Bauer, *Mexican War*, 290–95. For an account that gives emphasis to Robert E. Lee's role, see Freeman, *R. E. Lee*, 1:249–72.

23. Bauer, *Mexican War*, 295–98; Henry, *Story of the Mexican War*, 338–39.

24. RG 153, Records of General Courts-Martial, Case EE565, Court-Martial of Major B. L. E. Bonneville, testimony of Major Bonneville, Captain William Hoffman, and Lieutenant Edward Johnson, NA.

25. Ibid., testimony of Major Bonneville, Captain Hoffman, Lieutenant Johnson, and Lieutenant S. B. Buckner; Bauer, *Mexican War*, 298.

26. RG 153, Records of General Courts-Martial, Case EE565, testimony of Lieutenant L. A. Armistead, Lieutenant Ralph Kirkham, and Sergeant M. McCann, NA; Bauer, *Mexican War*, 298.

27. RG 153, Records of General Courts-Martial, Case EE565, testimony of William J. Worth, Captain Hoffman, Lieutenant Johnson, Sergeant H. P. Downs, et al., NA; Bauer, *Mexican War*, 298, 300; Smith, *War with Mexico*, 2:115–16.

28. Bauer, *Mexican War*, 298–301; Ripley, *War with Mexico*, 2:255, 257–58, 268–69, 272; Smith, *War with Mexico*, 2:115–16; Henry, *Story of the Mexican War*, 340–41; Reports of William J. Worth, Newman S. Clarke, Benjamin L. Bonneville, and William Hoffman, in U.S. Congress, House of Representatives, *Message from the President at the Commencement of the First Session of the Thirtieth Congress*, House Executive Document 8, 30th Cong., 1st sess., 315–22, A55, A62–64; WHTW to wife, undated [August 1847?], Walker Papers; John Sedgwick, *Correspondence of John Sedgwick, Major General*, 2 vols. (New York: DeVinne Press, 1902), 1:115.

29. U.S. Congress, House of Representatives, *Message from the President*, House Executive Document 8, 317, 320, A55, 62–64.

30. Cullum, *Biographical Register*, 936; WHTW to Roger Jones, September 9, 1848, NA M567, Roll 398, Item W734; WHTW to wife, undated [August 1847?], Walker Papers.

31. Wilcox, *Mexican War*, 636–37; Bauer, *Mexican War*, 301 and 305, n. 38.

32. RG 153, Records of General Courts-Martial, Case EE565, testimony of B. L. E. Bonneville, Assistant Surgeon DeLeon, and others, NA.

33. Bauer, *Mexican War*, 306–8; WHTW to wife, July 27, 1847, and undated [August 1847?], Walker Papers.

34. See Bauer, *Mexican War*, 308–11; Smith, *War with Mexico*, 2:140–47; Ripley, *War with Mexico*, 2:357–84; Henry, *Story of the Mexican War*, 351–55; and Wilcox, *Mexican War*, 429–42, for the attack on Molino del Rey.

35. Bauer, *Mexican War*, 309; Wilcox, *Mexican War*, 433, 437, 441; Byrne, "Sixth Regiment of Infantry," 487; Ripley, *War with Mexico*, 2:368; Smith, *War with Mexico*, 2:143–45; Kirkham, *Mexican War Journal*, 58; Raphael Semmes, *Service Afloat and Ashore During the Mexican War* (Cincinnati: William H. Moore, 1851), 439; Reports of W. J. Worth and B. L. E. Bonneville, in U.S. Congress, Senate, *Message from the President at the Commencement of the First Session of the Thirtieth Congress*, Senate Executive Document 1, 30th Cong., 1st sess., 365, A138–39.

36. W. H. T. Walker Biographical Sketch, Civil War Miscellany—Personal Papers, GDAH: *Augusta Chronicle and Sentinel*, March 17, 1861; *Augusta Constitutionalist*, August 25, 1864; *Kennesaw Gazette*, September 15, 1889; Kirkham, *Mexican War Journal*, 58, 67; WHTW to Frederick Townsend, August 1, 1848, Frederick Townsend Papers, Albany Institute of History and Art.

37. Bauer, *Mexican War*, 311; Blackwood, ed., *To Mexico with Scott*, 216–17; Wilcox, *Mexican War*, 636–37; Freeman, *R. E. Lee*, 1:275.

38. Cullum, *Biographical Register*, 936; Wilcox, *Mexican War*, 636; WHTW to wife, November 26, December 8, 1847, Walker Papers, Kirkham; *Mexican War Journal*, 72.

39. William Montgomery Gardner, "The Memoirs of William Montgomery Gardner," ed. Elizabeth McKinne Gardner (typescript), 32–34, Richmond County Historical Society, Augusta, Ga.

40. RG 153, Records of General Courts-Martial, Case EE565, NA.

CHAPTER 6. HERO AND FAMILY MAN, 1848–1854

1. WHTW to wife, April 30, May 4, 19, July 27, undated [August ?], November 26, 1847, Walker Papers; Register, First Presbyterian Church, Albany, N.Y.; obituary of Mary Walker Schley, January 10, 1910, *Savannah Morning News*; Frederick Townsend to Mary C. Walker (Uncle Fred to Molly), December 9, 1853, Walker Papers; Mary T. Walker to Frederick Townsend, January 21, 1848, Folder 3, Frederick Townsend Papers, Albany Institute of History and Art.

2. Hannah Townsend to Frederick Townsend, 30 [December 1847?], and unknown [Hannah Townsend?] to Frederick Townsend, January 21, 1848, Folder 3, Frederick Townsend Papers; WHTW to wife, December 8, 1847, Walker Papers.

3. RG 94, Orders and Special Orders by Generals Butler and Worth to the Army in Mexico, SO 8, February 29, 1848, SO 10, March 3, 1848, SO 11, March 4, 1848, NA.

4. *Augusta Constitutionalist*, August 25, 1864; *Augusta Chronicle and Sentinel*, May 11, 1848; WHTW to Roger Jones, May 17, 1848, NA M567, Roll 396, Item W339. This report to the adjutant general was in Mary Walker's handwriting with WHTW's shaky signature affixed.

5. *Augusta Constitutionalist*, August 25, 1864; W. Ewing Johnston to Frederick Townsend, May 17, June 21, 1848, Folder 4, Frederick Townsend Papers; WHTW to Frederick Townsend, August 1, 1848, Folder 3, ibid., WHTW to Roger Jones, July 19, 1848, NA M567, Roll 384, Item M833, and Jones to WHTW, July 29, 1848, NA M565, Roll 16, Vol. 25, p. 264, No. 1533.

6. WHTW to Jones, October 1, November 4, December 31, 1848, NA M567, Roll 398, Items W808, W899, and W1023.

7. Hannah Townsend to Solomon Townsend, March 1, 1849, Walker Papers; NA M665, Rolls 66 and 67, 6th Infantry Returns, December 1848–April 1849; Byrne, "Sixth Regiment of Infantry," 488; Cornelius W. Lawrence and William Schley to President Zachary Taylor, January 24, 29, 1849, NA M567, Roll 419, Item W56, and Roll 420, Item W77. Lawrence was cousin to the Townsends and president of the Bank of New York. Schley was owner and president of Richmond Factory near Augusta. *DAB*, 4:557; Cullum, *Biographical Register*, 755; Smith, *War with Mexico*, 2:185–88; Bauer, *Mexican War*, 371; Henry, *Story of the Mexican War*, 378, 382–83.

8. Grady McWhiney, *Braxton Bragg and Confederate Defeat*, Vol. 1 (1969; reprint, Tuscaloosa: University of Alabama Press, 1991), 117–18, 120; WHTW to Jones, June 2, July 1, 1848, NA M567, Roll 421, Items W300 and W344; WHTW to George W. Crawford, July 10, 1849, and William Seward to Zachary Taylor, M567, Roll 421, Item W359; Arthur F. Hoskins to George W. Crawford, "to be laid before the President," August 13, 1849, M567, Roll 407, Item H546. Hoskins was leader of the Whig party in Alabama and former supreme court justice of that state.

9. WHTW to Jones, August 14, 1849, NA M567, Roll 421, Item W408; Jones to WHTW, August 17, 1849, RG 94, Recruiting Service LS, Vol. 5, p. 506, No. 1336, NA; WHTW to Jones, December 31, 1849, M567, Roll 422, Item W614; Jones to WHTW, January 25, 1850, RG 94, Recruiting Service LS, Vol. 6, p. 15, No. 1415, NA; Register, First Presbyterian Church, Albany; WHTW to wife, undated [October 21, 1853?], Walker Papers.

10. WHTW to Jones, April 23, 1850, NA M567, Roll 439, Item W169; Jones to WHTW, May 14, 1850, RG 94, Recruiting Service LS, Vol. 6, p. 47, No. 77, NA; WHTW to W. G. Freeman, June 5, 1850, NA Microfilm Publication M1635, LR, HQA, Roll 14, Item W58; Freeman to WHTW, July 1, 1850, NA Microfilm Publication M857, LS, HQA, Roll 3, Vol. 7/5, p. 338, No. 249.

11. Russell F. Weigley, *History of the United States Army* (New York: Macmillan, 1967), 193–94, 286–87.

12. Georgia House of Representatives, *House Journal 1847*, 114.

13. *Augusta Constitutionalist*, May 19, 21, 22, 23, 1850; Minutes of Augusta City Council, May 20, 1850. *Augusta Chronicle and Sentinel*, May 25, 1850; Fredrika Bremer, *The Homes of the New World* (New York: Harper and Brothers, 1853), 367–69. The sword is now the property of Hugh M. Walker, Jr., of North Augusta, S.C. He has loaned it for exhibit to the Atlanta History Center, Atlanta.

14. WHTW to Jones, October 3, 14, 23, 1850, NA M567, Roll 440, Items W462, W474, and W490; NA M665, Roll 67, Return for 6th Infantry, November 1850; *Kennesaw Gazette*, September 15, 1889; Cullum, *Biographical Register*, 709, 936; WHTW to Jones, January 5, February 4, March 1, 31, April 30, June 1, 1851, M567, Roll 455, Items W50, W106, W133, W199, and W223, Roll 456, Item W251. Cullum's letters to Jones for the period when his itinerary coincided with Walker's are November 30 and December 31, 1850, and January 31, February 28, March 31, and April 30, 1851, M567, Roll 426, Item C704, Roll 443, Items C51, C121, and C149, Roll 444, Items C218 and C240. The Italian guide book, *Murray's Handbook for Central Italy and Rome*, is the property of Hugh M. Walker, Jr.

15. WHTW to Jones, June 25, 1851, NA M567, Roll 456, Item W257; Jones to WHTW, June 28, July 11, 1851, RG 94, Recruiting Service LS, Vol. 6, p. 182, No. 191, and p. 186, No. 204, NA; *Hoffman's Albany Directory and City Register, 1852–53*; WHTW to Jones, April 3, 1852, M567, Roll 474, Item W178; Meadows, *Walker Genealogy*, 162; WHTW to Jones, July 12, 1852, M567, Roll 475, Item W323; WHTW to wife, undated [September 1852?], Walker Papers.

16. William R. Plum, *The Military Telegraph During the Civil War in the United States*, 2 vols. (Chicago: Jansen, McClurg, 1882), 2:86–106; WHTW to wife, March 3, 1855, Walker Papers; *Savannah Daily Morning News*, January 8, 1855; *Augusta Chronicle and Sentinel*, March 7, 1855; CCSC Deed Book 3N, 38–39; WHTW to wife, September 30, 1852, Walker Papers.

17. United States Military Academy, *Annual Report*, 1876, obituary of M. C. M. Hammond; Edgefield County Probate Records (microfilm), wills of Wyatt W. Starke, Apartment 71, Package 2868, and Sarah Davies Starke, Apartment 73, Package 2951, South Carolina Department of Archives and History; CCSC Deed Books 3L, 224, and 3N, 273; WHTW to wife, undated (postmarked September 22) and September [October] 9, 1852, Walker Papers.

18. WHTW to wife, September [October] 9, October 21, 23[?], 24[?], 25, 27, 28, 31, 1852, Walker Papers; CCSC Deed Book 3N, 38–39.

19. Georgia General Assembly, *Acts of the General Assembly of the State of Georgia, 1853–54*, 396–97; CCSC Deed Books 3N, 37, and 3U, 323–24; *Savannah Daily Morning News*, January 1, 1861; WHTW to wife, June 30, July 5, 19, 1863, Walker Papers.

20. WHTW to wife, October 28, 1852, Walker Papers.

21. WHTW to Commissioner of Pensions, September 2, 1852; Land Warrant 22282, December 27, 1852, Unindexed Bounty Land Claims, Records of the Veterans Administration (RG 15); Abstract of Bounty Land Warrants; RG 49, Records of the Bureau of Land Management, NA; WHTW to wife, February 19, 21[?], 1855, Walker Papers.

22. Hannah Townsend to Anne T. Martin, September 9, 1851; WHTW to wife, September 30, October 2, 3, 21, 31, 1852, Walker Papers; *Augusta Chronicle and Sentinel*, December 1, 1852; Hannah Townsend to Mary T. Walker and Justine Van Rensselaer to Mary T. Walker, both November 30, 1852, Walker Papers.

23. Wyatt-Brown, *Southern Honor*, 66, 134–35.

24. WHTW to wife, September 23, 30, October 13[?], 21, 27, 1852, Walker Papers; Letters of Administration, Isaiah Townsend, Vol. 9D, 227, Albany County, N.Y., Surrogate Court. John Townsend died in 1854. His will was proven September 20, 1854: Will Vol. 15, 199, Albany County Surrogate Court.

25. Wyatt-Brown, *Southern Honor*, 65.

26. Ibid., 73. Walker's complaints about military service and his search for an alternative career are in WHTW to wife, September 23, 28, 30, October 13[?], 21, 1852, Walker Papers.

27. Paul R. Goode, *The United States Soldiers' Home: A History of Its First Hundred Years* (Washington, D.C.: Privately printed, 1957), 28–31, 37; Lynda L. Crist and Mary S. Dix, eds., *The Papers of Jefferson Davis*, Vol. 5: *1853–1855*, Vol. 6: *1856–1860* (Baton Rouge: Louisiana State University Press, 1985, 1989), 163, 266, 461; Jeanne Twiggs Heidler, "The Military Career of David Emanuel Twiggs" (Ph.D. dissertation, Auburn University, 1988), 147–48.

28. WHTW to Western Division, December 11, 1852, Records of the U.S. Army Continental Army Commands, 1821–1920, RG 393, Western Division Register of LR, 1852, Item W87, NA; Western Division to WHTW, December 15, 1852, RG 393, Western Division LS, Vol. 12/12, 89, NA; WHTW to W. W. Bliss, August 1, 1853, Western Division Register of LR, Item W48, and WHTW to W. W. Bliss (copy), NA M1635, Roll 19, Item W107; Western Division to WHTW, August 16, 1853, Western Division LS, Vol. 12/12, 145; HQA to WHTW, August 29, 1853, NA M857, Roll 4, Vol. 8/6, p. 38, No. 102; WHTW to L. Thomas (HQA), September 2, 1853, NA M1635, Roll 19, Item W119; and WHTW to G. W. Lay (Western Division), September 2, 1853, Western Division LR, Item W55; RG 231, Records of the Soldiers' Home, Correspondence, Reports, and Orders Relating to Regulations, and Administrative Memoranda, NA. Walker's monthly reports to each headquarters were dated December 1852–March 1853, Augusta; April 1853, Savannah; May 1853, Augusta; June–November 1853, Albany; December 1853–June 1854, Augusta. In September 1852 Adjutant General Roger Jones died and was replaced by Colonel Samuel Cooper.

CHAPTER 7. COMMANDANT OF CADETS, 1854–1856

1. This favorable view of Jefferson Davis as secretary of war, although not universally held, is supported by David Sansing, "A Happy Interlude: Jefferson Davis and the War Department, 1853–1857," *Journal of Mississippi History* 51 (November 1989): 297–312. Another opinion on Davis as secretary of war, not necessarily contradictory, is William C. Davis, *Jefferson Davis: The Man and the Hour* (New York: Harper Collins, 1991), 223–39.

2. WHTW to wife, October 30, 1852, and undated [October 23, 1853?], Walker Papers; WHTW to Jefferson David, February 8, 1854, Jefferson Davis Papers, Transylvania University, Lexington, Ky.

3. *Augusta Chronicle and Sentinel*, March 16, 31, 1854; Secretary of War to WHTW, June 24, 1854, WHTW to Samuel Cooper, July 4, 1854, NA M567, Roll 507, Items W260 and W245; Order 13, HQCC, July 31, 1854, Orders Corps of Cadets, RG 88, Vol. 2, USMA Archives.

4. Ambrose, *Duty, Honor, Country*, 141; Freeman, *R. E. Lee*, 1:347–48; Crist and Dix, eds., *Papers of Jefferson Davis*, 5:70, 82, 364.

5. Ambrose, *Duty, Honor, Country*, 131–37, 162; Forman, *West Point*, 138–39; *Army Register*, 1854, 1855, 1856; "Memoirs of Samuel Wragg Ferguson" (typescript), 45, Samuel Wragg Ferguson Papers, Duke University, Durham, N.C.

6. See USMA Archives, RG 88, Orders, Corps of Cadets, 143, Register of Letters Received [from the Commandant of Cadets], and 140 and 144, Letters Received from the Commandant of Cadets, for July 1854 to May 1856, for examples of cadet violations and Walker's administration of discipline.

7. USMA Archives, RG 88: Order 36, August 28, 1855; SO 8, February 20, 1856; RG 144: February 24, 1856; RG 88: August 19, 1854; SO 19, August 20, 1854; RG 88: Order 20, July 6, 1855; RG 144: January 24, 1856; RG 88: Order 31, August 31, 1855; Order 3, February 7, 1856; RG 88, Order 44, December 29, 1855; RG 88: Order 2, May 2, 1855.

8. John G. Barnard to Joseph G. Totten, August 3, 1856, NA Microfilm Publication M1089, Letters Sent by the Superintendent of the U.S. Military Academy, 1838–1902, Roll 1, Vol. 3.

9. Ambrose, *Duty, Honor, Country*, 143; George William Cushing to his father, December 29, 1854, January 3, 1855, George William Cushing Papers, USMA Library; USMA Archives, RG 88: SO 1, January 2, 1855; Order 2, January 3, 1855; RG 143: January 5, 1855.

10. Crist and Dix, eds., *Papers of Jefferson Davis*, 5:136–37, 403; R. E. Lee to Mrs. M. Hetzel, January 31, 1855, John G. Barnard to Joseph G. Totten, November 12, 22, 1855, March 20, 1856, NA M1089, Roll 1, Vol. 3; USMA Archives, RG 88: SO 2, January 4, 1855; SO 14, August 6, 1855; SO 8, February 20, 1856; RG 143: January 4 and August 5, 1855; RG 144: February 24, 1856; Freeman, *R. E. Lee*, 1:344; WHTW to wife, March 2, 1855, Walker Papers.

11. USMA AOG, *Register of Graduates*; Ezra J. Warner, *Generals in Gray* (Baton

Rouge: Louisiana State University Press, 1959), and Warner, *Generals in Blue* (Baton Rouge: Louisiana State University Press, 1964).

12. Nathaniel C. Hughes, *General William J. Hardee, Old Reliable* (Baton Rouge: Louisiana State University Press, 1965), 41–44; Crist and Dix, eds., *Papers of Jefferson Davis*, 5:341, 351.

13. Hughes, *Hardee*, 44.

14. Ambrose, *Duty, Honor, Country*, 134–35; Hughes, *Hardee*, 44; WHTW to Samuel Cooper, August 17, November 26, 1854, NA M567, Roll 508, Items W303 and W479; WHTW to Robert J. Pruyn, June 21, 1855, Confederate Miscellany Collection, Emory University, Atlanta, Ga.

15. WHTW to General W. Smith, February 16, 1855, Gratz and Dreer Autograph Collections, Historical Society of Pennsylvania, Philadelphia; Theodore J. Crackel, "The Oldest Quarters at West Point," *Assembly* 49 (July 1991): 26–28; NA Microfilm Publication 444, Orders and Endorsements Sent by the Secretary of War, 1846–70, Roll 3, Frame 392, Endorsement 8140, John Gibbon to Chief of Engineers, June 16, 1856, endorsed by Jefferson Davis, July 7, 1856; Mary T. Walker to WHTW, November 19, 1855, Walker Papers.

16. *Augusta Chronicle and Sentinel*, November 5, 1854; Register, Albany Rural Cemetery, Albany, N.Y., Section 45, Lot 4; Robert Townsend to WHTW, October 31, 1854, Walker Papers.

17. USMA Archives, RG 143, January 20, 1855; SO 20, HQMA, January 20, 1855, NA M617, Roll 1414; WHTW to Adam [Johnston?], January 4, 1855, WHTW to wife, February 8, 19, 1855, Walker Papers.

18. Robert M. Utley, *Frontiersmen in Blue: The United States Army and the Indian, 1848–1865* (New York: Macmillan, 1867), 12–13; Crist and Dix, eds., *Papers of Jefferson Davis*, 5:96–98, 389–90; WHTW to wife, March 7, 1855, Walker Papers.

19. WHTW to wife, February 13, 19, March 3, 7, 1855, Walker Papers; Jefferson Davis to WHTW et al., March 9, 1855, NA M1635, Roll 27, Item W34; *Augusta Constitutionalist*, March 10, 1855; WHTW to Cooper, March 14, 1855, NA M567, Roll 530, Item W119; Freeman, *R. E. Lee*, 1:350–51.

20. WHTW to Cooper, April 6, 1855, NA M567, Roll 530, Item W174; AGO, SO 63, April 11, 1855, GO, SO, and Circulars, NA; McCain, "Military Career of Walker," 41–44.

21. SO 186, Headquarters, Military Academy, November 7, 1855, and SO 207, December 13, 1855, NA M617, Roll 1414; Mary T. Walker to WHTW, November 19, 1855, Walker Papers; WHTW to Joseph Totten, December 11, 1855, with endorsement by Jefferson Davis, December 1855, RG 77, Records of the Office of the Chief of Engineers, LR 1855, Item W1692, NA; McCain, "Military Career of Walker," 43–44.

22. WHTW to wife, undated [July 1856?], Walker Papers; WHTW to Cooper, May 20, 1856, NA M567, Roll 551, Item W203; McCain, "Military Career of Walker," 44.

CHAPTER 8. FAREWELL TO ARMY BLUE, 1856–1861

1. Mary Walker's feelings about her husband's resignation are reflected in his letters to her, undated [July 1856?] and Thursday [July 10, 1856?], Walker Papers; Meadows, *Walker Genealogy*, 181; obituary of W. H. T. Walker, Jr., *Augusta Chronicle*, April 24, 1948; Molly Walker to Grandmama [Mary Cresswell Walker], February 26, 1856, and Molly to Cousin Anna [Anna Walker Robinson], February 29, 1856, Walker Papers.

2. WHTW to wife, undated [July 1856?], Walker Papers.

3. Ibid., and WHTW to wife, Thursday [July 10, 1856?], ibid. The rumor was not true. Worth was junior to Thayer.

4. Cooper to WHTW, May 28, 1856, NA M1635, Roll 33, Item W58; Irvin McDowell to WHTW, May 29, 1856, RG 108, Records of the Headquarters of the Army, SO Vol. 3 (1849–58), SO 40, NA; WHTW to wife, 19 [June 1856?] and February [21, 1855?], Walker Papers.

5. WHTW to wife, undated [July 1856?] and Monday [June 23, 1856?], Walker Papers.

6. S. V. Seyburn, "The Tenth Regiment of Infantry," in *The Army of the United States*, ed. Theophilus F. Rodenbough and William L. Haskins (New York: Merrill, Maynard and Co., 1896), 532–33; Warner, *Generals in Blue*, 67, 455; Cullum, *Biographical Register*, 410, 1015.

7. Headquarters, 10th Infantry to WHTW, Regimental Order No. 45, June 12, 1856, NA M567, Roll 551, Item W263; WHTW to wife, Thursday [July 10, 1856?], Walker Papers.

8. WHTW to wife, undated [June 20, 1856?], Sunday night [June 1856?], undated [July 1856?], July 5 [1856?], Thursday [July 10, 1856?], July 18 [1856?], Walker Papers; Walker to Cooper, July 27, August 28, 1856, NA M567, Roll 551, Items W341 and W411. The July letter was written from Albany and the August one from West Point.

9. NA M665, Roll 113, 10th Infantry returns for September and October 1856; Cullum, *Biographical Register*, 1432.

10. Mary T. Walker to "My dear niece," November 9, 1856, Walker Papers.

11. WHTW to Lorenzo Thomas, January 27, 1857, with enclosure dated November 25, 1856, NA M1635, Roll 38, Item W4; NA M665, Roll 113, Return for 10th Infantry, November 1856.

12. WHTW to wife, July 5 [1856?], July 18 [1856?], Walker Papers.

13. RCSC Deed Book 2L, 714–15; Screven County, Georgia, Superior Court Deed Book T (12P), 551–52; RCPC Accounts Books 2B, 306–20, and 2C, 402–3; WHTW to wife, December 16, 1863, Walker Papers; Dixon Hollingsworth, *Screven County History* (Dallas: Curtis Media Corp., 1989), 35–36.

14. Doyce B. Nunis, "Colonel Archibald Campbell's March from Savannah to Augusta, 1779," *GHQ* 45 (1961): 275–86; Hollingsworth, *Screven County*, 29–30, 34–35; *De Bow's Review* 11 (October 1851): 400–402.

15. CCSC Deed Book 3L, 224.

16. WHTW to Cooper, November 3, 1858, NA M567, Roll 594, Item W377; WHTW to wife, September 2, 1858, Walker Papers; Death Certificate of Freeman Valentine Walker, January 21, 1933, South Carolina State Board of Health, Bureau of Vital Statistics, Registration District 601, File 109.

17. WHTW to daughter, August 21 [1858?], and to wife, April [4?], May 5, December 11, 16, 1863, April 2, 1864, Walker Papers; *Augusta City Directory, 1861; DGB*, 2:591–92; *DAB*, 10:549.

18. NA Microfilm Publication M653, Eighth Census of the United States, 1860, Roll 135, Richmond County, 952, and Roll 151, Screven County Slave Schedules, 359; WHTW to wife, September 2, 1858, April 2, June 2, 1864, Walker Papers; Hollingsworth, *Screven County*, 33, 219–21, 288–89. Seaborn Jones is sketched in Robert M. Myers, *The Children of Pride* (New Haven: Yale University Press, 1972), 1566–67. His full name was Augustus Seaborn Jones.

19. WHTW to Irvin McDowell, February 3, 1858, NA M1635, Roll 44, Item W28; McDowell to WHTW, February 10, 1858, NA M857, Roll 5, Vol. 9/7, p. 282, No. 64; McDowell to WHTW, March 10, 1859, ibid., p. 502, No. 86; WHTW to Cooper, December 1, 1858, NA M567, Roll 594, Item W204; WHTW to Cooper, M567, Roll 617, Item W157; RG 108, Records of the Headquarters of the Army, GO, HQA, Vol. 178 (1849–61), GO 7, March 29, 1860; WHTW to L. Thomas, April 10, 1860, M1635, Roll 55, Item W52, with certificate of Dr. H. L. Steiner; certificate of Dr. H. L. Steiner, June 4, 1860, enclosure to WHTW to Cooper, June 4, 1860, and WHTW to Cooper, May 12, 1860, M567, Roll 635, Items W218 and W186.

20. Coffman, *Old Army*, 82–84 and notes; Heidler, "Military Career of Twiggs," 186; Russell K. Brown, "An Old Woman with a Broomstick: General David E. Twiggs and the U.S. Surrender in Texas, 1861," *Military Affairs* 48 (April 1984): 57–61.

21. Taylor, *Destruction and Reconstruction*, 23; Clark, *Lost Arcadia*, 71.

22. F. N. Boney, "The Politics of Expansion and Secession," in Kenneth Coleman, gen. ed., *A History of Georgia* (Athens: University of Georgia Press, 1977), 148–49.

23. Florence Fleming Corley, *Confederate City: Augusta, Georgia, 1860–1865* (Columbia: University of South Carolina Press, 1960), 30–31, 106; *Augusta Chronicle and Sentinel*, November 8, 1860. Precise numbers of ballots cast for each candidate are hard to come by. On the same day, November 8, on two different pages, the *Chronicle and Sentinel* printed different totals for each. Douglas received about 1,050 votes, Bell 850, and Breckinridge 400.

24. Boney, "Politics of Expansion," 149–50; T. Conn Bryan, *Confederate Georgia* (Athens: University of Georgia Press, 1953), 1–3; Joseph H. Parks, *Joseph E. Brown of Georgia* (Baton Rouge: Louisiana State University Press, 1977), 111–14; Louise B. Hill, *Joseph E. Brown and the Confederacy* (Chapel Hill: University of North Carolina Press, 1939), 36–39; *CRG*, 1:19–57, 157–205.

25. John A. Garraty and Robert A. McCaughey, *The American Nation*, 2 vols. (New York: Harper & Row, 1987), 1:418.

26. Bryan, *Confederate Georgia*, 3; Parks, *Brown*, 114–17, 123; Hill, *Brown*, 39; *CRG*, 1:739–47.

27. WHTW to Cooper, December 15, 1860, NA M567, Roll 636, Item W490; *Augusta Chronicle and Sentinel*, December 20, 21, 1860, May 28, 1861; *CRG*, 1:740–41, 2:8–9; WHTW to Henry C. Wayne, January 8, 1860 [1861], Incoming Correspondence to the Adjutant General, Henry C. Wayne; Henry C. Wayne to Joseph E. Brown, December 19, 1860, Outgoing Correspondence from Adjutant General Henry C. Wayne, 1860–62, RG 22, GDAH; Parks, *Brown*, 123. The U.S. adjutant general's letter accepting Walker's resignation, dated December 19, 1860, is the property of Hugh Walker, Jr.

28. Warner, *Generals in Gray*, 329; Northern, *Men of Mark in Georgia*, 3:202; *DGB*, 2:1043; Crist and Dix, eds., *Papers of Jefferson Davis*, 5:238, 425–26, 429, 6:95, 385–89; Alexander A. Lawrence, ed., "Some Letters from Henry C. Wayne to Hamilton Fish," *GHQ* 43 (1959): 392.

29. *CRG*, 2:275.

30. *Augusta Chronicle and Sentinel*, December 21, 1860; *Augusta Constitutionalist*, December 25, 1860.

31. Corley, *Confederate City*, 31–32; *Augusta Chronicle and Sentinel*, December 25, 1860; *CRG*, 1:97–99. Edward J. Cashin, *The Story of Augusta* (Augusta: Richmond County Board of Education, 1980), 115, recounts the story of the meeting but places Walker's intervention on January 2 rather than December 24.

32. *Augusta Chronicle and Sentinel*, January 8, 11, 13, 1861.

33. Isaac W. Avery, *History of the State of Georgia from 1850 to 1881* (New York: Brown and Derby, 1881), 144–45; WHTW to Editor, *Augusta Chronicle and Sentinel*, January 11, 1861; WHTW to Henry C. Wayne, January 8, 1861, RG 22, GDAH.

CHAPTER 9. ANTICIPATION AND FRUSTRATION, 1861

1. Parks, *Brown*, 121; Bryan, *Confederate Georgia*, 4–6; Boney, "Politics of Expansion," 150–51; Corley, *Confederate City*, 32, 107; "Georgian" to the Editor, *Augusta Chronicle and Sentinel*, January 13, 1861.

2. Parks, *Brown*, 127–28; Hill, *Brown*, 44–45; Bryan, *Confederate Georgia*, 6–10; Boney, "Politics of Expansion," 149–52, 187.

3. Parks, *Brown*, 128–29; Bryan, *Confederate Georgia*, 10–11; Hill, *Brown*, 45; Corley, *Confederate City*, 32.

4. Parks, *Brown*, 124–25; Hill, *Brown*, 41–42; Bryan, *Confederate Georgia*, 6; Boney, "Politics of Expansion," 188; Joseph T. Derry, *Georgia*, Vol. 6 (extended ed.), in Clement A. Evans, ed., *Confederate Military History*, 12 vols. (Atlanta:

Confederate Publishing Company, 1899), 5–8; *OR*, Ser. I, Vol. 1, pp. 318–19. All references are to Series I unless otherwise indicated. Warner, *Generals in Gray*, 175; Cullum, *Biographical Register*, 998; Northern, *Men of Mark in Georgia*, 3:185; *DAB*, 11:61.

5. Meadows, *Walker Genealogy*, 167, 169–73; NA M617, Roll 56, Returns from United States Military Posts, Augusta Arsenal, December 31, 1860; *Augusta Constitutionalist*, January 25, 1861; Corley, *Confederate City*, 35–37; Charles C. Jones, Jr., and Salem Dutcher, *Memorial History of Augusta, Georgia* (1890; reprint, Spartanburg, S.C.: Reprint Co., 1980), 178; *Augusta Chronicle and Sentinel*, February 1, 1861; *OR*, 1:320–23.

6. Parks, *Brown*, 128, 134; Bryan, *Confederate Georgia*, 15; *OR*, Ser. IV, Vol. 1, p. 117; *CRG*, 1:710–11; William H. Bragg, *Joe Brown's Army* (Macon, Ga.: Mercer University Press, 1987), ix. Walker's commission, dated February 1, 1861, is in AGO Letter Book, Vol. B44, pt. 1, 20, and AGO Commission Book B49, 3, GDAH. The names of all the officers of both regiments up to that date were printed in the *Augusta Chronicle and Sentinel*, February 17, 1861.

7. WHTW to Wayne, February 1, 4, 6, 7 (3 letters), 15, 18, 21, 22, 1861, Adjutant General Wayne's Incoming Correspondence, RG22, GDAH; Wayne to WHTW, February 21, 22 (2 letters), 1861, AGO Letter Book B44, 131, 133, 138, GDAH; WHTW to Wayne, February 5, 1861, Henry C. Wayne Papers, Duke University, Durham, N.C.; Parks, *Brown*, 135.

8. H. E. Boney, "War and Defeat," in Coleman, gen. ed. *History of Georgia*, 187; Bryan, *Confederate Georgia*, 12–14.

9. Parks, *Brown*, 128, 134; Hill, *Brown*, 50; *CRG*, 3:18–20; *OR*, Ser. IV, Vol. 1, p. 117; Bryan, *Confederate Georgia*, 15.

10. *CRG*, 3:20–39; Parks, *Brown*, 136–37; Hill, *Brown*, 51–52.

11. WHTW to Joseph E. Brown, March 10, 1861, William P. Palmer Civil War Collection, Item P644, Western Reserve Historical Society, Cleveland, Ohio; *CRG*, 1:710–11; *OR*, Ser. IV, Vol. 1, pp. 167–68; McWhiney, *Bragg*, 152; L. P. Walker to Brown, March 22, 1861, *CRG*, 3:33–34.

12. Robert Toombs to L. P. Walker, March 21, 1861, and Walker to Toombs, March 22, 1861, *CRG*, 3:31–32; Brown to [L. P. Walker?], undated [April 20, 1861?], ibid., 57; Parks, *Brown*, 138–39, 142; Lillian Henderson, ed., *Roster of the Confederate Soldiers of Georgia, 1861–1865*, 6 vols. (Hapeville, Ga.: Longino and Porter, 1955–62), 1:307; WHTW to Brown, March 14, 1861, RG 22, GDAH.

13. *CRG*, 1:744, 3:53; Parks, *Brown*, 141; Avery, *History of Georgia*, 186; Bryan, *Confederate Georgia*, 15.

14. Warner, *Generals in Gray*, 149; Northern, *Men of Mark in Georgia*, 3:421; *DAB*, 9:543; *DGB*, 1:513; Parks, *Brown*, 125.

15. *Augusta Chronicle and Sentinel*, March 17, 1861; Wayne to WHTW, March 22, 1861, AGO Letter Book B44, 208; AGO Commission Book B49, 87; Wayne to WHTW, March 28, 1861, AG Secretaries' Letter Book, Vol. 2, 420, GDAH.

16. *CRG*, 3:40, 50–51, 53, 55–58, 64–65; Brown to WHTW, April 23, 1861, Joseph E. Brown Papers, Hargrett Rare Book and Manuscript Library, University of Georgia, Athens; WHTW to L. P. Walker, and Walker to WHTW, April 25, 1861, *OR*, Ser. IV, Vol. 1, pp. 238–39; WHTW to L. P. Walker, April 25, 1861, NA Microfilm Publication M618, Telegrams Received by the Confederate Secretary of War, 1861–65, Roll 2; L. P. Walker to WHTW, April 25, 1861, Walker to Joseph E. Brown, April 29, 1861, NA Microfilm Publication M524, Telegrams Sent by the Confederate Secretary of War, 1861–65 (RG 109, Chapter 9, Vol. 33, NA); WHTW to Robert E. Lee, April 23, 1861, and Lee's response, April 23, 1861, RG 109, War Department Collection of Confederate Records, Virginia Forces, Letters Received, File 108, NA.

17. H. C. Wayne to WHTW, May 7, 1861, AG Secretaries' Letter Book, Vol. 3, p. 177, GDAH; Octavia LeVert et al. to L. P. Walker, NA Microfilm Publication M331, Compiled Service Records of Confederate General and Staff Officers and Non-Regimental Enlisted Men, Roll 257, WHTW; T. R. R. Cobb to wife, April 30, 1861, T. R. R. Cobb Papers, Hargrett Rare Book and Manuscript Library, University of Georgia; *Augusta Chronicle and Sentinel*, May 28, 1861; WHTW to Samuel Cooper, May 28, 1861, Chapter 1, Vol. 45, Register of Letters Received by the Confederate Adjutant and Inspector General, Item W127, RG 109, NA. Samuel Cooper had resigned his U.S. Army commission and had been appointed Confederate adjutant and inspector general in March 1861.

18. *Augusta Chronicle and Sentinel*, May 29, 1861; WHTW to Cooper, May 3 [30?], 1861, Chapter 1, Vol. 45, Item W89, RG 109, NA; WHTW to wife, June 2, 1861, Walker Papers.

19. Brown, "An Old Woman with a Broomstick," 57–61. Fort Monroe was held by Union forces throughout the war. Two other Federal posts, Fort Taylor at Key West and Fort Jefferson in the Dry Tortugas, were never seriously threatened by Confederate troops.

20. David Yulee to Joseph Finegan or George W. Call, January 5, 1861, *OR*, 1:442; *CRG*, 2:16–19; Parks, *Brown*, 125; Hill, *Brown*, 42; Slemmer to Samuel Cooper, January 10, February 5, 1861, *OR*, 1:334–42; Lorenzo Thomas to Israel Vogdes, January 21, 1861, and Vogdes to Thomas, February 7, March 17, 1861, ibid., 352, 357–58, 360–61; Vodges to AAG, Department of the East, April 16, 1861, ibid., 378; Winfield Scott to Harvey Brown, April 1, 1861, and Brown to Erasmus D. Keyes, Secretary to the General in Chief, April 18, 1861, ibid., 365–66, 378–79; Montgomery Meigs to Joseph Totten, Chief of Engineers, April 25, 1861, and Harvey Brown to E. D. Townsend, AAG, May 2, 1861, ibid., 393–99, 400–405. A good account of the early activities at Pensacola is Bruce Catton, *The Coming Fury* (Garden City, N.Y.: Doubleday, 1961), 271–82. An account by a participant is J. H. Gilman, "With Slemmer in Pensacola Harbor," in *B&L*, 1:26–32. The official documentation is in *OR*, 1:331–473.

21. *OR*, 1:354, 445; *ORN*, 4:67, 74, 92–93, 212–14; Catton, *Coming Fury*, 274; Gilman, "With Slemmer," 29–32.

22. *OR*, 1:338, 354; Gilman, "With Slemmer," 31; McWhiney, *Bragg*, 157–61.

23. *OR*, 1:448–50, 455; Bragg to Samuel Cooper, March 10, 1861, William P. Palmer Collection of Braxton Bragg Papers, Folder 1, Western Reserve Historical Society; McWhiney, *Bragg*, 154–56, 164; Catton, *Coming Fury*, 275–76. Catton errs in saying Bragg had thousands of men by mid-March. Thousands were on the way, but few had arrived.

24. *OR*, 1:457; *ORN*, 4:90, 109–10; McWhiney, *Bragg*, 166–70.

25. *ORN*, 4:110–11, 115, 118, 135–37; *DAB*, 20:531; *OR*, 1:460; McWhiney, *Bragg*, 171.

26. *ORN*, 4:117–19; *OR*, 1:378–79, 458, 460–61, 463, 465–66; McWhiney, *Bragg*, 171; Bragg to Cooper, April 14, 1861, Oversized Vol. 1, Bragg Papers, Western Reserve. Additional arrivals of troops were reported May 9 and 17.

27. Bragg to Cooper, May 11, 1861, Folder 2, Bragg Papers, Western Reserve; Chapter 1, Vol. 86, Register of Appointment of Officers, pt. 1, p. 5, RG 109, NA. The register says Walker's commission was delivered to him at his residence at Augusta, Georgia, on October 29, 1861. This is an obvious error.

28. WHTW to wife, June 2, July 3, 1861, Walker Papers; Bragg to Cooper, June 3, 1861, Oversized Vol. 1, Bragg Papers, Western Reserve; *Army Register*, *1854, 1855, 1856*, 3 vols. (for staff at West Point). See McWhiney, *Bragg*, 171–72, for an exchange at Pensacola of letters between Bragg and an old army friend on the Northern side, Henry J. Hunt.

29. Bragg to Cooper, May 18, 30, 1861, Folder 2, Bragg Papers, Western Reserve; *OR*, 1:468; McWhiney, *Bragg*, 176–77, 182; Abstract of Return for Confederate Troops at Pensacola for September 1, 1861 (the closest available date to Walker's tenure), *OR*, 6:725; WHTW to wife, June 13, 1861, Walker Papers; S. A. M. Wood to L. P. Walker, August 8, 1861, *OR*, 1:469–70; WHTW to Cooper, July 13, 1861, NA Microfilm Publication 437, Letters Received by the Confederate Secretary of War, Roll 5, Item 2412.

30. WHTW to wife, July 3, 1861, Walker Papers; *CRG*, 3:41, 43; Corley, *Confederate City*, 38, 108; Bragg to Cooper, August 7, 13, 1861, Oversized Vol. 1, Bragg Papers, Western Reserve; *Augusta Chronicle and Sentinel*, July 12, 1861.

31. WHTW to wife, June 13, July 3, 12, 1861, to daughter, undated [July 10?], 1861, Walker Papers.

32. WHTW to wife, July 12, 1861, ibid.

33. WHTW to wife, July 3, 12, undated [July?], 1861, to daughter, July 10[?], 1861, ibid.; WHTW to Cooper, July 13, 1861, NA M437, Roll 5, Item 2412. John James Walker was the brother of Leroy P. Walker.

34. WHTW to wife, July 12, 21, undated [July?], 1861, to daughter, July [10?], 1861, Walker Papers; WHTW to Cooper, July 13, 1861, NA M437, Roll 5, Item 2412; Bragg to Cooper, August 2, 1861, Folder 2, Bragg Papers, Western Reserve, and *OR*, 1:469; SO 179, Headquarters, C.S. Troops near Pensacola, August 2, 1861, NA M331, Roll 257, WHTW. For comments about sickness among the troops see WHTW to wife, July 12, 21, 1861, Walker Papers; S. A. M. Wood to L. P. Walker,

OR, 1:469–70; Bragg to Cooper, July 28, 1861, Folder 2, Bragg Papers, Western Reserve.

35. *Augusta Chronicle and Sentinel,* August 6, 10, 1861.

36. WHTW to wife, August 11, 26, 1861, Walker Papers; Mary Boykin Chesnut, *Mary Chesnut's Civil War,* ed. C. Vann Woodward (New Haven: Yale University Press, 1981), 149–52. Mrs. Chesnut referred to Walker as "Shotpouch." J. B. Jones, *A Rebel War Clerk's Diary,* 2 vols. (Philadelphia: J. B. Lippincott, 1866), 1:61–62. Jones gave the date of the confrontation in the adjutant general's office as July 12. He must have meant August 12. *OR,* 5:797, 809.

37. WHTW to wife, September 1, 4, 8, 1861, Walker Papers; *OR,* 5:825; Terry L. Jones, *Lee's Tigers: The Louisiana Infantry in the Army of Northern Virginia* (Baton Rouge: Louisiana State University Press, 1987), 5, 6, 10, 35–36, 39–40, 111, 238–44, 249–50; GO 49, Order Book 1861, Container 21, Microfilm Roll 4, P. G. T. Beauregard Papers, Library of Congress; WHTW to Thomas Jordan, October 26, 1861, NA M437, Roll 14, Item 7335. The army was directed to turn the murder suspects over to local civilian authorities. See A. T. Bledsoe to P. G. T. Beauregard, November 8, 1861, NA Microfilm Publication M522, Letters Sent by the Confederate Secretary of War, 1861–65, Roll 2, Vol. 2, p. 455.

38. Taylor, *Destruction and Reconstruction,* 22–23.

39. *New Orleans Picayune,* September 4, 5, 7, 1861. A laudatory article from the *New Orleans Delta* was reprinted in the *Augusta Chronicle and Sentinel,* September 15, 1861.

40. Henry E. Handerson, *Yankee in Gray: The Civil War Memoirs of Henry E. Handerson, with a Selection of His Wartime Letters,* intro. by Clyde L. Cummer (Cleveland: Press of Western Reserve University, 1962), 33.

41. Douglas S. Freeman, *Lee's Lieutenants,* 3 vols. (New York: Charles Scribner's Sons, 1942–44), 1:87–88. Another version is that Wheat said, "I don't feel like dying yet" (Mark M. Boatner, *The Civil War Dictionary* [New York: David McKay, 1959]); Jones, *Lee's Tigers,* 55; SO 287, Order Book 1861, Container 21, Microfilm Roll 4, Beauregard Papers.

42. WHTW to wife, July 3, September 4, 8, 9, 11, 24, 1861, Walker Papers; Corley, *Confederate City,* 63; *Ancestoring* (publication of the Augusta Genealogical Society) 12 (1987): 41; obituary of Mary G. Walker, *Augusta Constitutionalist,* July 18, 1862.

43. WHTW to wife, March 30, 1847, September 8, 1861, Walker Papers; RG 109, Chap. 1, Vol. 46, Items W429, W430, W515, W543, NA; Samuel Cooper to WHTW, September 15, 21, 1861, NA Microfilm Publication M627, Letters and Telegrams Sent by the Confederate Adjutant and Inspector General, 1861–65, Roll 2, Vol. 36; *Appleton's Cyclopedia of American Biography,* 3:106; NA M331, Roll 72, Aaron Davis, Roll 123, Thomas R. Heard, Roll 231, Stokes A. Smith; SO 437, Order Book 1861, Container 21, Microfilm Roll 4, Beauregard Papers; Andrew B. Booth, ed., *Records of Louisiana Confederate Soldiers and Louisiana Confederate Com-*

mands, 3 vols. (New Orleans: Commissioner of Louisiana Military Records, 1920), 2:549, 3:Book A, 241, 3:Book B, 630.

44. Thomas Jordan to WHTW, September 6, 27, October 5, 21, 1861, Letterbook A, Container 13, Microfilm Roll 2; SO 288, 315, 420, 450, 451, 453, 455, 463, Order Book 1861, Container 21, Microfilm Roll 4, Beauregard Papers.

45. *Augusta Constitutionalist*, October 27, 1861; *Augusta Chronicle and Sentinel*, August 30, 1861.

46. *OR*, 5:2, 6, 11, 12, 15–17, 575; George B. McClellan, *McClellan's Own Story* (New York: Charles L. Webster, 1887), 66–67, 76–78.

47. *OR*, 5:824, 884, 932–33, 52, pt. 2:275; Joseph E. Johnston, *Narrative of Military Operations Directed During the Late War Between the States* (1874; reprint, Bloomington: Indiana University Press, 1959), 77.

48. *New Orleans Picayune*, October 4, 1861; *DAB*, 10:144, 12:115; Cullum, *Biographical Register*, 927; Robert M. McLane, *Reminiscences, 1827–1897* (1903; reprint, Wilmington, Del.: Scholastic Resources, Inc., 1972), 65; RG 153, Records of the Proceedings of General Courts-Martial, Case CC193, NA. McLane testified on Walker's behalf. Gilbert E. Govan and James W. Livingood, *A Different Valor: The Story of General Joseph E. Johnston, C.S.A.* (Indianapolis: Bobbs-Merrill, 1956), 17; WHTW to wife, July 18, 1864, Lydia McL. Johnston to Mary T. Walker, July 29, [1864], Walker Papers.

49. Freeman, *Lee's Lieutenants*, 1:111–13; Johnston, *Narrative*, xiii–xiv; Joseph B. Cumming, *A Sketch of the Descendants of David Cumming and Memoirs of the War Between the States*, ed. Mary Gairdner Smith Cumming (Augusta, Ga.: Privately printed, 1925), 56; E. T. Sykes, *History of Walthall's Brigade* (Columbus, Miss.: Mississippi Historical Society, 1905), 597–98.

50. Freeman, *Lee's Lieutenants*, 1:113–15; Johnston, *Narrative*, xiv–xv, 70–73; Govan and Livingood, *Different Valor*, 66–71.

51. Freeman, *Lee's Lieutenants*, 1:102–9, 671; *OR*, 5:850–51, 877, 904–5, 945, 51, pt. 2:339.

52. WHTW to wife, September 24, 1861, Walker Papers; Freeman, *Lee's Lieutenants*, 1:121, 162–63; *OR*, 5:798–99, 881; Warner, *Generals in Gray*, 280; Cullum, *Biographical Register*, 1118.

53. Johnston, Beauregard, and Smith to Benjamin, September 28, 1861, Letterbook copy, Military Papers, Container 54, Microfilm Roll 9, Beauregard Papers; *OR*, 5:882–83.

54. Thomas Jordan to WHTW, September 28, 1861, Letterbook A, Container 13, Microfilm Roll 2; SO 374, Order Book 1861, Container 21, Microfilm Roll 4, Beauregard Papers.

55. Thomas Jordan to WHTW, September 25, 1861, Letterbook A; SO 374 and 376, Order Book 1861, Beauregard Papers; WHTW to wife, October 2, 1861, Walker Papers; *Augusta Constitutionalist*, October 5, 15, 1861; *Augusta Chronicle and Sentinel*, October 15, 1861; *New Orleans Picayune*, October 11, 1861. Two different

versions of the expedition appeared in the *Picayune* on the same day. One was datelined October 1 and signed by "Zounpetros," the other October 2, signed by "H.P." See Jones, *Lee's Tigers*, 25–26, 55–56.

56. *New Orleans Picayune*, October 15, 1861.

57. McClellan, *McClellan's Own Story*, 167.

58. Johnston, *Narrative*, 75–77; Govan and Livingood, *Different Valor*, 74–75; *OR*, 5:881–82, 884–87.

59. *OR*, 5:892–95.

60. Warner, *Generals in Gray*, see under individual names.

61. Freeman, *Lee's Lieutenants*, 1:119–20, 349–50; *OR*, 5:913–14; Johnston, *Narrative*, 73–74; Govan and Livingood, *Different Valor*, 78; Jones, *Lee's Tigers*, 10; *New Orleans Picayune*, October 29, 1861.

62. Chap. 1, Vol. 47, Item W682, RG 109, NA; *New Orleans Picayune*, November 1, 6, 1861; *Augusta Constitutionalist*, November 1, 3, 1861, *Augusta Chronicle and Sentinel*, November 1, 3, 1861.

63. Cullum, *Biographical Register*, 1119; Warner, *Generals in Gray*, 194–95; WHTW to Adam [Johnston?], January 4, [1855?], Walker Papers.

64. Benjamin to WHTW, October 2, 1861, NA M522, Roll 3, Vol. 3; Taylor, *Destruction and Reconstruction*, 23–24.

65. *New Orleans Picayune*, November 1, 6, 1861; *Augusta Constitutionalist*, November 1, 3, 1861; *Augusta Chronicle and Sentinel*, November 1, 3, 1861.

66. *New Orleans Picayune*, November 1, 6, 1861; *Augusta Constitutionalist*, November 1, 3, 1861; *Augusta Chronicle and Sentinel*, November 1, 3, 1861.

67. *Augusta Constitutionalist*, November 3, 1861; Chesnut, *Civil War*, 235; Jones, *Lee's Tigers*, 43–44; Warner, *Generals in Gray*, 9–10.

68. *New Orleans Picayune*, November 11, 1861.

69. *OR*, 5:892.

70. Parks, *Brown*, 129–323; Hill, *Brown*, 48–265; Bryan, *Confederate Georgia*, 80–100.

71. Parks, *Brown*, 209; WHTW to wife, October 1, 1863, Walker Papers; Warner, *Generals in Gray*, 149–50; H. C. Wayne to J. P. Benjamin, January 17, 1862, quoted in Lawrence, ed., "Some Letters from Henry C. Wayne to Hamilton Fish," 393.

72. Brown to WHTW, November 16, 1861, quoted in *Augusta Chronicle and Sentinel*, November 28, 1861.

73. *DAB*, 10:365–66; Warner, *Generals in Gray*, 323–34; WHTW to wife, September 4, 24, 1861, to daughter, October 24, 1861, Walker Papers.

74. *Augusta Chronicle and Sentinel*, November 3, 1861; *OR*, 5:954.

CHAPTER 10. GEORGIA CINCINNATUS, 1861–1862

1. *OR*, 4:579–94, 6:168, 185; *ORN*, 6:119–45, 12:230; Boatner, *Civil War Dictionary*, 385, 663; Freeman, *R. E. Lee*, 1:606.

2. *OR*, 6:3, 185, 203–4; *ORN*, 12:259, 261; Freeman, *R. E. Lee*, 1:608; Daniel Ammen, "DuPont and the Port Royal Expedition," in *B&L*, 1:671–91.

3. *OR*, 6:309, Freeman, *R. E. Lee*, 1:607–9.

4. *OR*, 6:304–5, 313–14, 323–24, 364; *ORN*, 12:295; Freeman, *R. E. Lee*, 1:609–10; Bryan, *Confederate Georgia*, 67.

5. *OR*, 6:312–14, 320, 53:186–87; Freeman, *R. E. Lee*, 1:609–10; Ellison Capers, *South Carolina*, Vol. 5 in Clement A. Evans, ed., *Confederate Military History*, 12 vols. (Atlanta: Confederate Publishing Co., 1899), 36–37.

6. Freeman, *R. E. Lee*, 1:613; Derry, *Georgia*, 58. Bryan, *Confederate Georgia*, 254, gives a somewhat different version of the defensive positions.

7. *CRG*, 2:45–50, 52–55, 69–70, 93; Bryan, *Confederate Georgia*, 25–26, 82; Bragg, *Joe Brown's Army*, 5–6; Parks, *Brown*, 165–66, 168; Hill, *Brown*, 66.

8. *CRG*, 2:93–94, 131–34, 138, 143, 146; Parks, *Brown*, 167–68; *Augusta Constitutionalist* and *Augusta Chronicle and Sentinel*, November 28, 1861; Joseph E. Brown to WHTW, November 11, 16, 1861, Governor's Letter Book, GDAH; Henry C. Wayne to WHTW, November 29, 1861, AG Secretaries' Letter Book, 5:363, GDAH; WHTW to Wayne, December 1, 1861, Incoming Correspondence to the Adjutant General, RG 22, GDAH.

9. *OR*, 6:306–7.

10. *CRG*, 3:141; *OR*, 53:184, 6:362, 365; Freeman, *R. E. Lee*, 1:617; Bryan, *Confederate Georgia*, 68–69, 84; Wayne to Governor Brown, October 1, 1861, Outgoing Correspondence from Henry C. Wayne, 1860–62, GDAH; Lawton to Wayne, November 6, and Wayne to Lawton, November 13, 1861, Telamon Cuyler Collection, Box 17, Georgia Confederate, Adjutant General Papers, Folder 2, Hargrett Collection, University of Georgia, Athens.

11. *Savannah Daily Morning News*, November 12, 1861; Charles C. Jones, Jr., to his father, November 13, 1861, in Myers, *Children of Pride*, 794, and map in frontispiece; AG Secretaries' Letter Book, 5:443, GDAH; *Augusta Constitutionalist*, December 20, 1861; *OR*, 6:365.

12. *CRG*, 2:47; WHTW to Wayne, January 2, 1861 [1862], Incoming Correspondence to the Adjutant General, RG 22, GDAH.

13. WHTW to Henry R. Jackson, January 4, 1862, Henry R. Jackson Letter Book, Letters Received, 1862, GDAH.

14. Brown to WHTW, January 7, 1862, Henry R. Jackson to Brown, January 8, 1862, Brown to Jackson, undated, Governor's Letter Book, Wayne to WHTW, January 1, 1862, AG Secretaries' Letter Book, 5:780, GDAH.

15. *CRG*, 2:131–33, 199–201; WHTW to H. R. Jackson, January 2, 7, 10, February 4, 10, 1862, Henry R. Jackson Letter Book, Letters Received, 1862, GDAH; Wayne to WHTW, AG Secretaries' Letter Book, 5:584, 672, 770, 843, GDAH; WHTW to Jackson, January 2, 1862, Henry R. Jackson Letter Book, Arms, GDAH. The names of the individual companies and the regiments and battalions they belonged to can be found in summary form in the Civil War Miscellaneous Information Index, GDAH.

16. WHTW to Jackson, January 18, 23, 24, 1862, H. R. Jackson Order Book, AGO B47, GO 20, GDAH; Avery, *History of Georgia*, 228.

17. *ORN*, 12:324–28, 382, 386, 403; *OR*, 6:32–33; Freeman, *R. E. Lee*, 1:615; Bryan, *Confederate Georgia*, 68; Derry, *Georgia*, 59; Parks, *Brown*, 166–67.

18. Parks, *Brown*, 176–82; Bryan, *Confederate Georgia*, 83; *CRG*, 2:249–50, 3:146–47.

19. Bryan, *Confederate Georgia*, 68; WHTW to H. R. Jackson, January 20, 24, 27, 1862, Jackson Letter Book, GDAH; Civil War Miscellaneous Information Index, GDAH; Henderson, ed., *Roster of the Confederate Soldiers from Georgia*, 1:182.

20. Henry R. Jackson Order Book, AGO B47, GDAH; *Savannah Daily Morning News*, February 10, 1862; George A. Mercer Diary (typescript), Vol. 2, March 27, 1862, Mercer Family Papers, Georgia Historical Society, Savannah; *Charleston Tri-Weekly Mercury*, March 11, 1862; A. R. Lawton to H. R. Jackson, February 3, 1862, Jackson Letter Book, Item 140, GDAH.

21. *OR*, 6:143–44, 146–47, 153–56; Derry, *Georgia*, 82; Bryan, *Confederate Georgia*, 70–71; Charles H. Olmstead, "The Siege of Fort Pulaski," *GHO* 1 (1917): 101–2; Olmstead, "The Memoirs of Charles Olmstead," pt. 6, ed. Lilla Mills Hawes, *GHQ* 44 (1960): 65–67; Quincy A. Gillmore, "Siege and Capture of Fort Pulaski," in *B&L*, 2:2–6.

22. Freeman, *R. E. Lee*, 1:617, 623–26; Bryan, *Confederate Georgia*, 71; Parks, *Brown*, 192–94; *OR*, 6:379–80, 386–87, 389–91, 396; *ORN*, 12:491–505, 522–28, 590–92; *CRG*, 3:151–52; Derry, *Georgia*, 82–91; *Charleston Tri-Weekly Mercury*, March 11, 1862. William R. Boggs, *Military Reminiscences of General William R. Boggs, C.S.A.* (Durham, N.C.: Seeman Printery, 1913), 24–26, says Governor Brown directed that works be prepared below the city at this time and Boggs laid out the line. This is an error in recollection; Lee already had such work well under way. Boggs was colonel and chief engineer of the Georgia State Troops at the time.

23. Parks, *Brown*, 194; Freeman, *R. E. Lee*, 1:617, 625–26; *OR*, 6:377, 398, 400, 403–4; *CRG*, 3:152; *Charleston Tri-Weekly Mercury*, March 11, 1862.

24. *Charleston Tri-Weekly Mercury*, March 29, 1862; Boggs, *Reminiscences*, 25–26; Myers, *Children of Pride*, 854; Mercer Diary, April 14, 1862; Capers, *South Carolina*, 191–92; E. Milby Burton, *The Siege of Charleston, 1861–1865* (Columbia: University of South Carolina Press, 1970), 121–23; *ORN*, 13:566, 818; Jackson Order Book, AGO B47, GO 23, February 7, and GO 42, March 30, 1862, GDAH; *OR*, 14:853–54, 856–57, 916; Freeman, *R. E. Lee*, 1:628–29; *OR*, 6:400, 407; Warner, *Generals in Gray*, 232; Cullum, *Biographical Register*, 917.

25. *OR*, 6:133–47, 157–67; Olmstead, "Pulaski," 102–5; Olmstead, "Memoirs," pt. 6, 69–72; Gillmore, "Siege and Capture of Fort Pulaski," 7–12; Derry, *Georgia*, 88–91; *ORN*, 12:730–32; Bryan, *Confederate Georgia*, 71–72; Parks, *Brown*, 194.

26. Editor's note to Gillmore, "Siege and Capture of Fort Pulaski," *B&L*, 2:11–12; Derry, *Georgia*, 89–90; George Cary Eggleston, *A Rebel's Recollections* (1875; reprint, Bloomington, Indiana University Press, 1959), 137–39.

27. *CRG*, 2:250–52, 3:183–88, 191–99, 200–201, 203, 205–9; Parks, *Brown*, 193–97; *OR*, Ser. IV, Vol. 1, pp. 1111–13; Bragg, *Brown's Army*, 8; AG Secretaries' Letter Book, 6:420, GDAH; *Augusta Chronicle and Sentinel* and *Augusta Constitutionalist*, April 15, 1862. For Capers and Harrison see Northern, *Men of Mark in Georgia*, 3:166–68, 141, and *DGB*, 1:171–72, 513–14. Harrison is sometimes confused with his son, George P. Harrison, Jr., who was colonel of the 5th Regiment, Georgia State Troops, and later colonel of the 32nd Georgia, CSA.

28. Hill, *Brown*, 164–65.

29. Corley, *Confederate City*, 41, 43, 46–60, 63–66.

30. WHTW to daughter, January 16, 1862, Walker Papers; WHTW to Henry C. Wayne, February 26, 1862, Civil War Collection, Box 62, Item EG, Henry E. Huntington Library, San Marino, Calif.; WHTW to wife, undated [fall 1862?], and December 12, 1863, Walker Papers; *Augusta Constitutionalist*, July 18, 1862; Clark, *Lost Arcadia*, 73–75; *Augusta Chronicle and Sentinel*, October 4, 1862, January 28, 1871, April 22, May 24, 1863.

CHAPTER 11. RETURN TO THE FRAY, FEBRUARY–AUGUST 1863

1. Capers, *South Carolina*, 78–79; Burton, *Siege of Charleston*, 92–93; Walter B. Cisco, *States Rights Gist* (Shippensburg, Pa.: White Mane Press, 1991), 75–77; *OR*, 6:377, 379.

2. *OR*, 6:257–58; Derry, *Georgia*, 101, 105–7; Capers, *South Carolina*, 76–77, 101–6; *OR*, 14:20–27, 144–89; *ORN*, 13:399–406.

3. Burton, *Siege of Charleston*, 94–96; Capers, *South Carolina*, 82; *OR*, 14:13–15, 502, 506; *ORN*, 13:53. Cullum, *Biographical Register*, 891; Warner, *Generals in Blue*, 30; Burton, *Siege of Charleston*, 101–11, 113; Capers, *South Carolina*, 83–92; *OR*, 14:41–104; *ORN*, 13:102–10; Cisco, *Gist*, 77–80. The Appendix to *OR*, Vol. 14, contains the correspondence pertaining to Benham's case.

4. Burton, *Siege of Charleston*, 123–31; Capers, *South Carolina*, 192–93; Derry, *Georgia*, 103–5; *ORN*, 14:111, 228, 269, 417, 447, 458, 536, 577–623.

5. Burton, *Siege of Charleston*, 112, 114, 116; Capers, *South Carolina*, 94, 100–101; *OR*, 14:2, 561, 570, 594, 597, 601, 603, 630, 632, 633, 636, 641; P. G. T. Beauregard, "The Defense of Charleston," in *B&L*, 4:1–3; Cisco, *Gist*, 81–82.

6. Burton, *Siege of Charleston*, 116; Capers, *South Carolina*, 96–99; *OR*, 14:615, 619–21, 633–35; Beauregard, "Charleston," 2–3.

7. *OR*, 14:642; *ORN*, 13:376; Burton, *Siege of Charleston*, 117–19; Capers, *South Carolina*, 107–10; Cisco, *Gist*, 83.

8. *ORN*, 13:221, 453, 543, 626, 635, 696; *OR*, 14:211–23; Derry, *Georgia*, 201–4; Beauregard, "Charleston," 9–10; C. R. P. Rodgers, "Du Pont's Attack at Charleston," in *B&L*, 4:33; Warner, *Generals in Gray*, 10.

9. *OR*, 14:759–61.

10. Ibid., 765; A. W. Kenan to Jefferson Davis, received February 6, 1863, Chapter 1, Register of Letters Received by the Adjutant and Inspector General, Vol. 54, Item 210, RG 109, NA.

11. Undated, unidentified newspaper clipping, Walker Papers; Satterfield, *Madame LeVert*, 223–24; Beauregard to Mrs. O. W. LeVert, October 5, 1862, Beauregard to WHTW, December 19, 1862, Letter book copies, Personal Letterbook, June 30, 1862–February 9, 1863, Container 6, Microfilm Roll 1, Beauregard Papers.

12. WHTW to wife, undated [fall 1862?], Walker Papers; Boggs, *Reminiscences*, 27.

13. George Randolph to A. H. Kenan, September 27, 1862, NA M522, Roll 5 (War Department Collection of Confederate Records, RG 109, Chapter 1, Vol. 8, 48).

14. *Augusta Constitutionalist*, May 8, 1863.

15. WHTW to daughter, January 16, 1862, March 10, 1863, Walker Papers.

16. Warner, *Generals in Gray*, 216; WHTW to daughter, March 10, 1863, Walker Papers.

17. Samuel Cooper to WHTW, February 9, 19, March 3, 1863, Cooper to Thomas Jordan, February 26, 1863, Cooper to P. G. T. Beauregard, March 3, 1863, NA M627, Roll 4 (Chapter 1, Vols. 38 and 39, 76, 89, 100, 109, RG 109, NA); *OR*, 14:778, 809; *Augusta Constitutionalist*, February 17, 1863; Chapter 1, Vol. 86, Register of Appointment of Officers, 10, RG 109, NA.

18. Cumming, *Memoirs*, 55–57; *Savannah Daily Morning News*, March 3, 1863.

19. *OR*, 14:824, 774–75; WHTW to daughter, March 10, to wife, April [4?], 1863, Walker Papers; Lucian Lamar Knight, *Georgia's Landmarks, Memorials and Legends*, 2 vols. (Atlanta: Byrd Printing, 1913), 1:395; Warner, *Generals in Gray*, 339; Derry, *Georgia*, 44, 51–52; Henderson, ed., *Roster of the Confederate Soldiers of Georgia*, 3:89, 161, 427, 437, 497.

20. *OR*, 14:864–77.

21. NA M331, Roll 139, Henry R. Jackson, Roll 249, N. O. Tilton; Bragg, *Joe Brown's Army*, 117; *Augusta City Directory*, 1861; Henderson, ed., *Roster of the Confederate Soldiers of Georgia*, 1:290. Warner, *Generals in Gray*, and other sources state erroneously that the senior Jackson served on Walker's staff. They have confused father with son. Charles Edgeworth Jones, *Georgia in the War, 1861–1865* (Atlanta: Foote and Davies, 1909), 97–98, and Joseph H. Crute, Jr., *Confederate Staff Officers, 1861–1865* (Powhatan, Va.: Derwent Press, 1982), 202, give substantially correct lists of Walker's staff for the different periods he was a Confederate general officer.

22. *OR*, 14:218–23; *ORN*, 13:716–34, Derry, *Georgia*, 203–4; WHTW to wife, April [4?], 1863, Walker Papers.

23. *OR*, 14:285–86, 788, 840, 881, 887, 889, 899, 918; Beauregard to Governor Joseph E. Brown, February 18, 1863, Telegram Book, Container 29, Microfilm Roll 6, Thomas Jordan to Hugh W. Mercer, March 31, 1863, Container 53, Micro-

film Roll 8, Beauregard Papers; Capers, *South Carolina*, 188–90, 194; Beauregard, "Charleston," 10; Rodgers, "DuPont's Attack," 35; WHTW to wife, April [4?], 9, to daughter, April 15, 1863, Walker Papers; Bragg, *Joe Brown's Army*, 55–56; Cisco, *Gist*, 85; G. A. B. Walker to Governor Joseph E. Brown, July 3, 1863, Governor's Incoming Correspondence, RG 1, Box 49, Location 3335–11, GDAH; *Augusta Chronicle and Sentinel*, April 8, 16, 1863; *Charleston Mercury*, April 8, 10, 15, 1863; *Charleston Daily Courier*, April 10, 1863. Both newspapers referred to the Georgia State Line regiments as the Georgia State Troops.

24. Burton, *Siege of Charleston*, 135–37; *ORN*, 14:xvii–xviii, 718, 727; Rodgers, "DuPont's Attack," 33–35.

25. Burton, *Siege of Charleston*, 136–40; Capers, *South Carolina*, 195–96; *ORN*, 14:5–9, 76–77; Beauregard, "Charleston," 10–12; Rodgers, "DuPont's Attack," 35–37, 39.

26. Burton, *Siege of Charleston*, 142; *ORN*, 14:3, 30–31, 123–24, 132, 295–96, 311; Rodgers, "DuPont's Attack," 46; *OR*, 14:437–39.

27. *OR*, 14:891, 899–901, 925; Augustus P. Adamson, *A Brief History of the Thirtieth Georgia Regiment* (Griffin, Ga.: Mills Printing Co., 1912), 28.

28. WHTW to daughter, April 15, 1863, Walker Papers; J. B. Cumming to wife, April 17, 1863, in W. Kirk Wood, ed., *A Northern Daughter and a Southern Wife: The Civil War Reminiscences and Letters of Katherine H. Cumming, 1860–1865* (Augusta: Phoenix Printing Co., 1976), 67. Like W. H. T. Walker and Henry C. Wayne, Joseph B. Cumming had married a woman from New York. Mary Granger, ed., *Savannah River Plantations* (Savannah: Georgia Historical Society, 1947), 442–43.

29. WHTW to wife, June 13, undated [July?], 1861, July 7, [1856?], Walker Papers.

30. WHTW to wife, May 5, 1863, ibid.; *Charleston Daily Courier*, April 30, 1863; *Augusta Constitutionalist*, May 1, 8, 1863.

31. Bruce Catton, *Grant Moves South* (Boston: Little, Brown, 1960), 324–46; Ulysses S. Grant, *Personal Memoirs of U. S. Grant* (1885; reprint, New York: Da Capo Press, 1982), 219–28; *OR*, 17, pt. 1:605–10; *ORN*, 23:590–93, 606–8, 611–15. George W. Morgan, "The Assault on Chickasaw Bluffs," in *B&L*, 3:462–70, gives a lucid account of that operation, including a fairly damning indictment of Sherman's tactics and attitude.

32. Catton, *Grant Moves South*, 377–87; Grant, *Memoirs*, 232–37; *ORN*, 24:243–49, 279, 282–84, 291–93, 474–80, 490–92, 498–501.

33. Catton, *Grant Moves South*, 407–25; Grant, *Memoirs*, 237–52, *ORN*, 24:553–54, 717.

34. Catton, *Grant Moves South*, 426–28; Grant, *Memoirs*, 252–59; *OR*, 24, pt. 3:250–59.

35. Catton, *Grant Moves South*, 436–37; Johnston, *Narrative*, 170–71; Govan and Livingood, *Different Valor*, 194–96.

36. Catton, *Grant Moves South*, 429; Johnston, *Narrative*, 171–72; Govan and

Livingood, *Different Valor*, 195–97; *OR*, 14:923–26, 931–39, 944, 947, 953–54, 956. Upon arrival in Mississippi the 47th Georgia was attached to Breckinridge's division (*OR*, 24, pt. 3:1039).

37. J. B. Cumming to wife, April 17, 1863, in Wood, ed., *Northern Daughter*, 67; WHTW to wife, May 5, 1863, Walker Papers; *OR*, 14:925–26; Cisco, *Gist*, 87–88.

38. *OR*, 14:216, 926, 945, 24, pt. 3:833, 1041; Mercer Diary, May 4, 1863; Capers, *South Carolina*, 203–4; Derry, *Georgia*, 220; Cisco, *Gist*, 89; Henderson, ed. *Roster of the Confederate Soldiers of Georgia*, 4:924; Arthur W. Bergeron, *Guide to Louisiana Confederate Military Units, 1861–1865* (Baton Rouge: Louisiana State University Press, 1989), 157–58.

39. WHTW to wife, May 5, 7, 1863, Walker Papers; *Augusta Chronicle and Sentinel*, April 22, May 24, 1863; Cumming, *Memoirs*, 57; J. B. Cumming to father, May 27, 1863, Cumming Family Papers, Richmond County Historical Society, Augusta, Ga.

40. Chapter 1, Vol. 86, Register of Appointments of Officers, 10, RG 109, NA.

41. Cisco, *Gist*, 90–91; *OR*, 14:956; Mercer Diary, May 31, 1863; "Extracts from the Diary of Lieutenant Colonel John G. Pressley of the Twenty-Fifth South Carolina Volunteers," *SHSP* 14 (1886): 46–47.

42. Arthur J. L. Fremantle, *The Fremantle Diary*, ed. Walter Lord (Boston: Little, Brown, 1954), 90; *OR*, Ser. IV, 2:769.

43. Johnston, *Narrative*, 172–75; Govan and Livingood, *Different Valor*, 197–98; Catton, *Grant Moves South*, 440; *OR*, 24, pt. 1:215; Cisco, *Gist*, 92.

44. Catton, *Grant Moves South*, 436–37; Grant, *Memoirs*, 259–61.

45. *OR*, 24, pt. 1:704–6, 736–39; Grant, *Memoirs*, 261; Catton, *Grant Moves South*, 439; Johnston, *Narrative*, 175.

46. Johnston, *Narrative*, 177; Govan and Livingood, *Different Valor*, 199; Cisco, *Gist*, 92–93; Capers, *South Carolina*, 207; *OR*, 24, pt. 1:785, pt. 3:877, 881–82.

47. *OR*, 24, pt. 1:749–51, 753–54, 785–87; Capers, *South Carolina*, 204–8; Johnston, *Narrative*, 177; Grant, *Memoirs*, 264–65; Catton, *Grant Moves South*, 440.

48. Fremantle, *Diary*, 93–94.

49. Grant, *Memoirs*, 265–68; Catton, *Grant Moves South*, 440–42; Johnston, *Narrative*, 176, 178–80; Govan and Livingood, *Different Valor*, 199–202; *OR*, 24, pt. 2:6–128.

50. Grant, *Memoirs*, 269–75; Catton, *Grant Moves South*, 442–46; Johnston, *Narrative*, 182–85; Govan and Livingood, *Different Valor*, 202–4; *OR*, 24, pt. 2:128–43; Warner, *Generals in Gray*, 193.

51. Grant, *Memoirs*, 276–78, 284–86; Catton, *Grant Moves South*, 448–53, 466–68.

52. Johnston, *Narrative*, 189–90, 198; Govan and Livingood, *Different Valor*, 205–7; Grant, *Memoirs*, 278; Cisco, *Gist*, 93; *OR*, 24, pt. 1:242.

53. Warner, *Generals in Gray*, 93; Cullum, *Biographical Register*, 1180; *OR*, 24,

pt. 1:190–91, 194; Chapter 1, Vol. 86, Register of Appointment of Officers, 4, RG 109, NA. The actual date of appointment was June 27 to rank from May 23. Walker's commission was delivered to him August 12. He was confirmed by the Senate January 25, 1864.

54. *ORN*, 25:342, 373; Reynolds, ed., *Albany Chronicles*, 602; *National Cyclopedia of American Biography*, 4:458–59; Harsha, *Noted Living Albanians*, 408–16; *Appleton's Cyclopedia*, 6:148; *OR*, 2:86, 16, pt. 1:1161, 20, pt. 1:403, Ser. III, Vol. 3, pp. 166–68; WHTW to wife, undated [June 1863?], Walker Papers.

55. *OR*, 24, pt. 3:925, 978.

56. NA Microfilm Publication M266, Compiled Service Records of Confederate Soldiers Who Served in Organizations from the State of Georgia, Roll 73, Nelson's Cavalry Company, Muster Roll for July–August 1863, Henderson, ed., *Roster of the Confederate Soldiers of Georgia*, 1:552.

57. J. G. McCown, "About Ector's and McNair's Brigades," *Confederate Veteran* 9(1901): 113.

58. *OR*, 24, pt. 3:919–20, 957–58; Cisco, *Gist*, 93–94.

59. *OR*, 24, pt. 1:243; Capers, *South Carolina*, 209; Johnston, *Narrative*, 189, 191, 200; Govan and Livingood, *Different Valor*, 204, 208; Catton, *Grant Moves South*, 469–70; Grant, *Memoirs*, 279, 282; WHTW to wife, June 6, 1863, Walker Papers.

60. Cisco, *Gist*, 154; NA M331, Roll 28, James A. Bowers, Roll 162, Lawson Magruder, Roll 250, J. Robert Troup; Crute, *Confederate Staff Officers*, 202; Jones, *Georgia in the War*, 97–98; Joseph Jones, "Roster of the Medical Officers of the Army of Tennessee," *SHSP* 22 (1894): 176–77; NA Microfilm Publication M627, Roll 4, Vol. 38, 345; NA Microfilm Publication M258, Compiled Service Records of Confederate Soldiers Who Served in Organizations Raised Directly by the Confederate Government, Roll 49, Martin's Battalion, Robert Martin.

61. WHTW to Johnston, May 31, June 4, 6, 15, 1863, *OR*, 24, pt. 3:939–40, 946–47, 951, 965, pt. 2:439–42; John W. Hagan to wife, June 4, 1863, in *Confederate Letters of John W. Hagan*, ed. Bell I. Wiley (Athens: University of Georgia Press, 1954), 19. Hagan was a private and later sergeant in the 29th Georgia.

62. *OR*, 24, pt. 3:960; Johnston, *Narrative*, 202–4; Govan and Livingood, *Different Valor*, 213–14; Catton, *Grant Moves South*, 469–70; Grant, *Memoirs*, 286–88; Capers, *South Carolina*, 210; Cisco, *Gist*, 94.

63. WHTW to daughter, June 26, 1863, to wife, July 5, 1863, Walker Papers; Cumming, *Memoirs*, 58; Cisco, *Gist*, 95; John W. Hagan to wife, July 5, 1863, in Hagan, *Letters*, 21; Adamson, *Thirtieth Georgia*, 29–30.

64. *OR*, 24, pt. 2:651; Johnston, *Narrative*, 204–6, 564; Govan and Livingood, *Different Valor*, 214; Capers, *South Carolina*, 211.

65. Grant, *Memoirs*, 301–2; Govan and Livingood, *Different Valor*, 215; Capers, *South Carolina*, 210; *OR*, 24, pt. 2:533–34, 555–56, 574.

66. *OR*, 24, pt. 2:535, 556, 575; Johnston, *Narrative*, 207, 564–66; Govan and

Livingood, *Different Valor*, 216; Capers, *South Carolina*, 211; John W. Hagan to R. Roberts, E. W. Roberts, and J. S. Roberts, July 15, 20, 1863, in Hagan, *Letters*, 22–27; *Augusta Chronicle and Sentinel*, August 15, 1863.

67. *OR*, 24, pt. 2:535–36, 550, 658; Johnston, *Narrative*, 208–10; Govan and Livingood, *Different Valor*, 219–20; Capers, *South Carolina*, 210; John W. Hagan to R. Roberts, E. W. Roberts, and J. S. Roberts, July 15, 20, 1863, in Hagan, *Letters*, 23, 26; WHTW to wife, July 19, 1863, Walker Papers.

68. Cumming, *Memoirs*, 59.

69. WHTW to wife, July 19, 1863, Walker Papers.

70. *OR*, 24, pt. 2:536–37, 576; Johnston, *Narrative*, 210; Govan and Livingood, *Different Valor*, 220–21; Capers, *South Carolina*, 211; Catton, *Grant Moves South*, 482–83.

71. *OR*, 24, pt. 2:536; Johnston, *Narrative*, 228, 567; Govan and Livingood, *Different Valor*, 229–30; Hughes, *Hardee*, 158; Capers, *South Carolina*, 210–11; Grant, *Memoirs*, 303; WHTW to wife, July 23, August 2, 1863, Walker Papers.

72. Catton, *Grant Moves South*, 473–76; *OR*, 24, pt. 3:546, 1010–11, 1031–32, 1034; Johnston, *Narrative*, 566–67; Govan and Livingood, *Different Valor*, 215, 218.

73. WHTW to wife, July 19, August 2, 1863, Walker Papers.

CHAPTER 12. CHICKAMAUGA, SEPTEMBER–DECEMBER 1863

1. Thomas L. Connelly, *Autumn of Glory: The Army of Tennessee, 1862–1865* (Baton Rouge: Louisiana State University Press, 1971), 126–34; Glenn Tucker, *Chickamauga: Bloody Battle of the West* (Dayton, Ohio: Morningside Bookshop, 1984), 15–22; Jerry Korn, *The Fight for Chattanooga: Chickamauga to Missionary Ridge* (Alexandria, Va.: Time-Life Books, 1985), 18–34.

2. Connelly, *Autumn of Glory*, 138–39, 149–52; Tucker, *Chickamauga*, 96–97.

3. *OR*, 30, pt. 4:516; WHTW to daughter, August 24, 1863, Walker Papers.

4. *OR*, 30, pt. 4:538; George W. Brent Journal, August 27, 31, 1863, Folder 22, Bragg Papers, Western Reserve; Adamson, *Thirtieth Georgia*, 33.

5. *OR*, 30, pt. 4:561, 594; Brent Journal, August 28, September 4, 5, 1863, Bragg Papers, Western Reserve.

6. Connelly, *Autumn of Glory*, 73–74; Tucker, *Chickamauga*, 23–30; Daniel H. Hill, "Chickamauga, the Great Battle of the West," in *B&L*, 3:639–41.

7. *OR*, 30, pt. 1:40–47, 169; "The Opposing Forces at Chickamauga, Ga.," *B&L*, 3:672–76; Thomas L. Livermore, *Numbers and Losses in the Civil War* (1900; reprint, Bloomington: Indiana University Press, 1957), 105–6; Tucker, *Chickamauga*, 15.

8. Judith Lee Hallock, *Braxton Bragg and Confederate Defeat*, Vol. 2 (Tuscaloosa: University of Alabama Press, 1991), 40–42; Brent Journal, September 5, 1863, Bragg Papers, Western Reserve; St. John R. Liddell, *Liddell's Record*, ed. Nathaniel C. Hughes (Dayton, Ohio: Morningside Press, 1985), 136, 138–39; *OR*, 30, pt. 2:14,

17, 244, 257–58, 286–87, 495, 499, 32, pt. 3:688; WHTW to wife, September 15, 1863, Walker Papers.

9. Liddell, *Liddell's Record*, 135–37, 168; Sykes, *Walthall's Brigade*, 597.

10. WHTW to wife, September 15, 1863, Walker Papers.

11. McWhiney, *Bragg*, 323–24, 326–27, 329–36, 374–92; William M. Polk, *Leonidas Polk, Bishop and General*, New ed., 2 vols. (New York: Longmans, Green, 1915), 2:199–211; Joseph H. Parks, *General Leonidas Polk, the Fighting Bishop* (Baton Rouge: Louisiana State University Press, 1962), 294–302; Johnston, *Narrative*, 161–62; Govan and Livingood, *Different Valor*, 178–83, 185–86.

12. Polk, *Polk*, 2:238–44; Parks, *Polk*, 326–30; Connelly, *Autumn of Glory*, 174–88; Tucker, *Chickamauga*, 60–71; OR, 30, pt. 2:29–32; Brent Journal, September 10–13, 1863, Bragg Papers, Western Reserve.

13. Liddell, *Record*, 140.

14. Polk, *Polk*, 2:240–42; Parks, *Polk*, 328–30; Hallock, *Bragg*, 61–62.

15. Connelly, *Autumn of Glory*, 193; Hallock, *Bragg*, 63; OR, 30, pt. 4:643, 649, 652; Brent Journal, September 15, 1863, SO 244, September 13, and SO 245, September 17, 1863, Oversize Vol. 4, pp. 213–14, Bragg Papers, Western Reserve; WHTW to wife, September 15, 1863, Walker Papers.

16. James Longstreet, *From Manassas to Appomattox* (1896; reprint, Secaucus, N.J.: Blue and Grey Press, 1984), 433–35; Connelly, *Autumn of Glory*, 150–52; Tucker, *Chickamauga*, 86–89, 92–93; Brent Journal, September 16, 1863, Bragg Papers, Western Reserve.

17. Brent Journal, September 15–17, 1863, Circular, Headquarters, Army of Tennessee, September 18, 1863, Oversize Vol. 4, p. 221, Bragg Papers, Western Reserve; OR, 30, pt. 4:657–63; Connelly, *Autumn of Glory*, 193–97.

18. Connelly, *Autumn of Glory*, 197–98; Tucker, *Chickamauga*, 112–15, 117; OR, 30, pt. 2:239, 251, 271–72, 357, 524; Cumming, *Memoirs*, 62. Cumming says Walker crossed at Landrum's Ford but no other source supports this. Maps of the field show a Lambert's Ford downstream from Alexander's Bridge but no Landrum's.

19. George W. Brent to WHTW, September 18, 1863 (four times), Folder 10, Bragg Papers, Western Reserve.

20. Tucker, *Chickamauga*, 118–19, 126; Connelly, *Autumn of Glory*, 199–200.

21. Tucker, *Chickamauga*, 127–37; Connelly, *Autumn of Glory*, 202–3; Cumming, *Memoirs*, 63; OR, 30, pt. 2:240, 248–49, 251–52, 258, 273–74.

22. Connelly, *Autumn of Glory*, 203–7; Tucker, *Chickamauga*, 141–45, 152–63; Irving A. Buck, *Cleburne and His Command* (New York: Neale Publishing Company, 1908), 127.

23. Longstreet, *From Manassas to Appomattox*, 438; Connelly, *Autumn of Glory*, 208–10; Tucker, *Chickamauga*, 213, 217; Hal Bridges, *Lee's Maverick General, Daniel Harvey Hill* (New York: McGraw-Hill, 1961), 206–7; Hill, "Chickamauga," 652.

24. Connelly, *Autumn of Glory*, 210–16; Tucker, *Chickamauga*, 213–15; Bridges, *Hill*, 206–12; Hill, "Chickamauga," 652–53.

25. Connelly, *Autumn of Glory*, 216–19; Tucker, *Chickamauga*, 222–25; Bridges, *Hill*, 212–15, 225; Hill, "Chickamauga," 653.

26. Connelly, *Autumn of Glory*, 221; Bridges, *Hill*, 212, 218; Hill, "Chickamauga," 653, 655.

27. Connelly, *Autumn of Glory*, 221–22; Tucker, *Chickamauga*, 233–39; Bridges, *Hill*, 218–19; Hill, "Chickamauga," 655–56.

28. Tucker, *Chickamauga*, 99–100; Cisco, *Gist*, 98–101; Capers, *South Carolina*, 283–84; *OR*, 30, pt. 2:245, 249.

29. *OR*, 30, pt. 2:241, 245.

30. Ibid., 142, 241, 245.

31. Liddell, *Record*, 144–45; *Atlanta Intelligencer*, October 4, 13, 1863; J. F. Wheless, "Confederate Data: Reminiscences of the Battle of Chickamauga," 2–3, Civil War Collection, Tennessee State Library and Archive; *Augusta Chronicle and Sentinel*, October 20, 1863. On another occasion, Hill allegedly endorsed the leave application of a bugler, "Disapproved. Shooters before tooters."

32. Cisco, *Gist*, 102; Capers, *South Carolina*, 285–87; Connelly, *Autumn of Glory*, 222; Tucker, *Chickamauga*, 246–47; Bridges, *Hill*, 219–21; *OR*, 30, pt. 2:245–46, 249.

33. *OR*, 30, pt. 2:144, 253, 259, 265, 274–75; "Address of Col. Archer Anderson on the Campaign and Battle of Chickamauga," *SHSP* 9 (1881): 414; Hill, "Chickamauga," 657.

34. *OR*, 30, pt. 2:241.

35. Connelly, *Autumn of Glory*, 223–25; Tucker, *Chickamauga*, 252–304; Longstreet, *From Manassas to Appomattox*, 448–50.

36. *OR*, 30, pt. 1:855, 860, 862, 867, pt. 2:144, 241; Hill, "Chickamauga," 660; Bridges, *Hill*, 221–22.

37. *OR*, 30, pt. 1:475, pt. 2:144–45, 241, 246, 249, 253, 259–60, 275–76; Cisco, *Gist*, 103–4; Tucker, *Chickamauga*, 359–63.

38. McCown, "About Ector's and McNair's Brigades," 113.

39. *OR*, 30, pt. 2:242.

40. Ibid., 241–42. Walker's memory was slightly faulty; he had only three batteries at Chickamauga, Ferguson having been left on the road from Rome. Bledsoe's battery was with Gregg's brigade in Bushrod Johnson's division.

41. Sykes, *Walthall's Brigade*, 532.

42. *OR*, 30, pt. 2:243–44, 256, 271; William H. Reynolds to Mrs. W. J. [Anna] Dickey, September 22, 1863, Dickey Family Letters, Civil War Miscellany—Personal Papers, GDAH; Cumming, *Memoirs*, 64; J. B. Cumming to wife, September 24[?], 1863, in Wood, ed., *Northern Daughter*, 76.

43. WHTW to wife, October 1, 1863, Walker Papers. The rumor of Walker's death may have been based on the report of Lieutenant Colonel Frank Erdelmeyer, 32d Indiana, who claimed he found the dead body of the general while passing over the battlefield on September 20. See *OR*, 30, pt. 1:547.

44. Connelly, *Autumn of Glory*, 212–13; Hallock, *Bragg*, 78; Livermore, *Numbers and Losses*, 69; *OR*, 30, pt. 1:179.

45. Hallock, *Bragg*, 80–87; Connelly, *Autumn of Glory*, 229–34; WHTW to wife, September 30, 1863, Walker Papers.

46. Hallock, *Bragg*, 89–92; Connelly, *Autumn of Glory*, 235–36; Polk, *Polk*, 2:293–99, 303–5; Parks, *Polk*, 344; Bridges, *Hill*, 232.

47. Circular, Army of Tennessee, September 22, 1863, Vol. 4, p. 213, Brent Journal, September 24, 1863, both in Bragg Papers, Western Reserve; Liddell, *Record*, 149; Hallock, *Bragg*, 270.

48. William W. Mackall to wife, October 10, 1863, William W. Mackall Papers, Southern Historical Collection, University of North Carolina, Chapel Hill.

49. WHTW to wife, October 1, November 9, 1863, Walker Papers.

50. Longstreet, *From Manassas to Appomattox*, 464–65; Hallock, *Bragg*, 95–96; Connelly, *Autumn of Glory*, 238–40; Bridges, *Hill*, 234–36; Steven E. Woodworth, *Jefferson Davis and His Generals* (Lawrence: University Press of Kansas, 1990), 240; Liddell, *Record*, 151–52; *OR*, 30, pt. 2:65–66.

51. Hallock, *Bragg*, 94–95, 98–107; Connelly, *Autumn of Glory*, 241–42, 245–49, 251; Polk, *Polk*, 2:298, 300; Parks, *Polk*, 349–51; Bridges, *Hill*, 236–42; Woodworth, *Davis and His Generals*, 241–45.

52. Special Order No. 294, Army of Tennessee, November 12, 1863, and Circular, "Organization of the Army Artillery," November 20, 1863, Folder 11, Bragg Papers, Western Reserve; *OR*, 31, pt. 2:487, 716, pt. 3:685–86, 30, pt. 2:244, 495, 32, pt. 3:694; Connelly, *Autumn of Glory*, 250; Warner, *Generals in Gray*, 118–19.

53. *OR*, 31:660; Christopher Losson, *Tennessee's Forgotten Warriors* (Knoxville: University of Tennessee Press, 1989), 119, 133; G. W. Brent to George Maney, October 29, 1863, Oversize Vol. 3, Bragg Papers, Western Reserve.

54. WHTW to wife, November 9, 1863, Walker Papers; *OR*, 31, pt. 1:685.

55. Special Order No. 292, November 10, 1863, Oversize Vol. 3, 519, Bragg Papers, Western Reserve; *Augusta Chronicle and Sentinel*, November 14, 1863.

56. James Lee McDonough, *Chattanooga: A Death Grip on the Confederacy* (Knoxville: University of Tennessee Press, 1984), 45–48, 63; Hallock, *Bragg*, 109–10; Connelly, *Autumn of Glory*, 233.

57. Grant, *Memoirs*, 312–16, 321. Grant's narrative on Chattanooga is substantially reprinted in *B&L*, 3:679–711. McDonough, *Chattanooga*, 49, 53–54, 74, 95; Hallock, *Bragg*, 122, 129; Warner, *Generals in Blue*, 233–35.

58. McDonough, *Chattanooga*, 76–85, 87; Hallock, *Bragg*, 122; Connelly, *Autumn of Glory*, 258.

59. Longstreet, *From Manassas to Appomattox*, 473; McDonough, *Chattanooga*, 85, 87–88; Hallock, *Bragg*, 122–23; Connelly, *Autumn of Glory*, 256–60; *OR*, 31, pt. 1:220–22, 52, pt. 2:546, 547, 550, 553, 556.

60. Longstreet, *From Manassas to Appomattox* 475–77; McDonough, *Chattanooga*, 88–94; Connelly, *Autumn of Glory*, 260–61; Hallock, *Bragg*, 123.

61. Longstreet, *From Manassas to Appomattox*, 471, 474–75, 477; McDonough, *Chattanooga*, 88; Connelly, *Autumn of Glory*, 256, 260–61; Hallock, *Bragg*, 123–24.

62. Connelly, *Autumn of Glory*, 262–67; Woodworth, *Davis and His Generals*, 248;

Longstreet, *From Manassas to Appomattox*, 480–81; Hallock, *Bragg*, 109, 125–26, 130; McDonough, *Chattanooga*, 98–101, 110.

63. *OR*, 31, pt. 2:13; Connelly, *Autumn of Glory*, 270–71; McDonough, *Chattanooga*, 108–9, 182–85; Hallock, *Bragg*, 130–31, 136–37; Boatner, *Civil War Dictionary*, 147.

64. McDonough, *Chattanooga*, 110–13; Grant, *Memoirs*, 331–32.

65. McDonough, *Chattanooga*, 113–14, 124–25; Connelly, *Autumn of Glory*, 272; Losson, *Forgotten Warriors*, 121–22; Hallock, *Bragg*, 131.

66. Field returns for Walker's division, October 15 and 22, 1863, Folder 10, Return of the Strength of each Regiment . . . in Polk's Corps, October 22, 1863, Folder 10, Tabular Statement of the Organization of Walker's Division, November 3, 1863, Folder 11, Statement of the Strength of the Army of Tennessee in the Engagements Before Chattanooga . . . , December 24, 1863, Folder 11, Bragg Papers, Western Reserve; *OR*, 31, pt. 2:660; James C. Nisbet, *Four Years on the Firing Line*, ed. Bell I. Wiley, (Jackson, Tenn.: McCowat-Mercer Press, 1963), 141–42. Nisbet incorrectly states that Wilson was already dead when his regiment arrived at the Army of Tennessee. He also exaggerates the number of men he brought to the army, saying the combined strength of the 66th Georgia and 26th Georgia Battalion was fifteen hundred. This must have been the aggregate strength when the units were recruited because on the return of December 14, 1863, the combined strength of the 66th and 26th was 634 total present and 1,016 aggregate present and absent (*OR*, 31, pt. 3:824). In my opinion, Nisbet's memoir of his service with the Army of Tennessee is one long fabrication strung on a thin narrative of truth. By his own account, Nesbit was everywhere, did everything, and remembered it with perfect clarity fifty years later. Yet a careful comparison of only a few of his facts with other accounts proves them to be false, exaggerated, or uninformed. For instance, in regard to Gist commanding Walker's division on Missionary Ridge in November 1863, Nisbet said that Walker had been wounded at Chickamauga and when he returned to the army he went to a different division (*Four Years*, 156–57). This is a ridiculous statement from a man who served directly under Walker's command in the same division for more than seven months. Nisbet has been used as a source, but care has been taken to point out the variations between his "facts" and those reported by others.

67. McDonough, *Chattanooga*, 130–39; Grant, *Memoirs*, 335–36; Losson, *Forgotten Warriors*, 122–24; Hallock, *Bragg*, 131–34; Sykes, *Walthall's Brigade*, 599; Korn, *Fight for Chattanooga*, 136.

68. McDonough, *Chattanooga*, 120–24; Grant, *Memoirs*, 333–34.

69. Connelly, *Autumn of Glory*, 273–76; McDonough, *Chattanooga*, 140, 143–205; Hallock, *Bragg*, 134–42; Losson, *Forgotten Warriors*, 125–27; Grant, *Memoirs*, 337–40; Joseph S. Fullerton, "The Army of the Cumberland at Chattanooga," *B&L*, 3:723–26.

70. Losson, *Forgotten Warriors*, 127–28; McDonough, *Chattanooga*, 206–9; Hal-

lock, *Bragg*, 142; Connelly, *Autumn of Glory*, 276; Cisco, *Gist*, 111; Nisbet, *Four Years*, 160–61.

71. McDonough, *Chattanooga*, 209, 220–25; Losson, *Forgotten Warriors*, 128–29; Cisco, *Gist*, 111–14; Hallock, *Bragg*, 144; Nisbet, *Four Years*, 161–63; *Augusta Chronicle and Sentinel*, December 3, 1863.

72. *OR*, 31, pt. 2:88, 402, 480, 486–87, 684, 716–17, pt. 3:827, 32, pt. 3:694; Howard M. Madaus and Robert D. Needham, *The Battle Flags of the Confederate Army of Tennessee* (Milwaukee: Milwaukee Public Museum, 1976), 62, 108; *Augusta Chronicle and Sentinel*, December 3, 8, 1863.

73. Major Robert Martin to General G. T. Beauregard, December 9, 1863, NA Microfilm Publication M258, Roll 49, Martin's Battalion, Robert Martin.

74. *Augusta Constitutionalist*, August 25, 1864; Cumming, *Memoirs*, 65; WHTW to wife, November 28, December 2, 3, 1863, Walker Papers; *Augusta Chronicle and Sentinel*, December 6, 1863.

75. Connelly, *Autumn of Glory*, 277–78; Hallock, *Bragg*, 147–52; Losson, *Forgotten Warriors*, 129–30.

76. Richard M. McMurry, *Two Great Rebel Armies: An Essay in Confederate Military History* (Chapel Hill: University of North Carolina Press, 1989), 7–8.

77. WHTW to wife, December 3, 1863, Walker Papers. For support of Bragg see letters from the generals named in Folders 11 and 12, Bragg Papers, Western Reserve, and Hallock, *Bragg*, 153–54.

78. Thomas L. Connelly and Archer Jones, *The Politics of Command: Factions and Ideas in Confederate Strategy* (Baton Rouge: Louisiana State University Press, 1973), 72.

79. McDonough, *Chattanooga*, 139–40; *OR*, 31, pt. 2:684–91, 695–96, 705, 722, 732. Moore and Pettus called Jackson by name in their criticism; Walthall referred to him only as "the brigadier general commanding." See Sykes, *Walthall's Brigade*, 539; Losson, *Forgotten Warriors*, 124–25.

80. WHTW to wife, December 3, 1863, Walker Papers; *OR*, 31, pt. 3:783, 827, 850, 885; Statement of the Strength of the Army of Tennessee in the Engagements Before Chattanooga . . . , Folder 11, Bragg Papers, Western Reserve.

81. *OR*, 31, pt. 3:873; Johnston, *Narrative*, 260; WHTW to wife, December 1863[?], July 18, 1864, Walker Papers.

82. WHTW to wife, June 30, 1863, Walker Papers.

83. See Govan and Livingood, *Different Valor*, 236–39, for discussion of Johnston's reappointment to command.

84. Warner, *Generals in Gray*, 339, 291–92; *OR*, 30, pt. 2:242; NA M331, Roll 236, Service Record of C. H. Stevens, Roll 270, C. C. Wilson; Nisbet, *Four Years*, 142, 169; *Augusta Chronicle and Sentinel*, December 4, 1863. Walker's letter of condolence to Mrs. Wilson was printed in the *Chronicle* on December 18.

85. Wood, ed., *Northern Daughter*, 17; WHTW to daughter, December 22, 1863, Walker Papers.

CHAPTER 13. EMANCIPATION, JANUARY 1864

1. WHTW to wife, January 1, 1864, Walker Papers.

2. Cisco, *Gist*, 115; WHTW to wife, January 7, 1864, Walker Papers.

3. Steve Davis, "That Extraordinary Document: W. H. T. Walker and Patrick Cleburne's Emancipation Proposal," *Civil War Times Illustrated* 16 (December 1977): 15; WHTW to Braxton Bragg, March 8, 1864, Item P77, Palmer Civil War Collection, Western Reserve. Steve Davis has generously shared with me his original text and notes as well as his personal insight into this affair.

4. Davis, "That Extraordinary Document," 15; WHTW to Bragg, March 8, 1864, Item P77, Palmer Civil War Collection, Western Reserve.

5. Cleburne's document is printed in full in *OR*, 52, pt. 2:586–92, and in Buck, *Cleburne*, 215–23.

6. Davis, "That Extraordinary Document," 15–16.

7. WHTW to Bragg, March 8, 1864, Item P77, Palmer Civil War Collection, Western Reserve; WHTW to Jefferson Davis, January 12, 1864, *OR*, 52, pt. 2:595; Davis, "That Extraordinary Document," 16.

8. WHTW to wife, February 13, 23, 1855, October 30, 1852, Walker Papers.

9. RCPC Minute Book C, 157, 206; RCSC Deed Books 2A, 270, 2B, 91, 2H, 307, 2L, 714–15, 2M, 622; NA M653, Eighth Census of the United States, 1860, Roll 151, Slave Schedules, Screven County, Georgia, 359; WHTW to wife, August 2, December 16, 1863, October 28, 1852, April 4, 1863, Walker Papers.

10. WHTW to Henry C. Wayne, February 26, 1862, Civil War Collection, Huntington Library.

11. WHTW to wife, September 27, October 24, 1852, February 10, 1855, Walker Papers.

12. WHTW to wife, October 28, 1852, undated [fall 1862?], ibid.

13. WHTW to daughter, December 22, 1863, ibid.

14. *Augusta Chronicle and Sentinel*, January 11, 1861; WHTW to wife, February 24, 1864, Walker Papers.

15. WHTW to wife, January 7, 1864; Buck, *Cleburne*, 213; Davis, "That Extraordinary Document," 16; WHTW to Bragg, March 8, 1864, Item P77, Palmer Civil War Collection, Western Reserve.

16. Davis, "That Extraordinary Document," 16–17; *OR*, 52, pt. 2:593–94; WHTW to Bragg, March 8, 1864, Item P77, Palmer Civil War Collection, Western Reserve; J. Patton Anderson to WHTW, January 9, 1864, W. H. T. Walker Letters, Houghton Library, Harvard University, Cambridge, Mass.; William B. Bate to WHTW, January 9, 1864, Carter L. Stevenson to WHTW, January 9, 1864, Civil War Collection, Huntington Library; Alexander P. Stewart to WHTW, January 9, 1864, Letterbook copy, W. H. T. Walker–A. P. Stewart Correspondence, Georgia Historical Society, Savannah.

17. Thomas C. Hindman to WHTW, January 9, 1864, *OR*, 32, pt. 2:532; B. F.

Cheatham to WHTW, January 10, 1864, Huntington Library; WHTW to Bragg, March 8, 1864, Item P77, Palmer Civil War Collection, Western Reserve; Losson, *Forgotten Warriors*, 137.

18. Frank E. Vandiver, *Their Tattered Flags* (New York: Harper's Magazine Press, 1970), 264; J. P. Anderson to Leonidas Polk, January 14, 1864, *OR*, 52, pt. 2:598–99; Chesnut, *Civil War*, 545.

19. Davis, "That Extraordinary Document," 18; WHTW to Jefferson Davis, January 12, 1864, *OR*, 52, pt. 2:595.

20. WHTW to Jefferson Davis, January 16, 1864, Civil War Collection, Huntington Library; Davis, "That Extraordinary Document," 18.

21. Jefferson Davis to WHTW, January 23, 1864, *OR*, 52, pt. 2:596 (wherein the letter is incorrectly dated January 13), and Dunbar Rowland, *Jefferson Davis, Constitutionalist: His Letters, Papers and Speeches* (Jackson: Mississippi Department of Archives and History, 1923), 159; *OR*, 52, pt. 2:606–9; Buck, *Cleburne*, 213–14; Govan and Livingood, *Different Valor*, 245.

22. Hallock, *Bragg*, 163, 180; William C. Davis, *Breckinridge: Statesman, Soldier, Symbol* (Baton Rouge: Louisiana State University Press, 1974), 402–3; Connelly, *Autumn of Glory*, 319–21.

23. S. R. Gist to Bragg, February 27, 1864, Folder 12, Bragg Papers, Western Reserve. Bragg's answer is not extant but is quoted in Walker's letter of March 8.

24. Gist to Bragg, March 9, 1864, ibid.

25. WHTW to Bragg, March 8, 1864, Item P77, Palmer Civil War Collection, Western Reserve.

26. Davis, "That Extraordinary Document," 20.

27. Fred C. Ainsworth, *Memorandum Relative to General Officers Appointed by the President in the Armies of the Confederate States* (Washington, D.C.: U.S. Military Secretary's Office, 1905), 3–7. Warner, *Generals in Gray*, passim; Cullum, *Biographical Register*, passim.

28. *OR*, 52, pt. 2:606.

29. WHTW to wife, July 12, 1864, Walker Papers.

30. WHTW to wife, Sunday night [February 14, 1864?], ibid. The exact date of Walker's return is not known, but a letter from General Hardee to the division commander was addressed to S. R. Gist on February 10 and another to W. H. T. Walker on February 13, Folder 6 (typescript of Hardee letterbook in Folder 5), William J. Hardee Papers, Alabama Department of Archives and History, Montgomery; *OR*, 31, pt. 3:885.

31. *OR*, 32, pt. 2:588, pt. 3:868; Losson, *Forgotten Warriors*, 119, 133, 135; Hughes, *Hardee*, 190; WHTW undated endorsement, NA M267, Compiled Service Records of Soldiers Who Served in Organizations from the State of South Carolina, Roll 337, 24th South Carolina, Ellison Capers Service Record.

32. Warner, *Generals in Gray*, 150–51; *OR*, 32, pt. 3:868.

33. Johnston, *Narrative*, 277; Nisbet, *Four Years*, 166; Cisco, *Gist*, 116; WHTW to wife, December 11, 1863, February 29, 1864, Walker Papers; Richard Irvine

Manning to his mother, January 28, 1864, Williams-Chesnut-Manning Family Papers, South Caroliniana Library, University of South Carolina, Columbia.

34. *OR*, 32, pt. 2:776, 820.

35. Connelly, *Autum of Glory*, 289–91; Johnston, *Narrative*, 265–66; James L. McDonough and James P. Jones, *War So Terrible: Sherman and Atlanta* (New York: Norton, 1987), 55–56.

36. McDonough and Jones, *War So Terrible*, 56; Losson, *Forgotten Warriors*, 142; Johnston, *Narrative*, 278; Govan and Livingood, *Different Valor*, 244; Joseph E. Brown to J. E. Johnston, February 10, 1864, *OR*, 52, pt. 2:616; Governor Joseph E. Brown's Letter Book, 1860–65, 597, RG 1, GDAH.

37. McDonough and Jones, *War So Terrible*, 56; Govan and Livingood, *Different Valor*, 243; Losson, *Forgotten Warriors*, 142; *OR*, 31, pt. 3:657, 32, pt. 2:586, 776, pt. 3:602, 657, 720, 866.

38. McDonough and Jones, *War So Terrible*, 56; Govan and Livingood, *Different Valor*, 242–43; Losson, *Forgotten Warriors*, 142; Cisco, *Gist*, 116; Nisbet, *Four Years*, 175.

39. McDonough and Jones, *War So Terrible*, 57; Losson, *Forgotten Warriors*, 142; *OR*, 32, pt. 2:602, 670.

40. Connelly, *Autumn of Glory*, 290, 305; Johnston, *Narrative*, 278–79; *OR*, 32, pt. 3:685–86, 694.

41. WHTW to wife, February 14[?], 22, Sunday 12 A.M. [February 28?], March 10, 1864, Walker Papers; Hughes, *Hardee*, 193; *Augusta Constitutionalist*, August 25, 1864; Katherine H. Cumming to J. B. Cumming, December 11, 1863, in Wood, ed., *Northern Daughter*, 78.

42. WHTW to wife, December 18, 1863, February 14[?], 28[?], March 1, 1864, Walker Papers.

43. WHTW to wife, February 22[?], March 10, 24, 1864, ibid.; Maria Cumming to her mother, February 18, 1864, Cumming Family Papers, Richmond County Historical Society. Matthew Talbot married Mary Elizabeth Reid of Eatonton, Georgia, on February 4, 1864, family genealogy, collection of Adele Shearer.

44. Cumming, *Memoirs*, 66; WHTW to wife, April 2, March 1, 4, 1864, Walker Papers; NA M627, Roll 4 (RG 109, Chapter 1, Vol. 39, NA), 52; Henderson, ed., *Roster of the Confederate Soldiers of Georgia*, 1:290, 6:795; NA, M331, Roll 216, William H. Ross Service Record.

45. *OR*, 32, pt. 1:8–11; Connelly, *Autumn of Glory*, 294; Hughes, *Hardee*, 194–96; Buck, *Cleburne*, 225–27; Losson, *Forgotten Warriors*, 140; WHTW to wife, February 22[?], 24, 28[?], 1864, Walker Papers.

46. WHTW to wife, February 24, 28[?], 1864, Walker Papers.

47. Lawson W. Magruder to his father, March 26[?], 1864, Magruder Family Papers.

48. Ibid.

49. Family Genealogy, Magruder Family Papers; NA M653, Eighth Census of

the United States, 1860, Roll 586, Madison County, Mississippi, 104; *OR*, 30, pt. 2:242; NA M331, Roll 67, Joseph B. Cumming Service Record; Lawson W. Magruder to his father, March 26[?], 1864, Magruder Genealogy, Magruder Family Papers.

50. WHTW to wife, March 24, 1864, Walker Papers; Lawson W. Magruder to his father, March 26[?], 1864, Magruder Family Papers.

51. WHTW to wife, March 24, 1864, Walker Papers; WHTW and Mary Walker to Molly Walker, April 12, 14, 1864, ibid.

52. WHTW to wife, March 24, 1864, ibid.

53. WHTW and Mary Walker to Molly Walker, April 12, 14, 1864, ibid.; NA M331, Roll 162, Lawson W. Magruder Service Record.

54. *OR*, 47, pt. 3:856; Sykes, *Walthall's Brigade*, 491, 577; Registers of Commissions, 1887–91, 1891–95, Mississippi Department of Archives and History, Jackson; Magruder Genealogy, Lawson W. Magruder to his father, March 26[?], 1864, Magruder Family Papers.

55. Wyatt-Brown, *Southern Honor*, 53–54.

56. WHTW and Mary Walker to Molly Walker, April 12, 14, 1864, WHTW to wife and daughter (two letters), June 2, 1864, Walker Papers; Cumming, *Memoirs*, 66; Wood, ed., *Northern Daughter*, 18–19; NA M331, Roll 151, DeRosset Lamar.

57. WHTW and Mary Walker to Molly Walker, April 14, 1864, L[ee] M. Butler to Miss Walker, May 2, 1864, Walker Papers; Meadows, *Walker Genealogy*, 193.

58. W. W. Mackall to his wife, Tuesday [April 26?], April 29, May 2, 1864, Mackall Papers, Southern Historical Collection, University of North Carolina.

59. WHTW to wife, February 14[?], 22, March 1, 10, 1864, Walker Papers; Cisco, *Gist*, 119.

60. John Bell Hood, *Advance and Retreat*, ed. Richard N. Current (1880; reprint, Bloomington: Indiana University Press, 1959), 67–68; Richard M. McMurry, *John Bell Hood and the War for Southern Independence* (Lexington: University of Kentucky Press, 1982), 85–93; Bridges, *Hill*, 254–55; Warner, *Generals in Gray*, 142–43; Cullum, *Biographical Register*, 1622; WHTW to wife, February 28[?], 1864, Walker Papers.

61. WHTW to wife, March 1, April 2, 1864, Walker Papers; McMurry, *Hood*, 100; Extract from the Journal of Melancthon Smith, April 7, 1864, Folder 18, Benjamin F. Cheatham Papers, Tennessee State Library and Archives and History, Nashville.

62. George W. Gordon, "The Famous Snowball Battle in the Confederate Army at Dalton, Ga., 1864," in Ben LaBree, ed., *Camp Fires of the Confederacy* (Louisville: Courier-Journal Job Printing Company, 1898), 48; Steve Davis, "The Great Snow Battle of 1864," *Civil War Times Illustrated* 15 (June 1976): 32–33; Nisbet, *Four Years*, 176; W. J. Hardee to WHTW, February 13, 1864, Letterbook, Hardee Papers, Alabama Department of Archives and History, Montgomery.

63. William H. Reynolds to his sister, Mrs. W. J. [Anna] Dickey, March 25, 1864,

Dickey Family Letters, Civil War Miscellany—Personal Papers, GDAH; Buck, *Cleburne*, 227–28; Davis, "Great Snow Battle," 33–34.

64. Gordon, "Snowball Battle," 49–51; Davis, "Great Snow Battle," 34–35; William G. Bentley, "The Great Snowball Battle," *Civil War Times Illustrated* 5 (January 1967): 22–23; McDonough and Jones, *War So Terrible*, 63–64; Losson, *Forgotten Warriors*, 136–37; John B. Lindsley, ed., *The Military Annals of Tennessee: Confederate* (1886; reprint, Spartanburg, S.C.: Reprint Co., 1974), 199; Nisbet, *Four Years*, 175–76.

65. Gordon, "Snowball Battle," 52–53; Davis, "Great Snow Battle," 35; Diary of the Quartermaster Officer of the 65th Georgia Regiment [Captain James J. Goodrum?], KNMP; McDonough and Jones, *War So Terrible*, 64.

66. W. W. Mackall to wife, May 2, 1864, Mackall Papers; Hughes, *Hardee*, 198; Cumming, *Memoirs*, 66; Wood, ed., *Northern Daughter*, 18; "Journal of Campaign with the Army of Tennessee in 1864," George A. Mercer Diary (typescript) May 7, 1864, Mercer Family Papers, Georgia Historical Society; Cisco, *Gist*, 119; WHTW to wife, May 12, 1864, Walker Papers.

CHAPTER 14. THE LAST CAMPAIGN, FEBRUARY–JULY 1864

1. Grant, *Memoirs*, 357–59; Grant to Sherman, April 4, 1864, *OR*, 32, pt. 3:245–46.

2. Sherman to Grant, April 10, 1864, to Cyrus B. Comstock, April 5, 1864, *OR*, 32, pt. 3:313, 362.

3. McDonough and Jones, *War So Terrible*, 67–72; Connelly, *Autumn of Glory*, 287–88, 291–94, 299, 301–5, 307–8, 311, 321–24; Johnston, *Narrative*, 263–69, 272–75, 287–301; Govan and Livingood, *Different Valor*, 242, 249–53, 255–57; Hood, *Advance and Retreat*, 89–95.

4. *OR*, 38, pt. 1:89–102, 115; McDonough and Jones, *War So Terrible*, 28–31; Warner, *Generals in Blue*, 233–35, 237–39, 358–59.

5. *OR*, 38, pt. 1:103–10, 115; McDonough and Jones, *War So Terrible*, 31–32; Jacob D. Cox, *Atlanta* (1882; reprint, Dayton, Ohio: Morningside House, 1987), 21; Warner, *Generals in Blue*, 127–28, 281–83, 306–8.

6. *OR*, 38, pt. 1:111–14, 115; McDonough and Jones, *War So Terrible*, 32–33; Warner, *Generals in Blue*, 425–26; *Army Register, 1856.*

7. *OR*, 38, pt. 3:675–76, 638–44; McDonough and Jones, *War So Terrible*, 65; Hood, *Advance and Retreat*, 79–80; McMurry, *Hood*, 98; Hughes, *Hardee*, 191.

8. *OR*, 32, pt. 3:788, 38, pt. 3:614, 639, 643, 676; Johnston, *Narrative*, 302; "Journal of Campaign," Mercer Diary, Mercer Family Papers, Georgia Historical Society; Diary of Robert Davis Smith, 62 (typescript), KMNP; Samuel McKittrick to wife, May 4, 1864, Samuel McKittrick Letters, KMNP.

9. Cox, *Atlanta*, 27–28, 241; E. C. Dawes, "The Confederate Strength in the

Atlanta Campaign," *B&L*, 4:281. For comparative examples of Union and Confederate returns see *OR*, 38, pt. 1:115–17, and pt. 3:675–80. RG 109, Chapter 2, Vol. 245, Morning Reports of Brigadier General John K. Jackson's Brigade, April 1862–March 5, 1864, NA, is an example of all the present and absent categories.

10. Johnston, *Narrative*, 271, 302; Govan and Livingood, *Different Valor*, 208; Cox, *Atlanta*, 28; Connelly, *Autumn of Glory*, 385.

11. Cox, *Atlanta*, 241–44; Dawes, "Confederate Strength," 281–83; Richard M. McMurry, "Resaca: A Heap of Hard Fitin," *Civil War Times Illustrated* 9 (May 1970): 6; *OR*, 38, pt. 3:676. Hood, for his own purposes, also asserted that Johnston's army was stronger than claimed in May 1864. See Hood, *Advance and Retreat*, 70–88.

12. William T. Sherman, *Memoirs of Gen. W. T. Sherman*, 2 vols. (New York: Charles L. Webster, 1891), 2:25; McDonough and Jones, *War So Terrible*, 98; Cox, *Atlanta*, 31; McMurry, "Resaca," 7.

13. Connelly, *Autumn of Glory*, 334–35; McMurry, *Hood*, 101; McDonough and Jones, *War So Terrible*, 97; Johnston, *Narrative*, 305; Govan and Livingood, *Different Valor*, 262.

14. See Connelly, *Autumn of Glory*, 326–30, and Jones and McDonough, *War So Terrible*, 91–97, for detailed analyses of the Confederate position at Dalton. Johnston's apologia for standing at Dalton is in his *Narrative*, 276–78.

15. McDonough and Jones, *War So Terrible*, 98–99; Cox, *Atlanta*, 31.

16. McDonough and Jones, *War So Terrible*, 100–103; McMurry, *Hood*, 101–2; McMurry, "Resaca," 7–8; Connelly, *Autumn of Glory*, 334–37.

17. "Journal of Campaign," May 8, 1864, Mercer Diary; *OR*, 38, pt. 3:713.

18. McDonough and Jones, *War So Terrible*, 102–6; Buck, *Cleburne*, 232–33; Connelly, *Autumn of Glory*, 337–41; McMurry, "Resaca," 8, 10–11; McMurry, *Hood*, 102–3; Johnston, *Narrative*, 305–9; Govan and Livingood, *Different Valor*, 265–68. Nisbet, *Four Years*, 177–84, contends that the 66th Georgia had been sent to Resaca on May 1 and bore the brunt of the fighting at Snake Creek Gap on May 9 with only two regiments of Cantey's brigade. The only other evidence that any element of the Georgia Division was at Resaca on that date was the statement that Grigsby's Kentucky cavalry brigade expected to find a company of Georgia infantry at the entrance to Snake Creek Gap. See W. C. P. Breckinridge, "The Opening of the Atlanta Campaign," *B&L*, 4:279. Further refuting Nisbet's recollection, on May 29, 1864, Sergeant John M. Davis of the 66th Georgia wrote to his wife, "Our regiment has not been in no general engagement before [today]." In describing the alleged action on May 9, Nisbet recorded that Captain C. M. Jordan of his regiment was wounded in the leg and later died in the hospital. Lillian Henderson shows that Captain Columbus Jordan was wounded on May 18, although she does say at Resaca, and died in Atlanta on May 29. In the lists of wounded arriving in Atlanta hospitals from the front printed in the *Atlanta Intelligencer* on an almost daily basis beginning on May 12, no casualties from the 66th Georgia appeared

until May 18, when Jordan's and one other name were printed. Jordan's death was announced on May 31. He was probably wounded on the retreat to Cassville. See John M. Davis to Mrs. Mary N. Davis, Malcolm Letters, Hargrett Rare Book and Manuscript Library, University of Georgia; Henderson, *Roster of Confederate Soldiers of Georgia*, 6: 702; *Atlanta Intelligencer*, May 21, 31, 1864.

19. "Journal of Campaign," May 10, 1864, Mercer Diary; W. W. Mackall to wife, May 12, 1864, Mackall Papers, Southern Historical Collection, University of North Carolina; Hamilton M. Branch to mother, May 18, 1864, Hamilton Branch Letters, Hargrett Rare Book and Manuscript Library, University of Georgia, Athens; Charles A. J. Martin to "My Dear Parents," May 12, 1864, J. K. P. Martin Letters (typescript), KMNP.

20. WHTW to wife, May 12, 1864, Walker Papers; Joseph B. Cumming to wife, May 13, 1864, Wood, ed., *Northern Daughter*, 83.

21. *OR*, 38, pt. 2:862, 892, 903, pt. 3:399, 420; McMurry, "Resaca," 11; McDonough and Jones, *War So Terrible*, 110.

22. *OR*, 38, pt. 3:713, pt. 4:701–2, 706–7; Cisco, *Gist*, 120; "Journal of Campaign," May 12, 1864, Mercer Diary; Walter A. Clark, *Under the Stars and Bars, or Memories of Four Years Service with the Oglethorpes of Augusta, Georgia* (Augusta: Chronicle Printing Co., 1900), 98. Hamilton Branch to his mother, May 13, 1864, Hamilton Branch Letters, Hargrett Rare Book and Manuscript Library, University of Georgia. Some of the events in Capers's chronology in *OR* may be misdated by one day; for example, he says the crossing to Calhoun occurred on May 11; see note 32, below.

23. McMurry, "Resaca," 11; McDonough and Jones, *War So Terrible*, 107, 109–10; McMurry, *Hood*, 103, 105; Connelly, *Autumn of Glory*, 342.

24. McMurry, "Resaca," 11–12, 44; McDonough and Jones, *War So Terrible*, 109–14; Cox, *Atlanta*, 43–46; Johnston, *Narrative*, 310–12; Govan and Livingood, *Different Valor*, 269–70; Oliver O. Howard, "The Struggle for Atlanta," *B&L*, 4:301–2; *OR*, 38, pt. 3: 978.

25. *OR*, 38, pt. 3:714 (see note 31 below), 978–79, pt. 4:709, 711; William O. Norrell Diary, May 14, 1864, KMNP; Hamilton Branch to his mother, May 16, 1864, Hamilton Branch Letters, Hargrett Rare Book and Manuscript Library, University of Georgia; Adamson, *Thirtieth Georgia*, 39; "Journal of Campaign," May 14, 1864, Mercer Diary; Clark, *Under the Stars and Bars*, 98–99, 108–9; Walter B. Capers, *The Soldier-Bishop, Ellison Capers* (New York: Neale, 1912), 97–98.

26. *OR*, 38, pt. 3:399–400, 420–21, pt. 4:196; McMurry, "Resaca," 44; McDonough and Jones, *War So Terrible*, 116–17.

27. "Journal of Campaign," May 14, 15, 1864, Mercer Diary; McMurry, "Resaca," 44, 46–47; McDonough and Jones, *War So Terrible*, 115–17; Connelly, *Autumn of Glory*, 342–43; Johnston, *Narrative*, 311–14; Govan and Livingood, *Different Valor*, 269–70; McMurry, *Hood*, 105–6; Losson, *Forgotten Warriors*, 145–46.

28. *OR*, 38, pt. 3:400–401, 421–22, pt. 4:196; McMurry, "Resaca," 47.

29. *Augusta Constitutionalist*, May 21, 29, June 19, 1864; "Journal of a Campaign," May 15, 1864, KMNP.

30. *OR*, 38, pt. 3:33, 377, 401, 422, pt. 4:189, 197; Hamilton Branch to his mother, May 16, 1864, Hamilton Branch Letters, Hargrett Rare Book and Manuscript Library, University of Georgia; Calathiel Helms to his wife, May 13 [15?], 1864, Calathiel Helms Letters, United Daughters of the Confederacy Collection of Letters from Confederate Soldiers, 2:444, GDAH; *Atlanta Intelligencer*, June 4, 1864; RG 109, Chapter VI, Vol. 748, Letters, Orders, and Circulars Sent and Received, Medical Director's Office, Army of Tennessee, 181, NA.

31. Albert Castel, *Decision in the West* (Lawrence: University of Kansas Press, 1992), 178–79. Professor Castel had advised me that he has revised these passages for the second printing of his book.

32. *OR*, 38, pt. 3:714; Cisco, *Gist*, 120–21, 178; Capers, *Soldier-Bishop*, 97–98. In his report, Ellison Capers also said Walker's division first crossed to the south side of the Oostanaula on May 11 whereas all other indications are that it was the twelfth. Hamilton Branch wrote that Mercer's brigade and presumably the rest of the division marched to Resaca on May 11 and then back three miles. Then they marched through Resaca and across the river on May 12. This countermarch may have led to Capers's confusion of dates, which is understandable in a report written four months after the action. See Hamilton Branch to his mother, May 13, 1864, Hamilton Branch Letters, Hargrett Rare Book and Manuscript Library, University of Georgia. S. R. Gist's biographer, like Castel, used Capers's report to infer that Gist remained near Calhoun on May 14 and was summoned back to Resaca on the fifteenth; see Cisco, *Gist*, 120–21, and notes, 178.

33. Captain J. H. Steinmeyer Diary, 25 (typescript), KMNP; *OR*, 38, pt. 3: 979.

34. Samuel McKittrick to "Dear Companion," May 16, 1864, McKittrick Letters, KMNP.

35. *OR*, 38, pt. 3:420–21, 714.

36. *OR*, 38, pt. 4:713.

37. Steinmeyer Diary, 33–34, KMNP.

38. *OR*, 38, pt. 3:981; Johnston, *Narrative*, 314; Govan and Livingood, *Different Valor*, 270–71; McMurry, "Resaca," 47; McDonough and Jones, *War So Terrible*, 117–18; Connelly, *Autumn of Glory*, 343; Nisbet, *Four Years*, 185–87.

39. McMurry, "Resaca," 48; Connelly, *Autumn of Glory*, 343–44.

40. *OR*, 38, pt. 3:401–2, 714–15, 722; "Journal of Campaign," May 16, 1864, Mercer Diary.

41. Nisbet, *Four Years*, 188–91.

42. Richard M. McMurry, "Cassville," *Civil War Times Illustrated* 10 (December 1971): 4–8; Connelly, *Autumn of Glory*, 344–46; McDonough and Jones, *War So Terrible*, 124–25, 128–29, 131; Johnston, *Narrative*, 319–21; Govan and Livingood, *Different Valor*, 271–74; Buck, *Cleburne*, 241–42; Losson, *Forgotten Warriors*, 147–48.

43. McMurry, "Cassville," 8–9; Hood, *Advance and Retreat*, 99–104; McMurry,

Hood, 108; Polk, *Polk,* 2:356; McDonough and Jones, *War So Terrible,* 133–36; Connelly, *Autumn of Glory,* 346–48; Johnston, *Narrative,* 321–22; Govan and Livingood, *Different Valor,* 274–75.

44. Connelly, *Autumn of Glory,* 348; Johnston, *Narrative,* 319, 321; Govan and Livingood, *Different Valor,* 271–72; Cox, *Atlanta,* 243; Dawes, "Confederate Strength;" 281–82; *OR,* 38, pt. 3:686.

45. Buck, *Cleburne,* 243; Derry, *Georgia,* 307–8; "Journal of Campaign," May 19, 1864, Mercer Diary; Clark, *Under the Stars and Bars,* 99; *OR,* 38, pt. 3:715–16, 686. Cumming, *Memoirs,* 68.

46. RG 109, Chapter 6, Vol. 748, Letters, Orders and Circulars Sent and Received, Medical Director's Office, Army of Tennessee, 1862–65, 181, NA.

47. McMurry, "Cassville," 9, 45; Hood, *Advance and Retreat,* 104–5; Polk, *Polk,* 2:356, 377–79; McDonough and Jones, *War So Terrible,* 137; Connelly, *Autumn of Glory,* 349; Johnston, *Narrative,* 322–23; Govan and Livingood, *Different Valor,* 276.

48. McMurry, "Cassville," 45, 47; Polk, *Polk,* 2:356–57, 380–81; Parks, *Polk,* 378–79; Connelly, *Autumn of Glory,* 348–52; Johnston, *Narrative,* 323–24; Govan and Livingood, *Different Valor,* 276; Hood, *Advance and Retreat,* 106–9; McMurry, *Hood,* 109; McDonough and Jones, *War So Terrible,* 137–39; *OR,* 38, pt. 3:716, 984; Buck, *Cleburne,* 244. Hardee's biographer makes no mention of the meeting at Cassville and his subject's opinion (Hughes, *Hardee,* 204).

49. McMurry, "Cassville," 8, 45, 47; Connelly, *Autumn of Glory,* 351; John W. Hagan to his wife, May 18, 1864, in Hagan, *Confederate Letters,* 36–37; Thomas B. Mackall Journal, May 20, 1864, Joseph E. Johnston Papers, College of William and Mary, Williamsburg, Va.; Govan and Livingood, *Different Valor,* 276–78.

50. Buck, *Cleburne,* 244; Samuel G. French, *Two Wars* (Nashville: Confederate Publishing Company, 1901), 198; McMurry, "Cassville," 47.

51. *OR,* 38, pt. 3:985; Richard M. McMurry, "The Hell Hole: New Hope Church," *Civil War Times Illustrated* 11 (February 1973): 33–34; McDonough and Jones, *War So Terrible,* 144–45.

52. "Journal of Campaign," May 20, 1864, Mercer Diary; Reminiscences of John L. Keen, Civil War Miscellany—Personal Papers, GDAH; *OR,* 35, pt. 2: 447. On May 2, before the regiment arrived in his army, Johnston wrote to Adjutant General Samuel Cooper that the 57th, in the opinion of Mercer, would not fight and did not consider itself properly exchanged after Vicksburg. See *OR,* 52, pt. 2: 664.

53. McMurry, "Hell Hole," 33–36; McDonough and Jones, *War So Terrible,* 145, 147–49; Johnston, *Narrative,* 327.

54. McMurry, "Hell Hole," 36–37; McDonough and Jones, *War So Terrible,* 149–54; Johnston, *Narrative,* 327–28.

55. McMurry, "Hell Hole," 37–38; McDonough and Jones, *War So Terrible,* 154–55.

56. McMurry, "Hell Hole," 38; *OR,* 38, pt. 3:705, 716; "Journal of Campaign,"

May 26, 1864, Mercer Diary; McDonough and Jones, *War So Terrible*, 155; Buck, *Cleburne*, 247; Johnston, *Narrative*, 329.

57. McMurry, "Hell Hole," 38; *OR*, 38, pt. 3:706; McDonough and Jones, *War So Terrible*, 155–57.

58. McMurry, "Hell Hole," 38, 40; McDonough and Jones, *War So Terrible*, 159–66; Johnston, *Narrative*, 329–31.

59. Hughes, *Hardee*, 204; Losson, *Forgotten Warriors*, 149–51; "Journal of Campaign," May 27, 1864, Mercer Diary; Clark, *Under the Stars and Bars*, 100, 112.

60. McMurry, "Hell Hole," 40–43; McDonough and Jones, *War So Terrible*, 166–69; *OR*, 38, pt. 3:989–90.

61. RG 109, Chapter 6, Vol. 748, 183, NA; *Atlanta Intelligencer*, June 4, 1864. The total loss of fifty-four hundred given in *OR*, 38, pt. 3:687, is incorrect. The division and brigade figures for the Army of Tennessee have been added twice. The numbers for Walker's and Cantey's divisions were left out of the summary.

62. WHTW to daughter, June 2, 1864, Walker Papers; Wyatt-Brown, *Southern Honor*, 107.

63. WHTW to wife, June 2, 1864, Walker Papers; *Augusta Chronicle and Sentinel*, May 28, 31, 1864; Augusta *Constitutionalist*, June 21, 1864.

64. WHTW to wife, June 2, 1864, Walker Papers; Norrell Diary, June 1, 1864, KMNP.

65. *OR*, 38, pt. 4:741; Myron W. House, "History of the First Volunteer Regiment of Georgia, 1864–1865" (M.A. thesis, Emory University, 1973), 17, 21; Olmstead, "Memoirs," pt. 9, *GHQ* 44 (1960): 422; Dawes, "Confederate Strength," 281–82; Johnston, *Narrative*, 574. Hamilton Branch said the 1st Georgia Volunteers arrived in camp on May 29. See Hamilton Branch to his mother, May 29, 1864, Hamilton Branch Letters, Hargrett Rare Book and Manuscript Library, University of Georgia.

66. McDonough and Jones, *War So Terrible*, 171; *OR*, 38, pt. 1:115, 117.

67. Richard M. McMurry, "Kennesaw Mountain," *Civil War Times Illustrated* 8 (January 1970): 20, 22–23; McDonough and Jones, *War So Terrible*, 172–74; *OR*, 38, pt. 3:707, 716; Mackall Journal, June 10, 1864, Johnston Papers, College of William and Mary; Olmstead, "Memoirs," pt. 9, 424–26; John W. Hagan to his wife, June 17, 1864, in Hagan, *Confederate Letters*, 40–41.

68. McMurry, "Kennesaw Mountain," 22; Jones and McDonough, *War So Terrible*, 174–77; Connelly, *Autumn of Glory*, 358; Johnston, *Narrative*, 337; Polk, *Polk*, 2:372–74; Parks, *Polk*, 382–83; *Augusta Chronicle and Sentinel*, June 15, 1864; *Atlanta Intelligencer*, June 15, 1864.

69. Sydney C. Kerksis, "Action at Gilgal Church, Georgia, June 15–16, 1864," *Atlanta Historical Bulletin* 15 (Fall 1970): 9–14, 17, 37; "Journal of Campaign," June 15, 16, 1864, Mercer Diary; John W. Hagan to his wife, June 17, 1864, in Hagan, *Confederate Letters*, 40.

70. *OR*, 38, pt. 1:295, 334; Derry, *Georgia*, 315; "Journal of Campaign," June 18,

1864, Mercer Diary; French, *Two Wars*, 203; Clark, *Under the Stars and Bars*, 101, 117–24. The text of Walker's letter of commendation to the 63d Georgia, addressed to General Mercer, is printed in Dixon Hollingsworth, *Screven County History*, 44. Lieutenant Colonel George R. Black of the 63d was a Screven native.

71. Olmstead, "Memoirs," pt. 9, 426–27; "Journal of Campaign," June 18, 1864, Mercer Diary; *OR*, 38, pt. 1:408.

72. John W. Hagan to his wife, June 21, 22, 1864, in Hagan, *Confederate Letters*, 41–43.

73. "Journal of Campaign," June 20, 22, 1864, Mercer Diary; Hamilton Branch to his mother, June 22, 1864, Hamilton Branch Letters, Hargrett Rare Book and Manuscript Library, University of Georgia; Calathiel Helms to his wife, June 22, 1864, Calathiel Helms Letters, United Daughters of the Confederacy Collection of Letters from Confederate Soldiers, 2:448, GDAH; Charles L. Thiot to his wife, June 22, 1864, Charles L. Thiot Letters, Emory University, Atlanta, Ga.; Blanton B. Fortson to father, June 24, 1864, Civil War Miscellany—Personal Papers, GDAH; RG 109, Chapter 6, Vol. 748, 181, 183, 185, NA.

74. *OR*, 38, pt. 1: 223–24, 243–44, 246, 883–84, pt. 3: 716, pt. 4: 545, 557; J. H. Booker, Reminiscences, Civil War Miscellany—Personal Papers, GDAH; Letter of Commendation from General Gist to the 46th Georgia, Civil War Miscellany—Unit File, GDAH; Steinmeyer Diary, 25, KNMP; *Augusta Chronicle and Sentinel*, June 22, 23, 1864; Henderson, *Roster of Confederate Soldiers*, 4:924–1026.

75. McMurry, "Kennesaw Mountain," 23; McDonough and Jones, *War So Terrible*, 178–80; Johnston, *Narrative*, 338–39.

76. McMurry, "Kennesaw Mountain," map on 26–27; McDonough and Jones, *War So Terrible*, 180; Johnston, *Narrative*, 338–39.

77. McMurry, "Kennesaw Mountain," 24; McDonough and Jones, *War So Terrible*, 177–78, 181–83.

78. McMurry, "Kennesaw Mountain," 24, 31; John W. Hagan to his wife, June 28, 1864, in Hagan, *Confederate Letters*, 45; William R. Hurst to wife and family, June 29, 1864, Hurst Family Letters (typescript), KNMP; McDonough and Jones, *War So Terrible*, 182–84; *OR*, 38, pt. 4:797; Cox, *Atlanta*, 119–20.

79. McMurry, "Kennesaw Mountain," 25, 28; Johnston, *Narrative*, 342; McDonough and Jones, *War So Terrible*, 186.

80. Clark, *Under the Stars and Bars*, 101–2, 130–36; Clark's account of the adventures of his company is especially vivid. Norrell Diary, June 27, 1864, KNMP; "Journal of Campaign," June 27, 1864, Mercer Diary; McMurry, "Kennesaw Mountain," 28.

81. McMurry, "Kennesaw Mountain," 28–29; Olmstead, "Memoirs," pt. 9, 430; McDonough and Jones, *War So Terrible*, 186.

82. Clark, *Under the Stars and Bars*, 136; *OR*, 38, pt. 4:798.

83. *OR*, 38, pt. 4:799.

84. Ibid., pt. 3:900–901, 968, 716, pt. 4:802; Johnston, *Narrative*, 342.

85. C. Helms Letter, "Kennesaw Mountings, near Maryetta, Ga.," June 28, 1864 (typescript), KMNP.

86. *Augusta Chronicle and Sentinel*, July 6, 1864.

87. McMurry, "Kennesaw Mountain," 29–31; Losson, *Forgotten Warriors*, 153–60; Buck, *Cleburne*, 259–60; McDonough and Jones, *War So Terrible*, 187; Johnston, *Narrative*, 342–43; Govan and Livingood, *Different Valor*, 293–94.

88. McMurry, "Kennesaw Mountain," 31–32; Johnston, *Narrative*, 345; Cox, *Atlanta*, 122–24.

89. McMurry, "Kennesaw Mountain," 33; Govan and Livingood, *Different Valor*, 295; Clark, *Under the Stars and Bars*, 136; Ellison Capers to Joseph E. Johnston, July 28, 1874, Joseph E. Johnston Papers, College of William and Mary; *OR*, 38, pt. 3:703, 901.

90. RG 109, Chapter 6, Vol. 748, 185, NA. Obvious disparities between the official records and the numbers recorded by unit members must be explained by faulty reporting. For example, George A. Mercer's list of casualties up to June 22 far exceeds in killed the number reported for Mercer's brigade up to July 4 by the army's medical director (see text at note 73 above).

91. *Augusta Chronicle and Sentinel*, July 7, 1864.

92. WHTW to daughter, June 27, 1864, Walker Papers.

93. Cumming, *Memoirs*, 69.

94. Johnston, *Narrative*, 345; McDonough and Jones, *War So Terrible*, 191–92.

95. William W. Mackall to wife, July 4, 1864, Mackall Papers, Southern Historical Collection, University of North Carolina; Olmstead, "Memoirs," pt. 9, 431–32; "Journal of Campaign," July 3, 4, 1864, Mercer Diary; *Augusta Chronicle and Sentinel*, July 7, 1864.

96. *OR*, 38, pt. 3:648, 655, 679, pt. 4:802, pt. 5: 866; Johnston, *Narrative*, 575; William J. M. Gardner, Reminiscences, Civil War Miscellany—Personal Papers, GDAH; Warner, *Generals in Gray*, 150–51; William R. Hurst to wife, July 4, 1864, Hurst Family Letters, KMNP.

97. Nisbet, *Four Years*, 255–56; NA M266, Roll 277, 26th Georgia Battalion, John W. Nisbet Service Record.

98. *OR*, 38, pt. 3:642, 652; Joseph H. Crute, Jr., *Units of the Confederate States Army* (Midlothian, Va.: Derment Press, 1987), 70–71; NA M258, Roll 24, 10th Confederate Cavalry, Thaddeus G. Holt.

99. Francis A. Shoup, "Dalton Campaign—Works at the Chattahoochee River—Interesting History," *Confederate Veteran* 3 (1895): 262–64; Howell Perdue and Elizabeth Perdue, *Pat Cleburne, Confederate General* (Hillsboro, Texas: Hill Junior College Press, 1973), 337; Norrell Diary, July 5, 1864, KMNP; Hamilton Branch to his mother, July 6, 1864, Hamilton Branch Letters, Hargrett Rare Book and Manuscript Library, University of Georgia.

100. William L. Adams to sister, July 10, 1864, Adams Family Papers, William L. Dickey to Anna Dickey, July 13, 1864, Dickey Family Letters, Civil War Miscellany—Personal Papers, GDAH.

101. John M. Davis to his wife, July 6, 1864, Malcolm Letters, Hamilton Branch to his mother, July 7, 1864, Hamilton Branch Letters, Hargrett Rare Book and Manuscript Library, University of Georgia; Calathiel Helms to his wife, July 6, 1864, United Daughters of the Confederacy Collection of Letters from Confederate Soldiers, 2:449, GDAH.

102. McDonough and Jones, *War So Terrible*, 85, 200–201, 203–5; Johnston, *Narrative*, 345; Govan and Livingood, *Different Valor*, 296–300, 305–6; Connelly, *Autumn of Glory*, 361–65, 391; Woodworth, *Davis and His Generals*, 279–82; *OR*, 38, pt. 5:867, 873.

103. Connelly, *Autumn of Glory*, 392–96; McDonough and Jones, *War So Terrible*, 194–97, 199; Johnston, *Narrative*, 346–47; Cox, *Atlanta*, 137–40.

104. *OR*, 38, pt. 5:868, 872–73; "Journal of Campaign," July 9, 1864, Mercer Diary.

105. Warner, *Generals in Gray*, 293–94.

106. WHTW to daughter, July 2, 1864, Walker Papers.

107. WHTW to wife, July 12, 1864, ibid.

108. W. W. Mackall to wife, June 22, 1864, Mackall Papers, Southern Historical Collection, University of North Carolina; Warner, *Generals in Gray*, 52–53.

CHAPTER 15. DEATH OF A GENERAL, JULY 1864

1. WHTW to wife, July 12, 1864, Walker Papers.

2. Hallock, *Bragg*, 191–92; Johnston, *Narrative*, 348; Govan and Livingood, *Different Valor*, 309; WHTW to daughter, July 15, 1864, Walker Papers; W. W. Mackall to wife, July 13, [14?], 15, 1864, Mackall Papers, University of North Carolina.

3. Connelly, *Autumn of Glory*, 363–64, 398–99, 411, 413–18, 421; McMurry, *Hood*, 117–21; Govan and Livingood, *Different Valor*, 309–12, 316; McDonough and Jones, *War So Terrible*, 205; Woodworth, *Davis and His Generals*, 282, 285; Johnston, *Narrative*, 348, 350–51; *OR*, 38, pt. 5: 881–83, 52: pt. 2: 692–95, 704; Hallock, *Bragg*, 191–95.

4. Connelly, *Autumn of Glory*, 418–19, 421; McMurry, *Hood*, 121–23; Johnston, *Narrative*, 349; Govan and Livingood, *Different Valor*, 311–12, 316–17; McDonough and Jones, *War So Terrible*, 205, 207–8; Woodworth, *Davis and His Generals*, 283–85; Johnston, *Narrative*, 348–49; Hood, *Advance and Retreat*, 126; Hughes, *Hardee*, 215–16; *OR*, 38, pt. 5: 885, 887, 52: pt. 2: 707. Robert D. Little advances the theory that Johnston and Hood were the wrong choices to command the Army of Tennessee. In Little's opinion, the best choice would have been a nonorthodox soldier such

as Nathan B. Forrest. Little believes that if Jefferson Davis insisted on having a man who was familiar with the army's operations, it should have been Hardee. See Robert D. Little, "General Hardee and the Atlanta Campaign," *GHQ* 29 (1945): 1–22.

5. Connelly, *Autumn of Glory*, 422–24; Hood, *Advance and Retreat*, 126–28; McMurry, *Hood*, 123; Govan and Livingood, *Different Valor*, 317–18, 323; Johnston, *Narrative*, 349–50; Woodworth, *Davis and His Generals*, 285–86; Johnston, *Narrative*, 349–50, 369; Nisbet, *Four Years*, 206; *OR*, 38, pt. 3: 717, pt. 5: 887–91, 52: pt. 2: 708–9; Lydia M. Johnston to Mary T. Walker, July 29, 1864, Walker Papers.

6. Hamilton Branch to his mother, July 19, 1864, Hamilton Branch Letters, Hargrett Rare Books and Manuscripts Library, University of Georgia, Athens.

7. WHTW to wife, July 18, 1864, Walker Papers.

8. Robert E. Lee, *The Wartime Papers of R. E. Lee*, Clifford Dowdey and Louis H. Manarin, eds. (Boston: Little Brown, 1961), 821–22; Govan and Livingood, *Different Valor*, 313–15.

9. *OR*, 38, pt. 3: 697, 52, pt. 2: 713; Hughes, *Hardee*, 218; Connelly, *Autumn of Glory*, 419, 423, 451; WHTW to wife, July 18, 1864, Walker Papers. The quotation is from Shakespeare: "Evenhanded justice commends the ingredients of our poisoned chalice to our own lips" (*Macbeth*, Act 1, scene 7).

10. Losson, *Forgotten Warriors*, 173; Hughes, *Hardee*, 220; *OR*, 38, pt. 5: 892.

11. *Augusta Chronicle and Sentinel*, July 28, 1864, quoting *Atlanta Intelligencer* of unknown date.

12. McDonough and Jones, *War So Terrible*, 209; McMurry, *Hood*, 127; Hood, *Advance and Retreat*, 165–66; Connelly, *Autumn of Glory*, 439–40.

13. *OR*, 38, pt. 3: 717, pt. 5: 887; Connelly, *Autumn of Glory*, 363–64, 399–400.

14. Losson, *Forgotten Warriors*, 174; McDonough and Jones, *War So Terrible*, 209–10; McMurry, *Hood*, 127–28; Hood, *Advance and Retreat*, 166; Connelly, *Autumn of Glory*, 440; Hughes, *Hardee*, 219–20; *OR*, 38, pt. 3: 630.

15. McDonough and Jones, *War So Terrible*, 212–13, 215–16; McMurry, *Hood*, 128; Hood, *Advance and Retreat*, 167–68; Connelly, *Autumn of Glory*, 440–43; Hughes, *Hardee*, 220–22.

16. *OR*, 38, pt. 1: 290, 297, 306, 326, pt. 3: 698; McDonough and Jones, *War So Terrible*, 213–14; Connelly, *Autumn of Glory*, 443.

17. *OR*, 38, pt. 1: 298, 306, pt. 2: 328; "Journal of Campaign," July 20, 1864, Mercer Diary; Olmstead, "Memoirs," part 10, *GHQ* 45 (1961), 44; Nisbet, *Four Years*, 209–10; *New York Tribune*, July 28, 1864; Connelly, *Autumn of Glory*, 443.

18. Hamilton Branch to his mother, July 21, 1864, Branch Letters, University of Georgia.

19. *OR*, 38, pt. 1: 298, pt. 2: 328; Losson, *Forgotten Warriors*, 175–76; Buck, *Cleburne*, 268–69.

20. Steve Davis, "The Battles of Atlanta: Actions from July 10 to September 2,

1864," *Blue and Gray Magazine* 6 (August 1989): 17; McDonough and Jones, *War So Terrible*, 217–18; McMurry, *Hood*, 128–30; Hood, *Advance and Retreat*, 169–72; Connelly, *Autumn of Glory*, 443–44; Hughes, *Hardee*, 223–25.

21. *OR*, 38, pt. 3: 698, 756; Rolls of South Carolina Volunteers in the Confederate States Provisional Army ("Memory Rolls"), Vols. 2 and 3, Infantry, 16th and 24th South Carolina, South Carolina Department of Archives and History, Columbia. Only those clearly identified as Peach Tree Creek casualties have been counted. Dozens of others are included for "Atlanta" with no date or place of wound shown.

22. Nisbet, *Four Years*, 210; "Battlefield Letters to Mother and Sweetheart," *Atlanta Journal Magazine*, April 25, 1943, 8; Henderson, ed., *Roster of the Confederate Soldiers of Georgia*, 6:717; J. M. Hurst to Mary, undated, Hurst Family Letters, KMNP; J. W. Hagan to wife, July 21, 1864, *Confederate Letters*, 52; Warner, *Generals in Gray*, 291–92; newspaper clipping, "Walker's Division That Was (Correspondence of the *Savannah Republican*), Atlanta, July 25, 1864," Walker Papers; *Augusta Chronicle and Sentinel*, July 26, 1864, *Augusta Constitutionalist*, July 28, 1864. Warner, *Generals in Gray*, and others err in saying Stevens died in Atlanta. After he was wounded, he was taken to the home of Leroy Napier in Vineville, near Macon, where he expired.

23. William Napier to Mrs. Briggs H. Napier, July 25, 1864, Briggs H. Napier Letters, Civil War Miscellany-Personal Papers, GDAH; NA M258, Compiled Service Records of Confederate Soldiers Who Served in Organizations Raised Directly by the Confederate Government, Roll 58, Records of the 1st Georgia Confederate Regiment, George A. Smith Service Record, Certificate of George A. Smith, August 11, 1864; "Journal of Campaign," July 22, 1864, Mercer Diary.

24. Connelly, *Autumn of Glory*, 444–45; McDonough and Jones, *War So Terrible*, 219–20; Buck, *Cleburne*, 270–72.

25. McDonough and Jones, *War So Terrible*, 221–22; Connelly, *Autumn of Glory*, 444; McMurry, *Hood*, 130; Hood, *Advance and Retreat*, 175–76.

26. McDonough and Jones, *War So Terrible*, 222–23; Connelly, *Autumn of Glory*, 445–46; McMurry, *Hood*, 130–31; Hood, *Advance and Retreat*, 173–74, 176–77; Hughes, *Hardee*, 226.

27. Hughes, *Hardee*, 226–27; Cumming, *Memoirs*, 71; Losson, *Forgotten Warriors*, 177; *OR*, 38, pt. 3: 737, 750; Wilbur G. Kurtz, "Civil War Days in Georgia: The Death of Major General W. H. T. Walker," *Atlanta Constitution Magazine*, July 27, 1930, 6. A condensed version of Kurtz's article appeared in *Civil War History* 6 (June 1960): 174–79. Hood, *Advance and Retreat*, 177, 178.

28. Hood, *Advance and Retreat*, 181–82; Cumming, *Memoirs*, 71.

29. Kurtz, "Civil War Days," 16; Wilbur G. Kurtz Papers, Notebook 12, p. 160, Atlanta History Center, Atlanta, Ga.; McDonough and Jones, *War So Terrible*, 223–24; Connelly, *Autumn of Glory*, 445; Hughes, *Hardee*, 227.

30. Philip D. Stephenson, "War Memoirs," Louisiana and Lower Mississippi

Valley Collection, Louisiana State University Library, Baton Rouge. I am indebted to Nathaniel C. Hughes, Jr., who is editing Stephenson's memoir for publication, for bringing this exerpt to my attention.

31. Connelly, *Autumn of Glory*, 447, 448; McDonough and Jones, *War So Terrible*, 224–25; Losson, *Forgotten Warriors*, 178–79; Kurtz, "Civil War Days," 16; William B. Bate, Report of Operations (typescript), KMNP; Hughes, *Hardee*, 227; *OR*, 38, pt. 3: 737.

32. Cumming, *Memoirs*, 71–72; Jeffrey S. Mosser, "I Shall Make Him Remember This Insult," *Civil War Times Illustrated* 32 (1993): 24; Kurtz, "Civil War Days," 16; Hughes, *Hardee*, 229; McDonough and Jones, *War So Terrible*, 225.

33. Kurtz, "Civil War Days," 16; Mosser, "Insult," 24; Cumming, *Memoirs*, 72.

34. Kurtz, "Civil War Days," 16; *OR*, 38, pt. 3: 642, 652, 758–59; Cumming, *Memoirs*, 72; Crute, *Units of the Confederate States Army*, 70–71; NA M258, Roll 23, 10th Confederate Cavalry, J. F. Bass; Wilbur C. Kurtz to Joseph B. Cumming (Major Cumming's grandson), May 26, 1951, Box 24, Folder 3, Kurtz Papers.

35. Kurtz Papers, Notebook 10, p. 6; Samuel Carter III, *The Siege of Atlanta* (New York: St. Martin's Press, 1973), 234; "Valuable finds on view for you," *Atlanta Historical Society Newsletter*, January–February 1990, 3; author's interview with William Erquitt, Curator, Civil War Collection, Atlanta History Center, November 1990.

36. *OR*, 38, pt. 3: 631; Hood, *Advance and Retreat*, 179, 183; Hughes, *Hardee*, 230.

37. *OR*, 38, pt. 3: 369, 384, 407, 475; W. H. Chamberlin, "Hood's Second Sortie at Atlanta," *B&L*, 4: 326; Connelly, *Autumn of Glory*, 448; Hughes, *Hardee*, 228; Losson, *Forgotten Warriors*, 177.

38. *OR*, 38, pt. 3: 370, 738, 747; Buck, *Cleburne*, 280; Losson, *Forgotten Warriors*, 178–79; Bate, Report, KMNP.

39. *OR*, 38, pt. 3: 370, 407, 738, 747; McDonough and Jones, *War So Terrible*, 226–27; W. H. Chamberlin, "Recollections of the Battle of Atlanta," in *The Atlanta Papers*, comp. Sydney C. Kerksis (Dayton, Ohio: Press of the Morningside Bookshop, 1980), 457–60; Robert N. Adams, "The Battle and Capture of Atlanta," ibid., 473–80; William K. Strong, "The Death of General James B. McPherson," ibid., 518–20, 537–38.

40. *OR*, 38, pt. 3: 369–70, 407, 475; Chamberlin, "Second Sortie," 326.

41. "Battle of the Fairgrounds," *Savannah Daily Morning News*, August 15, 1864, reprinted in the *Augusta Chronicle and Sentinel*, August 17, 1864. In the author's opinion, the probable source for this detailed account of the battle on July 22 was Lieutenant Hamilton Branch. Branch was wounded at Atlanta on July 24 and was at home recuperating until late September. See Henderson, ed., *Roster of the Confederate Soldiers of Georgia*, 5:576, where the date is incorrectly given as June 24.

42. "Battle of the Fairgrounds;" NA M258, Roll 58, 1st Georgia Confederate Regiment, George A. Smith; *Macon Daily Telegraph*, July 28, 1864; Nisbet, *Four Years*, 212.

43. "Battle of the Fairgrounds;" Cisco, *Gist*, 128.

44. "Battle of the Fairgrounds;" Olmstead, "Memoirs," *GHQ* 45 (1961): 45; *OR*, 38, pt. 3: 758–59; "Journal of Campaign," July 22, 1864, Mercer Diary.

45. "Battle of the Fairgrounds;" Nisbet, *Four Years*, 212–15; *OR*, 38, pt. 3: 475–76, 502; Madaus and Needham, *Battle Flags*, 149. The other color lost was the flag of Ferguson's South Carolina battery on the retreat from Missionary Ridge in November 1863.

46. Connelly, *Autumn of Glory*, 449; McDonough and Jones, *War So Terrible*, 227–29, 231–36; Losson, *Forgotten Warriors*, 179–80.

47. "Battle of the Fairgrounds;" *OR*, 38, pt. 3: 754; Hamilton Branch to his mother, July 23, 1864, Branch Letters, University of Georgia.

48. *OR*, 38, pt. 1: 75, pt. 3: 21; Hood, *Advance and Retreat*, 181; McDonough and Jones, *War So Terrible*, 236. Logan's first estimate was made on July 24. By the time he wrote his final report in September, he had backed off to the point where he cited individual numbers of dead and captured that totaled fifty-five hundred. See *OR*, 38, pt. 3: 29.

49. *OR*, 38, pt. 3: 476.

50. Cisco, *Gist*, 128; newspaper clipping, "Walker's Division That Was," Walker Papers; Warner, *Generals in Gray*, 281–82.

51. *Augusta Chronicle and Sentinel*, May 3, 1868; J. H. Steinmeyer to Ellison Capers, March 18, 1880, Ellison Capers Papers, Duke University, Durham, N.C.

52. Nisbet, *Four Years*, 212, 216; Kurtz to Joseph B. Cumming, May 26, 1951 (not mailed), Box 24, Folder 3, Kurtz Papers.

53. *Augusta Constitutionalist*, July 24, 1864; *OR*, 38, pt. 3: 758–59.

54. Olmstead, "Memoirs," Part 10, *GHQ* 45 (1961): 44–45.

55. *OR*, 38, pt. 3: 760; Henderson, ed., *Roster of the Confederate Soldiers of Georgia*, 1:113, 5:917; "Journal of Campaign," July 22, 1864, Mercer Diary.

56. Kurtz, "Civil War Days," 16; *Augusta Chronicle and Sentinel*, July 24, 1864; Cumming, *Memoirs*, 71–72; J. H. Steinmeyer to Ellison Capers, March 18, 1880, Capers Papers, Duke University.

57. Cumming, *Memoirs*, 72; *OR*, 38, pt. 3: 713–18, 754, 758–59; Capers, *Soldier-Bishop*, 79–83; NA, M267, Compiled Service Records of Confederate Soldiers Who Served in Organizations from the State of South Carolina, Roll 337, 24th South Carolina, Ellison Capers Service Record.

58. Joseph B. Cumming, "Address of Joseph B. Cumming at the Unveiling of the Monument to Maj. Gen'l. William Henry Talbot Walker on the Battle Field of Atlanta, July 22, 1902," in *Occasional Addresses*, variously printed, 1873–1902, n.d., n.p.

59. "Battlefield Letters to Mother and Sweetheart," *Atlanta Journal Magazine*, April 25, 1943, 8; "Civil War Teamster Has Unique Record," *Atlanta Journal*, August 28, 1909, 4.

60. Castel, *Decision in the West*, 394 and note, 608; author's interview with

William Erquitt, November 15, 1990; "Memo of Information from J. W. McWilliams," Folder 11, Box 35, Kurtz Papers; Henderson, ed., *Roster of the Confederate Soldiers of Georgia*, 4: 545.

61. "Memo of Information from J. W. McWilliams," Folder 11, Box 35, Kurtz to Cumming, May 26, 1951, Paper Read by Wilbur B. Kurtz at the Atlanta Symposium, January 31, 1955, Folder 3, Box 24, Kurtz Papers.

62. WHTW to wife, March 27, 1847, June 23, 1856[?], July 12, 1861, to daughter, September 1863[?], to wife, December 1863[?], Walker Papers.

63. Chesnut, *Civil War*, 151–52; Eggleston, *Rebel's Recollections*, 137–39; Richard I. Manning to his father, July 4, 1863, to his mother, July 19, 1863, Williams-Chesnut-Manning Family Papers, South Caroliniana Library, University of South Carolina, Columbia; W. W. Mackall to wife, July 4, 1864, Mackall Papers, Southern Historical Collection, University of North Carolina.

64. Bate, Report, KMNP.

65. *OR*, 38, pt. 1: 75; Sherman, *Memoirs*, 2:92–93; Hughes, *Hardee*, 230; Connelly, *Autumn of Glory*, 450; Losson, *Forgotten Warriors*, 182; Hood, *Advance and Retreat*, 221.

66. RG 109, War Department Collection of Confederate Records, Chapter VI, Vol. 748, Letters, Orders and Circulars Sent and Received, Medical Director's Office, Army of Tennessee, 1862–65, 196–97, NA; *OR*, 38, pt. 1: 159.

67. T. B. Roy, "General Hardee and the Military Operations Around Atlanta," *SHSP* 8 (1880): 367; *OR*, 38, pt. 3: 21.

68. *OR*, 38, pt. 3: 408, 419, 451, 477, 733, 741, 748; Losson, *Forgotten Warriors*, 183; Ed Porter Thompson, *History of the Orphan Brigade* (Louisville, Ky.: Lewis N. Thompson, 1898), 263.

69. RG 109, Chapter VI, Vol. 748: 196–97, NA; *OR*, 38, pt. 3: 756; Letter of William A. O'Neal, Civil War Miscellany-Personal Papers, GDAH; "Battlefield Letters to Mother and Sweetheart," *Atlanta Journal Magazine*, April 25, 1943, 8.

70. Henderson, ed., *Roster of the Confederate Soldiers of Georgia*, 1:1–113, 3:89–183, 427–575, 4:924–1026, 6:571–771; "Memory Rolls," South Carolina Department of Archives and History. Besides those identified at Peach Tree Creek or Decatur, the memory rolls list another forty-three killed and thirty-nine wounded at Atlanta.

71. *OR*, 38, pt. 3: 756; Henderson, ed., *Roster of the Confederate Soldiers of Georgia*, 1:113–213, 5:620–731, 917–1023, 6:369–487.

72. Hood, *Advance and Retreat*, 221. Steve Davis similarly estimates Confederate losses to be in excess of five thousand, not the eight thousand Sherman claimed ("Battles of Atlanta," 25).

73. *New York Tribune*, July 26, 31, 1864. The *Cincinnati Commercial* article was reprinted in the *Tribune* on July 31.

74. Losson, *Forgotten Warriors*, 183; Buck, *Cleburne*, 286; *OR*, 38, pt. 3: 732, 739, 740, 747, 748. Wilkinson Drive in East Atlanta, the site of Walker's monument, was named for Colonel Wilkinson.

75. *OR*, 38, pt. 3: 661–62, 759; Henderson, ed., *Roster of the Confederate Soldiers of Georgia*, 3:497, 5:620; *Macon Daily Telegraph*, July 28, 1864; NA M266, Compiled Service Records of Confederate Soldiers Who Served in Organizations from the State of Georgia, Roll 236, 8th Georgia Battalion, Edward F. Morgan Service Record, Roll 368, 25th Georgia, William J. Winn Service Record, Roll 397, 30th Georgia, James S. Boynton Service Record, Roll 478, 46th Georgia, Samuel J. C. Dunlap Service Record, Roll 527, 54th Georgia, William H. Mann and Morgan Rawls Service Records; "Journal of Campaign," July 22, 1864, Mercer Diary; Cisco, *Gist*, 128; Hughes, *Hardee*, 231.

76. John W. Hagan to his wife, July 28, 1864, *Confederate Letters*, 53; J. J. McKinney to Mrs. McKittrick, July 25, 1864, "Report of Deaths in Company I, 16th South Carolina," July 23, 1864, McKittrick Letters, KMNP. McKinney told Mrs. McKittrick that her husband was shot in the lungs but the official report gave cause of death as "wound in the groin."

77. *OR*, 38, pt. 3: 631, 699; Hood, *Advance and Retreat*, 183; Hughes, *Hardee*, 231–32; Cox, *Atlanta*, 176; Roy, "Military Operations Around Atlanta," 337–87.

78. Davis, "Battles of Atlanta," 25; Connelly, *Autumn of Glory*, 449; McMurry, *Hood*, 132; McDonough and Jones, *War So Terrible*, 237.

79. Cumming, *Memoirs*, 71; *OR*, 38, pt. 3: 732.

CHAPTER 16. POSTLUDE

1. *Augusta Chronicle and Sentinel*, July 24, 1864; Wood, ed., *Northern Daughter*, 20. Katherine Cumming said her husband accompanied the general's body, but in his eulogy in 1902, Joseph B. Cumming said that after he left Walker to deliver an order, he never saw him again "in life or in death." See *Augusta Chronicle*, April 27, 1948, obituary of W. H. T. Walker, Jr.; W. H. T. Walker Biographical Sketch, GDAH; *Augusta Constitutionalist*, July 28, 1864.

2. *Augusta Chronicle and Sentinel* and *Augusta Constitutionalist*, July 26, 1864.

3. *Augusta Chronicle and Sentinel*, July 28, 1864.

4. Lydia M. Johnston to Mary T. Walker, July 29, 1864, Walker Papers.

5. Typescript journal, 143, Samuel Wragg Ferguson Papers, Duke University, Durham, N.C.; Hood, *Advance and Retreat*, 182; E. Porter Alexander, *Fighting for the Confederacy*, ed. Gary W. Gallagher (Chapel Hill: University of North Carolina Press, 1989), 494.

6. *OR*, 38, pt. 5:907, 39, pt. 2:855, 45, pt. 1:667, 739, 52, pt. 2:713; "Journal of Campaign," July 25, 26, 1864, Mercer Diary; Connelly, *Autumn of Glory*, 451; Olmstead, "Memoirs," pt. 10, 46.

7. Connelly, *Autumn of Glory*, 452–534, passim; James L. McDonough and Thomas L. Connelly, *Five Tragic Hours: The Battle of Franklin* (Knoxville: University of Tennessee Press, 1983), 127–29, 161–66; Cisco, *Gist*, 140–45; Joseph B.

Cumming, "How I Knew That the War Was Over," *Confederate Veteran* 9 (1901): 18; Cumming, *Memoirs*, 85–86; *OR*, 47, pt. 1:1065, 1088.

8. Meadows, *Walker Genealogy*, 181; *Augusta Chronicle and Sentinel*, September 24, 1864; RCPC Account Book 2C (1871–72), 402–3; Hollingsworth, *Screven County History*, 40; Screven County Superior Court, Deed Book T (12P), 551–52; RCSC Deed Book 3C, 282; *Augusta Chronicle*, January 28, 1871.

9. Mary "Molly" Walker from various locations in New York to "Charlie" [C. C. Schley] in Savannah, fifteen letters, July to October 1865, Frederick Townsend to Molly, November 15, 1865, Walker Papers; R. A. Brock, ed., *The Appomattox Roster* (1887; reprint, New York: Antiquarian Press, 1962), 212; Meadows, *Walker Genealogy*, 197; Records of Laurel Grove Cemetery (typescript), Georgia Historical Society, Savannah; *Savannah Morning News*, January 19, 20, 1910. The date of Molly's marriage to Schley was January 6, 1866; Meadows gives the date incorrectly as 1892.

10. Mary T. Walker to Molly Walker, October 13, 21, November 23, December 2, 1868, Walker Papers; *Albany Argus*, December 28, 1868; *Augusta Chronicle*, December 29, 1868; Louise Dumont, "Walker Cemetery Tombstone Inscriptions," 25 (bound typescript), Richmond County Historical Society.

11. Copy of Mary Walker's will, Walker Papers; Albany County, N.Y. Surrogate Court, Will Book 21, 327. Both files contain some of the letters of administration of Franklin and Frederick Townsend.

12. Correspondence between Willie Walker, Jr., in Cornwall, N.Y., and his sister in Savannah from 1869 to 1871 is in the Walker Papers. His pleas to be returned to the family were in letters dated January 20 and 28, 1869; his dismissal from school was reported on April 7, 1871 (Meadows, *Walker Genealogy*, 192–93; interviews with Karen Allmond, 1990–91).

13. RCPC, Will Book E, 65–66; Allmond interviews; Meadows, *Walker Genealogy*, 192–93; *Augusta Chronicle*, April 24, 1948; interviews with Ella Nuite and Kenneth Kitchens, December 1989; Works Progress Administration, American Guide Series, *Augusta* (Augusta: Tidwell Printing Supply Co., 1938), 163–64.

14. Meadows, *Walker Genealogy*, 193, 197; Clark, *Lost Arcadia*, 76–77; Register of the Albany Rural Cemetery; Sidney Herbert, *A Complete Roster of the Volunteer Organizations of the State of Georgia* (Atlanta: James P. Harrison, 1878), n.p.; Heitman, *Biographical Register*, 1:995; *Savannah Morning News*, January 22, 1933; Dumont, "Walker Cemetery Inscriptions," 23–24.

15. For the lives of Mary Townsend's siblings, see the sources listed in Chapter 3; *New York Times*, November 15, 1866; Reynolds, *Genealogical and Family History of Southern New York and the Hudson River Valley*, 1007–8.

16. Warner, *Generals in Gray*, 151, 150, 43, 9, 330, 217, 143, 162, 31; Bragg, *Joe Brown's Army*, 117–18; *Augusta Chronicle*, May 15, 1922.

17. Ruby M. M. Pfadenhauer, "History of Augusta Arsenal," *Richmond County History* 2 (Summer 1970): 7; Meadows, *Walker Genealogy*, 167.

18. Cashin, *Story of Augusta*, 146–47.

19. "Honor to Gen. W. H. T. Walker," *Confederate Veteran* 10 (1902): 402–7. The removal of the monument from its original to its present location was noted in the *Augusta Herald*, May 21, 1937.

20. A photograph of Walker's statue on the Confederate monument in Augusta appears in Thomas B. Allen, *The Blue and the Gray* (Washington, D.C.: National Geographic Society, 1992), 5.

CHAPTER 17. THE SOLDIER AND THE MAN

1. WHTW to wife, April 30, 1847, Walker Papers (quotation).

2. Daughters of the American Revolution, *Historical Collections of the Joseph Habersham Chapter*, 2 vols. (Atlanta: Blosser, 1902), 2:229.

3. *Kennesaw Gazette*, September 15, 1889.

4. *Augusta Chronicle and Sentinel*, May 3, 1868; [Edgefield, S.C.?] *Advertiser* clipping, March 19, 1864, Walker Papers; Sykes, *Walthall's Brigade*, 597–98; Maria Cumming Lamar to her mother, February 18, 1864, Cumming Family Papers, Richmond County Historical Society.

5. WHTW to wife, July 12, 1861, and undated [February 28, 1864?], Walker Papers.

6. Isaac Hermann, *Memoirs of a Confederate Veteran, 1861–1865* (Lakemont, Ga.: CSA Printing and Binding, 1974), 121–26.

7. Clark, *Under the Stars and Bars*, 108–9.

8. Taylor, *Destruction and Reconstruction*, 23; Hood, *Advance and Retreat*, 182; Sykes, *Walthall's Brigade*, 598.

9. Cumming, *Memoirs*, 56; *Kennesaw Gazette*, September 15, 1889.

10. Sam R. Watkins, *"Co. Aytch," Maury Grays, First Tennessee Regiment* (1882; reprint, New York: Collier Books, 1962), 123; Hermann, *Memoirs*, 100–101.

11. *Kennesaw Gazette*, September 15, 1889; Liddell, *Liddell's Record*, 168.

12. McMurry, *Hood*, 123. Biographies of Richard Taylor and J. Johnston Pettigrew are T. Michael Parrish, *Richard Taylor, Soldier Prince of Dixie* (Chapel Hill: University of North Carolina Press, 1992), and Clyde N. Wilson, *Carolina Cavalier: The Life and Mind of James Johnston Pettigrew* (Athens: University of Georgia Press, 1990).

13. McDonough and Jones, *War So Terrible*, 242–43; *OR*, 38, pt. 5: 266, 273, 307, 522–23.

14. James Compton, "The Second Division of the 16th Army Corps in the Atlanta Campaign," in *Atlanta Papers*, ed. Kerksis, 256; McDonough and Jones, *War So Terrible*, 246–47; *OR*, 38, pt. 5: 252–53.

15. Warner, *Generals in Blue*, 115–16, 343–44.

16. Brown, "Old Woman with a Broomstick," 57–61; Russell K. Brown, "David Emanuel Twiggs," *Richmond County History* 15 (Summer 1983): 13–16.

17. Coffman, *Old Army*, 66–67; McWhiney, *Bragg*, 26–51; Grant, *Memoirs*, 343.

18. WHTW to wife, [December 12, 1846?], Walker Papers.

19. WHTW to wife, December 16, 1863, Walker Papers; WHTW to Jefferson Davis, July 30, 1855, Davis Papers, Transylvania University; WHTW to Henry C. Wayne, January 8, [1861], Adjutant General's Incoming Correspondence, RG 22, GDAH.

20. SO 282, October 31, 1863, Oversize Vol. 3, 487, Bragg Papers, Western Reserve; Clark, *Under the Stars and Bars*, 135; WHTW to wife, July 8, 1864, Walker Papers. Regail Reab survived his captivity to marry the daughter of Octavia LeVert (Meadows, *Walker Genealogy*, 192, 197).

21. WHTW to wife, July 16, 1864, Walker Papers.

22. WHTW to wife, undated [June 23, 1856?], September 27, 1852, ibid.

23. WHTW to wife, February 24, 1864, ibid.

24. Clark, *Lost Arcadia*, 71.

25. WHTW to wife, February 24, 1864, Walker Papers.

26. Taylor, *Destruction and Reconstruction*, 22; Sykes, *Walthall's Brigade*, 598; WHTW to wife, September 4, 1861, Walker Papers.

27. *Augusta Constitutionalist*, August 25, 1864.

28. Cumming, "Address."

BIBLIOGRAPHY

MANUSCRIPTS

Official Records in the National Archives

Records of the Veterans Administration (Record Group 15)
    Unindexed Bounty Land Claims
Records of the Bureau of Land Management (Record Group 49)
    Abstracts of Bounty Land Warrants
Records of the Office of the Chief of Engineers (Record Group 77)
    Letters Received
Records of the Adjutant General's Office, 1780s–1917 (Record Group 94)
    General Orders, Special Orders, and Circulars
    Letters Received, Main Series
    Letters Sent, Main Series
    Letters Sent, Recruiting Service
    Muster Rolls
    Orders and Special Orders by Generals Butler and Worth to the Army in Mexico
    Records of the Army in Florida, Letters Sent
    Register of Recruits
Records of the Office of the Secretary of War (Record Group 107)
    Letters Received
    Letters Sent
Records of the Headquarters of the Army (Record Group 108)
    General Orders and Special Orders
    Letters Received
    Letters Sent

War Department Collection of Confederate Records (Record Group 109)
  Register of Letters Received by the Adjutant and Inspector General, Chapter 1, Vols. 45, 46, 54
  Register of Appointment of Officers, Chapter 1, Vol. 86
  Letters, Orders, and Circulars Sent and Received, Medical Director's Office, Army of Tennessee, Chapter 6, Vol. 748
  Virginia Forces, Letters Received
Records of the Office of the Judge Advocate General (Army) (Record Group 153)
  Records of the Proceedings of General Courts-Martial, 1809–90
Records of the Soldiers Home (Record Group 231)
  Administrative Memoranda
  Correspondence, Reports, and Orders Relating to Regulations
  Records Relating to East Pascagoula, Mississippi
Records of the U.S. Army Continental Commands, 1821–1920 (Record Group 393)
  Western Department and Division, Letters Received and Sent

Microfilm Records from the National Archives

Microfilm Publication M6, Letters Sent by the Secretary of War Relating to Military Affairs, 1800–1889
Microfilm Publication M22, Register of Letters Received by the Office of the Secretary of War, Main Series, 1800–1870
Microfilm Publication M127, Letters Sent to the President by the Secretary of War, 1800–1863
Microfilm Publication M221, Letters Received by the Secretary of War, Registered Series, 1800–1870
Microfilm Publication M253, Consolidated Index to Compiled Service Records of Confederate Soldiers
Microfilm Publication M258, Compiled Service Records of Confederate Soldiers Who Served in Organizations Raised Directly by the Confederate Government
Microfilm Publication M266, Compiled Service Records of Confederate Soldiers Who Served in Organizations from the State of Georgia
Microfilm Publication M267, Compiled Service Records of Confederate Soldiers Who Served in Organizations from the State of South Carolina
Microfilm Publication M331, Compiled Service Records of Confederate General and Staff Officers, and Non-Regimental Enlisted Men
Microfilm Publication M409, Index to Letters Received by the Confederate Secretary of War, 1861–65
Microfilm Publication M410, Index to Letters Received by the Confederate Adjutant and Inspector General and by the Confederate Quartermaster General, 1861–65
Microfilm Publication M432, Seventh Census of the United States, 1850
  Roll 471, Albany City, New York
  Roll 852, Edgefield County, South Carolina

Microfilm Publication M437, Letters Received by the Confederate Secretary of War, 1861–65

Microfilm Publication M444, Orders and Endorsements Sent by the Secretary of War, 1846–70

Microfilm Publication M469, Letters Received by the Confederate Quartermaster General, 1861–65

Microfilm Publication M474, Letters Received by the Confederate Adjutant and Inspector General, 1861–65

Microfilm Publication M522, Letters Sent by the Confederate Secretary of War, 1861–65

Microfilm Publication M524, Telegrams Sent by the Confederate Secretary of War, 1861–65

Microfilm Publication M565, Letters Sent by Office of the Adjutant General, Main Series, 1800–1890

Microfilm Publication M567, Letters Received by the Adjutant General of the Army, Main Series, 1822–60

Microfilm Publication M617, Returns from United States Military Posts, 1800–1916

    Roll 56, Augusta Arsenal, 1860–84

    Roll 404, Fort Gibson, 1824–44

    Roll 1287, Fort Towson, 1841–54

    Roll 1412, West Point, 1829–38

    Roll 1414, West Point, 1853–65

Microfilm Publication M618, Telegrams Received by the Confederate Secretary of War, 1861–65

Microfilm Publication M627, Letters and Telegrams Sent by the Confederate Adjutant and Inspector General, 1861–65

Microfilm Publication M653, Eighth Census of the United States, 1860

    Roll 135, Richmond County, Georgia

    Roll 151, Screven County, Georgia, Slave Schedules

    Roll 586, Madison County, Mississippi

Microfilm Publication M665, Returns from Regular Army Infantry Regiments, 1821–1916

    Rolls 65–68, 6th Infantry, 1837–55

    Roll 113, 10th Infantry, 1855–1862

Microfilm Publication M688, U.S. Military Academy Cadet Application Papers, 1805–66

    File 1831/96, Application of W. H. T. Walker

Microfilm Publication M711, Register of Letters Received by Office of the Adjutant General, 1812–89

Microfilm Publication M857, Letters Sent by the Headquarters of the Army, Main Series, 1828–1903

Microfilm Publication M1089, Letters Sent by the Superintendent of the U.S. Military Academy, 1838–1902

Microfilm Publication M1094, General Orders, Special Orders, and Circulars Issued by the Adjutant General of the Army, 1809–60

Microfilm Publication M1105, Registers of the Records of the Proceedings of the U.S. Army General Courts-Martial, 1809–90

Microfilm Publication M1635, Letters Received by the Headquarters of the Army, 1828–1903

Official Records in the U.S. Military Academy Archives

Proceedings of the Academic Board (Staff Records) (Record Group 14), Vols. 1 and 2

Orders, Corps of Cadets (Record Group 88), Vol. 2

Bimonthly and Semi-Annual Muster Rolls (Record Group 96), Vol. 4

Letters Received from the Commandant of Cadets, 1845–66 (Record Group 140)

Register of Letters Received [from the Commandant of Cadets], 1853–61 (Record Group 143)

Letters Received [from the Commandant of Cadets], 1853–61 (Record Group 144)

Post Orders, 1828–1904 (Record Group 167), Vol. 6

State Archives Collections

Alabama Department of Archives and History, Montgomery
William J. Hardee Papers

Georgia Department of Archives and History, Atlanta
Adjutant General's Office Commission Book, B49
Adjutant General's Office Letter Book, B44
Adjutant General's Secretaries' Letter Books
Governor Joseph E. Brown's Letter Books (Record Group 1)
Civil War Index
Civil War Miscellany—Personal Papers
Adams Family Papers
J. H. Booker Reminiscences
Dickey Family Letters
Blanton B. Fortson Letters
William J. M. Gardner Reminiscences
John L. Keen Reminiscences
Briggs H. Napier Letters
William A. O'Neal Letters
W. H. T. Walker Biographical Sketch
Civil War Miscellany—Unit File
Incoming Correspondence to Governor Joseph E. Brown (Record Group 1)

Incoming Correspondence to the Adjutant General, Henry C. Wayne (Record Group 22)

Henry R. Jackson Letter Book, Letters Received

Henry R. Jackson Order Book, B47, General Orders

Outgoing Correspondence from Adjutant General Henry C. Wayne, 1860–62 (Record Group 22)

United Daughters of the Confederacy Collection

Letters from Confederate Soldiers

George A. B. Walker Diary (microfilm)

Mississippi Department of Archives and History, Jackson

Register of Commissions, 1887–91 and 1891–95

South Carolina Department of Archives and History, Columbia

Edgefield County Probate Records (microfilm). Wills of Wyatt W. Starke and Sarah Davies Starke

Rolls of South Carolina Volunteers in the Confederate States Provisional Army ("Memory Rolls")

South Carolina State Board of Health, Columbia

Death Certificate of Freeman Valentine Walker

Tennessee State Library and Archives, Nashville

Benjamin F. Cheatham Papers

Civil War Collection

J. F. Wheless Reminiscences

Local Government Records Collections

Albany County, New York

Surrogate Court Letters of Administration Books

Surrogate Court Will Books

Augusta, Georgia

Minutes of City Council, 1850

Chatham County, Georgia

Probate Court Will Books

Superior Court Deed Books

Richmond County, Georgia

Court of Ordinary Minute Books

Probate Court Accounts Books

Probate Court Letters of Administration Books

Probate Court Marriage Books

Probate Court Will Books

Superior Court Deed Books

Superior Court Minute Books

Screven County, Georgia

Superior Court Deed Books

Personal Papers and Manuscript Collections

Albany Institute of History and Art, Albany, N.Y.
    Franklin Townsend Family Papers
    Frederick Townsend Papers
    Howard Townsend Collection
    Isaiah Townsend Papers
Albany Rural Cemetery, Albany, N.Y.
    Register
Karen Allmond
    Walker Family books, papers, and photographs
Atlanta History Center, Atlanta, Ga.
    Wilbur G. Kurtz Papers
    W. H. T. Walker Personality File
Library of Congress, Washington, D.C.
    P. G. T. Beauregard Papers
Duke University, Durham, N.C.
    Ellison Capers Papers
    Samuel Wragg Ferguson Papers
    Thomas H. Kenan Papers
    W. H. T. Walker Papers
    Henry C. Wayne Papers
Emory University, Atlanta, Ga.
    Confederate Miscellany Collection
        W. H. T. Walker Letter
    Charles L. Thiot Letters (microfilm)
First Presbyterian Church of Albany, N.Y.
    Church Register
Georgia Historical Society, Savannah, Ga.
    Confederate States Army Papers
        W. H. T. Walker–A. P. Stewart Correspondence
    Mercer Family Papers
        Correspondence
        George A. Mercer Diary (typescript)
    Register of Chatham County Marriages (typescript)
    Register of Laurel Grove Cemetery (typescript)
Harvard University, Houghton Library, Cambridge, Mass.
    W. H. T. Walker Letters
Historical Society of Pennsylvania, Philadelphia
    Gratz and Dreer Autograph Collections
        W. H. T. Walker Letters

Henry E. Huntington Library and Art Gallery, San Marino, Calif.
  Civil War Collection
    W. H. T. Walker Correspondence
Kennesaw Mountain National Battlefield Park, Kennesaw, Ga.
  William B. Bate Report (typescript)
  Diary of the Quartermaster Officer of the 65th Georgia Regiment [Captain James J. Goodrum?] (typescript)
  C. Helms Letter (typescript)
  Hurst Family Letters (typescript)
  Samuel McKittrick Letters (typescript)
  J. K. P. Martin Letters (typescript)
  William O. Norrell Diary (typescript)
  Robert Davis Smith Diary (typescript)
  J. H. Steinmeyer Diary (typescript)
Louisiana State University Library, Baton Rouge, La.
  Louisiana and Lower Mississippi Valley Collection
    Philip D. Stephenson, "War Memoirs"
Colonel Lawson W. Magruder, Jr.
  Magruder Family Papers
Richmond County Historical Society, Augusta, Ga.
  Cumming Family Papers
  Dumont, Louise. "Walker Cemetery Tombstone Inscriptions" (bound typescript)
  Gardner, William Montgomery. "The Memoirs of William Montgomery Gardner" (typescript). Edited by Elizabeth McKinne Gardner.
  Reese, Morton L. "Cemetery Records, Mostly from Richmond County, Georgia." 3-vol. bound typescript.
Adele Shearer
  Walker Family Papers
Transylvania University, Lexington, Ky.
  Jefferson Davis Papers
U.S. Military Academy Library, West Point, N.Y.
  George William Cushing Papers
  W. H. T. Walker's Cullum File
University of Georgia, Hargrett Rare Book and Manuscript Library, Athens
  Hamilton Branch Letters
  Joseph E. Brown Papers
  T. R. R. Cobb Papers (typescript)
  John M. Davis Letters in the Malcolm Letters
  Georgia Adjutant General Papers in the Telamon Cuyler Collection
  W. H. T. Walker Letter

University of North Carolina, Southern Historical Collection, Chapel Hill
    Daniel C. Govan Papers
        St. John R. Liddell, "Record of the Civil War" (microfilm)
        William W. Mackall Papers (microfilm)
University of South Carolina, South Caroliniana Library, Columbia
    Williams-Chesnut-Manning Family Papers
Hugh McLean Walker, Jr.
    W. H. T. Walker books, papers, and photographs
Western Reserve Historical Society, Cleveland, Ohio
    William P. Palmer Collection of Braxton Bragg Papers (microfilm)
    William P. Palmer Civil War Collection W. H. T. Walker Letters
College of William and Mary, Williamsburg, Va.
    Joseph E. Johnston Papers (microfilm)
Laurie Wolfe
    Walker Family Papers

PRINTED DOCUMENTS

Ainsworth, Fred C. *Memorandum Relative to General Officers Appointed by the Presi-dent in the Armies of the Confederate States.* Washington, D.C.: U.S. Military Secretary's Office, 1905.
Candler, Allen D., ed. *Confederate Records of the State of Georgia.* 6 vols. Atlanta: State Printer, 1909–11.
Georgia General Assembly. *Acts of the General Assembly of the State of Georgia, 1853–1854.*
Georgia House of Representatives. *House Journal, 1847.*
Lowrie, Walter, and Matthew Clarke, eds. *American State Papers, Military Affairs.* 7 vols. Washington, D.C.: Gales and Seaton, 1828–61.
U.S. Congress. House. *Correspondence, Secretary of War and Commanding Officer in Florida.* 27th Cong., 2d sess. House Executive Document 262. Serial 405.
———. *Message from the President at the Commencement of the First Session of the Thirtieth Congress.* 30th Cong., 1st sess. House Executive Document 8. Serial 515.
———. *Mexican War Correspondence.* 30th Cong., 1st sess. House Executive Document 60. Serial 520.
U.S. Congress. Senate. *Official Report of Action of 25th December 1837 with the Seminole Indians.* 25th Cong., 2d sess. Senate Document 227. Serial 316.
———. *Message from the President at the Commencement of the First Session, Thirtieth Congress.* 30th Cong., 1st sess. Senate Executive Document 1. Serial 503.
U.S. Military Academy. *Regulations for the U.S. Military Academy at West Point, New York.* New York: John F. Trow, 1853.
U.S. Navy Department. *Official Records of the Union and Confederate Navies in the War*

of the Rebellion. 30 vols. Washington, D.C.: U.S. Government Printing Office, 1896–1922.

U.S. War Department. *The War of the Rebellion: A Compilation of the Official Records of the Union and Confederate Armies.* 128 vols. Washington, D.C.: U.S. Government Printing Office, 1880–1901.

PERIODICALS AND NEWSPAPERS

Ancestoring [Magazine of the Augusta Genealogical Society]
Atlanta Intelligencer
Augusta Chronicle and Sentinel
Augusta Constitutionalist
Augusta Herald
Charleston Mercury
Charleston Daily Courier
Charleston Tri-Weekly Mercury
Daily Albany Argus
Edgefield (S.C.) *Weekly Advertiser*
Kennesaw Gazette
New Orleans Delta
New Orleans Picayune
New York Times
New York Tribune
Savannah Daily Morning News

ACCOUNTS OF PARTICIPANTS

Adams, Robert N. "The Battle and Capture of Atlanta." In *The Atlanta Papers.* Compiled by Sydney C. Kerksis. Dayton, Ohio: Press of the Morningside Bookshop, 1980. 465–86.

Adamson, Augustus P. *A Brief History of the Thirtieth Georgia Regiment.* Griffin, Ga.: Mills Printing Co., 1912.

Alexander, E. Porter. *Fighting for the Confederacy.* Edited by Gary W. Gallagher. Chapel Hill: University of North Carolina Press, 1989.

Anderson, Archer. "Address of Colonel Archer Anderson on the Campaign and Battle of Chickamauga." *Southern Historical Society Papers* 9 (1981): 385–418.

Ballentine, George. *Autobiography of an English Soldier in the United States Army.* New York: Stringer and Townsend, 1853.

"Battlefield Letters to Mother and Sweetheart." *Atlanta Journal Magazine,* April 25, 1943, p. 8.

Beauregard, G. T. "The Defense of Charleston." In *Battles and Leaders of the Civil War.* Edited by Robert V. Johnson and Clarence C. Buel. 4 vols. 1887–88. Reprint. New York: Thomas Yoseloff, 1956. 4:1–23.

Blackwood, Emma Jerome, ed. *To Mexico with Scott: Letters of Captain E. Kirby Smith to His Wife.* Cambridge, Mass.: Harvard University Press, 1917.

Boggs, William R. *Military Reminiscences of General William R. Boggs, C. S. A.* Durham, N.C.: Seeman Printery, 1913.

Breckinridge, W. C. P. "The Opening of the Atlanta Campaign." In *Battles and Leaders of the Civil War.* Edited by Robert U. Johnson and Clarence C. Buel. 4 vols. 1887–88. Reprint. New York: Thomas Yoseloff, 1956. 4:277–81.

Bremer, Fredrika. *The Homes of the New World.* New York: Harper and Brothers, 1853.

Buck, Irving A. *Cleburne and His Command.* New York: Neale, 1908.

Calhoun, W. L. *History of the 42nd Regiment Georgia Volunteers (Infantry), Confederate States of America.* Atlanta: Sisson, 1900.

Chamberlin, W. H. "Hood's Second Sortie at Atlanta." In *Battles and Leaders of the Civil War.* Edited by Robert U. Johnson and Clarence C. Buel. 4 vols. 1887–88. Reprint. New York: Thomas Yoseloff, 1956. 4:326–31.

———. "Recollections of the Battle of Atlanta." In *The Atlanta Papers.* Compiled by Sydney C. Kerksis. Dayton, Ohio: Press of the Morningside Bookshop, 1980. 451–63.

Chesnut, Mary Boykin. *Mary Chesnut's Civil War.* Edited by C. Vann Woodward. New Haven: Yale University Press, 1981.

Clark, Walter A. *A Lost Arcadia, or The Story of My Old Community.* Augusta: Chronicle Job Printer, 1909.

———. *Under the Stars and Bars, or Memories of Four Years Service with the Oglethorpes of Augusta, Georgia.* Augusta: Chronicle Printing Co., 1900.

Compton, James. "The Second Division of the 16th Army Corps in the Atlanta Campaign." In *The Atlanta Papers,* compiled by Sydney C. Kerksis. Dayton, Ohio: Press of the Morningside Bookshop, 1980. 235–57.

Cox, Jacob D. *Atlanta.* 1882. Reprint. Dayton Ohio: Morningside House, 1987.

Crist, Lynda L., and Mary S. Dix, eds. *The Papers of Jefferson Davis.* Vol. 5: 1853–1855; Vol. 6: 1856–1860. Baton Rouge: Louisiana State University Press, 1985 and 1989.

Cumming, Joseph B. "Address of Joseph B. Cumming at the Unveiling of the Monument to Maj. Gen'l. William Henry Talbot Walker on the Battle Field of Atlanta, July 22, 1902." *Occasional Addresses.* Variously published 1873–1902, n.p., n.d.

———. "How I Knew That the War Was Over." *Confederate Veteran* 9 (1901):18.

———. *A Sketch of the Descendants of David Cumming and Memoirs of the War Between the States.* Edited by Mary Gairdner Smith Cumming. Augusta, Ga.: Privately printed, 1925.

Dawes, E. C. "The Confederate Strength in the Atlanta Campaign." In *Battles and Leaders of the Civil War*. Edited by Robert U. Johnson and Clarence C. Buel. 4 vols. 1887–88. Reprint. New York: Thomas Yoseloff, 1956. 4:281–83.

Eggleston, George Cary. *A Rebel's Recollections*. 1875. Reprint. Bloomington: Indiana University Press, 1959.

Fremantle, Arthur J. L. *The Fremantle Diary*. Edited by Walter Lord. Boston: Little, Brown, 1954.

French, Samuel G. *Two Wars*. Nashville: Confederate Publishing Co., 1901.

Fullerton, Joseph S. "The Army of the Cumberland at Chattanooga." In *Battles and Leaders of the Civil War*. Edited by Robert U. Johnson and Clarence C. Buel. 4 vols. 1887–88. Reprint. New York: Thomas Yoseloff, 1956. 3:719–26.

Gillmore, Quincy A. "Siege and Capture of Fort Pulaski." In *Battles and Leaders of the Civil War*. Edited by Robert U. Johnson and Clarence C. Buel. 4 vols. 1887–88. Reprint. New York: Thomas Yoseloff, 1956. 2:1–12.

Gilman, J. H. "With Slemmer in Pensacola Harbor." In *Battles and Leaders of the Civil War*. Edited by Robert U. Johnson and Clarence C. Buel. 4 vols. 1887–88. Reprint. New York: Thomas Yoseloff, 1956. 1:26–32.

Gordon, George W. "The Famous Snowball Battle in the Confederate Army at Dalton, Ga., 1864." In Ben LaBree, ed., *Camp Fires of the Confederacy*. Louisville: Courier-Journal Job Printing Co., 1898.

Grant, Ulysses S. *Personal Memoirs of U. S. Grant*. 1885. Reprint in 1 vol. New York: DaCapo Press, 1982.

Hagan, John W. *Confederate Letters of John W. Hagan*. Edited by Bell I. Wiley. Athens: University of Georgia Press, 1954.

Handerson, Henry E. *Yankee in Gray: The Civil War Memoirs of Henry E. Handerson, with a Selection of His Wartime Letters*. Introduction by Clyde L. Cummer. Cleveland: Press of Western Reserve University, 1962.

Hermann, Isaac. *Memoirs of a Confederate Veteran, 1861–1865*. Lakemont, Ga.: CSA Printing and Binding, 1974.

Hill, Daniel H. "Chickamauga—The Great Battle of the West." In *Battles and Leaders of the Civil War*. Edited by Robert U. Johnson and Clarence C. Buel. 4 vols. 1887–88. Reprint. New York: Thomas Yoseloff, 1956. 3:638–62.

"Honor to Gen. W. H. T. Walker." *Confederate Veteran* 10 (1902): 402–7.

Hood, John Bell. *Advance and Retreat*. 1880. Edited by Richard N. Current. Bloomington: Indiana University Press, 1959.

Howard, Oliver O. "The Struggle for Atlanta." In *Battles and Leaders of the Civil War*. Edited by Robert U. Johnson and Clarence C. Buel. 4 vols. 1887–88. Reprint. New York: Thomas Yoseloff, 1956. 4:293–325.

Johnston, Joseph E. *Narrative of Military Operations Directed During the Late War Between the States*. 1874. Reprint. Bloomington: Indiana University Press, 1959.

Jones, J. B. *A Rebel War Clerk's Diary*. 2 vols. Philadelphia: J. B. Lippincott, 1866.

Jones, Joseph. "Roster of the Medical Officers of the Army of Tennessee." *Southern Historical Society Papers* 22 (1894): 165–280.

Lawrence, Alexander A., ed. "Some Letters from Henry C. Wayne to Hamilton Fish." *Georgia Historical Quarterly* 43 (1959): 391–409.

Lee, Robert E. *The Wartime Papers of R. E. Lee*. Edited by Clifford Dowdey and Louis H. Manarin. Boston: Little, Brown, 1961.

Liddell, St. John R. *Liddell's Record*. Edited by Nathaniel C. Hughes. Dayton, Ohio: Morningside Press, 1985.

Lindsley, John B., ed. *The Military Annals of Tennessee: Confederate*. 1886. Reprint. Spartanburg, S.C.: Reprint Co., 1974.

Longstreet, James. *From Manassas to Appomattox*. 1896. Reprint. Secaucus, N.J.: Blue and Grey Press, 1984.

McClellan, George B. *McClellan's Own Story*. New York: Charles L. Webster, 1887.

McCown, J. G. "About Ector's and McNair's Brigades." *Confederate Veteran* 9 (1901): 113.

McLane, Robert M. *Reminiscences, 1827–1897*. 1903. Reprint. Wilmington, Del.: Scholastic Resources, Inc., 1972.

Morgan, George W. "The Assault on Chickasaw Bluffs." In *Battles and Leaders of the Civil War*. Edited by Robert U. Johnson and Clarence C. Buel. 4 vols. 1887–88. Reprint. New York: Thomas Yoseloff, 1956. 3:462–70.

Nisbet, James C. *Four Years on the Firing Line*. Edited by Bell I. Wiley. Jackson, Tenn.: McCowat-Mercer Press, 1963.

Olmstead, Charles H. "The Memoirs of Charles H. Olmstead." Edited by Lilla Mills Hawes. *Georgia Historical Quarterly*, pt. 1, 42 (1958): 389–408; pts. 2–5, 43 (1959): 60–74, 170–86, 261–80, 378–91; pts. 6–9, 44 (1960): 56–74, 186–219, 306–20, 419–34, pts. 10–11, 45 (1961): 42–56, 137–55.

———. "The Siege of Fort Pulaski." *Georgia Historical Quarterly* 1 (1917): 98–105.

"The Opposing Forces at Chickamauga, Ga." In *Battles and Leaders of the Civil War*. Edited by Robert U. Johnson and Clarence C. Buel. 4 vols. 1887–88. Reprint. New York: Thomas Yoseloff, 1956. 3:672–75.

Oswandal, J. Jacob. *Notes of the Mexican War, 1846–47–48*. Philadelphia, 1885.

Polk, William M. *Leonidas Polk, Bishop and General*. New ed., 2 vols. New York: Longmans, Green, 1915.

Pressley, John G. "Extracts from the Diary of Lieutenant Colonel John G. Pressley of the Twenty-Fifth South Carolina Volunteers." *Southern Historical Society Papers* 14 (1886): 35–62.

Ripley, Roswell S. *The War with Mexico*. 2 vols. New York: Harper and Brothers, 1849.

Rodgers, C. R. P. "DuPont's Attack at Charleston." In *Battles and Leaders of the Civil War*. Edited by Robert U. Johnson and Clarence C. Buel. 4 vols. 1887–88. Reprint. New York: Thomas Yoseloff, 1956. 4:32–47.

Roy, T. B. "General Hardee and the Military Operations Around Atlanta." *Southern Historical Society Papers* 8 (1880): 337–87.

Sedgwick, John. *Correspondence of John Sedgwick, Major General.* 2 vols. New York: DeVinne Press, 1902.

Semmes, Raphael. *Service Afloat and Ashore During the Mexican War.* Cincinnati: William H. Moore, 1851.

Sherman, William T. *Memoirs of Gen. W. T. Sherman.* 2 vols. New York: Charles L. Webster, 1891.

Shoup, Francis A. "Dalton Campaign — Works at the Chattahoochee River — Interesting History." *Confederate Veteran* 3 (1895): 262–65.

Sprague, John T. *The Origin, Progress, and Conclusion of the Florida War.* 1848. Facsimile ed. Gainesville: University of Florida Press, 1964.

Starke, Wyatt W. "A Georgia Planter." *De Bow's Review* 11 (October 1851): 400–402.

Strong, William K. "The Death of General James B. McPherson." In *The Atlanta Papers.* Compiled by Sydney C. Kerksis. Dayton, Ohio: Press of the Morningside Bookshop, 1980. 505–39.

Sykes, E. T. *History of Walthall's Brigade.* Columbus, Miss.: Mississippi Historical Society, 1905.

Taylor, Richard. *Destruction and Reconstruction.* New York: D. Appleton, 1879.

Thompson, Ed Porter. *History of the Orphan Brigade.* Louisville, Ky.: Lewis N. Thompson, 1898.

Watkins, Sam R. *"Co. Aytch," Maury Grays, First Tennessee Regiment.* 1882. Reprint. New York: Collier Books, 1962.

Wilcox, Cadmus M. *History of the Mexican War.* Edited by Mary Rachel Wilcox. Washington, D.C.: Church News Publishing Co., 1892.

Wood, W. Kirk, ed. *A Northern Daughter and a Southern Wife: The Civil War Reminiscences and Letters of Katherine H. Cumming, 1860–1865.* Augusta: Phoenix Printing Co., 1976.

SECONDARY SOURCES

Allen, Thomas B. *The Blue and the Gray.* Washington, D.C.: National Geographic Society, 1992.

Ambrose, Stephen E. *Duty, Honor, Country: A History of West Point.* Baltimore: Johns Hopkins Press, 1966.

Appleton's Cyclopedia of American Biography. 6 vols. New York: D. Appleton, 1888.

Army Register, 1854–56.

Association of Graduates, U.S. Military Academy. *Annual Register of Graduates and Former Cadets.* 1990 ed.

Augusta City Directory. 1841, 1859, 1861.

Avery, Isaac W. *History of the State of Georgia from 1850 to 1881*. New York: Brown and Derby, 1881.

Bauer, K. Jack. *The Mexican War, 1846–1848*. New York: Macmillan, 1974.

Bentley, William G. "The Great Snowball Battle." *Civil War Times Illustrated* 5 (January 1967): 22–23.

Bergeron, Arthur W. *Guide to Louisiana Confederate Military Units, 1861–1865*. Baton Rouge: Louisiana State University Press, 1989.

Blewitt, Octavian. *A Hand-book for Travellers in Central Italy* . . . London: John Murray, 1850; cover title: *Murray's Hand-book, Central Italy and Rome*. [W. H. T. Walker's annotated copy].

Boatner, Mark M. *The Civil War Dictionary*. New York: David McKay, 1959.

Booth, Andrew B., comp. *Records of Louisiana Confederate Soldiers and Louisiana Confederate Commands*. 3 vols. New Orleans: Commissioner of Louisiana Military Records, 1920.

Bowen, Eliza A. *The Story of Wilkes County, Georgia*. Marietta, Ga.: Continental Book Publishing Co., 1950.

Bragg, William H. *Joe Brown's Army*. Macon, Ga.: Mercer University Press, 1987.

Bridges, Hal. *Lee's Maverick General, Daniel Harvey Hill*. New York: McGraw-Hill, 1961.

Brock, R. A., ed. *The Appomattox Roster*. 1887. Reprint. New York: Antiquarian Press, 1962.

Brown, Joseph M. *The Mountain Campaigns of Georgia*. 5th ed. Buffalo: Art Printing Works, 1890.

Brown, Russell K. "David Emanuel Twiggs." *Richmond County History* 15 (Summer 1983): 13–16.

——. *Fallen in Battle: American General Officer Combat Fatalities from 1775*. Westport, Conn.: Greenwood Press, 1988.

——. "An Old Woman with a Broomstick: General David E. Twiggs and the U.S. Surrender in Texas, 1861." *Military Affairs* 48 (April 1984): 57–61.

Bryan, T. Conn. *Confederate Georgia*. Athens: University of Georgia Press, 1953.

Burton, E. Milby. *The Siege of Charleston, 1861–1865*. Columbia: University of South Carolina Press, 1970.

Byrne, Charles. "The Sixth Regiment of Infantry." In *The Army of the United States*, edited by Theophilus F. Rodenbough and William L. Haskins. New York: Maynard, Merrill, 1896.

Capers, Ellison. *South Carolina*. Vol. 5 in Clement A. Evans, ed., *Confederate Military History*. 12 vols. Atlanta: Confederate Publishing Co., 1899.

Capers, Walter B. *The Soldier-Bishop, Ellison Capers*. New York: Neale, 1912.

Carter, Samuel, III. *The Siege of Atlanta*. New York: St. Martin's Press, 1973.

Cashin, Edward J. *The Story of Augusta*. Augusta: Richmond County Board of Education, 1980.

Castel, Albert. *Decision in the West.* Lawrence: University of Kansas Press, 1992.

Catalog of the Officers and Students in Yale College, 1839–1840. New Haven: N.p., 1840.

Catton, Bruce. *The Coming Fury.* Garden City, N.Y.: Doubleday, 1961.

———. *Grant Moves South.* Boston: Little, Brown, 1960.

"Ceded Lands": Records of St. Paul's Parish and Early Wilkes County, Georgia. Albany, Ga.: Delwyn Associates, 1964[?].

Cisco, Walter B. *States Rights Gist.* Shippensburg, Pa.: White Mane Press, 1991.

"Civil War Teamster Has Unique Record." *Atlanta Journal,* August 28, 1909, p. 4.

Claus, Errol M. "The Atlanta Campaign, July 18 to September 2, 1864." Ph.D. dissertation, Emory University, 1965.

Coffman, Edward M. *The Old Army: A Portrait of the American Army in Peacetime, 1784–1898.* New York: Oxford University Press, 1986.

Coleman, Kenneth, gen. ed. *A History of Georgia.* Athens: University of Georgia Press, 1977.

Coleman, Kenneth, and Charles S. Gurr, eds. *Dictionary of Georgia Biography.* 2 vols. Athens: University of Georgia Press, 1983.

Connelly, Thomas L. *Autumn of Glory: The Army of Tennessee, 1862–1865.* Baton Rouge: Louisiana State University Press, 1971.

Connelly, Thomas L., and Archer Jones. *The Politics of Command: Factions and Ideas in Confederate Strategy.* Baton Rouge: Louisiana State University Press, 1973.

Corley, Florence Fleming. *Confederate City: Augusta, Georgia, 1860–1861.* Columbia: University of South Carolina Press, 1960.

Crackel, Theodore J. "The Oldest Quarters at West Point." *Assembly* 49 (July 1991): 26–28.

Crute, Joseph H., Jr. *Confederate Staff Officers, 1861–1865.* Powhatan, Va.: Derwent Press, 1982.

———. *Units of the Confederate States Army.* Midlothian, Va.: Derwent Press, 1987.

Cullum, George W. *Biographical Register of the Officers and Graduates of the United States Military Academy at West Point, New York.* 3d ed. Boston: Houghton Mifflin, 1891.

Daniel, Larry J. *Soldiering in the Army of Tennessee.* Chapel Hill: University of North Carolina Press, 1991.

Daughters of the American Revolution. *Historical Collections of the Joseph Habersham Chapter.* 2 vols. Atlanta: Blosser, 1902.

Davis, Robert S., Jr., comp. *The Wilkes County Papers, 1773–1833.* Easley, S.C.: Southern Historical Press, 1979.

Davis, Steve. "The Battles of Atlanta: Actions from July 10 to September 2, 1864." *Blue and Gray Magazine* 6 (August 1989): 9–62.

———. "A Georgia Firebrand: Major General W. H. T. Walker, C.S.A." *Georgia Historical Quarterly* 63 (Winter 1979): 447–60.

———. "The Great Snow Battle of 1864." *Civil War Times Illustrated* 15 (June 1976): 32–35.

———. "That Extraordinary Document: W. H. T. Walker and Patrick Cleburne's Emancipation Proposal." *Civil War Times Illustrated* 16 (December 1977): 14–20.

Davis, William C. *Breckinridge: Statesman, Soldier, Symbol.* Baton Rouge: Louisiana State University Press, 1974.

———. *Jefferson Davis: The Man and the Hour.* New York: Harper Collins, 1991.

Derry, Joseph T. *Georgia.* Vol. 6 (extended ed.) in Clement A. Evans, ed., *Confederate Military History.* 12 vols. Atlanta: Confederate Publishing Co., 1899.

Dyer, Brainard. *Zachary Taylor.* Baton Rouge: Louisiana State University Press, 1946.

Faust, Patricia L., ed. *The Historical Times Illustrated Encyclopedia of the Civil War.* New York: Harper & Row, 1986.

Forman, Sidney. *West Point: A History of the United States Military Academy.* New York: Columbia University Press, 1950.

Freeman, Douglas S. *Lee's Lieutenants.* 3 vols. New York: Charles Scribner's Sons, 1942–44.

———. *R. E. Lee: A Biography.* 4 vols. New York: Charles Scribner's Sons, 1948.

Garraty, John A., and Robert A. McCaughy. *The American Nation.* 6th ed. 2 vols. New York: Harper & Row, 1987.

Goode, Paul R. *The United States Soldiers' Home: A History of Its First Hundred Years.* Washington, D.C.: Privately printed, 1957.

Govan, Gilbert E., and James W. Livingood. *A Different Valor: The Story of General Joseph E. Johnston, C.S.A.* Indianapolis: Bobbs-Merrill, 1956.

Granger, Mary, ed. *Savannah River Plantations.* Savannah: Georgia Historical Society, 1947.

Hallock, Judith Lee. *Braxton Bragg and Confederate Defeat.* Vol. 2. Tuscaloosa: University of Alabama Press, 1991.

Harsha, David A. *Noted Living Albanians.* Albany, N.Y.: Weed, Parsons and Co., 1891.

Heidler, Jeanne Twiggs. "The Military Career of David Emanuel Twiggs." Ph.D. dissertation, Auburn University, 1988.

Heitman, Francis B. *Biographical Register and Dictionary of the United States Army, 1789–1903.* 2 vols. Washington, D.C.: U.S. Government Printing Office, 1903.

Henderson, Lillian, ed. *Roster of the Confederate Soldiers of Georgia, 1861–1865.* 6 vols. Hapeville, Ga.: Longino and Porter, 1955–62.

Henry, Robert Selph. *The Story of the Mexican War.* 2d ed. New York: Frederick Ungar, 1961.

Herbert, Sidney. *A Complete Roster of the Volunteer Military Organizations of the State of Georgia.* Atlanta: James P. Harrison, 1878.

Hill, Louise B. *Joseph E. Brown and the Confederacy.* Chapel Hill: University of North Carolina Press, 1939.

Hoffman's Albany Directory and City Register. 1852–53.

Hollingsworth, Dixon. *Screven County History*. Dallas: Curtis Media Corp., 1989.

House, Myron W. "History of the First Volunteer Regiment of Georgia, 1864–1865." M.A. thesis, Emory University, 1973.

Howell, George Rogers, and Jonathan Tenney. *History of the County of Albany, N.Y.* New York: W. W. Munsell, 1886.

Hughes, Nathaniel C. *General William J. Hardee, Old Reliable*. Baton Rouge: Louisiana State University Press, 1965.

Jones, Charles C., Jr., and Salem Dutcher. *Memorial History of Augusta, Georgia*. 1890. Reprint. Spartanburg, S.C.: Reprint Co., 1980.

Jones, Charles Edgeworth. *Georgia in the War, 1861–1865*. Atlanta: Foote and Davies, 1909.

Jones, Terry L. *Lee's Tigers: The Louisiana Infantry in the Army of Northern Virginia*. Baton Rouge: Louisiana State University Press, 1987.

Kerksis, Sydney C. "Action at Gilgal Church, Georgia, June 15–16, 1864." *Atlanta Historical Bulletin* 15 (Fall 1970): 9–43.

——, comp. *The Atlanta Papers*. Dayton, Ohio: Press of the Morningside Bookshop, 1980.

Knight, Lucian Lamar. *Georgia's Landmarks, Memorials and Legends*. 2 vols. Atlanta: Byrd Printing, 1913.

Korn, Jerry. *The Fight for Chattanooga: Chickamauga to Missionary Ridge*. Alexandria, Va.: Time-Life Books, 1985.

Kurtz, Wilbur G. "Civil War Days in Georgia: The Death of Major General W. H. T. Walker." *Atlanta Constitution Magazine*, July 27, 1930, pp. 5–6, 16, 20.

——. "The Death of Major General W. H. T. Walker, July 22, 1864." *Civil War History* 6 (June 1960): 174–79.

Little, Robert D. "General Hardee and the Atlanta Campaign." *Georgia Historical Quarterly* 29 (1945): 1–22.

Livermore, Thomas L. *Numbers and Losses in the Civil War*. 1900. Reprint. Bloomington: Indiana University Press, 1957.

Losson, Christopher. *Tennessee's Forgotten Warriors*. Knoxville: University of Tennessee Press, 1989.

Madaus, Howard M., and Robert D. Needham. *The Battle Flags of the Confederate Army of Tennessee*. Milwaukee: Milwaukee Public Museum, 1976.

Mahon, John K. *History of the Second Seminole War, 1835–1842*. Gainesville: University of Florida Press, 1967.

McCain, Paul M. "The Military Career of William Henry Talbot Walker." M.A. thesis, Duke University, 1948.

McDonough, James Lee. *Chattanooga: A Death Grip on the Confederacy*. Knoxville: University of Tennessee Press, 1984.

McDonough, James Lee, and Thomas L. Connelly. *Five Tragic Hours: The Battle of Franklin*. Knoxville: University of Tennessee Press, 1983.

McDonough, James Lee, and James P. Jones. *War So Terrible: Sherman and Atlanta.* New York: Norton, 1987.

McMurry, Richard M. "The Atlanta Campaign, December 23, 1863, to July 18, 1864." Ph.D. dissertation, Emory University, 1967.

——. "Cassville." *Civil War Times Illustrated* 10 (December 1971): 4–9, 45–48.

——. "The Hell Hole: New Hope Church." *Civil War Times Illustrated* 11 (February 1973): 32–43.

——. *John Bell Hood and the War for Southern Independence.* Lexington: University Press of Kentucky, 1982.

——. "Kennesaw Mountain." *Civil War Times Illustrated* 8 (January 1970): 19–34.

——. "Resaca: A Heap of Hard Fitin." *Civil War Times Illustrated* 9 (November 1970): 4–12, 44–48.

——. *Two Great Rebel Armies: An Essay in Confederate Military History.* Chapel Hill: University of North Carolina Press, 1989.

McWhiney, Grady. *Braxton Bragg and Confederate Defeat*, Vol. 1. 1969. Reprint. Tuscaloosa: University of Alabama Press, 1991.

Meadows, Mary. *The Genealogy of the Families Foremon-Boisclair, Walker, Beers, Lacy.* Easley, S.C.: Southern Historical Press, 1980.

Mellichamp, Josephine. *Senators from Georgia.* Huntsville, Ala.: Stroud, 1976.

Mosser, Jeffrey S. "I Shall Make Him Remember This Insult." *Civil War Times Illustrated* 32 (March–April 1993): 24, 49, 52–57, 60–62.

——. "William Henry Talbot Walker, C.S.A." *North South Trader's Civil War* 17 (1990): 18–22.

Munsell, Joel. *Collections on the History of Albany.* 3 vols. Albany, N.Y.: J. Munsell, 1870.

Myers, Robert M. *The Children of Pride.* New Haven: Yale University Press, 1972.

The National Cyclopedia of American Biography. 43 vols. New York: James T. White, 1891–1961.

Newsome, F. M., and Nell H. Newsome. *Wilkes County Cemeteries.* Washington, Ga.: Wilkes Publishing Co., 1970.

Northern, William J. *Men of Mark in Georgia.* 7 vols. 1907. Reprint. Spartanburg, S.C.: Reprint Co., 1973.

Nunis, Doyce B. "Colonel Archibald Campbell's March from Savannah to Augusta, 1779." *Georgia Historical Quarterly* 45 (1961): 275–86.

Parks, Joseph H. *General Leonidas Polk, C.S.A., the Fighting Bishop.* Baton Rouge: Louisiana State University Press, 1962.

——. *Joseph E. Brown of Georgia.* Baton Rouge: Louisiana State University Press, 1977.

Parrish, T. Michael. *Richard Taylor, Soldier Prince of Dixie.* Chapel Hill: University of North Carolina Press, 1992.

Perdue, Howell, and Elizabeth Perdue. *Pat Cleburne, Confederate General.* Hillsboro, Texas: Hill Junior College Press, 1973.

Pfadenhauer, Ruby M. M. "History of Augusta Arsenal." *Richmond County History* 2 (Summer 1970): 5–22.

Plum, William R. *The Military Telegraph During the Civil War in the United States.* 2 vols. Chicago: Jansen, McClurg, 1882.

Prucha, Francis P. *The Sword of the Republic: The United States Army on the Frontier, 1783–1846.* New York: Macmillan, 1969.

Reynolds, Cuyler, ed. *Albany Chronicles.* Albany, N.Y.: J. B. Lyon, 1906.

——, ed. *Genealogical and Family History of Southern New York and the Hudson River Valley.* 3 vols. New York: Lewis Historical Publishing Co., 1914.

Risch, Erna. *Quartermaster Support of the Army, 1775–1939.* Washington, D.C.: Center of Military History, 1989.

Rowland, Dunbar. *Jefferson Davis, Constitutionalist: His Letters, Papers and Speeches.* Jackson: Mississippi Department of Archives and History, 1923.

Sansing, David. "A Happy Interlude: Jefferson Davis and the War Department, 1853–1857." *Journal of Mississippi History* 51 (November 1989): 297–312.

Satterfield, Frances G. *Madame LeVert: A Biography of Octavia Walton LeVert.* Edisto Island, S.C.: Edisto Press, 1987.

Scarborough, William K. "Science on the Plantation." In *Science and Medicine in the Old South*, edited by Ronald L. Numbers and Todd L. Savitt. Baton Rouge: Louisiana State University Press, 1989.

Seyburn, S. V. "The Tenth Regiment of Infantry." In *The Army of the United States*, edited by Theophilus F. Rodenbough and William L. Haskins. New York: Merrill, Maynard, 1896.

Sifakis, Stewart. *Who Was Who in the Civil War.* New York: Facts on File Publications, 1988.

Smith, Justin H. *The War with Mexico.* 2 vols. New York: Macmillan, 1919.

Tucker, Glen. *Chickamauga: Bloody Battle of the West.* Dayton, Ohio: Morningside Bookshop, 1984.

U.S. Military Academy. *Annual Report, 1876.*

Utley, Robert M. *Frontiersmen in Blue: The United States Army and the Indian, 1848–1865.* New York: Macmillan, 1967.

"Valuable Finds on View for You." *Atlanta Historical Society Newsletter*, January–February 1990, p. 3.

Vandiver, Frank E. *Their Tattered Flags.* New York: Harper's Magazine Press, 1970.

Warner, Ezra J. *Generals in Blue.* Baton Rouge: Louisiana State University Press, 1964.

——. *Generals in Gray.* Baton Rouge: Louisiana State University Press, 1959.

Weigley, Russell F. *History of the United States Army.* New York: Macmillan, 1967.

Wilson, Clyde N. *Carolina Cavalier: The Life and Mind of James Johnston Pettigrew.* Athens: University of Georgia Press, 1990.

Woodworth, Steven E. *Jefferson Davis and His Generals.* Lawrence: University Press of Kansas, 1990.

Works Progress Administration, American Guide Series. *Augusta*. Augusta: Tidwell Printing Supply Co., 1938.

Wyatt-Brown, Bertram. *Southern Honor: Ethics and Behavior in the Old South*. New York: Oxford University Press, 1982.

INDEX